1992
The Supreme Court Review

1992
The

"Judges as persons, or courts as institutions, are entitled to
no greater immunity from criticism than other persons
or institutions . . . [J]udges must be kept mindful of their limitations and
of their ultimate public responsibility by a vigorous
stream of criticism expressed with candor however blunt."
—*Felix Frankfurter*

". . . while it is proper that people should find fault when
their judges fail, it is only reasonable that they should recognize the
difficulties. . . . Let them be severely brought to book,
when they go wrong, but by those who will take the trouble
to understand them."
—*Learned Hand*

THE LAW SCHOOL

THE UNIVERSITY OF CHICAGO

Supreme Court Review

EDITED BY

DENNIS J. HUTCHINSON

DAVID A. STRAUSS

AND GEOFFREY R. STONE

 THE UNIVERSITY OF CHICAGO PRESS

CHICAGO AND LONDON

INTERNATIONAL STANDARD BOOK NUMBER: 0-226-36247-7

LIBRARY OF CONGRESS CATALOG CARD NUMBER: 60-14353

THE UNIVERSITY OF CHICAGO PRESS, CHICAGO 60637

THE UNIVERSITY OF CHICAGO PRESS, LTD., LONDON

© 1993 BY THE UNIVERSITY OF CHICAGO, ALL RIGHTS RESERVED, PUBLISHED 1993

PRINTED IN THE UNITED STATES OF AMERICA

The paper used in this publication meets the minimum requirements of American National Standard for Information Sciences—Permanence of Paper for Printed Library Materials, ANSI Z39.48-1984. ∞

TO KEN AND LU

*On the occasion
of their 50th Anniversary*

CONTENTS

DAVID A. STRAUSS

ABORTION, TOLERATION, AND MORAL UNCERTAINTY

Planned Parenthood v Casey,[1] the most highly publicized decision of last Term, explicitly "reaffirmed" the "essential holding of *Roe v. Wade*"[2] that the Constitution protects the right to an abortion in certain circumstances. For all the attention it received, however, *Casey* may prove to be more important for its theoretical contributions than for its actual effects on the availability of abortion. As a practical matter, the significance of *Casey* is far from certain; the Court upheld a number of restrictions that the state of Pennsylvania placed on abortion and left it unclear how far states may go in the future in limiting access to abortions. More than any previous decision, however, *Casey* placed the constitutional right to abortion on a coherent and plausible theoretical basis.

Before *Casey*, the abortion debate in the courts had focused mostly on the question whether the Constitution protects the interest, usually described as a right to privacy, that is invaded by laws forbidding abortion. This debate was conditioned by the New Deal constitutional revolution—the development of a consensus that the

David A. Strauss is Harry N. Wyatt Professor of Law, the University of Chicago.

AUTHOR'S NOTE: I am grateful to many people who commented on an earlier version of this paper that made similar arguments without addressing *Casey:* participants in the University of Chicago Law School Work in Progress Workshop and the Yale Legal Theory Workshop, and Albert Alschuler, Mary Becker, Abner Greene, Elena Kagan, Andrew Koppleman, Larry Kramer, Larry Lessig, Michael McConnell, Geoffrey Miller, Richard Posner, Stephen Schulhofer, Louis Michael Seidman, Cass Sunstein, and Robin West. The Russell Baker Scholars Fund and the Russell J. Parsons Faculty Research Fund at the University of Chicago Law School provided financial support.

[1] 112 S Ct 2791 (1992).

[2] Id at 2804.

Supreme Court was wrong to strike down regulatory and welfare legislation. The perceived lesson of the New Deal era was that courts illegitimately violate popular sovereignty when they create rights not specified explicitly enough in the Constitution.

The legal debate about abortion usually took the same form: do the courts impermissibly invade popular sovereignty when they find an "unenumerated right to privacy" that encompasses the right to obtain an abortion? The academic legal debate has come to focus less on this issue, but until *Casey*, litigation (and Supreme Court confirmation hearings) were still dominated by this question.

This lawyers' debate, preoccupied with the last constitutional war, underemphasized the more difficult issues that are really at the heart of the abortion question. Those issues are, on the one hand, the social status of women; and on the other, the moral status of fetal life. Participants in the larger political (and moral and religious) debate have been more astute in recognizing that these are the issues on which the abortion controversy ought to turn. Neither side can make a convincing argument until these issues have been addressed—the question of women's status by the defenders of laws forbidding abortion, and the question of fetal life by the opponents of such laws.

The great contribution of *Casey* is that it began to recognize the centrality of these issues to the abortion debate. The status of women played a larger role in *Casey* than in any previous opinion of the Court's dealing with abortion. The Court considered the "essential holding of *Roe v. Wade*" to be a requirement that previability restrictions on abortion be specially justified,[3] and it continued to rest that requirement on the "liberty" guaranteed by the Fourteenth Amendment,[4] not—as some have suggested—on the premise that restrictions on abortion are suspect because they discriminate against women.[5] But in explaining the importance of this liberty interest, the Court specifically referred to the effect of

---

[3] Id at 2804, 2811.

[4] Id at 2807.

[5] See id at 2846–47 & n 4 (Blackmun concurring); see, for example, Ruth Bader Ginsburg, *Some Thoughts on Autonomy and Equality in Relation to Roe v. Wade*, 63 NCL Rev 375 (1985); Kenneth Karst, *Foreword: Equal Citizenship Under the Fourteenth Amendment*, 91 Harv L Rev 1, 53–59 (1977).

abortion laws on women's status.[6] And in justifying its reaffirmation of *Roe*, the Court explained that "[a]n entire generation has come of age free to assume *Roe*'s concept of liberty in defining the capacity of women to act in society, and to make reproductive decisions."[7]

Casey also recognized, again to a greater extent than any previous case upholding the right to an abortion, that the most powerful argument against its conclusion was the claim that fetal life has a status comparable to life that is unquestionably fully human. The weight to be given to the interest in fetal life, the Court said, not the constitutional basis of reproductive freedom, "was the difficult question faced in *Roe*."[8]

Implicit in *Casey*, I believe, is a persuasive argument for the unconstitutionality of anti-abortion laws that addresses the issues of the social status of women and the moral status of fetal life. This argument acknowledges—as the Court did in *Casey*, although perhaps not sufficiently—that there is fundamental uncertainty about the moral status of fetal life. Generally accepted methods of moral reasoning do not tell us the extent to which fetal life is morally entitled to the same protection as (undoubted) human life. The claim that anti-abortion laws are unconstitutional cannot rest on the premise that fetal life is morally entitled to no or minimal protection, because we do not know that premise to be true. We do not know whether it is true or false.

The question is how we are to act in the face of such uncertainty. A standard argument against *Roe* is that the political process exists precisely to decide unresolved moral questions of this kind.[9] That

---

[6] See 112 S Ct at 2807:

> [T]he liberty of the woman is at stake in a sense unique to the human condition and so unique to the law. . . . Her suffering is too intimate and personal for the State to insist, without more, upon its own vision of the woman's role, however dominant that vision has been in the course of our history and our culture. The destiny of the woman must be shaped to a large extent on her own conception of her spiritual imperatives and her place in society.

[7] Id at 2812.

[8] Id at 2817. See id at 2810–11: "Even on the assumption that the central holding of *Roe* was in error, that error would go only to the strength of the state interest in fetal protection, not to the recognition afforded by the Constitution to the woman's liberty."

[9] Id at 2873 (Scalia dissenting); see also *Cruzan v Director, Missouri Department of Health*, 497 US 261, 293 (1990) (Scalia concurring).

argument, however, is mistaken. Sometimes, high-stakes questions that are morally uncertain are properly resolved by the political process. But sometimes, the political process must leave each individual free to resolve such a question for himself or herself.

The clearest example is religious conviction.[10] In our relatively skeptical age, questions of religious truth often do not seem as important as many issues that arouse political controversy. But religious liberty is not premised on such skepticism. We would still believe in religious toleration even if we thought—as many do, and as people commonly did when the regime of religious toleration emerged during the Reformation—that questions of religious truth are of surpassing importance, more important than any issue of this world.

Religious toleration is, to be sure, only an analogy to the abortion issue. And it is not the case that *every* morally uncertain issue should be resolved by the individual rather than by the state. The point of the analogy to religious toleration is simply to disprove the argument that morally uncertain issues of life-or-death (or greater) importance cannot be left to individual judgment.

The question remains why abortion is an issue that should be resolved on the level of the individual, rather than on the level of the state. This is where the status of women becomes important. In cases of true moral uncertainty, an issue should be resolved at the level that minimizes the risk that some group of people will be unacceptably subordinated by the decision makers. That level may be the level of the nation-state; the level of some political unit smaller than the nation-state; or the level of the individual. In our society at least, a decision about abortion at any level other than the level of the individual would present an unacceptable risk of subordinating women.

Casey was perhaps more faithful to these principles in theory than in practice. While reaffirming a general right to an abortion, the Court upheld significant restrictions on that right: a requirement that physicians provide women with information that was calculated to discourage them from obtaining abortions; a mandatory 24-hour waiting period; and a requirement that minors obtain

---

[10] Although the Court in *Casey* did not explicitly compare its resolution of the abortion issue to religious toleration, it repeatedly alluded to the quasi-religious character of beliefs about the status of fetal life. See 112 S Ct at 2806–07.

either one parent's consent or approval from a court. The Court invalidated a requirement that a married woman who seeks an abortion must obtain the consent of her husband.[11]

To some extent the Court's resolution of these issues was consistent with the approach I suggest: when the Court invalidated the spousal notification provision, it emphasized the danger of the subordination of women,[12] and one of the reasons the prevailing opinion gave for upholding the other regulations—the need to "ensure that [the woman's] choice is thoughtful and informed"[13] —is consistent with a regime of toleration. But the specific restrictions that the Court upheld reflect an effort to influence a woman's decision in a way that cannot be squared with the analysis I have described; or so I will argue below. It is the theoretical approach implicit in *Casey*, more than the specific holdings, that seems to promise a new era in the abortion debate in the courts.

I. MORAL UNCERTAINTY AND FETAL LIFE

A. THE CONCEPT OF MORAL UNCERTAINTY

The Court in *Casey* took as a given the divergence of views about the status of fetal life. "Men and women of good conscience can disagree, and we suppose some always shall disagree, about the profound moral and spiritual implications of terminating a pregnancy, even at its earliest stage."[14] But the Court did not explain why mere disagreement, even persistent disagreement, is enough to justify rejecting the position about fetal life endorsed by a democratic majority.[15]

In fact, as I believe the Court perceived, something more than mere disagreement or controversy is needed. To a degree—not in every particular, but in important respects—the moral status of

---

[11] See id at 2822, 2803, 2826–31 (plurality opinion of O'Connor, Kennedy, and Souter).

[12] See id at 2829–31.

[13] Id at 2818 (plurality opinion).

[14] Id at 2806.

[15] The prevailing opinion in *Casey* did reaffirm the line, drawn by *Roe*, between pre- and postviability abortions, and this conclusion was based partly on its own evaluation of the moral significance of fetal life. See id at 2816–17 (plurality opinion of O'Connor, Kennedy, and Souter). In addition, Justice Stevens, in a concurring opinion, seemed to take the position that fetal life does not have intrinsic moral worth. Id at 2840. The plurality opinion did not endorse this view.

fetal life is not merely a controversial issue but a radically uncertain issue. Many highly controversial issues are not radically morally uncertain in the way that the status of fetal life is. The question of the just distribution of wealth is an example. It is a highly controversial issue, but people who disagree can reason about it in a way that at least holds out the hope of narrowing the disagreement. The disagreement will rest in part on empirical issues, such as the effects of various measures on incentives. Those issues are resolvable in principle. To the extent that there are nonempirical aspects of their disagreement, people who hold opposing views on wealth distribution can appeal to many arguments in the various traditions of political philosophy. They can supply utilitarian or social contractarian arguments for the various positions. They can, in short, provide each other with many reasons for their respective views.

The moral status of fetal life—the extent to which a fetus should be treated as a human being—is uncertain in a more fundamental sense. It is unresolvable not just in practice but in principle. An analogy to mathematics might help illustrate this point. There are problems that mathematicians have not yet solved and will never solve, because, for example, solving them would require too much computation time. Those problems are analogous to issues like the just distribution of wealth: they are intractable in practice, but they are resolvable in principle. Then there are mathematical problems that, in the current state of knowledge, are unsolvable in principle—for example, propositions that so far can neither be proved true nor be proved false.

If radically uncertain questions exist even in mathematics, we should expect to find radically uncertain moral questions as well. My suggestion, which I believe is also the best reading of *Casey*, is that claims about the moral status of fetal life—to be precise, claims about the moral status of fetal life that are strong enough to resolve the abortion controversy—are in this category. Some day moral reasoning may advance to the point where we can resolve the question of the moral status of fetal life, or at least to the point where we can agree on how we might go about resolving it. But at least for now, the question of the moral status of fetal life, unlike the question of the just distribution of wealth, is not characterized by even a primitive level of agreement. There appear to be few shared premises from which one might proceed to try to resolve this issue.

Perhaps that is why the lawyers' debate has instinctively steered clear of this question; an advocate's stock in trade is finding shared premises that might be used to persuade an antecedently neutral or hostile interlocutor.

This is the way in which the status of fetal life resembles matters addressed by religious doctrine. Opponents of anti-abortion laws sometimes argue that those laws are unacceptable in a society committed to religious neutrality because they reflect the domination of certain religious groups. But of course organized religious groups take positions on many issues, and many widely accepted legal prohibitions have roots in religious doctrine. The significant relationship between religious doctrine and an anti-abortion position is not the historical or political connection; it is the epistemological parallel. People of different religions often hold opposed beliefs that are not based on any agreed-upon set of premises. Consequently there is no way in which they can proceed toward a resolution of their disagreement. The same is true of disputes over the status of fetal life.

B. FETAL LIFE AND MORAL THEORY

What is the evidence that the status of fetal life is fundamentally uncertain in this way? The political debate over abortion is some evidence. The two sides do not join issue on this question in any significant way. In public debates over questions of wealth distribution, for example, the two sides cite data, make claims about the efficacy of various programs and the importance of competing demands on resources, and make arguments based on notions of equality and desert. Although similar arguments are sometimes offered in other aspects of the abortion debate, nothing comparable is heard when the subject is the status of fetal life.

It is probably fair to say that the pro-choice side often does not engage this question; that side either makes libertarian arguments about the impropriety of government restraints, or focuses on the status of women, or attempts to argue that the pro-choice position can be justified even if a fetus is the moral equivalent of a human being.[16] The anti-abortion side does occasionally make efforts to

---

[16] For similar criticism, see, for example, Kathleen McDonnell, *Not an Easy Choice: A Feminist Re-Examines Abortion* 53–54 (Women's Press, Toronto, 1984); Ruth Colker, *Feminist Litigation: An Oxymoron?*, 13 Harv Women's L J 137, 165–67 (1990).

engage in something that might be called argument on the question; the displays of pictures of aborted fetuses are an example. But the anti-abortion side often does not suggest any reasons that might convince someone who does not share its intuitive response to such pictures. To some extent the anti-abortion arguments are based on overtly religious views; that tends to confirm that there is no shared set of premises from which the problem can be addressed.

But the principal argument for the thesis of radical moral uncertainty is that the major theories in the tradition of moral philosophy do not provide a satsifactory way of analyzing a category of issues that includes the status of fetal life. The category concerns what might be called the boundaries of the moral universe—beings whose status as members of the moral universe is unclear. This includes not just fetuses but animals, severely mentally disabled individuals, and future generations. The principal traditional moral theories—which have much to say about the usual subjects of political controversy, such as wealth distribution—do not deal with the boundaries of the moral universe very well at all.

The important modern moral theories can roughly be categorized as either utilitarian theories or social contract theories.[17] Both define the moral universe in ways that are useful over a wide range of cases but are either vague or implausible at the boundaries. The deficiency is perhaps most obvious in the case of social contract theories. The essential idea of these theories is that certain social arrangements are justified because they adequately protect the interests of every person subject to them. We know that they adequately protect every person's interests because every person would accept them under certain idealized conditions.[18]

In these theories, however, the definition of a contracting party is usually just specified, not justified. Because that definition determines the boundaries of the moral universe, these theories have little useful to say about boundary issues, including the status of fetal life. If the definition includes all beings with a "potential" capacity to reason in some sense—to conceive a plan of life, or to

---

[17] For this division, see, for example, John Rawls, *A Theory of Justice* §§ 3, 27–30 (Harvard, 1971).

[18] For a leading account that describes the bases of social contract theory along these lines, see T. M. Scanlon, *Contractualism and Utilitarianism*, in Amartya Sen & Bernard Williams, eds, *Utilitarianism and Beyond* 103–28 (Cambridge, 1982).

act morally—it seems destined to be either too broad or too narrow, depending on how the vague term "potential" is understood. If, for example, an unfertilized egg has such a potential, the theory entails implausible obligations to bring lives into being. At the other end of the spectrum, if the definition is limited to beings with the actual capacity to reason, the theory is equally implausible at least because it excludes infants; the intuition against infancticide is so strong and widespread that a theory that can "resolve" the abortion issue only by justifying infanticide has not resolved the abortion issue (or perhaps has supplied a strong argument against allowing abortion).

Between those two end points there seems to be no nonarbitrary way to draw a line that resolves the status of fetal life. This is not a criticism of social contract views; it is achievement enough if they clarify moral issues that concern fully functioning adult humans. The point is that (perhaps as in the mathematical analogy) the existing state of theoretical knowledge does not resolve certain questions, including the question of the status of fetal life.[19]

Utilitarian theories often purport to deal with these questions in a more satisfactory way, but it is not clear that they come any closer to a resolution. Again the definition of a boundary either does not help with the question of fetal life, or is arbitrary, or leads to implausible conclusions. If a fetus is included in the moral universe on the ground that it has the capacity to feel pain, then animals must also be included.[20] That leads to implausible conclusions about the obligation of people to sacrifice themselves for animals. If a fetus is included on the ground that it has the potential for a utility function, then it is indistinguishable from other potential future beings, including those whose parents have not yet been born. That leads to some of the well-known problems that utilitari-

---

[19] For a related comparison of the abortion issue and the treatment of the severely disabled, see Louis Michael Seidman, *Confusion at the Border: Cruzan, "The Right to Die," and the Public/Private Distinction*, 1991 Supreme Court Review 47, 61–64.

[20] Bentham objected to the treatment of animals for just this reason. See *The Principles of Morals and Legislation* ch XVII, § I, subsection IV, n 1 (1789) (emphasis in original):

> The day *may* come when the rest of the animal creation may acquire those rights which never could have been witholden from them but by the hand of tyranny. . . . [A] full-grown horse or dog is beyond comparison a more rational, as well as a more conversable animal, than an infant of a day, or a week, or even a month, old. But suppose they were otherwise, what would it avail? The question is not, Can they reason? nor Can they *talk?* but *Can they suffer?*

anism faces with future beings.[21] If a fetus is excluded on the ground that it is not capable of formulating a plan of life or demonstrating preferences, then the problems with infants and disabled persons result.

One might ask why the outcome of the abortion dispute should be affected by the fact that abstract moral theories have difficulty dealing with the status of fetal life. Why is that not just a problem of concern to philosophers, with no significant consequences for the real-world abortion controversy? The answer, I believe, is that the deficiency of the leading moral theories reveals a blind spot in our thinking generally. The reason moral theories have trouble with this question is that no one really knows how to think about it systematically. Not only is the problem controversial, but no one knows quite how to go about solving it; that is what the deficiency of the leading moral theories reveals.

Moral theories are not just abstract designs of no relevance to actual controversies. A moral theory such as utilitarianism is an effort to organize widely held intuitions in a way that will help solve problems about which our intuitions are currently unclear or in conflict.[22] Although a moral theory often cannot resolve an ordinary controversy, such as over the just distribution of wealth, it can at least provide some reasons that people might use in trying to persuade each other. When the leading moral theories are seriously deficient in their approach to an issue, that suggests that we have few reasons we can offer to try to persuade each other. As I will attempt to elaborate below, it is the relative lack of reasons for holding any position on fetal life that makes that issue radically uncertain in a way that has consequences for the constitutional question.

II. The Good Samaritan Argument

I have said that a pro-choice argument must address the uncertain status of fetal life and that the Court in *Casey*, to its credit, recognized this. But one well-known defense of the pro-choice position (actually, more strongly, a defense of abortion)

---

[21] See, for an important discussion, Derek Parfit, *Reasons and Persons* chs 16–19 (Oxford, 1984).

[22] See, for this account, Rawls, *A Theory of Justice* 578–82 (cited in note 17).

claims to make it unnecessary to deal with the status of fetal life. The argument is that prohibiting abortion is equivalent to requiring a woman to assume duties of a Good Samaritan of an especially extraordinary form to the fetus.[23] This argument compares the responsibilities assigned to a woman by those who oppose abortion to the responsibilities of a conventional Good Samaritan. We do not require that a conventional Good Samaritan accept burdens comparable to those involved in a pregnancy even when an undoubted human life is at stake. It follows that we should not prohibit abortions even if we assume arguendo that fetal life is equivalent to human life.

None of the opinions in *Casey* (or in any other decision) relied on a form of this argument, and in my view the Good Samaritan argument does not succeed. The problem is that this argument depends on two libertarian premises: first, that obligations must be in some way commensurate with voluntary undertakings; and second, that there is a sharp distinction between bodily invasions and other impositions on individuals. These libertarian premises are not obviously true, are difficult to justify, and conflict with strongly held intuitions.

The first premise is needed to meet an obvious and superficial objection to the Good Samaritan argument—that, cases of rape and incest aside, no one becomes pregnant involuntarily. The burdens of pregnancy (it is therefore said), unlike the impositions on a Good Samaritan, are to some extent voluntarily assumed. This argument is insensitive to the many subtle forms of pressure and coercion that call into question the voluntariness of many pregnancies. But the principal answer to this argument offered by the proponents of the Good Samaritan view is that it is, in general, unrealistic and unfair to regard most pregnant women as voluntarily accepting the burdens of pregnancy in any meaningful sense.[24]

That answer seems correct, as far as it goes. But it assumes away the possibility that there are obligations and duties that arise without any voluntary act. They arise by virtue of status or just

---

[23] First advanced in Judith Jarvis Thomson, *A Defense of Abortion*, 1 Phil & Pub Aff 47 (1971), reprinted in *Rights, Restitution, & Risk* 1 (Harvard, 1986). See also Donald H. Regan, *Rewriting Roe v. Wade*, 77 Mich L Rev 1569 (1979).

[24] See Thomson, *Rights, Restitution, & Risk* 11–12 (cited in note 23).

because one happened to find oneself in a certain position.[25] Obligations to a political community are probably an example; efforts to
ground such obligations on voluntary undertakings are difficult to
sustain.[26] Obligations *to* a parent or to a sibling are also in this
category; they arise, at least in part, by virtue of status, not voluntary acts. One might, therefore, without taking any act of a kind
that would ordinarily lead to such strong obligations, find oneself
in the position of a parent who has obligations to her own unborn
child that she would not have to a stranger.

It might be responded that, while not all obligations have their
origin in voluntary acts, the anti-abortion position imposes unique
obligations on the mother, obligations of a kind that are never the
result of status alone. This response relies on the second libertarian
premise, about the distinctiveness of bodily invasions. No one
questions that parents have many burdensome obligations to their
children, such as the obligation to provide for their economic and
emotional support. Weighed just on some sort of quantitative scale
(such as how much one would pay to avoid the obligation, other
things equal), it is arguable that these burdens are greater than
those incurred by a pregnant mother. If pregnancy is an unacceptable obligation to impose on a person, that must be because it
involves a physical imposition that is qualitatively different from
other parental obligations.[27]

Obviously there is much to the point that physical invasions are
peculiarly objectionable. I will argue later that society's habitual
disregard for women's bodily integrity is an important reason for
insisting that the abortion decision not be made by the political
process. The Good Samaritan argument is also correct in saying
that ordinarily we do not insist that people subject themselves to
bodily impositions comparable to pregnancy, even when another

[25] See, for example, H. L. A. Hart, *Legal and Moral Obligation*, in A. I. Melden, ed, *Essays in Moral Philosophy* 103–4 (Univ of Washington, 1958), and the discussion of "natural duties" in Rawls, *A Theory of Justice* § 51 (cited in note 17).

[26] The classic discussion is David Hume, *Of the Original Contract*, in Charles W. Hendel, ed, *Political Essays* 43–61 (Bobbs-Merrill, 1953). For a recent discussion, see Jeremy Waldron, *Special Ties and Natural Duties*, 22 Phil & Pub Aff 1 (1993).

[27] See Thomson, *Rights, Restitution, and Risk* 8–9 (cited in note 23): "My own view is that if a human being has any just, prior claim to anything at all, he has a just, prior claim to his own body. . . . [N]obody has a right to use your kidneys unless you give him such a right." See also Judith Jarvis Thomson, *The Realm of Rights* 290–91 (Harvard, 1990).

life is at stake. The law does not require an individual to give up one kidney, for example, to save a stranger's life.

But people have stronger obligations to their children than to strangers, and it may be that parents have a moral obligation to sacrifice their physical integrity, to some degree, for the sake of their children. Parents may not refuse to give up their wealth or their labor, over an extended period, for the sake of their children. Why should a bodily intrusion, such as giving up a kidney, be regarded as necessarily more of an imposition than other parental sacrifices that are unquestionably obligatory? The implicit libertarian premise that bodily intrusion is a peculiarly unacceptable form of burden seems arbitrary.

It is true that in the current state of the law, parents are not generally required to sacrifice their bodily integrity even to save their children's lives. But that may just reflect institutional concerns about legal enforcement. It is certainly plausible that parents have a moral obligation to make such a sacrifice: a parent who did not give up a kidney to save a child's life, for example, would probably be widely reviled. It may be that there is no legal obligation to do so because the situations in which such a sacrifice would be called for are so few and so varied that it does not make sense to try to enact these moral obligations into law. It may be that trying to enforce such a legal obligation would be too threatening to other values. It is possible that when parents must make a one-time, heroic sacrifice for their children (which is what a sacrifice of bodily integrity, other than pregnancy, will typically be), they can generally be counted on to do so; legal enforcement is necessary only for long-term obligations, such as child support. Or, of course, it may simply be a defect in existing law.

In any event, it is difficult to see why a parent's extensive obligations to a child stop at the boundaries of the body. And if they do not—if it is not unacceptable to require a parent to give up a kidney for a child—then the Good Samaritan argument against restricting abortion loses much of its force.[28]

---

[28] A variant on the Good Samaritan argument is the claim that the defect of anti-abortion laws is that they require women, but not men, to bear physical impositions associated with childbirth and child rearing. Therefore, these laws constitute impermissible gender discrimination. See, for example, Cass R. Sunstein, *Neutrality in Constitutional Law (With Special Reference to Pornography, Abortion, and Surrogacy)*, 92 Colum L Rev 1, 29–44 (1992).

In short, a person might have the moral duties of parenthood even though he or she has not taken any voluntary act of a sort that usually has such momentous consequences. Unless the interest in bodily integrity is given enormous significance, beyond what can be easily justified, those duties might include sacrificing one's bodily integrity to save a child's life. Obviously there remains a great deal of force to the Good Samaritan argument. There is much room for dispute over the nature of the obligations a parent assumes, how one assumes them, and when those obligations might be consistent with having an abortion. But unless the two dubious libertarian premises are accepted, the abortion issue cannot be fully resolved on the assumption that fetal life is the moral equivalent of a child's life.

III. Abortion and the Regime of Toleration

A. THE ANALOGY TO RELIGIOUS TOLERATION

If the position that laws forbidding abortion are unconstitutional cannot easily be sustained on the assumption that fetal life is morally equivalent to human life, then that position must be reconciled with the uncertain status of fetal life. The Court in *Casey* seemed to recognize this, and it seemed also to perceive that religious toleration was a useful analogy, although it did not analyze the analogy closely.

I have suggested two limited ways in which religious toleration is analogous to the pro-choice position. First, questions about religious belief are characterized by radical uncertainty. There is no agreed-upon way of deciding the issues with which religious belief is concerned: issues, for example, about the nature of the soul and the afterlife, about the proper spiritual development of human beings and their relationship to some transcendent power. Second, religious issues, although they are issues of the greatest importance,

---

A difficulty with this argument is that, if it assumes fetal life to have the same moral status as undoubted human life, it does not entail that restrictions on abortion are wrong. The gender disparity can be removed by continuing to prohibit abortion while increasing fathers' obligations to undertake physical impositions to help their children. If abortion is the moral equivalent of killing an innocent person, that resolution of the gender disparity seems far preferable to permitting abortions. Failing that, unless gender discrimination is always impermissible, it would presumably have to be allowed if the alternative is the loss of innocent life. See id at 40 n 144.

are resolved on the level of the individual, not the level of the state. Religious toleration is therefore a counterexample to the argument made by the dissent in *Casey* that the political process is the proper way to resolve unsettled, but important, issues.

At one time, of course, it was widely accepted that religious issues were to be decided by the state, not by individuals. Indeed, at one time it would have seemed bizarre to say that individuals' spiritual development and the fate of their souls were not among the central concerns of the state. But the development of religious toleration, one of the great advances in Western culture, consisted precisely in deciding that matters of religious belief are to be resolved not at the level of the state, but at the level of each individual.

It might be objected that decisions about religion are different from decisions about abortion because decisions about one's own religious faith do not affect other people. Religiously inspired actions, as distinguished from beliefs, can affect other individuals, and (the argument would go) that is why actions can be regulated. A guarantee of absolute liberty applies only to beliefs, because an individual's belief affects no one else. Since an individual's decision whether to have an abortion affects a being that may have a moral status comparable to that of a human, the analogy to religious toleration does not sustain the pro-choice position.

But this view of religious belief as a private matter is decidedly modern, and slightly skeptical. When the regime of religious toleration arose, the more common view was that one person's religious belief affected others in the most profound ways possible. Aquinas argued for persecution on the ground that "forgers and other malefactors are put to death" and "it is a far graver matter to corrupt the faith which is the life of the soul than to falsify money which sustains temporal life."[29] More fundamentally, the idea that there are matters which are only one person's business is itself a modern artifact. A common justification for persecution was that the duty of love for one's neighbors required that they be saved from false belief and, therefore, from eternal damnation. It was a duty of love to destroy a heretic's body in order to save his or her soul.

These views are not prevalent today, but some people hold them,

---

[29] A. P. D'Entreves, ed, *Aquinas: Selected Political Writings* 157 (J. G. Dawson trans) (Blackwell, 1970).

and—more important—we do not have to establish their falsehood in order to believe that religious liberty is morally imperative. That is, some people believe that we will all be eternally damned if we do not persecute heretics; and we have no basis for concluding that that belief is false. But we still believe that people have a right to decide for themselves, free from persecution, whether to hold heretical beliefs. This demonstrates that some unsettled issues are to be resolved on the level of the individual, not the level of the state, even if the resolution might affect others besides the individual in the most profound ways possible.

B. DOES TOLERATION PRESUPPOSE THE FALSEHOOD OF CERTAIN BELIEFS?

It might be objected that in fact the regime of religious toleration does presuppose the falsehood of religious beliefs that would require persecution. If we really believed that we would all be eternally damned if we did not persecute heretics, for example, it is difficult to believe that we would be tolerant. By analogy, a regime of toleration for decisions about abortion could be justified only if we rejected the view that fetal life is morally equivalent to human life.

This objection can take one of two forms—a claim about the historical emergence of religious toleration that is surely correct but is beside the point, or a claim about the justification of religious toleration that seems incorrect.

1. No doubt as a historical matter, religious toleration could not have emerged in practice until most people came to accept, as a matter of religious doctrine, that heresy harmed only the heretic and not other people. It might be impossible to persuade people to be tolerant if they believed that the result would be their own damnation. So, it might be said, we cannot accept a regime of toleration for abortion until we conclude that abortion does not harm a being with a moral status comparable to that of humans.

This argument, however, fails to distinguish between the circumstances in which a regime of toleration is justified and the circumstances in which it might, as a factual matter, take hold. In parts of the world in which most people think they will be damned if they do not persecute heretics, religous toleration is unlikely to be widely accepted. But it would still be wrong to persecute people. Wc would still tell people in that part of the world that they ought to adopt a regime of toleration, and we would (other things equal) impose such a regime if it were in our power to do so.

2. The argument that the *justification* for religious toleration presupposes the falsehood of certain religious views is more difficult to answer. I believe that this claim is, however, inconsistent with the way we think about toleration. The reason is that if this argument is correct, then religious toleration becomes a sectarian view. One can believe in toleration only by accepting certain theological views and rejecting others. I do not think we ordinarily regard religious toleration as sectarian in that way. Rather, we would say that religious toleration is the correct view for good secular reasons—reasons having to do with the proper respect for others, for example—that everyone in society should accept.

The reason we do not allow persecution, even by those who believe they have a religious duty to engage in it, is that we believe for secular reasons that toleration is the only acceptable regime; and if we are to have a regime of toleration, we cannot allow persecution, no matter what the claims of religious duty. If we encountered people who believed they had a religious duty to engage in persecution, we would tell them they could not act on their conception of their religious duty. We would not, however, feel that we had to tell them that their religious beliefs were wrong. Indeed we would probably consider it inappropriate to tell them that their religious beliefs were wrong. Rather we would tell them that one of the conditions of living in organized society is that they cannot act on certain religious beliefs, however obligatory. People who hold these views must then make their peace, as best they can, with the conflict between their religious and political obligations. Similarly, in our society, we would not permit people to engage in, for example, human sacrifice or, in certain contexts, racial discrimination, even if they felt a religious obligation to do so. The reasons would be the same: not that the religious views that require such practices are wrong, but that for secular reasons we cannot permit such practices even when the reason for engaging in them is religious compulsion.[30]

---

[30] For a somewhat similar account of the relationship between toleration and uncertainty, see Thomas Nagel, *Equality and Partiality* 162–68 (Oxford, 1991).

The analogy to abortion is this: we can adopt a regime of toleration, in which the abortion decision is made on the level of the individual rather than the level of society, without rejecting the arguments of those who believe that fetal life is morally equivalent to human life. People who hold that view of fetal life will be forbidden from acting on it in certain ways. For example, they may not use force to obstruct abortions, even if people generally may use force to prevent the killing of an innocent person. But the reason is not that we know they are wrong in their view. It is that we have adopted a regime of toleration for abortion, one of the premises of which is that we cannot know for certain whether they are right or wrong in their view. If that regime is justified, then they cannot act in ways inconsistent with it.

To summarize: under both the regime of religious toleration and its counterpart for abortion, some people claim that the government is tolerating behavior that inflicts severe harm on innocent third parties. There are no generally accepted ways of reasoning that either confirm or disprove that claim. If toleration is nonetheless an acceptable regime in one area, then it is possible (so far, I have not shown more than this) that it is acceptable in the other area as well.

C. TOLERATION AND SUBORDINATION

The question remains: why should the abortion issue be decided on the level of the individual instead of on the level of the state? This is the point at which the status of women, properly emphasized by *Casey*, becomes important. Allowing the abortion decision to be made at the political level, instead of the individual level, would create an impermissible risk of subordinating women.

1. Subordination is a complex and vague notion. But it is an appropriate starting place for considering the constitutionality of anti-abortion laws, because the unconstitutionality of discrimination against women has become settled doctrine in the Supreme Court. Laws that discriminate on the basis of gender, somewhat like laws that discriminate on the basis of race, require special justification. Moreover, certain kinds of justifications—those resting on "old notions" and "archaic and overbroad generalizations" about women—are never sufficient to sustain the constitutionality

of a gender classification.[31] Although the Court has never made it entirely clear why discrimination against women is unconstitutional, it seems plausible to suppose that at least three aspects of the status of women in society, all relevant to the abortion issue, underlie this principle.

First, the political process has a persistent tendency generally to undervalue the interests of women. Although the Court has not given this as a reason for its hostility to gender discrimination, this is the *Carolene Products* explanation—perhaps the most conventional explanation—for requiring a special justification for laws that single out a group. In any event, the persistence of laws and practices that discriminate against women is evidence that their interests are undervalued.

Second, women's bodily integrity, in particular, is systematically undervalued. The Court's opinion in *Casey* alluded to this aspect of women's status. The prevalence of harassment and violence against women, and the widespread social attitudes that implicitly or explicitly condone those practices—for example, the relative respectability of domestic violence and the sexualization of violence against women—are evidence of this.

Third, women are treated as people whose principal responsibility is child bearing and child rearing. They are not seen as full participants in the labor market. The pattern of laws, economic arrangements, and social customs that discourages women from entering the labor market and encourages them to be mothers is evidence that this treatment exists. It is not obvious a priori that this treatment constitutes subordination. But throughout our history—for example, in the opposition to slavery, the exaltation of freedom of contract at the turn of the century, and the centrality of employment discrimination to civil rights issues today—the right to alienate one's labor has been highly valued, and that is evidence that a person is not regarded as fully human in our society unless he or she is allowed to participate in the labor market.[32]

---

[31] See, for example, *Mississippi University for Women v Hogan*, 458 US 718, 724–28 (1982); *Califano v Goldfarb*, 430 US 199, 211 (1977) (plurality opinion), quoting *Stanton v Stanton*, 421 US 7, 14 (1975), and *Schlesinger v Ballard*, 419 US 498, 508 (1975).

[32] Kristin Luker, *Abortion and the Politics of Motherhood* (University of California, 1984), argues that laws forbidding abortion are an outgrowth of this view of women. See also Reva Siegel, *Reasoning from the Body: A Historical Perspective on Abortion Regulation and Questions of*

This aspect of the status of women has been the most important in shaping the Court's view of gender discrimination. The Court's guiding principle in the area, as I said, has been that governments may not rely on "stereotyped" notions as justifications for classifying on the basis of gender. The stereotypes in question are those that view women as concerned primarily with children and the home and not as full participants in the labor market. And *Casey* emphasized the potential connection between these stereotypes and laws forbidding abortion.

2. The Court in *Casey* did not, however, make clear the exact connection between the status of women and the abortion issue. The connection, I believe, is this: the tendency to subordinate women in these three ways disqualifies the political process from resolving the moral uncertainty that is central to the abortion debate. There is too great a danger that if the political process decides the abortion issue, that decision will be an act of subordinating women in one or more of these ways.

The general undervaluing of women's interests is important because of the morally uncertain status of fetal life. It is often difficult to determine, in particular cases, when a group's interests are being undervalued; that is one of the notorious problems with the *Carolene Products* justification for strict judicial review. But we can say that a group's interests are undervalued if no reason can be given for imposing a burden on it. By the same token, if we can give good reasons for an imposition, then we have some assurance that the group's interests are not being undervalued.

The reason for the imposition that anti-abortion laws place on women is that the laws are needed to protect fetal life. It would be a mistake to say that this is no reason at all, in the sense that the imposition is arbitrary or whimsical. But the protection of fetal life is also not a completely satisfactory reason, because it rests on a premise—about the moral value of fetal life—that is, as I argued, radically uncertain in the sense that it cannot be defended on the basis of generally shared moral views.

This is, as I argued in Part I, the significance of the apparent

---

Equal Protection, 44 Stan L Rev 261 (1992). If that argument is correct, it is powerful additional support for my claim. But I am relying not on an argument like Luker's but on the (surely less controversial) proposition that the attitude that stereotypes women as child bearers and child rearers is prevalent.

fact that the leading moral theories have a difficult time addressing issues like the status of fetal life. Those theories are systematizations of widely held intuitions; their apparent inability to address these issues satisfactorily suggests that there is a dearth of widely accepted reasons that can be brought to bear on the issues. Ordinarily that would just be unfortunate. The political system would have to deal with the issue as best it could. But when there is a danger of subordination, the lack of widely shared reasons that could justify imposing a burden on a group suggests that the political process should not make the decision whether to impose the burden. That decision should be made at some other level, such as the level of the individual.

Anti-abortion laws directly implicate the other two aspects of subordination that I described. Both of these aspects of subordination played a role in the opinion in *Casey*. If society has a tendency to view women primarily as mothers, anti-abortion laws may reflect that view rather than an impartial weighing of the interest in fetal life against the woman's interests.

If we had a better way to reason about the status of fetal life, we might be more confident that, in enacting anti-abortion legislation, society had not given in to its tendency to undervalue women's interests in general, and in bodily integrity particularly, and to view them as childbearers. Therefore, this argument does not entail the implausible (and probably incoherent) conclusion that *no* decisions affecting women can be made by the political process. Other decisions—for example, resource allocation decisions—might also burden women, but the justification for the burden will not be a particular view about a morally uncertain issue like the moral status of fetal life. Instead it will be a claim that is controversial but not radically uncertain. Because such a claim provides a basis for reasoning from shared premises, the danger of subordination is reduced.

Similarly, if society did not have tendencies to undervalue women's bodily integrity and to see them as childbearers, then we would be more comfortable with allowing the radically uncertain issue about fetal life to be resolved by society, instead of by individuals. There is nothing intrinsically or necessarily undesirable about having morally uncertain issues resolved by the political process. There is no reason in general to think that the political process will do worse with such issues than an individual will. Both will make the decision without the benefit of theoretical guidance or a substantial weight of generally accepted reasons. But in the case of abortion, there is reason to be suspicious of the social decision and to favor the individual decision. The combination of moral uncertainty and a tendency toward subordination in society creates too serious a danger that an anti-abortion law is subordinating.

How do we know whether that danger is serious enough to require that the abortion decision be remitted to the level of the individual, where there is no (or at least a reduced) danger of subordination? There is no deductive answer to that question. But some decisions that might be of the greatest importance (such as decisions about religion) are made at the level of the individual. The moral uncertainty about fetal life seems to be severe. The subordination of women, at least along the lines I mentioned, is an ancient and persistent practice. A decision made at any level of the political process creates a danger of subordination. The most reasonable conclusion, therefore, is that this decision—like decisions implicating matters of religious doctrine—should be made at the level of the individual.

D. THREE OBJECTIONS AND THE PERMISSIBLE SCOPE OF REGULATION

There are at least three important objections that might be made to this argument for the unconstitutionality of restrictions on abortion. Those objections also help clarify the more narrow issue in *Casey:* the permissible scope of government regulation of abortion, within a regime of toleration. Although *Casey*'s specific conclusions about the scope of regulation are very questionable, some of what the Court said about the permissible scope of regulation further confirms that the Court implicitly accepted a view similar to the one I have outlined here.

1. First, it might be objected that the approach I have advocated, and attributed to the Court in *Casey*, only purports to assume that the moral status of fetal life is uncertain but covertly treats fetal life as if it is worth little. Agnosticism about the value of fetal life, it might be said, leads to no conclusion, not to a conclusion that a woman may choose whether to have an abortion. One way or another, we must assign some implicit value to fetal life.

It is true that radical uncertainty about moral matters has far more disturbing consequences than uncertainty in science or mathematics. In science or mathematics we can often just set uncertain matters aside. But society must reach some decision about how far to protect fetal life. Moreover, if society decides to allow the abortion decision to be made at the level of the individual, then individuals faced with the choice must make the decision. The radically uncertain status of fetal life will be a problem for the individual who must decide, too. In fact it is unclear how such an individual can best go about deciding.

It does not follow, however, that a social decision to adopt a regime of toleration resolves the uncertainty on the side of devaluing fetal life. The basis for the social decision is not that fetal life is worth little but that the danger of subordination will be reduced by allowing the status of fetal life to be decided at the level of the individual. It is analogous to saying that certain matters should be resolved by state or local governments rather than by the federal government. A pro-federalism decision about, say, criminal law enforcement does not necessarily resolve the merits of the underlying criminal law issue; similarly, a pro-toleration decision does not necessarily resolve the merits of the underlying abortion or religion issue.

There is, of course, a sense in which the approach I suggest attaches more value to avoiding subordination than to the likelihood that fetal life is morally equivalent to human life. But this alone does not suggest a low value for fetal life. We often allow the danger of subordination to outweigh the risk of loss of life. We allow local governments, in our system, to decide many life or death issues, as the criminal enforcement example suggests. Local governments determine the degree of risk that is acceptable in various government and private projects, the resources that are to be devoted to protecting against private violence, whether to authorize capital punishment, and so on. Of course, one reason those decisions are made on the local level is that local decision makers are more likely to make the right decision. But another reason is akin to an antisubordination argument: the national government would be seen as an outside force that did not give sufficient weight to local interests. This is an important argument for democracy in general, in preference, for example, to some form of technocracy. It is also the form of the argument for federalism, and for national sovereignty.

My argument is parallel. Because of the subordinating tendencies of the political process, any decision made at that level will seem to women as an alien decision made by those who have insufficient sympathy for their interests. Just as we are willing to run an increased risk of a wrong decision, even on a life or death matter, in order to avoid the kind of subordination that occurs when the national government instead of a local government makes a decision, so we should be willing to accept that risk in the case of abortion.

2. A related objection is that my argument overlooks the danger of subordination of the interests of the fetus. If allowing the government to decide whether abortions will be permitted creates too great a risk that women will be subordinated, then why does allowing the individual to make the decision not create a risk of subordination of the fetus? The only way to deny that that risk exists, it might be argued, is to take a position on the moral status of fetal life, the matter about which I claim not to take a position.

The answer to this objection is that the interests of the fetus and the interests of women are not symmetrical. The argument that women are systematically subordinated now, and therefore would be at risk of further subordination if the abortion decision were made by society, does not depend on any claims about radically uncertain matters. It rests on the three claims I made earlier, that society undervalues women's interests, that women's interest in bodily integrity is particularly discounted, and that women are regarded as primarily childbearers and child-rearers. If one could show that the interests of fetuses were subordinated by making similar claims—that is, claims that do not depend on premises about the status of fetal life—then the positions of women and fetuses would be symmetrical. But so far as I am aware, no one has plausibly made that case. The argument that fetuses are subordinated depends on a premise about the status of fetal life, a radically uncertain matter. The argument that women are subordinated does not depend on a radically uncertain premise.

If one accepts, as current equal protection doctrine does, the proposition that the political process tends to subordinate women (or even if one does not consider that proposition to be radically uncertain, but merely controversial in the usual way) then there is no symmetry between fetuses and women. The danger that the fetuses' interests will be subordinated, therefore, has not been shown to be a reason to allow restrictions on abortion.

3. Finally, it might be objected that deciding the question at the level of the individual is inappropriate because the woman herself has a stake in the decision. It is difficult to know how, exactly,

one should approach a matter about which there is radical moral uncertainty. But it is surely plausible to say that at least a decision under conditions of radical uncertainty ought to be made at a level that ensures the impartial consideration of all interests: in this case, the interests of both the woman's well-being and fetal life. The pregnant woman, it might be objected, will be disposed to be one-sided on these issues.

There are three possible answers to this objection.

a. One answer is that the woman's point of view will not be one-sided; the pregnant woman will have a strong inclination to identify with the fetus and to value its interests as well.[33] One should not be too quick to assume that because the woman has highly important interests of her own at stake, she is incapable of sympathizing with the fate of the fetus to a desirable degree.

b. Second, this objection suggests not that the abortion decision should be made at the political level rather than the individual level, but rather that there are, within a regime of toleration, permissible bases for regulating the abortion decision. It might be possible to identify a class of cases in which the likelihood of a "biased" decision by women—that is, a decision that did not adequately consider the interests of the fetus—is especially severe. If one could regulate that class of decisions precisely, so that the regulation did not affect other aspects of the abortion decision, then the approach I am suggesting would not rule out regulation. For example, it may be permissible to have a regulation designed to encourage careful thought by young women making the decision to have an abortion in highly stressful circumstances.

Again, there is an analogy to religious freedom. The regime of religious toleration does not obviously forbid the state from imposing some limits on the kinds of pressure that, for example, religious cults may apply in seeking to persuade people to convert, so long as the state does not interfere with the substance of the decision. The reason for the state's action is to create an environment in which an individual can reach the correct decision, not to impose a decision on the individual.

Here again the approach taken by the Court in *Casey* has important elements in common with what I am proposing. *Casey* upheld three restrictions that Pennsylvania imposed on women seeking abortions: a requirement that a physician inform the woman of

---

[33] See Robert D. Goldstein, *Mother-Love and Abortion* (University of California, 1988).

"the nature of the procedure, the health risks of the abortion and of childbirth, and the 'probable gestational age of the unborn child' ";[34] a requirement that amounted to a 24-hour waiting period; and a requirement that a minor seeking an abortion receive the consent of one parent, unless she could obtain approval from a court.[35] The Court invalidated a requirement that a woman obtain the consent of her husband.[36]

One of the justifications the pivotal members of the Court[37] gave for upholding the restrictions was the state's interest in insuring informed decision making by the woman. "[T]hroughout pregnancy," these Justices said, "the State may take measures to ensure that the woman's choice is informed."[38] This justification for regulating the abortion decision is consistent with a regime of toleration. Under such a regime, the reason for allowing the decision to be made at the individual level is not that an individual's decision is necessarily right, but rather that a decision by the government would risk being subordinating. It follows that there is a substantial and legitimate interest in ensuring that the decision is well-informed. In theory, all three of the restrictions that were upheld might have served this purpose.

Unfortunately, the Court did not evaluate the Pennsylvania restrictions by reference to this principle alone. Instead, the Court said that the state could also seek to persuade a woman to choose childbirth over abortion.[39] "Persuasive" efforts of the kind reflected in the Pennsylvania information provisions, at least, are difficult to reconcile with a regime of toleration. If the government is to remain truly agnostic on the moral status of fetal life, it is difficult to identify any plausible basis on which it might decide to favor child-

---

[34] 112 S Ct at 2822. Pennsylvania also required that women be told of the availability of materials published by the state that, among other things, described the fetus and provided information about fathers' child support obligations and about adoption and other services as an alternative to abortion. Id at 2822–23.

[35] See id at 2803.

[36] Id at 2826–31.

[37] This portion of the opinion was a plurality opinion by Justices O'Connor, Kennedy, and Souter. Justices Stevens and Blackmun would have invalidated all of these restrictions; the other justices would have upheld all of the restrictions.

[38] 112 S Ct at 2821 (plurality opinion).

[39] For example, id at 2821 (plurality opinion of O'Connor, Kennedy, and Souter). (I refer to the views of the Court because the dissenting opinions leave no doubt that four other members of the Court would have gone at least this far, and in fact further, in accepting the state's justifications for its restrictions.)

birth over abortion. And the decision that childbirth is to be favored over abortion might itself reflect the subordinating tendencies of the political order.

In addition, the Court in *Casey* established, as the standard for evaluating restrictions, not the relatively precise question whether they were conducive to a well-informed decision—a test that would be appropriate in a regime of toleration, provided it could be sensibly administered—but the far more amorphous question whether a restriction imposed an "undue burden" on the abortion right.[40] This, too, allowed the Court to uphold these restrictions despite objections that they did not serve to bring about a better-informed decision but only made it more difficult to obtain an abortion (and, in the case of the provision of information, constituted a kind of psychological coercion).

c. There is a third and more fundamental answer to the objection that, because of the woman's self-interest, the level of the individual is not the proper one for the resolution of the uncertain status of fetal life. In view of the moral uncertainty of the status of fetal life, it may be a mistake to base any conclusions on the supposition that there is a right answer to be found, if only we can identify the decision maker most likely to find it.

The system of religious toleration is not justified on the ground that it is most likely to produce the right decisions about religious issues. Similarly, perhaps the right approach to the abortion issue is to give up on trying to produce a correct decision and instead to try to avoid collateral bad effects—such as the subordination of women. As in the case of religion, we cannot assess even the probability that either the individual or the government will make a right decision about abortion. But we can say, with some assurance, that a decision by the government poses a risk of subordination that is absent (or greatly reduced) when the decision is made by an individual. Since we cannot determine which decision maker is more likely to be correct, the best course is to choose the decision maker who is less likely to be subordinating.

IV. Conclusion

The Court in *Casey* addressed, essentially for the first time, the issues that ought to be central to the legal debate over abortion:

---

[40] For example, id at 2819 (plurality opinion).

not whether there are "unenumerated rights" in the Constitution, but how to deal with fetal life, on the one hand, and the effect of abortion laws on the status of women, on the other. I have suggested that the Court adopted, however incompletely and inexplicitly, a plausible and coherent justification for a regime of toleration in the area of abortion. That justification is premised on, first, fundamental moral uncertainty about the status of fetal life; and, second, the danger that the political process will subordinate women, a danger that is a basis of the well-established constitutional principles governing gender discrimination.

Two possibly unexpected consequences follow from this justification. First, if society reached a point where the subordination of women was not a serious issue, the political process might again become the best way to determine the circumstances in which abortion should be allowed. There would still be libertarian arguments in favor of toleration, as well as practical arguments about the limits and disadvantages of legal enforcement of norms concerning intimate matters. But if society were free of gender bias, an important reason for prohibiting the political process from collectively determining the fate of entities like fetuses would be removed.

Second, and more relevant to present day concerns, it is an overstatement to say, as I generally have, that the moral status of fetal life is uncertain. The uncertainty is bounded. Probably few people would equate a hours-old zygote to an infant; probably few people would deny that a nine-month-old fetus has some substantial moral status. To the degree that moral issues about fetal life become less uncertain, the arguments for toleration that I have advanced become less applicable. Toleration may still be the appropriate regime, but for different reasons.

Moral knowledge, like other kinds of knowledge, can develop and change. If we gain more confidence in particular judgments about the status of fetal life, those judgments might be used as the basis for making a political decision. In the meantime, though, we must operate in an area characterized by radical moral uncertainty. In these circumstances, given the dangers of relying on the political process, the concern for the subordination of women should be decisive. That concern calls for the regime of toleration that *Casey*, imperfectly, solidified.

ELENA KAGAN

THE CHANGING FACES OF FIRST AMENDMENT NEUTRALITY: R.A.V. v ST. PAUL, RUST v SULLIVAN, AND THE PROBLEM OF CONTENT-BASED UNDERINCLUSION

Consider two cases—the most debated, as well as the most important, First Amendment cases decided by the Supreme Court in the past two Terms: *R.A.V. v St. Paul*,[1] invalidating a so-called hate speech ordinance, and *Rust v Sullivan*,[2] upholding the so-called abortion gag rule. On their face, the cases have little in common; certainly, the Justices deciding them saw no connection. Yet just underneath the surface, the cases have a similar structure, implicate an identical question, and fall within a single (though generally unrecognized) category of First Amendment cases. Along with many other cases to which neither has been assimilated, *R.A.V.* and *Rust* are, on this level, essentially the same—except that the one issue of First Amendment law they posed was answered by the Court in two different ways.

The equation of the cases at first glance is jarring, because an

Elena Kagan is Assistant Professor of Law, The University of Chicago Law School.

AUTHOR'S NOTE: I am grateful to Akhil Amar, Anne-Marie Burley, Richard Epstein, Abner Greene, Larry Lessig, Michael McConnell, Richard Posner, Jed Rubenfeld, and Cass Sunstein for very helpful comments on earlier drafts of this article. The Bernard G. Sang Faculty Fund and the Bernard Meltzer Fund provided financial assistance for this project.

[1] 112 S Ct 2538 (1992).

[2] 111 S Ct 1759 (1991).

orthodox understanding of First Amendment law highlights only the cases' dissimilarities. On such a view, the Court in *Rust* faced the new—and exceedingly difficult—First Amendment problem of selective funding of speech by the government.[3] The question was whether the federal government could fund a range of family planning services, but exclude from such funding abortion counseling, advocacy, or referral. Call this a selective subsidization question or call it an unconstitutional conditions question,[4] the essential nature of the inquiry is the same: it focuses on the government's ability to influence the realm of speech by distributing its own (wholly optional) largesse. By contrast, according to the orthodox view, the Court in *R.A.V.* faced the classic—and largely settled—First Amendment problem of the outright prohibition of a certain kind of speech by the government. The question was whether a municipality could criminalize the use of "fighting words" that provoke violence "on the basis of race, color, creed, religion, or gender." The focus was on the ability of the government to ban speech on the basis of content through use of the government's coercive power. Seen in this light, *Rust* and *R.A.V.* raised different problems, and it is no wonder that the cases provoked divergent responses: a stark rejection of the First Amendment claim in *Rust*, a powerful affirmation of the First Amendment claim in *R.A.V.*[5]

---

[3] To call such questions "new" is in a significant sense to compress history. The potential for these questions to emerge has existed in great measure since the rise of the regulatory state, and the Court has decided a number of First Amendment cases involving selective subsidization issues during the past decades. See, for example, *Speiser v Randall*, 357 US 513 (1958). Indeed, even prior to the creation of the regulatory state, issues of this kind could arise in such contexts as government property or employment. See, for example, *McAuliffe v Mayor of New Bedford*, 155 Mass 216, 29 NE 517 (1892). That these issues are still considered in any degree novel may have as much to do with their intractability—with the continuing inability of courts and commentators to resolve them—as with their timing.

[4] Phrased in the language of conditions, the question is whether the government could condition its grant of funding on the content of the recipient's speech.

[5] The variance—and, I will soon argue, the inconsistency—in the Court's responses to *Rust* and *R.A.V.* goes yet further than that suggested in the text. Four of the five Justices who voted to deny the First Amendment claim in *Rust* voted to sustain a broad First Amendment position in *R.A.V.* Those four were Chief Justice Rehnquist and Justices Scalia, Kennedy, and Souter; of the *Rust* majority, only Justice White rejected the broad First Amendment argument in *R.A.V.*, though concurring in the result on narrower grounds. Conversely, the two active Justices who wished to sustain the First Amendment claim in *Rust* (Justices Blackmun and Stevens) rejected the *R.A.V.* majority's broad First Amendment reasoning, though again concurring in the result. Justice O'Connor, who voted with the concurring Justices in *R.A.V.*, declined to take a position on the constitutional question in *Rust*, and in the interim between the two cases Justice Thomas, who joined the *R.A.V.* majority, replaced Justice Marshall, who joined the *Rust* dissent.

But is this the only—is this the best—way to view these cases? Or can they be recast—the issues in them redescribed—so that an underlying similarity leaps out? A few preliminaries at once suggest themselves. First, both cases involve speech of a particularly controversial—many believe deeply harmful—kind. That abortion advocacy is the bane of a certain segment of the political right and that racist speech is the bane of a certain segment of the political left must be considered, for First Amendment purposes, not a distinction, but a core likeness. Next, in each case the government responded to this controversy by engaging in a form of content discrimination, disfavoring certain substantive messages as compared to others. Both cases thus raise general questions of First Amendment neutrality: whether, when, and how the government may tip the scales for (or against) certain messages—or, stated otherwise, to what extent the government is required, with respect to the content of speech, to play a neutral role. But more than this must be said to assimilate the cases, for surely the question of First Amendment neutrality may present itself in different contexts, and different contexts may demand different approaches and legal rules. The key, then, to understanding the connection between R.A.V. and Rust is to note that in both cases, the issue of neutrality arises in the same way—that in both, the structure of the problem is the same.

How is this so? Briefly stated for now, Rust and R.A.V. both raise the question: If, in a certain setting, the government need not protect or promote any speech at all, may the government choose to protect or promote only speech with a certain content? Rust is easily seen in this light. The government, we believe, is not constitutionally required to promote speech through the use of federal funds.[6] May the government then fund whatever speech it wants? Or does it face constraints in selectively promoting expression? The question is similar in R.A.V. The government is not constitutionally required to tolerate any "fighting words" at all. May the government then permit some but not all fighting words? Or is it constitutionally constrained from selectively doling out this favor? The question posed in each case is in an important sense the question of First Amendment neutrality in its starkest form:

---

[6] There are exceptions to this widely accepted principle. See note 53. Yet the rule remains generally valid and served as the foundation for Rust.

when speech, considered broadly, has no claim to government promotion or protection, what limitations does government face in voluntarily advancing some messages, but not all?

This issue, which I will call the issue of content-based underinclusion, extends far beyond *Rust* and *R.A.V.* themselves. It links a wide variety of First Amendment cases and defines a largely unacknowledged First Amendment category. The question arises in cases involving selective funding of speech (such as *Rust*), selective prohibition of wholly proscribable speech (such as *R.A.V.*), selective bans on speech in non-public forums, and selective imposition of otherwise valid time, place, or manner restrictions (which may or may not involve the use of government property). At present, some of these cases—most notably, those involving funding decisions—are viewed as raising nasty, even intractable issues; others are seen as far more transparent. But if we recognize that all belong to one broad category, we may come to doubt our certainty as to some, even as we may gain guidance on others.

In this article, I view *R.A.V.* and *Rust* as reflecting on each other and, together, as reflecting on a broader range of First Amendment cases. My purpose is to elucidate connections that the Court's discourse has obscured, to explore what turns out to be a far-flung problem, and to essay some steps toward a solution. In Part I, I summarize the opinions in *R.A.V.* and *Rust*, showing how the majority opinion in *R.A.V.* echoes the principal dissent in *Rust* and how the majority opinion in *Rust* anticipates the principal concurrence in *R.A.V.* In Part II, I provide a fuller statement of the structural congruity of the cases and the issue they present, and I connect them with other kinds of First Amendment cases raising the question of content-based underinclusion. Part III considers two objections to this broad linkage: one based on the distinction between penalties and nonsubsidies, the other based on what appears to be the plenary power of the government to engage in speech itself. Finally, Part IV offers some tentative thoughts on the resolution of the problem of content-based underinclusion.

I

R.A.V. arose from the City of St. Paul's decision to charge a juvenile under the St. Paul Bias-Motivated Crime Ordinance for allegedly burning a cross on the property of an African-American family. The ordinance, as written, declared it a misdemeanor for any person to "place[] on public or private property a symbol, object, appellation, characterization or graffiti, including, but not limited to, a burning cross or Nazi swastika, which one knows or has reasonable grounds to know arouses anger, alarm or resentment in others on the basis of race, color, creed, religion or gender . . . ."[7]

The trial court dismissed the charge on the ground that the St. Paul ordinance was overbroad. The Minnesota Supreme Court reversed, holding that the ordinance, as properly construed, banned only expression not protected by the First Amendment. The court relied on *Chaplinsky v New Hampshire*, which declared that "fighting words"—defined as words "which by their very utterance inflict injury or tend to incite an immediate breach of the peace"—could be punished without "rais[ing] any constitutional problem."[8] According to the Minnesota Supreme Court, the St. Paul ordinance was constitutional because it extended only to expression that fell within the *Chaplinsky* formulation (although, of course, not to all such expression): the law covered "fighting words" that injured or provoked violence on the basis of race, color, creed, religion, or gender.[9]

All nine Justices agreed to strike down the ordinance as construed by the Minnesota Supreme Court, but none pretended to have achieved anything more than surface unanimity. Four of the Justices invalidated the law only because, in their view, the Minnesota Supreme Court had failed in its attempt to limit the ordinance to expression proscribable under *Chaplinsky;* the ordinance thus remained overbroad.[10] The majority declined to consider this argument, and the real controversy in the case lay elsewhere. It centered on the following question: Assuming the St. Paul ordinance

---

[7] Minn Stat § 292.02 (1990).

[8] 315 US 568, 572 (1942).

[9] See *In re Welfare of R.A.V.*, 464 NW2d 507, 510–11 (1991).

[10] In holding that the St. Paul ordinance reached only "fighting words" as defined by *Chaplinsky*, the Minnesota Supreme Court had suggested that the *Chaplinsky* definition included expression that by its very utterance caused (in the words of the St. Paul ordinance) "anger, alarm or resentment." 112 S Ct at 2559. The four concurring Justices objected to this sweeping understanding of *Chaplinsky*. The Justices stated, in accord with other post-*Chaplinsky* decisions, that the fighting words doctrine articulated in that case in no way allowed the restriction of speech that inflicted only such "injury" as "hurt feelings, offense, or resentment." Id.

reached only expression proscribable under *Chaplinsky*, did the ordinance remain invalid because it reached some, but not all, of this
expression—because it banned, on the basis of content, only certain fighting words?

Justice Scalia, writing for the majority,[11] answered the question
in the affirmative and invalidated the ordinance on this ground. In
prior cases, Justice Scalia readily admitted, the Court had made a
judgment that fighting words could be banned entirely—a judgment based on the view that such words are " 'of such slight social
value as a step to truth that any benefit that may be derived from
them is clearly outweighed by the social interest in order and morality.' "[12] The Court even had gone so far as to say that fighting
words and other similar categories of expression are " 'not within
the area of constitutionally protected speech' " and that the " 'protection of the First Amendment does not extend' " to them.[13] But
were these statements to be taken as "literally true"?[14] Did the First
Amendment vanish from the landscape because the government
had no obligation to permit the utterance of fighting words? Not
at all.

What remained fixed on the constitutional terrain was an obligation of content-neutrality, perhaps slightly relaxed in the context
of proscribable speech, but still with significant bite. No matter,
for example, that the government may proscribe libel; "it may not
make the further content discrimination of proscribing *only* libel
critical of the government."[15] No matter that a city may ban obscenity; it may not "prohibit . . . only that obscenity which in-

---

[11] The majority also included Chief Justice Rehnquist and Justices Kennedy, Souter, and
Thomas.

[12] 112 S Ct at 2543 (quoting *Chaplinsky*, 315 US at 572). Justice Scalia's opinion nowhere
questioned the fighting words doctrine as formulated in *Chaplinsky*; that doctrine was treated
throughout the opinion as a given. It is conceivable that some unstated discomfort with the
fighting words doctrine contributed to, or even caused, the *R.A.V.* decision; on this view,
the reasoning of the Court in *R.A.V.* operated as a kind of second-best surrogate for the
ideal but seemingly intemperate course of overruling the doctrine entirely. Cf. Richard A.
Epstein, *Foreword: Unconstitutional Conditions, State Power, and the Limits of Consent*, 102 Harv
L Rev 4, 28–31 (1988) (explaining various prohibitions on selective government action found
in unconstitutional conditions cases as a second-best means of constraining unwisely granted
government power). I assume here that the *R.A.V.* Court meant what it said and that its
rationale was something more than a pretext for limiting a doctrine it did not like, but felt
bound to tolerate.

[13] Id at 2543 (quoting, inter alia, *Roth v United States*, 354 US 476, 483 (1957), and *Bose
Corp. v Consumers Union*, 466 US 485, 504 (1984)).

[14] Id.

[15] Id (emphasis in original).

cludes offensive political messages."[16] Similarly, with respect to
the case at hand: no matter that a city may bar all fighting words;
it may not (as, the majority held, St. Paul did) bar only those
fighting words addressing a particular subject or expressing a particular viewpoint.[17] Although the category of fighting words is "unprotected"—although it has, "in and of itself, [no] claim upon the
First Amendment"—the government does not have free rein to
regulate selectively within the category.[18] Even wholly proscribable
categories of speech are not "entirely invisible to the Constitution,
so that they may be made the vehicles for content discrimination."[19]
To sustain all content discrimination within categories of speech,
simply because the categories as a whole are proscribable, would
be to engage in "a simplistic, all-or-nothing-at-all approach to First
Amendment protection . . . at odds with common sense."[20]

Justice White, in a concurring opinion,[21] took direct issue with
this reasoning: for him, the only relevant fact was that fighting
words as a category could be banned under the First Amendment.
Once the determination had been made that fighting words generally had no claim to First Amendment protection, the conclusion followed that the government could regulate such expression
freely—even if that regulation took the form of content discrimination. "It is inconsistent to hold that the government may proscribe
an entire category of speech . . . but that the government may not
treat a subset of that category differently without violating the
First Amendment; the content of the subset is by definition . . .
undeserving of constitutional protection."[22] Indeed, such a holding
foolishly would force the government to choose between regulating
all proscribable speech or none at all.[23] In Justice White's frame-

---

[16] Id at 2546 (emphasis deleted).

[17] Id at 2547.

[18] Id at 2545.

[19] Id at 2543.

[20] Id.

[21] Justice White's opinion was joined in full by Justice Blackmun and Justice O'Connor.
Justice Stevens joined only the portion of the opinion stating that the ordinance was overbroad; he specifically rejected both Justice White's and Justice Scalia's approaches to the
question discussed in the text. I discuss aspects of Justice Stevens's opinion in Part IV.

[22] Id at 2553.

[23] In this manner, Justice White was able to throw back upon Justice Scalia the charge
of all-or-nothingism. See id. Justice Stevens charged both opinions with manifesting that
apparently discredited approach to First Amendment questions. See id at 2562, 2567.

work, when speech had no claim to constitutional protection, government selectivity made no First Amendment difference;[24] if the government had no obligation to permit fighting words at all, then it faced no constraints in permitting some fighting words but not others.

Turn now to *Rust*, and compare the structure of the argument. The Department of Health and Human Services had issued regulations governing the allocation and use of Title X grants.[25] These regulations prohibited Title X–funded projects from providing abortion counseling or referrals (instead requiring them to provide referrals for prenatal care), as well as from encouraging, promoting, or advocating abortion. Title X grantees challenged the regulations, alleging (among other claims) that they violated the First Amendment.[26] The grantees argued in part that, by virtue of the regulations, the availability of subsidies now hinged on the content of speech—or, more specifically, its viewpoint: the government would subsidize a wide range of speech on family planning and other topics (including anti-abortion speech), but not abortion counseling, referral, or advocacy.

A majority of the Court, speaking through Chief Justice Rehnquist, rejected this argument. The starting point, for the Court, was that the Constitution required no subsidization of speech at all: " '[A] legislature's decision not to subsidize the exercise of a fundamental right does not infringe the right.' "[27] For the majority it followed that the government could also subsidize speech selec-

---

[24] Justice White stated that the Equal Protection Clause, as distinct from the First Amendment, would pose a barrier to differential treatment not rationally related to a legitimate government interest. See id at 2555. Ahkil Amar suggests that in acknowledging the relevance of the Equal Protection Clause, Justice White may have conceded the crucial point: that even within the realm of unprotected speech, some state action is illegitimate. See Akhil R. Amar, *Comment: The Case of the Missing Amendments: R.A.V. v. City of St. Paul*, 106 Harv L Rev 124, 130 & n 46. The question remains, though: Exactly what state action is illegitimate? Justice White's rational basis test, which would strike down legislation "based on senseless distinctions," 112 S Ct at 2556 n 9, will not lead to the same results as Justice Scalia's demanding First Amendment scrutiny.

[25] Such grants are made under Title X of the Public Health Service Act, 42 USC §§ 300–300a-6 (1988), which provides monies for family planning services. The HHS regulations appear at 42 CFR §§ 59.7–59.10 (1991).

[26] The grantees also argued that the regulations failed to comport with the governing statute and that they violated the Fifth Amendment right of women to choose to have an abortion. The Court rejected both these claims.

[27] 111 S Ct at 1772 (quoting *Regan v Taxation with Representation*, 461 US 540, 549 (1983)).

tively within broad limits:[28] the Court had rejected the proposition
"that if the government chooses to subsidize one protected right,
it must subsidize analogous counterpart rights."[29] In effect, the
"general rule that the Government may choose not to subsidize
speech" implied a corollary: the government may choose which
speech to fund.[30] And what of the usual First Amendment proscription against viewpoint discrimination? The Chief Justice suggested that in this context the term had no application: when the
government "has merely chosen to fund one [speech] activity to the
exclusion of the other[,]" the government "has not discriminated
on the basis of viewpoint."[31] In allotting funds, the government
was entitled to make "value judgment[s]."[32] The government could
subsidize speech promoting democracy, but not speech promoting
fascism;[33] the government could subsidize speech of family planning clinics (including anti-abortion speech) except for abortion
advocacy and referral. All followed from a simple point: "Title X
subsidies are just that, subsidies."[34] The statement echoes Justice
White in *R.A.V.*: Fighting words are just that, fighting words.
When the government has no general obligation, it has no obligation of neutrality.

Justice Blackmun's dissent in *Rust* vigorously disputed this proposition. Justice Blackmun acknowledged that the government generally has a choice whether to fund the exercise of a constitutional
right, but he insisted that "there are some bases upon which gov-

---

[28] Noting that funding by the government might not "invariably [be] sufficient to justify
government control over the content of expression," the Court proposed two potential
exceptions: when the subsidy was offered to a university or when the subsidy took the form
of providing a public forum. Id at 1776.

[29] Id at 1773.

[30] Id at 1776.

[31] It is conceivable that the Chief Justice intended to make a far narrower point than that
suggested in the text: he may have meant only that the particular funding decision at issue
did not involve viewpoint discrimination (as generally understood in First Amendment law),
because the HHS regulations merely drew a distinction, on the basis of subject matter,
between speech concerning preconception family planning and all other speech. In one
portion of the opinion, the Court indeed approaches this argument. See id at 1772. But the
argument, aside from being fallacious in light of the language of the regulations, see text at
note 99, cannot be thought to represent the whole, or even a major part, of the Court's
reasoniong: so narrow an interpretation of the decision makes most of the *Rust* opinion,
including the statements emphasized in the text, incomprehensible.

[32] Id at 1772.

[33] Id at 1773.

[34] Id at 1775 n 5.

ernment may not rest [a] decision" to fund expression.[35] Selective funding becomes impermissible when based upon the content— most clearly, upon the viewpoint—of the expression. The government may not " 'discriminate invidiously in its subsidies' " of speech by basing them on ideological viewpoint.[36] Thus, Justice Blackmun concluded, "[t]he majority's reliance on the fact that the Regulations pertain solely to funding decisions simply begs the question."[37] The point echoes Justice Scalia in *R.A.V.*: The concurrence's reliance on the fact that the St. Paul ordinance pertains solely to fighting words simply begs the question. Even in this circumstance, the government retains an obligation of neutrality.

Thus do the arguments in *Rust* and *R.A.V.* mirror each other. Between the two cases, the Court switched sides: the dissent in *Rust* became the *R.A.V.* majority, the majority in *Rust* became a concurrence in *R.A.V.* So too did most of the individual Justices trade positions; the difference in the outcome of the cases is hardly due to the change of mind of a single Justice.[38] But the structure of the dispute in the two cases is almost precisely the same. And that is because the *Rust* Court and the *R.A.V.* Court faced the same issue—a distinctive kind of First Amendment neutrality issue, extending far beyond *R.A.V.* and *Rust* themselves, which might best be labeled content-based underinclusion.

II

What, precisely, is content-based underinclusion? Suppose that the government, consistent with the First Amendment, may limit—by prohibiting or by refusing to subsidize—either an entire category of speech or all speech within a particular context. Now suppose that the government declines to go so far: rather than limiting speech to the full extent of its constitutional power, the government chooses to limit only some expression—and that on the basis of content. The resulting government action is, in the ordinary sense, narrower than the action stipulated to be constitutional. That is, the merely partial limitation allows more expres-

---

[35] Id at 1781.

[36] Id at 1780 (quoting *Regan*, 461 US at 548); see id at 1782.

[37] Id at 1781.

[38] See note 5.

sion. Yet this "narrower" action incorporates a content-based distinction: it picks and chooses among expression on the basis of what is said. The question thus becomes whether and when a government that has the power to restrict speech generally may instead limit select kinds of expression. Or, looked at from a different angle, the question is whether the government may voluntarily promote or protect some (but not all) speech on the basis of content, when none of the speech, considered in and of itself, has a constitutional claim to promotion or protection.

Such underinclusion—government may ban all speech in a category, but instead bans only some, defined by content—is a particular kind of content-based restriction, by no means equivalent to all government actions falling within the broad content-based category.[39] In many—indeed, most—cases of content-based speech restrictions, the question of inequality between different kinds of expression is wrapped in, and in practice inseparable from, a theoretically distinct issue: the permissibility of the burden placed on the speech affected. Consider, for example, a case arising from a statute that criminalizes in all contexts constitutionally protected speech—say, seditious advocacy. In deciding such a case, the Court usually will not ask whether the government has a sufficient reason to treat speech of one kind (seditious advocacy) differently from speech of another; rather, the Court will ask merely whether the government has a sufficient reason to restrict the speech actually affected.[40] The framing of the inquiry relates to the nature of the problem: in such a case, the issue is not underinclusion, for the government could not cure the constitutional flaw by extending the restriction to all speech regardless of its content.

By contrast, in a content-based underinclusion case, equality is

---

[39] Justice Scalia attempts in *R.A.V.* to avoid the term "underinclusiveness" in favor of the broader term "content discrimination," apparently because he thinks the former term more liable to the concurring opinions' charges of First Amendment absolutism. See 112 S Ct at 2545. But content-based underinclusion is no more than a distinctive kind of content-based distinction, and analysis explicitly focusing on underinclusion (when it exists) does no more than respond to the peculiar nature of the governmental action and the peculiar concerns it raises. Justice Scalia himself recognizes the need to distinguish among different kinds of content-based distinctions when he concedes that content-based analysis may take a somewhat different form in the context of wholly proscribable speech than in other First Amendment contexts. See id.

[40] See, e.g., *Brandenburg v Ohio*, 395 US 444 (1969) (per curiam); see generally Geoffrey R. Stone, *Content Regulation and the First Amendment*, 25 Wm & Mary L Rev 189, 202–3 (1983).

all that is at issue. Here, the Court usually will state the issue in terms of (and only in terms of) equal treatment. The Court will ask not whether the government has a sufficient reason for restricting the speech affected (taken in isolation), but whether the government has a sufficient reason for restricting the speech affected *and* not restricting other expression.[41] Once again, the framing of the inquiry follows from the structure of the problem. In these cases, by definition, the restriction is permissible but for the inequality, and the constitutional infirmity thus may be erased by extending the restriction to additional speech as well as by eliminating it entirely.[42] The First Amendment functions in these cases solely as a guarantee of some kind of equality on the plane of content.

The issue of content-based underinclusion arises in many settings—all superficially unlike, but all essentially similar.[43] One set of cases presenting the issue involves the selective imposition of otherwise reasonable time, place, or manner restrictions. Assume that a city may ban the use of noisy soundtrucks between sunset and sunrise in residential districts. Now assume that the city, rather than enacting this flat ban, exempts the use of soundtrucks to laud city government. One approach to this law holds that the burden imposed on speech is itself constitutionally permissible, but strikes down the law because of the content-based exemption.[44]

---

[41] On occasion the Court has focused on differential treatment without stating that a generally applied restriction of the same kind would be constitutional. But in almost all of the cases in which the Court has framed the question in this manner, such a general restriction on speech at least arguably would have satisfied constitutional standards. See, for example, *Police Dep't v Mosley*, 408 US 92 (1972).

[42] Justices frequently object to the Court's analysis in such cases precisely on the ground that it permits the enactment of a broader speech restriction. See 112 S Ct at 2553 (White concurring); id at 2561–62 (Stevens concurring); *Metromedia, Inc. v San Diego*, 453 US 490, 564 (1981) (Burger dissenting); *Carey v Brown*, 447 US 455, 475 (1980) (Rehnquist dissenting).

[43] See Geoffrey R. Stone, Louis M. Seidman, Cass R. Sunstein, and Mark V. Tushnet, *Constitutional Law* at 1337–62 (Little, Brown, 2d ed 1991), which organizes some cases along the lines I suggest in a section entitled "Equality and Free Expression."

[44] A court also might take either of two different approaches to the law. First, a court might ask whether the government has a compelling reason to burden the speech affected, without any exploration of the scope of the exemption. Under this approach, the content-based exemption serves to heighten the standard of review (to one of compelling interest); the ultimate inquiry, however, remains focused on the permissibility of the burden imposed, irrespective of the exemption. Second, a court might again focus on the permissibility of the burden imposed, but use the exemption not merely to heighten the standard of review, but to discredit the justification for the general speech restriction. For example, in the hypothetical given, a court might reason that if the city allows this exemption, then the city

Under this analysis, the permissibility of the general restriction is irrelevant: the government, even when it has discretion over allowing speech at all, may not grace a certain kind of speech with its special favor.[45]

Many Supreme Court cases reviewing limited time, place, or manner regulations incorporate this understanding of the content-based underinclusion problem and the analysis associated with it. In some of these cases, the regulations applied to the use of public forums. For example, in *Police Dept. v Mosley*,[46] the Court reviewed an ordinance that prohibited picketing on public streets near a school during certain hours, but exempted labor picketing from the general restriction. The Court held the ordinance unconstitutional because of the distinction between labor picketing and other picketing—because the ordinance worked a content-based "selective exclusion from a public place."[47] In other cases, the time, place, or manner restriction has applied outside the realm of public property. Thus, in *Metromedia v San Diego*,[48] the Court considered the

---

must view the interest in quiet during evening hours as insignificant, in which case the general restriction must fall. An analysis of this kind, although relying heavily on the exemption, in the end tests the constitutionality of the actual burden imposed on speech and finds that burden excessive. In other words, the exemption itself is not what is invalid; rather, the exemption proves the invalidity of a more general ban. See Stone, *Content Regulation and the First Amendment*, 25 Wm & Mary L Rev at 202–7 (cited in note 40).

[45] The Court in *R.A.V.* itself recognized the link between *R.A.V.* and cases of the kind discussed in the text. The Court compared the proscription of fighting words to the proscription of a noisy soundtruck. See 112 S Ct at 2544–45. The analogy implies that content-based distinctions within a generally proscribable category of speech (such as fighting words) present the same question as content-based distinctions superimposed on an otherwise valid time, place, or manner regulation.

[46] 408 US 92 (1972).

[47] Id at 94; see also *Carey v Brown*, 447 US 455 (1980) (invalidating on the same ground a statute prohibiting all picketing, except labor picketing, on streets surrounding residential places). *City of Lakewood v Plain Dealer Publishing Co.*, 108 S Ct 2138 (1988), presented the same issue in a different form. The case involved standards governing the allocation of city permits for newspaper vending machines. All assumed that the provision of city property (even public forum property) for vending machines was wholly optional, in the sense that the city government could choose whether it wished to allow any machines at all. The majority held that if the city chose to exercise this power, it must do so under standards that would safeguard against content discrimination. The dissent, written by Justice White and closely resembling his opinion in *R.A.V.*, concluded that because the First Amendment did not obligate the city to allow the placement of newsracks on city streets (or, in his words, because the placement of newsracks—like the use of fighting words—was not "protected by the First Amendment"), the city had no obligation to promulgate protective standards. In *Lakewood*, however, even Justice White agreed that were the city actually to engage in content discrimination in allocating newsrack permits, the First Amendment would come into play.

[48] 453 US 490 (1981).

legality of an ordinance restricting the use of billboards unless they fell within certain categories defined by content, such as political campaign signs or signs indicating the temperature or time. Here too, the Court struck down the law on the basis of its selectivity, entirely independent of the extent of the burden that the law imposed on the covered speech. The message in these cases, regardless whether public property was involved, was the same: even if speech generally may be regulated through reasonable time, place, or manner restrictions, such restrictions may not be imposed on speech only of a certain content.

All of these cases thus concern the same issue as *Rust* and *R.A.V.*, although they reach results identical only to the latter. In *Rust*, the Court permitted the government to favor (through funding) certain kinds of speech, on the ground that the government need not have favored any. In *Mosley* and *Metromedia*, the Court refused to allow the government to engage in similar selectivity: to favor (through donating public property or granting a regulatory exemption) certain kinds of speech on the ground that all speech could have been disfavored. If anything, as I will later discuss, *Rust* might be thought to raise a graver First Amendment problem, because the selectivity there was based on viewpoint, whereas in *Mosley* and *Metromedia*, it was based (at least facially) only on subject matter. In any event, the cases raised the same essential issue: the demands of First Amendment neutrality in a sphere in which government action respecting speech is in the first instance optional.

The Court often confronts the identical issue—but handles it differently—when dealing with speech restrictions applicable to non-public forums. Within broad limits, the government may choose to impose in such places sweeping restrictions on speech, so long as generally applicable.[49] Depending on the nature of the non-public forum, the government may have discretion to ban speech entirely. Frequently, however, the government chooses to restrict—in this context, up to the point of banning altogether—

---

[49] Restrictions must be "reasonable" in light of the nature and purposes of the non-public forum, but this standard frequently allows even wholesale prohibition of speech. For an example of the ease with which the reasonableness standard may be met in the context of non-public forums, see *International Society for Krishna Consciousness, Inc. v Lee*, 112 S Ct 2701 (1992). By contrast, in a public forum (whether traditional or designated), the government has only very narrow discretion to curtail speech generally, through limited time, place, or manner restrictions.

only speech of a certain content. Thus, the question once more arises: in circumstances in which the government need not allow or foster any speech, may it decide to allow or foster some speech on the basis of content?

Two cases will serve to illustrate how the issue arises—and how the Court has handled it—in this context. In *Lehman v City of Shaker Heights*,[50] the Court reviewed a municipal policy of refusing to sell advertising space on city buses to persons who wished to use the space to engage in political speech. After finding that the advertising space did not constitute a public forum, and thus that no general right of access applied, the Court was left with the question whether the municipality could bar only a certain kind of speech. Similarly, in *Greer v Spock*,[51] the Court considered whether a military base, also a non-public forum, could bar speeches and demonstrations of a partisan political nature, while allowing other kinds of expression. In these cases and others,[52] the Court has permitted some content-based distinctions (including those based on subject matter), but has drawn the line at distinctions that are based on viewpoint. The government may not use its broad discretion over the property it owns to advantage some viewpoints at the expense of others, but as in *Lehman* and *Greer* may make other distinctions based on content.

These cases too resemble *Rust* and *R.A.V.*, except in the rules the Court has established and the results it has reached. Banning all fighting words, as in *R.A.V.*, is no more problematic than banning all speech in a non-public forum. Yet in *R.A.V.*, the Court invalidated selective proscription, suggesting that even subject-matter distinctions violated the First Amendment, whereas in *Lehman* and *Greer*, the Court upheld such selective proscription. Perhaps, as I shall later discuss, the cases may be distinguished by virtue of the kind of content discrimination in each. But surely it should make no difference that the one case involves a selective ban within a wholly proscribable category of speech, the others a selective ban within a non-public forum. In both, what is at issue is the ability of the government to restrict some (but not all) speech

---

[50] 418 US 298 (1974).

[51] 424 US 828 (1976).

[52] See *Perry v Perry*, 460 US 37 (1983) (upholding statute granting preferential access to an interschool mail system); *Cornelius v NAACP*, 473 US 788 (1985) (upholding government policy limiting access to a charity drive aimed at federal employees).

when the government has the discretion to restrict the speech entirely.

From the discussion so far, it may come as little surprise to discover that even within a single setting—that of selective funding decisions—the problem of content-based underinclusion has bedeviled the Court. The government, as a general rule, need not fund any speech, whether through direct expenditures, tax exemptions, or other mechanisms.[53] But what if the government chooses to fund some (but not all) speech on the basis of content? Prior to *Rust*, the Court had confronted on several occasions this issue of selectivity in public funding decisions. In *Arkansas Writers' Project v Ragland*, for example, the Court considered the constitutionality of extending a tax exemption to religious, professional, trade, and sports journals, but not to general-interest magazines.[54] The Court struck down the exemption scheme because it rested on content distinctions, even though turning only on subject matter. In *Regan v Taxation with Representation*, by contrast, the Court approved a congressional decision to grant a tax subsidy to veterans' organizations, but not to other organizations, engaged in lobbying efforts.[55] There, the Court indicated (as it has in the non-public forum cases) that only viewpoint-based selectivity in government funding would violate the First Amendment.[56] Finally, as discussed

---

[53] This general rule is burdened with at least one prominent exception. The government has a broad obligation to permit speech in public forums; this donation of property for speech purposes is a form of funding. In addition, the government may have a duty to provide police protection and like services to speakers in certain circumstances. See *Edwards v South Carolina*, 372 US 229, 231–33 (1963); *Cox v Louisiana*, 379 US 536, 550 (1965). Once again, in providing these services, the government effectively funds expression. See generally Owen M. Fiss, *Why the State?*, 100 Harv L Rev 781, 786 (1987); Cass R. Sunstein, *Free Speech Now*, 59 U Chi L Rev 255, 273–74 (1992).

[54] 481 US 221 (1987).

[55] 461 US 540 (1983).

[56] The debate in *Ragland* and *Regan*, as in most such cases, focused explicitly on the question whether the government's power to refuse all funding implied a power to fund selectively. In dissent in *Ragland*, Justice Scalia saw as dispositive "the general rule that 'a legislature's decision not to subsidize the exercise of a fundamental right does not infringe the right.' " 481 US at 236 (quoting *Regan*, 461 US at 549). In *Regan*, the majority expounded this reasoning, citing the discretion of Congress over "this sort of largesse" and the absence of any First Amendment right to subsidization of speech. 461 US at 549. Other cases presenting substantially the same issue, in the context of government provision of services, are *Board of Education v Pico*, 457 US 853 (1982), in which the Court disapproved the removal of specified books from a school library over the objection that the government had no constitutional obligation to make available any book in a library, and *Southeastern Promotions v Conrad*, 420 US 546 (1975), in which the Court disapproved the exclusion of the musical "Hair" from a city auditorium over the objection that the city had substantial discretion to determine the nature of the entertainment it wished to support.

previously, the Court in *Rust* suggested that in the funding context even the prohibition on viewpoint discrimination docs not apply: the discretionary nature of funding decisions obviates any requirement of government neutrality among different kinds of expression.

What appears to emerge from the cases I have discussed—*Rust*, *R.A.V.*, and all the rest—is a set of diverse and contradictory responses to a single (and ubiquitous) First Amendment problem. All these cases, I have argued, pose the issue of content-based underinclusion, and yet the Court has failed to recognize this essential sameness. The argument, however, is so far only half complete. For although I have stated what bonds the cases, I have not yet explored what might be thought to unglue them. Perhaps there are real differences among these cases—-distinctions that reseparate in a principled manner what I have grouped together.

III

In this Part, I consider two objections to the proposition that *Rust* and *R.A.V.* belong to a single category of cases in which the government engages in content-based underinclusion. The first objection turns on the distinction between penalties and nonsubsidies, familiar from the Court's treatment of unconstitutional conditions cases. Cases such as *Rust*, it is said, involve nonsubsidies, whereas cases such as *R.A.V.* involve penalties; and selectivity with respect to nonsubsidies, but not penalties, is permissible. But the distinction between nonsubsidies and penalties founders in cases involving content-based underinclusion; perhaps more important, even if the distinction could be drawn, it would have no significance within this set of cases.

The second objection to viewing these cases as part of a single category relies on the government's plenary power to engage in speech itself. If the government has power to speak unrestrictedly, the argument runs, so too does the government have uncurtailed power to hire "agents" to engage in speech activities: thus does the government action in a case like *Rust*, but not in a case like *R.A.V.*, receive constitutional approval. But this approach also overlooks the distinctive character of content-based underinclusion cases, here by misunderstanding the way in which government action in these cases relates to the government's own expression. Both approaches fail to distinguish *Rust* and *R.A.V.*; both fail to fracture the category of content-based underinclusion; both fail to answer the question of First Amendment neutrality that category poses.

A

At the base of *Rust* lies the view that nonsubsidies and penalties are different—different in the sense that they can be distinguished from each other, and different also in the sense that the distinction matters. The government may not "penalize" a person for engaging in abortion advocacy, but the government may refuse to "subsidize" such speech, even if it subsidizes other, competing expression. The distinction between nonsubsidies and penalties runs across the gamut of unconstitutional conditions cases, whether or not involving the First Amendment; in these cases, the most common approach is to label governmental actions as either a penalty or a nonsubsidy, to declare the former coercive and unconstitutional, to declare the latter noncoercive and constitutionally permitted.[57]

This distinction prompts an obvious response to the argument I have been making. In discussing *Rust*, *R.A.V.*, and other cases, I have formulated the issue at stake in something like the following way: When may the government permit or subsidize some (but not all) speech on the basis of content in circumstances in which it need not permit or subsidize any? A skeptic might claim that the disjunctives in this statement are doing all the work—in other words, that I am conflating, through these simple "or"s, two separate inquiries. One question (raised, for example, by *Rust*) involves selective subsidies; the other (raised, for example, by *R.A.V.*) involves selective penalties. In that distinction, the argument further runs, lies a critical difference.

A first response to this argument contests the ease—or even the coherence—of an effort to sort out penalties from nonsubsidies in any content-based underinclusion case. In funding cases such as *Rust*, government action that seems to be a mere nonsubisdy becomes a penalty if viewed from a different, and no more contestable, perspective. Less obviously, the same is true (in reverse) of non-funding cases involving underinclusion, such as *R.A.V.*: gov-

---

[57] See, for example, *Regan*, 461 US 540; *Harris v McRae*, 448 US 297 (1980); *Speiser v Randall*, 357 US 513 (1958).

ernment action that seems, intuitively, a penalty becomes a mere nonsubsidy with a similar change in perspective.

Consider first a selective funding case like *Rust*, in which the difficulty of drawing the penalty/nonsubsidy distinction has frequently been noted.[58] In refusing to provide grants for abortion referrals, is the government penalizing or merely declining to subsidize this exercise of First Amendment rights? The answer rests upon the choice of a position—to use the inevitable jargon, a baseline—from which to measure the action. If the starting point assumes an absence of funding for any family planning services, including abortion referral, then the government action at issue is a nonsubsidy. If, by contrast, the starting point assumes funding for all family planning services, including abortion referral, then the government decision is a penalty.

The difficulty in such cases arises from the task of determining which position to adopt given that the action occurs within a realm of (frequently exercised) government prerogative. Presumably, the government action at issue should be viewed from the position of whatever state of affairs—funding or non-funding—is in some sense normal or natural. But in a world in which the government may and frequently does fund private speech and other activity, but has no general constitutional obligation to do so, the choice of this position is by no means obvious. What is the normal or natural state of affairs in such a world? Stated otherwise, what is a citizen (here, a family planning provider) entitled to expect? Nothing? Something? If the latter, what? The answers frequently are elusive.

Perhaps less obviously, the same difficulties attend any attempt to categorize the governmental action at issue (as penalty or nonsubsidy) in a case like *R.A.V.* A direct prohibition of speech, backed by sanctions, might seem the archetypal penalty. But the question in an underinclusion case, such as *R.A.V.*, is in fact more complicated. Remember that the government, acting within the Constitution, either may permit or may ban fighting words; the First Amendment has nothing to say respecting that decision. If that is so, we may measure the government action at issue from either of two perspectives. We may assume a perspective in which

---

[58] See, for example, Seth F. Kreimer, *Allocational Sanctions: The Problem of Negative Rights in a Positive State*, 132 U Pa L Rev 1293 (1984); Kathleen M. Sullivan, *Unconstitutional Conditions*, 102 Harv L Rev 1413 (1989); Cass R. Sunstein, *Why the Unconstitutional Conditions Doctrine Is an Anachronism*, 70 BU L Rev 593 (1990).

the government tolerates all fighting words; in that case, the prohibition of racial fighting words indeed smacks of a penalty. But alternatively, we may assume a perspective in which the government prohibits all fighting words; in that case, a ban on racial fighting words seems a mere nonsubsidy (with any exemption from the general prohibition counting as a subsidy).

As in the funding cases, the choice between the two stances—protection of fighting words or no protection of fighting words—is frequently unclear, and for much the same reason. Given a world in which the government may (and frequently does) but need not protect fighting words, either stance may seem justified. In this context too, it is no mean feat to determine the normal or natural state of affairs, or a citizen's entitlement. And thus in this context too, it is no mean feat to characterize the government action at issue as either a penalty or a nonsubsidy.

Consider, for example, two alternative avenues that a municipality might take to achieve the result of the St. Paul ordinance. First, suppose that a city government initially outlawed all fighting words and then, at some later date, repealed the measure except as to racial fighting words. The repealer in this example is as optional as the provision of funds in *Rust*. It follows that the remaining prohibition, no less than the refusal to fund abortion advocacy, can be considered a mere nonsubsidy. Or, second, suppose that a city government enacted a statute prohibiting fighting words generally, but then exempting, as a special act of legislative grace, non-racial fighting words. Here too, an obvious argument can be made that the exemption is a subsidy, all else nothing more than a refusal to subsidize.

This characterization seems more natural in the hypothetical cases than in *R.A.V.* itself, but that in no way undermines the point I am making. The characterization seems more apt because in choosing a stance from which to view government action, we instinctively consider how the world looked prior to the action and whether the action singles out certain speech for favorable or unfavorable treatment.[59] But this is—or, at the very least, should

---

[59] See Kreimer, 132 U Pa L Rev at 1359–71 (cited in note 58). Kreimer explicitly advocates the use of these factors to classify government action as a penalty or a nonsubsidy and to determine, on the basis of this classification, the action's constitutionality. My own proposed analysis does not depend on these considerations because it views as essentially irrelevant in the underinclusion context the determination whether government action constitutes a penalty or subsidy. See text following note 64.

be—as true in funding cases as in non-funding underinclusion cases
such as *R.A.V.* What the hypothetical cases show is that the same
debate over the proper characterization of government action may
arise in each of these contexts.

Thus far, the discussion suggests two points: first, that cases like
R.A.V. and *Rust* cannot easily be distinguished on the ground that
the one involves a penalty, the other a subsidy; and second, that
the distinction fails because, as shown previously, the cases alike
emerge from an area of government discretion. Lest it be at all
unclear, I emphasize that I am not, either here or elsewhere in
this essay, equating funding cases with all cases involving a direct
prohibition of speech. Rather, I am equating funding cases with a
specific kind of non-funding case—that involving underinclusion.
In these cases, as in funding cases, classification of the government
action at issue (as penalty or nonsubsidy) is problematic. It is so
because these cases, like funding cases, arise against a backdrop of
government prerogative: government may, but need not, act with
respect to the speech at issue. Were the Constitution to command
a certain action, the problem would evaporate. If the First Amendment, say, required the government to protect fighting words, the
requirement itself would establish the proper baseline, and any
deviation from the protection of fighting words would constitute a
penalty. Similarly in the funding cases, if the Constitution required
the government to pay for the exercise of speech rights, any refusal
to fund speech would penalize the speaker. The difficulty arises
when government has no such general obligation—when (assuming
no breach of applicable neutrality requirements) it can protect or
not protect, fund or not fund as it chooses.

The essential point applies well beyond the particular contexts
of *Rust* and *R.A.V.* As we have seen, general government prerogative exists in a number of First Amendment contexts: not only
when the government decides whether to fund speech (*Rust*), or to
ban speech falling within proscribable categories (*R.A.V.*), but also
when the government decides whether to prohibit speech in non-
public forums, as in *Greer*, or to issue reasonable time, place, or
manner regulations, as in *Mosley*. Here too we may ask whether
the government, in allowing only non-political speech on an army
base, has penalized political speech or subsidized non-political
speech. Or whether the government, in permitting only labor
speech around a school during certain hours, has granted a subsidy
to labor speech or imposed a penalty on all other expression.

In all of these underinclusion cases, we may play out endless arguments about whether government action with respect to some (but not all) speech has subsidized or penalized; we may say that the government has subsidized expressive activities in declining to exercise the full powers allotted to it under the First Amendment, or we may say that the government has penalized expressive activities in exercising only some subset of those powers. What alone is clear is that the subsidy/penalty line, properly understood, fails to separate any one of the contexts involving content-based underinclusion from the others. If one can be classified as a mere subsidy case, so too can they all.

The argument so far, however, seems subject to the objection that it disregards the ordinary meaning of the terms "subsidy" and "penalty." In common parlance, to subsidize speech means to pay for it; the government subsidizes expression when it picks up the costs of such activity, transferring them from a speaker to taxpayers generally. By contrast, to penalize speech means to impose a burden on a speaker—by fine or other means—that extends beyond requiring her to pay for her own expression.[60] From this standpoint, *Rust* involves a subsidy because the government is paying for speech (thus redistributing from taxpayers to speaker), whereas *R.A.V.* involves a penalty because the government is imposing an extra cost on the speaker (thus effectively redistributing in the opposite direction). Therein, it might be said, lies the difference.[61]

A bit of examination, however, reveals otherwise. The reason is simple: There are many ways for the government to pay for speech,

---

[60] Richard Epstein and Michael McConnell, in slightly different ways, build their conceptions of the whole unconstitutional conditions doctrine on this redistributive conception of the subsidy/penalty distinction (although McConnell also believes that some government actions counting as subsidies under this analysis still may violate the First Amendment). See Epstein (cited in note 12); Michael W. McConnell, *Unconstitutional Conditions: Unrecognized Implications for the Establishment Clause*, 26 San Diego L Rev 255 (1989).

[61] Under this approach, some "funding" cases of course will turn out to involve penalties, rather than subsidies. One example is *FCC v League of Women Voters*, 468 US 364 (1984), in which the Court invalidated a statute prohibiting broadcasters who received any federal monies from airing editorials; the effect of the statute was not merely to cut off government funding of editorials (a nonsubsidy under this approach), but to cut off funding of all the broadcaster's activities if it aired editorials (a penalty under this approach because the benefits withheld went beyond the costs of the speech). See Michael W. McConnell, *The Selective Funding Problem: Abortions and Religious Schools*, 104 Harv L Rev 989, 1016–17 (1991). The primary point I will make is different: that "non-funding" underinclusion cases like *R.A.V.* may turn out to involve subsidies under a test focusing on whether government is merely refusing to pay for speech or exacting some additional cost from the speaker.

and all content-based underinclusion cases—regardless whether they involve the writing of a check from tax revenues—involve some mechanism by which the government picks up some of the costs of a speaker's expression.

Consider in this regard the ordinance in *R.A.V.*, which regulated a brand of fighting words. Such expression, by definition, imposes a cost not merely on other individuals (the targets of the fighting words), but on society at large: fighting words "are of such slight social value as a step to truth that any benefit that may be derived from them is clearly outweighed by the social interest in order and morality."[62] It is indeed partly because of the social cost caused by fighting words that the Court has placed them in a wholly pro-scribable category. May it then not be said that in declining to regulate fighting words, the government picks up the cost of the speech, effectively paying (or forcing other citizens to pay) for it? The regulation of fighting words then appears a mere nonsub-sidy, the refusal to regulate a classic example of subsidization.[63] Under this approach to the penalty/subsidy distinction, there is no more a constitutional "penalty" on speech in *R.A.V.* than there was in *Rust*. Both involve decisions to subsidize some expressive activities and not others.

Other kinds of content-based underinclusion cases also raise, in this sense, the issue of selective subsidization. Return here to the non-public forum cases such as *Greer*, which involved speech on a military base. The donation of such public property—property whose ordinary use is to some extent incompatible with expres-sion—constitutes a subsidy, an absorption by the public of the costs associated with allowing expressive activity in the forum. The

---

[62] *Chaplinsky v New Hampshire*, 315 US 568, 572 (1942). The cost of fighting words may take a number of forms. If such words "by their very utterance inflict injury," they will at least impose a direct harm on their target; if they "tend to incite an immediate breach of the peace," they will impose as well a cost on the general public, including money spent for police protection.

[63] The same is true of the regulation of speech falling within any other category of wholly or partially proscribable expression, such as obscenity or some kinds of libel. Such regulation appears a mere nonsubsidy, in that it operates to prevent the speaker from transferring significant costs to the public; conversely, a refusal to regulate in these areas works as a subsidy, with the public determining to absorb the costs of the expression. For discussions of the way in which constitutional privileges in libel law subsidize speakers at the expense of those defamed, see Richard A. Posner, *Economic Analysis of Law* § 27.2 at 670 (Little, Brown, 4th ed 1992); Frederick Schauer, *Uncoupling Free Speech*, 92 Colum L Rev 1321, 1326–43 (1992).

denial of access to such property, by contrast, appears as a simple refusal to subsidize expression.[64] The same is true of cases arising from selective imposition of otherwise valid time, place, or manner restrictions, such as *Metromedia*. Here too, the government has determined that speech (in the form of billboards) imposes costs on the public. With respect to certain kinds of speech, that cost is absorbed by the taxpayers; with respect to other kinds of speech, the cost is thrown back on the speaker.

The ability to view all underinclusion cases in this manner again springs from their common grounding in a sphere of government discretion. As a general rule, the government has discretion to regulate or limit speech (assuming no violation of neutrality principles) precisely when such regulation plausibly may be described as a mere nonsubsidy in the sense just described. Thus, even if we view the subsidy/penalty line as appropriately defined by the direction of redistribution (from the speaker to the public or from the public to the speaker), cases such as *R.A.V.*—cases in which the government starts with general discretionary powers—appear not very different from direct funding cases like *Rust*. Whatever differences may exist in the form of the subsidy cannot be thought of constitutional significance.

But more than this may be said, for even if the penalty/subsidy distinction could serve to separate some underinclusion cases from others (*Rust*, for example, from *R.A.V.*), the distinction would remain, in the context of underinclusion cases, essentially irrelevant. Assume for the moment that the action involved in *R.A.V.* constitutes a "penalty." The First Amendment objection to the action cannot focus on the penalty itself—cannot focus, for example, on the extent to which it, relative to a subsidy, cuts off speech—given that the fighting words doctrine permits the government to penalize

---

[64] The relation of this analysis to public forum doctrine raises interesting questions. As previously noted, the government has a broad obligation to donate public forums for expressive purposes. The public forum cases thus might be viewed as stating an exception to the general rule that the government need not subsidize expression; indeed, I have considered public forums as forced subsidies at note 53. In keeping with the understanding of subsidies and penalties used in this discussion, however, we might consider the public forum cases not to involve subsidies at all. If public forums are at least in part defined as places compatible with expressive activity, then permitting speech in such places imposes few additional costs on the public. Cf. McConnell, *The Selective Funding Problem*, 104 Harv L Rev at 1033 (cited in note 61). This case, however, becomes more difficult to make as public forums are increasingly defined, as they have been in recent years, simply in terms of some historical criteria. See *International Society for Krishna Consciousness v Lee*, 112 S Ct 2701 (1992).

all speech of this kind. The objection instead must turn on government selectivity: the government has (dis)favored some speech on illegitimate grounds. In other words, if a selective penalty in a case like R.A.V. is constitutionally forbidden, the reason must have everything to do with the selection, and nothing to do with the penalty, which is, in and of itself, perfectly permissible. And if this is so, any distinction between a case like R.A.V. and a case like Rust cannot lie in the differing terms "penalty" and "subsidy." These terms should be viewed as constitutionally irrelevant; what has meaning in the cases—and in all underinclusion cases—is government selection. The Court's focus should be on this issue, and not on a set of terms bearing no real relation to it. The penalty/subsidy distinction provides meager aid in explaining Rust, R.A.V., or any other case of content-based underinclusion.

B

Unstated in any decision, but perhaps vaguely perceived by the Justices, is another notion—this one relating to the government's own speech—that may explain the divergent outcomes in Rust and R.A.V. and, more broadly, challenge the existence of a single category of content-based underinclusion cases encompassing Rust, R.A.V., and others. The argument starts from the premise—not undisputed but generally accepted—that the First Amendment places few limits on the government's own expressive activities; by and large, the government may speak as it chooses.[65] Of course, as a physical if not a constitutional matter, "the government" cannot speak; it can speak only through employees and agents. To say, then, that the First Amendment allows the government to speak is to say that the First Amendment allows the government (more precisely, its employees and agents) to hire employees and agents to do its speaking for it.[66]

---

[65] For purposes of this discussion, I accept the premise that the First Amendment imposes only minor limits on the government's own speech. For a lengthy and critical exploration of this premise, see Mark G. Yudof, *When Government Speaks* (University of California Press, 1983).

[66] The Supreme Court has indicated that the First Amendment protects even an individual's decision to hire or otherwise pay for a speaker, but also has suggested that the constitutional interest in such vicarious speech is of some lesser magnitude than the interest in direct speech. See *Buckley v Valeo*, 424 US 1 (1976) (discussing why a limitation on contributions to political campaigns poses fewer constitutional problems than a limitation on direct campaign expenditures).

From this premise emerges a claim that (at least some) government funding cases differ from all other cases of content-based underinclusion. When the government funds speech, even of hitherto private parties, the government is merely hiring agents to engage in speech for it. In paying for speech, it is speaking; if the latter is permissible, so is the former. Thus a decision like *Rust* becomes justifiable: in funding certain kinds of speech, the government effectively is engaging in the speech, and so the Constitution imposes few limits. But the same cannot be said, or so the argument goes, of a case like *R.A.V.*, which involves restrictions on the speech of private parties. The government's plenary power over its own speech provides a constitutional basis for decisions to fund expression of a particular kind, but provides no basis for decisions, even if wholly voluntary, to permit speech of a certain content.[67]

This argument can be contested on two independent grounds. The first disputes the equation of "government speech" and government funded speech. The second disputes the differentiation, with respect to "government speech," of funding decisions and other kinds of content-based underinclusion.

To appreciate some of the difficulties involved in equating government speech with government funding—because government can speak, it can fund others to speak—consider the following hypothetical: a city council enacts an ordinance providing that any person who endorses the actions of city government shall be entitled to a cash grant or tax exemption.[68] The city government itself—by which I mean municipal employees acting in their official capacity—constitutionally could engage in speech of this kind, and such speech might drown out, and hence render ineffective, countervailing expression. Given this power to speak, the hypothetical subsidy scheme cannot be attacked on the bare ground that it skews public debate about municipal government; the government's own speech also may have a skewing effect. And yet, the hypothetical

---

[67] I am grateful to my colleague Michael McConnell for raising this argument with me, though I do not think it should be taken (at least in this barebones form) as a statement of his position.

[68] Few would question the equivalence of a cash grant or other direct expenditure and a tax exemption, deduction, or credit in a scheme of this kind. As the Supreme Court has recognized, "Both tax exemptions and tax deductibility are a form of subsidy that is administered through the tax system." *Regan v Taxation with Representation*, 461 US 540, 544 (1983). Indeed, such tax provisions frequently are referred to as "tax expenditures." See Bernard Wolfman, *Tax Expenditures: From Idea to Ideology*, 99 Harv L Rev 491 (1985).

funding scheme seems (at the least) constitutionally problematic—far more so than what might be called direct government speech. The First Amendment problems also seem severe in a case, more closely analogous to *Rust*, in which the government makes cash grants not to the public at large, but to all political clubs for purposes of speech endorsing city government. Why do these funding programs appear to present greater constitutional difficulties than the government's own expression?[69]

As an initial matter, when the government itself speaks in favor of a position, we (the people) know who is talking and can evaluate the speech accordingly. (When the government speaks to laud itself, we may pay the speech little attention.) By contrast, when the government finances hitherto private parties to do its speaking, we may have little understanding of the source of the expression. This problem is particularly acute if we do not know of the existence of the funding scheme; then we will consistently mistake the interested for the impartial. But even if we know of the funding scheme, we will face a problem of attribution. The speakers may have engaged in the same expression without any government funding; alternatively, the speakers may have foregone their expression (or even espoused a different view) in the absence of a subsidy. We do not know whether to treat the speakers as independent or as hired guns. We thus may give the speech more (or less) weight than it deserves.

A related concern is that the funding scheme will operate to distort or influence the realm of private expression in a manner that systemically advantages public power. When the government speaks directly, it merely adds a voice (though perhaps a resounding one) to a conversation occurring among private parties. When the government speaks through subsidy schemes, it may change and reshape the underlying dialogue. What once were private choices—shall I praise the city government, criticize it, or say nothing at all?—now become in some measure governmental, as citizens calculate a set of economic incentives offered to them by government actors. The resulting choices by private individuals and organizations may give greater volume to the government's voice than the government could have achieved on its own. As

---

[69] For a related discussion of this question, see Cass R. Sunstein, *The Speech Market* (Free Press, forthcoming).

important, such funding schemes may subvert the very ability of a private sphere to provide a countermeasure to government power.

Rust illustrates the way in which government funding may have both more potent and more disruptive effects than direct government speech, even holding expenditures constant. The impact of the government's own speech on abortion questions likely pales in comparison to the impact of advice and counseling given to pregnant women by health care providers. (The reason relates not only to the source of the speech—an apparently independent professional—but also to the time at which it occurs.) How better, then, to communicate an anti-abortion message: through direct speech or through selective subsidization of health care providers? The latter course amplifies the government's own message at the same time as (and partly because) it wreaks havoc on the ability of those private parties in the best position to challenge the message to provide a counterweight to government authority.[70]

But even if, or to the extent that, government funding decisions can be equated with government speech, so too can other content-based underinclusive government actions. Suppose (to borrow a hypothetical from Justice Scalia's opinion for the Court in *R.A.V.*) a city council enacts an ordinance prohibiting those legally obscene works—but only those legally obscene works—that do not include an endorsement of the municipal government.[71] The hypothetical involves an exemption from otherwise permissible regulation, rather than a direct cash grant or an exemption from taxation. Yet, as shown previously, no reason exists for treating the one as different from the others. In the regulatory exemption case, the government is still paying for speech in every significant respect: the speaker receives a benefit for expressing views supportive of city government, and the government absorbs costs of the expression that normally would be borne by the speaker. The mechanism is different, but the essential act is the same. If the government

---

[70] I do not claim that every government funding program will pose these dangers or that no funding program should be assimilated to government speech. A funding program may be constructed in so narrow a fashion as to appear identical (or nearly so) to the government's own expression. This will be true when the constitutional concerns I have discussed are slight or absent. But as I will show, the same may be said of other (non-funding) decisions involving content-based underinclusion. The fact of funding is neither necessary nor sufficient to transform content-based underinclusive action into government expression.

[71] 112 S Ct at 2543.

"speaks" when it pays for speech by private parties, then the government is speaking in the *R.A.V.* Court's hypothetical.

The point can be made across the entire range of content-based underinclusion cases. In *Rust*, of course, the government made a direct cash grant for some kinds of expresssion, but not for others. In *R.A.V.*, which Justice Scalia saw as perfectly analogous to his obscenity hypothetical, the government offered some expression an exemption from otherwise applicable regulation of a proscribable speech category. The same mechanism is involved in cases, such as *Metromedia*, in which certain kinds of speech receive an exemption from otherwise reasonable time, place, or manner restrictions on expressive activity. And in some sense, the non-public forum cases bridge the gap: a rule that allows certain speech but not other speech on, say, a military base, as in *Greer*, can be viewed either as a direct grant (of certain rights in property, rather than of cash) or as an exemption from a generally applicable regulation prohibiting speech in a certain context. The key point is that the government actions in all these cases stand in a similar relation to government speech: in all, the government uses its powers, within a sphere of general discretion, to pick up the costs of speech—to pay for speech—of a particular content.

The argument based on government speech thus appears of limited consequence. The argument does not successfully challenge my central thesis: that there exists a single category of content-based underinclusion cases, all of which—regardless whether they involve direct funding—raise the same First Amendment issue. Nor does the government speech approach provide a comprehensive way of dealing with this issue. We can doubtless find instances of content-based underinclusion—again, some involving direct funding, some not—in which the government appears to be doing little more than speaking itself.[72] Yet surely, with respect to each

---

[2] In the non-public forum context, for example, we might wonder about a legal doctrine that would permit a general to speak to troops on a restricted military base about, say, alcohol use, but would preclude the general from inviting an expert on alcohol dependency to give a similar speech. An example of this kind suggests that courts might well recognize the possibility that, in a particular case, speech by a nominally private party should be treated as government speech. The inquiry should focus on the concerns mentioned above: whether the speech is clearly attributable to the government and whether the government's action, in promoting the speech, threatens to interfere with the realm of private discourse in a way direct government speech would not. Indeed, it is possible that even direct government expression should be tested by standards of a similar kind.

kind of content-based underinclusion mentioned, we will find many (almost certainly, many more) cases in which the government, through use of its discretionary funding or regulatory powers, is doing something more than speaking—is in fact influencing and shaping the world of private discourse in a way that accords with its own beliefs of what kinds of speech should be promoted. *R.A.V.* arguably is one example; *Rust* arguably is another. To treat all this as permissible government speech is to ignore the scope and effect of the government action and the constitutional problems such actions may raise. It is to evade the critical question: In a sphere of general discretion over speech, when may government prefer private speech of a certain content to private speech of another?

IV

The cases I have discussed raise a common First Amendment issue and call for a common constitutional analysis. I do not suggest that all cases of content-based underinclusion must "come out" in the same manner. I do not, for example, assert that if *R.A.V.* is right, then *Rust* must be wrong, or vice versa. I claim only that these cases, and others raising the issue of content-based underinclusion, should be subjected to the same constitutional standards.

Establishing those standards is no easy task. The problem of selective funding alone has confounded generations of judges and constitutional scholars. I have argued that selective funding cases must be assimilated to other instances of content-based underinclusion. The difficulty, therefore, far from being eased, is in fact broadened.

In this part, I thus offer a preliminary—and necessarily sketchy—view of the proper constitutional approach to cases raising the issue of content-based underinclusion. I start by sorting through, in a more concrete fashion than I have done before, the diverse and conflicting ways the Court has responded to this problem. I then suggest, taking into account the effect and motive of government action, a distinction between two kinds of content-based underinclusion: that involving subject matter, which generally is acceptable; and that involving viewpoint, which generally is not. Finally, harking back to *Rust* and especially to *R.A.V.*, I propose certain modifications to this simple division of the cases—instances in which subject matter–based distinctions should raise constitutional concern and, perhaps too, instances in which viewpoint-based distinctions should be tolerated.

The Court, failing to recognize the common problem of content-based underinclusion, has employed a variety of constitutional standards in the kinds of cases discussed in this article. At one extreme, the Court has indicated that within a sphere of general discretion, the government has near-complete freedom to make content-based distinctions with respect to speech. At the other extreme, the Court has stated that the government is barred (at least in the absence of the most compelling justification) from making any such distinctions. Between these two positions lie others, sometimes only half-articulated, premised on the notion that not all content-based distinctions are alike. Thus, the Court at times has indicated that within an area of general discretion, the government may restrict speech on the basis of subject matter or speaker, but not on the basis of viewpoint. These various standards sometimes correspond to the different contexts in which the problem of content-based underinclusion arises, so that in each context a single standard holds sway. More confusingly, a plurality of these standards may coexist and compete within even a single subcategory of content-based underinclusion cases.

The greatest disarray, as I have noted, appears in the selective funding cases, in which the Court has adopted the full range of positions just described. Prior to *Rust*, the Court had indicated that in the funding context, some kinds of content discrimination mattered profoundly, though precisely what kinds remained uncertain. Thus, in *Arkansas Writers' Project, Inc. v Ragland*,[73] the Court explicitly rejected any distinction between subject matter–based and viewpoint-based regulation, stating that all content-based regulation was subject to strict scrutiny.[74] By contrast, in *Regan v Taxation with Representation*,[75] the Court held that the government, in

---

[73] 481 US 221 (1987).

[74] Id at 230. The stringency of the Court's analysis may be attributable to a special concern about press regulation. The Court emphasized that "selective taxation of the press—either singling out the press as a whole or targeting individual members of the press—poses a particular danger of abuse by the State." Id at 228. A standard so strict applying to all funding decisions would prevent almost all government funding of expression.

[75] 461 US 540 (1983).

funding speech, could make some kinds of content-based distinctions, but suggested in dicta that funding on the basis of viewpoint would violate the Constitution.[76] Finally, in *Rust* the Court took the position that the government could fund expression as it wished, in accordance with its "value judgments."[77] In the context of funding, the whole question of content discrimination—including viewpoint discrimination—became irrelevant.

In each of the other contexts discussed in this article, the Court has concluded that even within a sphere of general discretion, the First Amendment prohibits the government from making certain kinds of content distinctions; the Court, however, has adopted a less rigorous approach in non-public forum cases than in others. In the non-public forum cases, the Court has denied the government only the power to make viewpoint distinctions; regulations based on subject matter or speaker identity, so long as they satisfy a toothless reasonableness inquiry, are permitted.[78] By contrast, in cases such as *Metromedia* or *Mosley*, in which the Court considered limited time, place, or manner regulations involving either no public property or a public forum, the Court generally has applied strict scrutiny to all content-based exemptions, regardless whether the exemptions pertain to particular viewpoints or to more general subject matter categories. Here, the Court repeatedly has held that the government "may not choose the appropriate subjects for public discourse," even if, in doing so, "the government does not favor one side over another."[79]

The Court in *R.A.V.* leaned toward the position taken in cases such as *Mosley*, although with numerous hedges and qualifications.

---

[76] Id at 548, 550 (disapproving funding decisions " 'aimed at the suppression of dangerous ideas' " (quoting *Cammarano v United States*, 358 US 498 (1959)); id at 551 ("[A] statute designed to discourage the expression of particular views would present a very different question.") (Blackmun concurring). The Court, in approving speaker-based funding decisions and disapproving viewpoint-based funding decisions, expressed no opinion on the permissibility of funding decisions based on the subject matter of speech. In other cases, however, the Court has treated similarly speaker-based and subject matter–based restrictions, distinguishing both from restrictions based on viewpoint. See, for example, *Perry v Perry*, 460 US 37 (1983); *Cornelius v NAACP*, 473 US 788 (1985).

[77] 111 S Ct at 1772.

[78] Thus, for example, the Court in *Greer v Spock*, 424 US 828 (1976), allowed a military base to exclude all partisan political speakers, and the Court in *Lehman v City of Shaker Heights*, 418 US 298 (1974), permitted a muncipal transportation system to refuse to post political advertisements. See also *Cornelius*, 473 US at 806; *Perry*, 460 US at 49.

[79] *Metromedia, Inc. v San Diego*, 453 US 490, 515, 518 (1981) (plurality); see *Carey v Brown*, 447 US 455, 460–61, 462 n 6 (1980); *Police Dep't v Mosley*, 408 US 92, 95, 99 (1972).

The *R.A.V.* Court, of course, ruled that at least some content-based distinctions within a proscribable category of speech violate the Constitution: "the First Amendment imposes . . . a 'content discrimination' limitation upon a State's prohibition of proscribable speech."[80] But what is the exact content of this limitation? The Court made clear that in the context of proscribable speech, the constitutional ban extends beyond explicit viewpoint-based distinctions; indeed, in the first statement of its holding, the Court declared the St. Paul law unconstitutional because it made distinctions "solely on the basis of the subjects the speech addresses."[81] Yet the Court declined to say that in this sphere the First Amendment renders suspect all content-based restrictions: "the prohibition against content discrimination is not absolute. It applies differently in the context of proscribable speech than in the area of fully protected speech."[82] Repeatedly asking whether a regulation would pose a "significant danger of idea or viewpoint discrimination," the Court listed a series of constitutionally unobjectionable content-based distinctions.[83] The list closed with the suggestion that, within a proscribable category of speech, content-based distinctions may be permissible so long as they present "no realistic possi-

---

[80] 112 S Ct at 2545.

[81] Id at 2542. The Court later concluded that the ordinance also discriminated with regard to viewpoint, but as I will discuss, this argument at least raised questions; the Court's decision thus depended heavily on the ban on subject matter restrictions. With respect to this ban, the majority opinion differed not only from Justice White's approach, but also from Justice Stevens's alternative analysis. Unlike Justice White, Justice Stevens would view certain content-based distinctions within proscribable categories of speech as constitutionally troubling. But Justice Stevens, unlike the *R.A.V.* majority, apparently would accord automatic strict scrutiny only to those content distinctions based explicitly on viewpoint. See id at 2568–69.

[82] Id at 2545.

[83] Id at 2545–47. First on the list were distinctions supported by the very factor that rendered the entire category of speech proscribable. To use one of Justice Scalia's examples, the government could prohibit, from the broad category of legally obscene materials, only the "most lascivious displays of sexual activity." Id at 2546. As each of the concurrences noted, this exception may have covered the St. Paul ordinance, which reasonably could be viewed as an attempt to prohibit, from the entire category of fighting words, those which "by their very utterance" inflict the greatest injury or pose the greatest danger of retaliatory violence. See id at 2556, 2565. Justice Scalia also excepted from rigorous constitutional scrutiny laws containing content distinctions based on the "secondary effects" (i.e., noncommunicative effects) of speech, as well as laws directed against conduct but incidentally covering a content-based subcategory of proscribable speech. See id at 2546–47. Finally, Justice Scalia would have viewed more leniently (although his reasoning on this count is mysterious) a prohibition of speech falling within a proscribable category that is "directed at certain persons or groups," id at 2548—yet another exception that reasonably could have been used to insulate the St. Paul ordinance from strict review.

bility that official suppression of ideas is afoot."[84] Whether a regulation prohibiting expression on certain subjects ever could fall within this "general exception" to the ban on content discrimination was left uncertain.

What then is the right approach? When, if ever, will some manner of content-based underinclusion invalidate a speech regulation? As I have said, the same constitutional standards should govern all of the various kinds of cases discussed in this article. I do not mean to suggest that the government interests underlying the underinclusive regulation of speech will be identical in all contexts. The nature of the government action at issue—for example, direct funding of speech or regulation of speech within a non-public forum—will sometimes provide distinctive justifications for content-based underinclusion.[85] Thus, in acting as manager of a military base, the government may have—as it claimed to have in *Greer*—peculiar reasons for restricting some speech, such as the interest in insulating a military establishment from partisan political causes. Similarly, in providing direct funding out of public coffers, the government frequently will have to take into account the limited availability of revenues devoted to a particular program or purpose. But because each kind of government action discussed in this article affects First Amendment rights in the same way, each should be held to the same set of justificatory burdens. The remaining question concerns the appropriate content of these burdens. That question is best approached by focusing on the nature of the First Amendment problem in all of these cases.

Thus recall what the Court confronts in each one of these contexts. The government is operating within a sphere of general discretion: it can refuse to promote or allow any speech at all. Instead, the government chooses to advance or permit some, but not other, speech on the basis of content. If the Court strikes down the action, citing content discrimination, the government can return to a general ban, becoming (in terms of total quantity of speech) more, rather than less, speech restrictive. The government can prohibit all fighting words, can bar all speakers from a military base, can

---

[84] Id at 2547. As an illustration of a content-based distinction posing no threat of censorship of ideas, Justice Scalia hypothesized an ordinance prohibiting only those obscene motion pictures featuring blue-eyed actresses.

[85] Cf. Sullivan, 102 Harv L Rev at 1503 (cited in note 58); Sunstein, *Why the Unconstitutional Conditions Doctrine Is an Anachronism*, 70 BU L Rev at 607 (cited in note 58).

prevent any person from using a noisy soundtruck, can decline to fund any speech. If all this is so, one way to approach the problem at least becomes clear. What we need to ask is when content discrimination resulting in more speech is of greater constitutional concern than content neutrality resulting in less. We can begin, in other words, to tackle the essential issue in all of these cases by rephrasing it (somewhat crudely) in the following terms: When is some speech worse than none?[86]

A proper response to this inquiry should focus on both the effects and the purposes of content-based underinclusive action. In other words, government regulation allowing some speech may raise greater constitutional problems than regulation allowing no speech at all either because the former has graver consequences than the latter or because the former more likely proceeds from an improper impulse. Both considerations suggest an initial, broad distinction between underinclusive action based on viewpoint and underinclusive action based on subject matter.

Consider first the possible consequences of underinclusive regulation of speech on the realm of public discourse.[87] Sometimes, such regulation will place particular messages at a comparative disadvantage and, in doing so, will distort public debate. An example is Justice Scalia's hypothetical ordinance prohibiting all legally obscene materials except those containing an endorsement of city government. Such a law leaves untouched speech supportive of city government, while restricting speech critical of city government, thereby skewing discourse on this issue. That obscenity (like fight-

---

[86] It might be argued that framing the inquiry in this way assumes unjustifiably that the government will respond to the invalidation of a content-based distinction by expanding the reach of the speech restriction, rather than by eliminating it entirely. This objection recognizes, quite correctly, that in some circumstances an apparently "greater" power is in fact practically or politically constrained; in that event, if the "lesser" power is removed, the government will not exercise its authority at all. See Kreimer, 132 U Pa L Rev at 1313 (cited in note 58). But in the settings discussed in this article, the objection appears to have only slight weight. The more expansive powers here—enacting limited time, place, or manner restrictions, establishing broad speech restrictions for non-public forums, declining to fund speech, proscribing categories of speech like fighting words or obscenity—are in most instances not merely theoretically but actually available; the government very frequently exercises such powers. We indeed may wish to keep in mind that in some cases, the government as a practical matter will not be able to—or, perhaps more frequently, will not wish to—expand the coverage of a speech restriction, but the central inquiry in these contexts remains as I have described it in the text.

[87] See Stone, *Content Regulation and the First Amendment*, 25 Wm & Mary L Rev at 198–200, 217–27 (cited in note 40), for a full discussion of these issues in connection not with content-based underinclusion, but with content-based discrimination generally.

ing words) is by definition unprotected makes no difference to the analysis; the distortion relates to ideas and messages extrinsic to that category. It is true that the distorting effect occurs at the margin; persons opposed to city government can communicate this message through means other than obscenity. Yet the ordinance remains more constitutionally problematic than a total ban on obscenity, which would have no skewing effect at all on the debate concerning city government.[88] Precisely the same point can be made in the context of direct funding. Assume our city council, informed of the decisions in *R.A.V.* and *Rust*, instead passed a law providing for public funding of all speech endorsing incumbent city officials in their campaigns for reelection. Such a law similarly provides a comparative advantage to messages of endorsement, thereby again skewing public debate. As with the obscenity statute, the skewing effect makes the statute more troublesome than a complete absence of public funding.[89]

Not all instances of content-based underinclusion, however, will have such problematic effects. Contrast to the viewpoint-based laws used above a set of regulations discriminating in terms of general subject matter. First, suppose that the city council enacts a law prohibiting all obscene materials except those dealing in any way with government affairs. It is no longer so clear that a total ban on obscenity would better serve First Amendment interests. At least facially, the law does not skew public debate about matters

---

[88] Of course, a total ban on obscenity removes all obscene messages from the world of public discourse, which in some other world might be thought a constitutional problem of large dimension. The premise here—accepted by the Supreme Court—is that eliminating obscenity per se from the realm of public debate raises no First Amendment problem whatsoever. A premise of similar kind exists in all cases of content-based underinclusion.

[89] The notion of a skewing effect, as set forth in the text, of course assumes that distortion arises from government, rather than from private, action. That assumption may be misplaced. If there is "too much" expression of a particular idea in an unregulated world, then government action specially disfavoring that idea might "un-skew," rather than skew, public discourse. See Fiss, 100 Harv L Rev at 786–87 (cited in note 53); Sunstein, *Free Speech Now*, 59 U Chi L Rev at 295–97 (cited in note 53). An understanding of this point has special relevance in considering underinclusive government action. With respect to such actions, the only constitutional worry is equality among ideas; restriction, taken alone, need not concern us. The situation is very different in the case of other kinds of speech restrictions, whose unconstitutionality may rest as much or more in considerations of personal autonomy as in considerations of equality. See generally David A. Strauss, *Persuasion, Autonomy, and Freedom of Expression*, 91 Colum L Rev 334 (1991). Nonetheless, I think the assumption used here to measure distortion is generally, although not invariably, proper. Any other would allow the government too great—and too dangerous—an authority to decide what ideas are overrepresented or underrepresented in the market.

involving government, as the viewpoint-based obscenity ordinance did.[90] Of course, the law allows the use of obscene materials to speak about government affairs, while restricting the use of those materials to speak about a host of other subjects. But neither those who wish to speak on such subjects nor their potential audience can claim in any real sense that the ordinance harms them more than would a ban on all obscene materials. The law, viewed solely in terms of effects on public debate, thus appears consistent with the First Amendment. And once again, the same is true of a similar statute involving the mechanism of direct funding. Assume that the city council passes a law providing for public funding of all candidates for elected office. Here too, the statute makes a content-based distinction: one kind of speech is funded, all other speech is not. But as long as the law covers all candidates and parties, no one can complain that the subsidy plan has effects on public debate that are constitutionally more troublesome than a refusal to subsidize at all.[91]

Yet effects are not all that matter in considering the permissibility of content-based underinclusion; we also must take into account the purposes underlying the government action.[92] Notwithstanding that another, more speech restrictive action could have been taken (assuming a proper purpose), the purpose of *this* action—the action in fact taken—must fall within the range of constitutional legitimacy. What objectives fall outside that range? It is a staple of First Amendment law that no government action may be taken because public officials disapprove of the message communicated. The flip side of this principle, as Geoffrey Stone has noted, is that "the government may not exempt expression from an otherwise general restriction because it agrees with the speaker's views."[93] Thus, as the *R.A.V.* Court stated: "The government may not regulate use [of fighting words] based on hostility—or favoritism—towards the

---

[90] I consider at text accompanying note 110 problems relating to viewpoint-differential consequences of such facially viewpoint-neutral laws. It may well be that this statute looks sufficiently odd to heighten concerns about such consequences.

[91] In covering all parties and candidates, the hypothetical statute stands on firmer ground than the subsidy scheme approved in *Buckley v Valeo*, 424 US 1 (1976), which funds some candidates and not others and thus may well distort debate on critical public matters.

[92] Again, Geoffrey Stone provides a fuller discussion of these issues, in the context of discussing content-based discrimination generally, in *Content Regulation and the First Amendment*, 25 Wm & Mary L Rev at 212–17, 227–33 (cited in note 40).

[93] Id at 228.

underlying message expressed."[94] Other constitutionally disfavored justifications for government action also appear in the cases—most notably, that the government may not restrict expression because it will offend others. Once again, as said in *R.A.V.*, selective limitations on speech may not be justified by "majority preferences."[95] Regardless whether the government could achieve the same or greater effects with another end in mind, the existence of such illegitimate aims should invalidate the action at issue.

The distinction between viewpoint-based restrictions and subject matter–based restrictions serves as a useful proxy in evaluating the purpose, as in evaluating the effects, of underinclusion. A return to the set of hypotheticals offered above illustrates this point. The actions singling out for favorable treatment endorsements of city government can be presumed to stem from an illegitimate motive: what legitimate reason could lie behind these regulations? A similar danger presents itself with regard to any government action favoring or disfavoring a particular viewpoint: if suppression of the viewpoint does not lie directly behind the action, at least attitudes toward the viewpoint may influence the decision.[96] By contrast, government actions covering speech of a variety of viewpoints, even if on a single topic, less probably emerge from government (or majority) approval or disapproval of a particular message, precisely because they apply to a range of diverse messages. So, for example, the statute providing funds for campaign speech likely stems from a desire to reduce corruption, and the ordinance granting an exemption to obscenity involving discussion of government affairs may arise from the view (common and usually permissible in First Amendment law, though reflecting a kind of favoritism) that political speech is of special constitutional value.[97] The key point is that just as subject matter restrictions will less often skew debate than viewpoint restrictions, so too will they less often arise from constitutionally improper justifications.[98]

---

[94] 112 S Ct at 2545.

[95] Id at 2548.

[96] See Stone, *Content Regulation and the First Amendment*, 25 Wm & Mary L Rev at 231 (cited in note 40).

[97] Again, however, this hypothetical regulation seems so eccentric that a closer examination into both purpose and effects might be in order. See note 90 and text at note 110.

[98] See Geoffrey R. Stone, *Restrictions of Speech Because of Its Content: The Peculiar Case of Subject-Matter Restrictions*, 46 U Chi L Rev 81, 108 (1978).

So far, then, we appear to have a simple way to test government action of the kind this article addresses. Viewpont-based regulation should receive the strictest constitutional scrutiny, both because it skews public debate in a way a general ban (or refusal to subsidize) would not and because it more likely arises from an impermissible motive. By contrast, subject matter–based regulation, which generally raises concerns of purpose and effect no greater than would a general ban, should receive less searching examination, involving (as in the case of content-neutral regulations) a general balancing analysis.

Thus, for example, in *Rust*, the Court first would decide whether the selective subsidization rested on the speaker's viewpoint. There seems little serious argument on this score: the regulations, quite explicitly, prohibited funded projects from "encourag[ing], promot[ing] or advocat[ing] abortion," as well as from engaging in abortion referral and counseling; at the same time, the regulations permitted funded projects to engage in anti-abortion advocacy and required them to refer women for prenatal care and adoption services.[99] Once the determination of viewpoint discrimination is made in this manner, a strong presumption of unconstitutionality would attach, rebuttable only upon a showing of great need and near-perfect fit. If the government could not make this showing, the subsidization scheme would be struck down, leaving the government with the option of funding either less or more speech relating to abortion.

This result accords with the principles, relating to the purpose and effects of government regulation, underlying a strict presumption against viewpoint-based underinclusion. The regulations at issue in *Rust* can hardly be understood except as stemming from government hostility toward some ideas (and their consequences) and government approval of others: the subsidization scheme, as the majority itself noted, reflected and incorporated a "value judgment."[100] Further, the regulations, in treating differently opposing points of view on a single public debate, benefitted some ideas at the direct expense of others and thereby tilted the debate to one side. For both these reasons, a refusal to fund any speech relating to

---

[99] 42 CFR §§ 59.8(a)(2), 59.8(b)(4), 59.10, 59.10(a) (1990); 53 Fed Reg 2927 (1988).
[100] 111 S Ct at 1772.

abortion would have been constitutionally preferable to the funding scheme that the regulations established.

Before this analysis becomes too comfortable, however, a final look at *R.A.V.* is in order. That case, far more than *Rust*, poses serious challenges—on every level—to the simple approach suggested so far: to the ability to distinguish between viewpoint-based and subject matter–based underinclusion, to the relaxed constitutional standard applying to subject matter–based underinclusion, and to the presumed impermissibility of viewpoint-based underinclusion. In so doing, *R.A.V.* forces modifications to the analytical structure presented thus far, as well as a continued willingness to test that structure against the concerns of purpose and effect giving rise to it.

To see the difficulties *R.A.V.* presents, we should consider, as an initial matter, whether the St. Paul ordinance discriminated on the basis of viewpoint or subject matter. This undertaking involves three separate inquiries: first, whether the ordinance on its face discriminated on the basis of viewpoint or subject matter; second, whether the ordinance in practice discriminated on the basis of viewpoint or subject matter; and third, which measure of discrimination (facial or operational) is to control if the answers to the first two questions differ. In exploring these issues, and attempting to draw more general lessons from them, I will refer frequently to Justice Scalia's and Justice Stevens's contrasting characterizations of the St. Paul ordinance.

Viewed purely on its face, the St. Paul ordinance, as construed by the Minnesota Supreme Court, appears to discriminate only on the basis of subject matter. The ordinance proscribed such fighting words as caused injury on the basis of race, color, creed, religion, or gender—that is, such fighting words as caused injury on the basis of certain selected topics. For this reason, Justice Stevens viewed the ordinance as at most a subject matter restriction:[101] all fighting words, uttered by any speaker of whatever viewpoint, concerning another person's "race, color, creed, religion, or gender" were forbidden. Even Justice Scalia frequently referred to the ordinance in this manner; in apparent acknowledgment of the

---

[101] Justice Stevens initially argued that the ordinance was based neither on viewpoint nor on subject matter, but only on the injury caused by the expression. 112 S Ct at 2570. For discussion of this point, see text at notes 116–17.

statutory language, he described the law as regulating expression "addressed to . . . specified disfavored topics," as policing "disfavored subjects," and as "prohibit[ing] . . . speech solely on the basis of the subjects the speech addresses."[102] Thus, if the analysis I have proposed is correct, and if a law is to be classified as viewpoint based or subject matter based solely by looking to the face of the statute, then Justice Scalia erred in finding the discrimination worked by the statute to be unconstitutional.

Beyond the question of facial discrimination, however, lurked another issue: Did the statute discriminate in its operation on the basis of viewpoint? Justice Stevens insisted that it did not. Describing how the ordinance would apply to both sides of a disputed issue, Justice Stevens noted: "[J]ust as the ordinance would prohibit a Muslim from hoisting a sign claiming that all Catholics were misbegotten, so the ordinance would bar a Catholic from hoisting a similar sign attacking Muslims."[103] Or (to take a simpler example) just as the ordinance would prevent the use of racial slurs by whites against blacks, so too would it prevent the use of racial slurs by blacks against whites.[104] Justice Scalia admitted this much, but nonetheless suggested that the ordinance operated in a viewpoint discriminatory manner. In some debates, Justice Scalia reasoned, the regulation would "license one side of a debate to fight freestyle, while requiring the other to follow Marquis of Queensbury Rules."[105] As an example, Justice Scalia noted that a sign saying that all Catholics were misbegotten would be prohibited, because the sign would insult on the basis of religion, but a sign saying that all anti-Catholic bigots were misbegotten would be permitted.

The conflict between Justice Scalia and Justice Stevens on this point serves as a reminder that the decision whether a statute dis-

---

[102] 112 S Ct at 2542, 2547; see id at 2570 (Stevens dissenting).

[103] 112 S Ct at 2571. Justice Stevens assumed in this example that the signs would constitute fighting words.

[104] Akhil Amar makes the interesting point that Justice Stevens seemed to go out of his way to avoid this obvious example, using instead a hypothetical involving two minority groups. Amar notes too that Justice White's opinion appeared to assume that the statute was asymmetrical, in the sense that it protected vulnerable social groups from dominant social groups, but not vice versa. See Amar, 106 Harv L Rev at 148–50 (cited in note 24). To the extent the statute is read in this manner—and Amar points out that the explicit examples in the statute (burning crosses and swastikas) are consistent with this reading—the viewpoint discrimination inherent in the statute becomes quite obvious.

[105] Id at 2548.

criminates on the basis of viewpoint may be highly contestable.[106] The very notion of viewpoint discrimination rests on a background understanding of a disputed issue. If one sees no dispute, one will see no viewpoints, and correspondingly one will see no viewpoint discrimination in any action the government takes.[107] Similarly, how one defines a dispute will have an effect on whether one sees a government action as viewpoint discriminatory. Justice Stevens understood the public debate on which the St. Paul ordinance acted as a dispute between racism of different stripes.[108] With respect to this dispute, the ordinance took a neutral position and effected a neutral result. Justice Scalia, by contrast, saw the dispute as one between racists and their targets and/or opponents. With respect to this dispute, the ordinance appeared to take a side. By prohibiting fighting words based on race, while allowing other fighting words, the law barred only the fighting words that the racists (and not the fighting words that their targets) would wish to use.

In this conflict, Justice Scalia seems to me to have the upper hand: the St. Paul ordinance, in operation, indeed effected a form of viewpoint discrimination. We can all agree that a law applies in a viewpoint discriminatory manner when it takes one side of a public debate. We should also all be able to agree that one way of taking sides is by handicapping a single contestant—and further, that one way of handicapping a contestant is by denying her a particular means of communication (such as fighting words).[109] The

---

[106] The difficulty may arise in considering either facial or operational viewpoint discrimination. Had the ordinance, on its face, prohibited all racist fighting words, the debate between Justice Scalia and Justice Stevens presumably would have been the same. Justice Stevens would have argued that the statute on its face did not discriminate on the basis of viewpoint because it prohibited all kinds of racist fighting words. Justice Scalia, by contrast, would have argued that the statute was facially viewpoint discriminatory because it prohibited the fighting words used by racists, but not the fighting words directed at them.

[107] See Catharine A. MacKinnon, *Feminism Unmodified* (Harvard, 1987) at 212 ("What is and is not a viewpoint, much less a prohibited one, is a matter of individual values and social consensus.").

[108] Justice Stevens at one point acknowledges a debate between proponents of bigotry and proponents of tolerance, but he insists that the ordinance also is neutral with respect to this debate. Thus, Justice Stevens says that the "response to a sign saying that 'all [religious] bigots are misbegotten' is a sign saying that 'all advocates of religious tolerance' are misbegotten.'" 112 S Ct at 2571. This statement has a lovely symmetry, but also a sense of unreality. Presumably, bigots wish to direct their speech not to abstract advocates of tolerance, but to members of a despised group. The question *R.A.V.* presents is whether the government can impose limits on the bigots' desire to do so. Here, Justice Stevens ignores this issue by reframing the public debate.

[109] That a regulation deprives a speaker only of a particular means of communication does not make the regulation any less an example of viewpoint discrimination. Indeed, almost all

St. Paul ordinance, it is true, handicaps both sides (and therefore neither side) when Jews and Catholics, whites and blacks scream slurs based on religion or race at each other. But surely race-based fighting words occur (indeed, surely they usually occur) in something other than this double-barreled context. In most instances, race-based fighting words will be all on one side, because only racists use race-based fighting words, and racists usually do not assail only each other. When the dispute is of this kind, the government effectively favors a side in barring only race-based fighting words. To put the point another way, if a law prohibiting the display of swastikas takes a side, no less does a law that punishes as well the burning of crosses.

Yet even if this is so, the question remains how to categorize a statute (such as the St. Paul ordinance) that discriminates on the basis of viewpoint only in operation, and not on its face. Do we classify the St. Paul ordinance as a subject matter restriction (in keeping with the face of the statute) or as a viewpoint restriction (in keeping with the way it works in practice)? Or, to put the question in a more meaningful way, regardless of the label we attach to the statute, do we treat it as discriminating on the basis of viewpoint or of subject matter?

When a statute has so unbalanced a practical effect as the St. Paul ordinance, I think, it must be treated in much the same manner as a statute that makes viewpoint distinctions on its face. I have argued that underinclusive actions based on subject matter generally should receive relaxed scrutiny because they pose little danger of skewing public debate on an issue or arising from an illegitimate motive; thus, they usually will be no worse (and because less speech restrictive, often a great deal better) than a refusal to allow or subsidize any speech at all. But a subject matter restriction of the kind in *R.A.V.* flouts this reasoning. Here, the restriction, although phrased in terms of subject matter, meaningfully applied only to one side of a debate and thus had a tilting effect as profound as a

---

cases of underinclusion function only to remove a particular means of communication from the speaker: the speaker may not use fighting words; the speaker may not use a noisy soundtruck; the speaker may not use the grounds of a military base; the speaker may not use government funds. In all of these cases, the government does not act to eliminate completely an idea from the realm of public discourse, but may nonetheless take a side. That the government's action deprives a speaker only of a means of communication is relevant, if at all, not to the question whether the action is viewpoint-based, but to the question whether, even if viewpoint-based, the action should be allowed.

viewpoint-based regulation; the ordinance, though facially prohibiting "race-based" fighting words, might as well have prohibited
racist fighting words—that is, fighting words expressing the view
of racism. And precisely because the law operated in this way, the
likelihood that it stemmed from impermissible motives must be
treated seriously; knowing that the ordinance would restrict only
a particular point of view, legislators might well have let their own
opinion, or the majority's opinion, of that viewpoint influence their
voting decision.[110] The ordinance thus presented the same dangers
as a facially viewpoint-based speech regulation.

It might be argued that in admitting this much, I have compromised fatally the position that underinclusive actions based on subject matter generally should not be subject to strict constitutional
scrutiny. After all, many subject matter restrictions have viewpoint-differential effects; in all such cases, it might be said, precisely the same arguments for strict scrutiny would apply. Further,
the argument might run, it may be difficult to distinguish these
subject matter restrictions from others, and it may be wise as a
general matter to overprotect speech; thus, we perhaps should look
upon all subject matter restrictions with suspicion. But this argument ignores the special feature of underinclusion cases: that in
such cases, invalidating a subject matter restriction will as likely
(perhaps more likely) lead to less, as to more, expression. In this
kind of case, a defensive, overprotective approach seems inappropriate: we should treat subject matter restrictions harshly only
when they pose real dangers of distorting effects or impermissible
motive. To the extent, then, that the *R.A.V.* opinion stands for
the proposition that all content-based underinclusion violates the
Constitution,[111] the opinion is in error.

This aspect of the analysis, no doubt, raises difficult questions.
One set involves the determination at what point the viewpoint
differential effects of a regulation that on its face involves subject
matter alone should begin to give rise to suspicion. Need we worry
only about statutes such as that involved in *R.A.V.*, in which the

---

[110] As the *R.A.V.* Court noted, St. Paul argued that the law was necessary, among other
reasons, to show that speech expressing hatred of groups was "not condoned by the majority." 112 S Ct at 2548. It is difficult to conceive of a more illegitimate purpose for regulating
speech.

[111] See text at notes 80–84 for discussion of the ambiguity of the *R.A.V.* opinion on this
question.

regulation effectively restricts one side alone, or need we worry too about statutes with lesser, but still noticeable, viewpoint-based effects? Another set of questions involves the technique used to identify troublesome regulations. Should we use case-by-case analysis, or should we try to devise some more general standard to separate out the most dangerous restrictions based facially on subject matter? Whatever the precise answers to these questions, though, the basic point remains: on some occasions, a regulation that on its face involves only subject matter must be treated as if it involved viewpoint; on most occasions, it need not.

In this statement, however, a final question lurks: When, if ever, may we tolerate viewpoint-based underinclusive actions? Suppose, for example, that the government wished to fund private speech warning of the dangers of tobacco. Would the government also be required to fund private speech minimizing the health risks associated with smoking? One answer to this question is to insist on strict viewpoint neutrality in the support of private speech; then, if the government wished to express an anti-smoking message, it would have to disdain private speech and do the job itself. Yet this answer runs contrary to many of our intuitions. The same point can be made by using a hypothetical along the lines of *R.A.V.* Suppose that the government banned all (but only) those legally obscene materials that featured actors smoking cigarettes. Would this action seem any more objectionable than the example Justice Scalia gave of innocuous selectivity within a proscribable category—the prohibition of all (but only) those obscene materials featuring blue-eyed actresses?[112] The smoking ordinance may seem, if anything, less troublesome; it, at least, has a reason. And yet the ordinance discriminates on the basis of viewpoint.

I cannot here consider in detail the circumstances in which viewpoint-based underinclusion should be upheld. I will note, however, a few points that may serve to structure future inquiry regarding this issue. These relate, first, to the possibility that some viewpoint-based underinclusion may be adequately justified even under a compelling interest test, and, second, to the more remote possibility that some viewpoint-based underinclusion need not be subjected at all to this most stringent standard.

---

[112] 112 S Ct at 2547.

The initial point is—or should be—obvious: strict scrutiny need not invalidate a viewpoint-based underinclusive action. The test, as stated by the Court, is whether the regulation is both necessary and narrowly tailored to serve a compelling interest.[113] In *R.A.V.*, the Court mistakenly interpreted this test to create a *per se* rule against viewpoint underinclusion. Action of this kind, the Court said, is never necessary, because the government can always enact a broader speech regulation.[114] But if the speech additionally covered by a broad regulation fails to advance the interest asserted, why must the government restrict it as well? Assume, for example, that the government has a compelling interest in ensuring that children do not start smoking; assume as well that speech extolling cigarettes in the immediate vicinity of a school leads children to start smoking. Must the government, to prevent this speech, enact a law that restricts speech in the vicinity of schools to the full extent allowed under the Constitution? Would such a law be either "necessary" or "narrowly tailored" to serve the asserted interest? The questions answer themselves. A viewpoint-based underinclusive action should not be held invalid (as it was in *R.A.V.*) on the mere ground that it is, by definition, underinclusive. If the government can show—if, for example, St. Paul could have shown—that it has a compelling interest, that it must regulate speech to achieve that interest, and that it has regulated all (but only) such speech as is necessary to achieve the interest, then the government action should pass strict scrutiny.[115]

The second point I make more tentatively: indeed, I pose it as a question: Must all viewpoint-based underinclusive actions be subject to strict scrutiny, or are there some "viewpoints" that in the context of underinclusion need not be treated as such? The examples I have used, relating to viewpoints on tobacco use, seem to suggest that not all viewpoints are alike, although it is difficult to fashion a principled reason why. If our intuitions rebel against the idea that the government cannot fund speech discouraging

---

[113] See, for example, *Perry v Perry*, 460 US 37, 45 (1983); *Cornelius v NAACP*, 473 US 788, 800 (1985).

[114] See 112 S Ct at 2550.

[115] See *Burson v Freeman*, 112 S Ct 1846 (1992), for a recent First Amendment case in which the Court understood the compelling interest standard in this manner (although perhaps misapplied it). In keeping with the essential thesis of this article, I believe this standard should govern in all cases of viewpoint-based underinclusion, including funding decisions.

smoking without also funding its opposite, they do so for some combination of three reasons, each of which exists in tension with common First Amendment principles. First, the debate in this case, by its nature, offers the hope of right and wrong answers— answers subject to verification and proof. Second, society has reached a shared consensus on the issue; the answers, in addition to being verifiable, are widely believed. And third—and most important—one side of the debate appears to do great harm. When these factors join, a viewpoint regulation may appear justifiable whenever a more general regulation could exist. Then, government disapproval of a message may seem no longer illegitimate, because the disapproval emerges from demonstrable and acknowledged harms; then too, the distortion of debate resulting from the government action may appear not vice, but virtue. Some speech here seems better than none.

Justice Scalia's and Justice Stevens's opinions in *R.A.V.* included a debate on just these issues. Justice Stevens first characterized the St. Paul ordinance not as viewpoint-based, not even as subject matter–based, but as injury-based: the ordinance banned speech that caused a special and profound harm. Justice Scalia mocked this approach, dismissing it as "word-play": "What makes the [injury] produced by violation of this ordinance distinct from the [injury] produced by other fighting words is nothing other than the fact that it is caused by a distinctive idea, conveyed by a distinctive message."[116] Replied Justice Stevens: the Court failed to comprehend "the place of race in our social and political order"; were it to do so, it would recognize that race-based fighting words were a grave social evil, causing "qualitatively different" harms from other fighting words.[117] St. Paul, on this view, had done nothing more than respond, neutrally and legitimately, to real-life concerns; and any resulting skewing effect, given these concerns, need hardly trouble us. To put the position most starkly (more starkly than Justice Stevens did): Even if, in some technical sense, the statute involved viewpoint, it was viewpoint we could cease to recognize as such for purposes of constitutional analysis.

The position of Justice Stevens cannot be right as a general matter. Almost all viewpoint-based regulations can be viewed as "harm-based" regulations, responding neutrally not to ideas as

---

[116] 112 S Ct at 2548.
[117] Id at 2565, 2570 n 9.

such, but to their practical consequences. We may indeed take as a given that almost all viewpoints anyone would wish to restrict cause arguable harms in some fashion. So, for example, in *Rust*, supporters of the regulations might argue that the selective funding corresponds not to viewpoints, but to demonstrable injuries (in the eyes of many) produced by abortion advocacy and counseling. And were we to treat such a case differently on the ground that there is no consensus on the "harmfulness" of this speech's consequences, then we would transform the First Amendment into its opposite—a safe haven for only accepted and conventional points of view.

Yet Justice Scalia's studied refusal to acknowledge or discuss the injuries caused by the speech in *R.A.V.* remains troubling. Here we have speech that, taken alone, has no claim to constitutional protection. The government responds to the special nature of this speech—to the special evil it causes—by in fact refusing to protect it. Perhaps this harm should be evaluated only in determining whether the government has met its high burden of justifying a distinction based on viewpoint. (Certainly, contrary to Justice Scalia's approach, the harm should be evaluated for this purpose.) The question that remains open for me is whether profound and indisputable harms can be taken into account for the purpose of lowering the standard of review applicable to viewpoint-based underinclusion—whether and when they may negate our usually justifiable concerns about the effects and motive of such government action. It may be possible to develop guidelines for this purpose— guidelines that will isolate and harshly confine a set of underinclusion cases in which viewpoint distinctions should be tolerated. But until we perform this feat, we could do far worse than to rely on a no-viewpoint distinction rule to handle cases of content-based underinclusion.

V

For now, it may be less important to solve the problem of content-based underinclusion than to understand that there is a problem to be solved. My claim throughout this article has been that a certain set of cases—cases generally treated as if they have nothing in common with each other—raise a common issue and demand a common answer. The cases come in four general categories. The two most recently treated by the Court (though in widely divergent ways) are typified by *Rust* and *R.A.V.*, the former involving selective funding of speech, the latter involving selective bans on speech within a wholly proscribable speech category. Add to these two others: cases involving selective bans on speech within a non-public forum and cases involving selective imposition of otherwise reasonable time, place, or manner restrictions, whether or not related to government property. The cases differ in context, but they share a structure transcending dissimilarities—a structure calling for acknowledgment by the Court and an effort to devise a uniform approach.

The problem these cases present is a problem of First Amendment neutrality, in as stark a form as can be found. In all these cases, the government may refuse to allow or subsidize any speech; the question remains when the government may refuse to allow or subsidize some (but not all) speech on the basis of content—when the government may give a special preference to expression of a certain kind. The cases cannot be distinguished by means of the subsidy/penalty distinction. The government action in all of these cases can be viewed as a subsidy; in each, the government voluntarily favors—and pays for—a certain kind of expression. More, labeling the action a subsidy or penalty is in these cases immaterial; assuming the government action constitutes a penalty, the problem lies not in the penalty itself, but in the government's selectivity—a problem that remains in the exact same form if the action is viewed a subsidy. For much the same reasons, the cases also cannot be distinguished by resort to an expansive notion of government speech. The action in all of these cases can be so characterized; and unless the government speech analogy has a power so far unsuspected in First Amendment law, it cannot displace the core issue in the cases. That issue must be confronted in whatever context it arises: when the government need not protect or promote any speech—when the speech itself has no claim upon the First Amendment—what limits remain on the government's power of selection?

I have suggested one approach to the problem; no doubt there are others worthy of attention. And were the Supreme Court to address the question in this way, no doubt the Justices would differ with respect to the solution. At least then, however, the debate in these cases would concern what under the First Amendment should matter. The answer might remain unclear, but the Court would have understood the question.

LILLIAN R. BEVIER

REHABILITATING PUBLIC FORUM DOCTRINE: IN DEFENSE OF CATEGORIES

In the companion cases of *International Society for Krishna Consciousness v Lee* and *Lee v International Society for Krishna Consciousness*,[1] the Supreme Court finessed an important opportunity to chart a clear future course for public forum doctrine. Instead of clarifying the law, shifting majorities of justices aligned themselves behind two seemingly inconsistent results, as the Court sustained an airport authority's ban on solicitation of money and invalidated its ban on distribution of literature. The opinions reveal that the Court is deeply divided and that it is mired in substantive and methodological confusion. A doctrinal consensus that once seemed to be emerging has now dissolved, and uncertainties abound on the crucial question of how intensively the Court will review regulations of speech on public property.

This disarray is exacerbated by the confusing set of opinions issued in two other recent decisions concerning the scope and content of First Amendment rights on public property. In *Forsyth County, Georgia v Nationalist Movement*,[2] the Court invalidated a parade permit ordinance because it authorized the county administrator to adjust the permit fee without prescribing adequate stan-

Lillian R. BeVier is Doherty Professor of Law, University of Virginia.

AUTHOR'S NOTE: Thanks to Paul Stephan for his generous reading of an earlier draft. Thanks also to Christopher Schneider, Class of '94, and Julia Rasnake, Class of '95, for their cheerful and indispensable research help.

[1] 112 S Ct 2701 (1992); 112 S Ct 2709 (1992); 112 S Ct 2711 (1992).

[2] 112 S Ct 2395 (1992).

dards to guide his discretion in doing so.[3] In *Burson v Freeman*, the Court subjected a Tennessee law prohibiting electioneering within 100 feet of a polling place to exacting scrutiny, but sustained the law because it served the state's "compelling" interest in election integrity and in protecting citizens' rights "to vote freely for the candidates of their choice."[4]

Of the three cases, *Lee* is the most significant, in part because it addressed a long-simmering controversy over whether airports are traditional public fora.[5] Unfortunately, *Lee* is also significant because, although it "answered" the question by holding that airports are not public fora, it cannot be said to have "settled" the issue. To the contrary, if anything, it unsettled it.

Lee invites analysis at two levels. First, what does the cacophony of opinions tell us about the current state of the public forum? In Part I, I address that question. I will describe not only the doctrinal antecedents of *Lee*, but also the uncertainties left in its wake. Second, there is the question of First Amendment theory. In Part II, I consider the theoretical framework into which public forum doctrine best fits. I conclude that the disagreements that surfaced in *Lee* reflect fundamentally different conceptions of the goals of the First Amendment. In that light, I offer a perspective on the public forum issue that casts the constitutional stakes in somewhat different terms than those in which they ordinarily appear. A few preliminary words will suggest the direction of the analysis.

Scholars generally have been critical of the last two decades of public forum decisions.[6] They have faulted the Court's craftsman-

---

[3] Id at 2401–03.

[4] 112 S Ct 1846, 1851 (1992).

[5] Prior to *Lee*, the Supreme Court had granted review in one other case presenting the question of whether airports are public forums, but it found the ordinance invalid on its face and thus did not address the public forum issue. *Jews for Jesus v Board of Airport Commissioners*, 482 US 569, 573–74 (1987). Lower federal courts have considered the question on many occasions. See, for example, *Gannet v Berger*, 894 F2d 61 (3d Cir 1990); *International Caucus of Labor Committees v Chicago*, 816 F2d 337 (7th Cir 1987); *Jamison v City of St. Louis*, 828 F2d 1280 (8th Cir 1987); *Africa/Nambia Trade and Cult. Council v United States*, 708 F2d 760 (DC Cir 1983); and *Fernandes v Limmer*, 663 F2d 619 (5th Cir 1981).

[6] Justice Brennan succinctly but with devastating accuracy summarized the current scholarly consensus in *United States v Kokinda*, 497 US 720, 741; n 1 (1990):

> See, *e.g.*, L. Tribe, American Constitutional Law 993 (2d ed. 1988) ("[A]n excessive focus on the public character of some forums, coupled with inadequate attention to the precise details of the restrictions on expression, can leave speech inade-

ship and they have sharply criticized what has seemed to them to be the Court's lack of sensitivity to First Amendment values. The prevailing scholarly consensus is that the Court's primary responsibility in public forum cases is to maximize the opportunities of citizens to engage in expressive activity. There is considerable scholarly support for the view that the Court's public forum decisions in the last twenty years have failed to sustain an appropriately "uninhibited, robust, wide-open"[7] debate on public issues. In Part II, I offer a competing vision of the goal of judicial review in public forum cases. I suggest that the Court's goal in developing the law of the public forum has not been to promote "uninhibited, robust, wide-open" debate but to craft a doctrinal structure that will reduce the systemic opportunities for public forum regulators to abuse their governmental power. From this perspective, the question to ask about public forum doctrine is not whether it provides "enough" opportunities for citizens to speak, but whether it is sufficiently correlated with differing degrees of First Amendment risk to play an effective role in translating First Amendment theory, appropriately conceived, into legal practice.

I. Public Forum Doctrine

Detailed accounts of the doctrinal road that led to *Lee* have been ably provided by others.[8] I shall offer a general overview in

---

quately protected in some cases, while unduly hampering state and local authorities in others") (footnotes omitted); Dienes, The Trashing of the Public Forum: Problems in First Amendment Analysis, 55 Geo. Wash. L. Rev. 109, 110 (1986) ("[C]onceptual approaches such as that embodied in the nonpublic-forum doctrine simply yield an inadequate jurisprudence of labels"); Farber & Nowak, The Misleading Nature of Public Forum Analysis: Content and Context in First Amendment Adjudication, 70 Va. L. Rev. 1219, 1234 (1984) ("Classification of public places as various types of forums has only confused judicial opinions by diverting attention from the real first amendment issues involved in the cases"); Post, Between Governance and Management: The History and Theory of the Public Forum, 34 U.C.L.A. L. Rev. 1713, 1715–1716 (1987) ("The doctrine has in fact become a serious obstacle not only to sensitive first amendment analysis, but also to a realistic appreciation of the government's requirements in controlling its own property. It has received nearly universal condemnation from commentators"); Stone, Content-Neutral Restrictions, 54 U. Chi. L. Rev. 46, 93 (1987) (current public forum analysis is plagued by a "myopic focus on formalistic labels" that "serves only to distract attention from the real stakes").

[7] *New York Times v Sullivan*, 376 US 254, 270 (1964).

[8] The best recent summary is Robert C. Post, *Between Governance and Management: The History and Theory of the Public Forum*, 34 UCLA L Rev 1713 (1987).

order to identify recurrent themes and isolate the most pervasively divisive issues. From the Court's first apparent recognition, in *Hague v CIO*,[9] of a First Amendment right of access to publicly owned property, the theoretical underpinnings of the right have been obscure. The Justices have never joined issue over the different presuppositions that have informed their judgments or examined the fundamental premises of the doctrine.

A. THE EARLIEST CASES: DAVIS AND HAGUE

From the point of view of those who advocate a broad public forum right, the law governing the First Amendment constraints on government's power to regulate speech in publicly owned property had an inauspicious beginning. In *Davis v Massachusetts*,[10] the Supreme Court sustained the criminal conviction of a defendant for speaking on the Boston Common without a permit, in violation of an ordinance prohibiting such activity. Echoing the rationale of the Massachusetts Supreme Judicial Court,[11] Chief Justice White analogized the state's rights as owner to those of a private owner. Thus, the Court held that "[t]he right to absolutely exclude all right to use, necessarily includes the authority to determine under what circumstances such use may be availed of, as the greater power contains the lesser."[12]

The *Davis* rule that state ownership entailed unreviewable state power to control speech in public places did not survive. Some thirty years later it yielded to the combined pressures of the modern activist state and the perseverance of civil liberties claimants. The case that effectively overruled *Davis* was *Hague v CIO*,[13] in which the Court voided an ordinance requiring permits for the holding of meetings "in or upon the public streets, highways, pub-

---

[9] 307 US 496 (1939).

[10] 167 US 43 (1897).

[11] Speaking through Justice Holmes, at the time still a member of that court, the Massachusetts court had said, "For the Legislature absolutely or conditionally to forbid public speaking in a highway or public park is no more an infringement of rights of a member of the public than for the owner of a private house to forbid it in his house." *Commonwealth v Davis*, 39 NE 113 (Mass 1895).

[12] *Davis*, 167 US at 48.

[13] 307 US 496 (1939).

lic parks or public buildings of Jersey City."[14] In a plurality opinion, Justice Roberts uttered the famous dictum that has become the paradigm of rhetoric supportive of speech rights in public places. Ironically, the dictum also contained the latent ambiguities that continue to plague public forum doctrine to this day:[15]

> Wherever the title of streets and parks may rest, they have immemorially been held in trust for the use of the public and, time out of mind, have been used for purposes of assembly, communicating thoughts between citizens, and discussing public questions. Such use of the streets and public places has, from ancient times, been part of the privileges, immunities, rights, and liberties of citizens. The privilege of a citizen of the United States to use the streets and parks for communication of views on national questions may be regulated in the interest of all; it is not absolute, but relative, and must be exercised in subordination to the general comfort and convenience, and in consonance with peace and good order; but it must not, in the guise of regulation, be abridged or denied.

Justice Roberts's words, which rejected the notion that ownership alone could provide a predicate for unreviewable state power to exclude speech from public places, took on the *rhetorical* "aura of a large democratic principle"[16] of guaranteed access to public places. The passage also points in a quite different direction, however, for in its own terms it applies only to streets and parks. Moreover, the Roberts dictum does not specify the principle's lineage: was it born of constitutional command or was it simply a by-product of entrenched historical practice?[17] Finally, the dictum provided no *analytical* guidance on the criteria for determining the appropriate application of the principle in the future. This analytical gap remains unfilled.

---

[14] Id at 502, n 1.

[15] Id at 515–16.

[16] Harry Kalven, Jr., *The Concept of the Public Forum: Cox v. Louisiana*, 1965 Supreme Court Review 1, 13.

[17] Despite the rhetorical generosity of the "title to the streets" notion, the actual basis for invalidation of the ordinance was not the failure to grant access but rather the "discretionary administration of the permit system governing street and park meetings." Note, *The Public Forum: Minimum Access, Equal Access and the First Amendment*, 28 Stan L Rev 117, 122 (1975).

B. FROM HAGUE TO THE CIVIL RIGHTS MOVEMENT: ESTABLISHING
   THE VAGUENESS CONSTRAINT

In the thirty years following *Hague*, the Court decided a number of cases involving speech in public places.[18] Many of these arose in the context of as-applied challenges to broadly worded breach-of-the-peace or disorderly conduct ordinances.[19] In this context, the Court found it unnecessary to address the substantive ambiguities of the Roberts dictum because it was able to resolve the disputes by developing a number of the second order doctrinal tools which now represent important—and unwavering—side constraints on governmental behavior.

The most significant, and the most coherent, of these side constraints is the vagueness doctrine. The vagueness doctrine does not dictate the substantive resolution of First Amendment questions. Instead, the doctrine

> requires legislatures to set reasonably clear guidelines for law enforcement officials and triers of fact in order to prevent "arbitrary and discriminatory enforcement." Where a statute's literal scope, unaided by a narrowing state court interpretation, is capable of reaching expression sheltered by the First Amendment, the doctrine demands a greater degree of specificity than in other contexts.[20]

In cases involving defendants accused of unlawfully engaging in expressive activity on publicly owned property, the vagueness doctrine enabled the Court to overturn convictions rendered pursuant to broad breach-of-the-peace statutes or permit requirements that conferred standardless discretion upon low level officials. In these settings, the vagueness doctrine played an indispensable systemic role in establishing and enforcing rule of law values as the regulatory norm in public forum cases.

> The rule of law signifies the constraint of arbitrariness in the exercise of government power. . . . [I]t means that the agencies of official coercion should, to the extent feasible, be guided by rules—that is, by openly acknowledged, relatively stable, and

---

[18] For a sampling from the most well-known of these, see *Schneider v State*, 308 US 147 (1939); *Cantwell v Connecticut* 310 US 296 (1940); *Cox v New Hampshire*, 312 US 569 (1941).

[19] See, for example, *Cantwell v Connecticut*, 310 US 296 (1940); *Terminiello v Chicago*, 337 US 1 (1949); *Feiner v New York*, 340 US 315 (1951).

[20] *Smith v Goguen*, 415 US 566, 572–73 (1974).

generally applicable statements of proscribed conduct. The evils to be retarded are caprice and whim, the misuse of government power for private ends, and the unacknowledged reliance on illegitimate criteria of selection.[21]

The vagueness doctrine enforces the rule of law norm in the public forum in two principal ways. First, by invalidating convictions for expressive activity under broadly worded statutes, the doctrine forestalls the use of "illegitimate criteria of selection" to decide what speech to regulate. This application of the doctrine promotes rule of law values, not because it averts the threat "that the universe of opportunities for expression will be curtailed," but because it averts the threat "that the opportunities for speech will be differentially constrained, depending on the speaker's point of view."[22]

The vagueness doctrine also enforces the rule of law norm through its effect on official decision making about speech uses of public property. Early in its public forum jurisprudence, the Court indicated that while it would overturn convictions for expressive activity obtained under vaguely worded statutes, it might nonetheless defer to legislative judgments prohibiting the same activity if such judgments were embodied in statutes "narrowly drawn to define and punish specific conduct."[23] The Court apparently sought not only to foreclose the use of illegitimate criteria, but also to shift the responsibility for the selection of criteria to accountable decision makers. In effect, then, the Court used the vagueness doctrine to compel public forum decision makers to specify their regulatory needs, to tailor their regulations to the particular locus, to announce the regulations clearly in advance, and to avoid aiming their prohibitions explicitly at disfavored viewpoints.

C. THE CIVIL RIGHTS MOVEMENT: HARRY KALVEN COINS A PHRASE

Apart from establishing the vagueness constraint, the cases decided between 1939 and the early 1960s did little to resolve the substantive ambiguities that were latent in the *Hague* dictum. That

---

[21] John Calvin Jeffries, Jr., *Legality, Vagueness, and the Construction of Penal Statutes*, 71 Va L Rev 189, 212 (1985).

[22] Id at 217.

[23] *Cantwell v Connecticut*, 310 US 296, 311 (1940).

there were many unanswered questions became evident when the civil rights movement took to the streets in the mid-1960s, and a variety of local attempts to curb public protests in the South reached the Court for review. In 1965, Harry Kalven wrote for this journal his classic article on the public forum[24] in which he became the first expressly to propose

> that in an open democratic society the streets, the parks, and other public places are an important facility for public discussion and political process. They are in brief a *public forum* that the citizen can commandeer . . . [a]nd . . . what is required is in effect a set of Robert's Rules of Order for the new uses of the public forum.[25]

Kalven's article did more than coin the phrase that has defined for a generation a central First Amendment issue. It also gave shape and content to the *Hague* dictum and poured substance into the concept of a First Amendment right of access to at least some public places—streets and parks.

During the decade or so following Kalven's article, commentators and Court decisions probed the limits and the rationale of this right. Citizens claimed, and sometimes the Court appeared to grant, a First Amendment right to protest in public places that had little in common with streets and parks.[26] Commentators suggested that a presumptive First Amendment right of access to public places (where citizens otherwise have a "right to be") ought to be the baseline against which any governmental decision to exclude must be justified on a case-by-case basis.

As already noted, the Court in the past had indicated that it would defer to specific legislative judgments about regulatory needs on public property. During the civil rights era, this suggestion was called sharply into question, as cases challenging specific legislative judgments began replacing cases challenging convictions under broadly worded breach-of-the-peace statutes on the Court's docket.

In response to such cases, the Court might have deferred to

---

[24] Harry Kalven, Jr., *The Concept of the Public Forum: Cox v. Louisiana*, 1965 Supreme Court Review 1.

[25] Id at 11–12.

[26] See, for example, *Brown v Lousiana*, 383 US 131 (1966) (public library); *Tinker v Des Moines School District*, 393 US 503 (1969) (public high school). But see *Adderley v Florida*, 385 US 39 (1966) (curtilage of jail).

specific legislative judgments regulating expressive activity on public property. The Court would not, in other words, make its own determination of whether the speech was compatible with the other uses of the property. This deference need not have gone as far as the earlier public ownership model implied, for the Court had clearly established that it would not countenance deliberate viewpoint discrimination. Apart from that, the deferential response would have entailed minimal judicial review of the substance of public forum decision making.

Alternatively, the Court might have scrutinized the substantive underpinnings of even the most specific legislative judgments to ensure the broadest possible accommodation of expressive activity. This more activist response would have engaged the Court in case-by-case review of forum managers' decisions to exclude expressive activity from public property.

In 1972, the Court in *Grayned v City of Rockford* sustained an ordinance that prohibited any noise near a school that "disturbs . . . the peace and good order of such school."[27] Although the Court upheld the ordinance, the opinion appeared to contemporary observers to endorse the activist approach. *Grayned* appeared to offer "a comprehensive, intelligible approach"[28] to the public forum right, for it suggested in dictum that the Court must decide *in every case* "whether the manner of expression is basically incompatible with the normal activity of the particular place at the particular time."[29] The implication was that the government would have to satisfy the Court in every case that its decision to exclude was justified by such a showing of incompatibility.

This implication was short-lived. In *Lehman v City of Shaker Heights*,[30] a political candidate challenged the constitutionality of the city of Shaker Heights' refusal to sell him car card space in the city's buses for his campaign ads. In the face of the city's policy of displaying only commercial advertisements, Lehman argued that the car cards "constitute a public forum protected by the First Amendment, and that there is a guarantee of nondiscriminatory

[27] 408 US 104, 108 (1972).

[28] Geoffrey R. Stone, *Fora Americana: Speech in Public Places*, 1974 Supreme Court Review 233, 253.

[29] 408 US at 116.

[30] 418 US 298 (1974).

access to such publicly owned and controlled areas of communication."[31] The argument looked like a winner. Because the car cards were already devoted to communicative purposes, Lehman's proposed use could hardly be called "basically incompatible" with them. Nonetheless, Justice Blackmun's plurality opinion declared that "[n]o First Amendment forum is here to be found,"[32] and it deferred to the city's decision to deny access.

Public forum jurisprudence since *Grayned* and *Lehman* has reflected a struggle to strike a sensible balance between *Grayned*'s call for judicial review of every denial of First Amendment access and *Lehman*'s call for deference to the decisions of forum managers.

D. FROM GRAYNED AND LEHMAN TO LEE:
BUILDING THE FRAMEWORK[33]

In retrospect, *Lehman* appears to be the watershed case. Although its implications were not obvious at the time, and it left much

---

[31] Id at 301.

[32] Id at 304.

[33] Three First Amendment developments of the last two decades that do not bear directly on the question of speech rights on publicly owned property are worthy of note. They tend to provide support for the explanation of public forum doctrine that I offer in Part II.

First, the Court refused to extend First Amendment rights of speech access to privately held resources. In *CBS, Inc. v Democratic Nat'l Comm*, 412 US 94 (1973), for example, the Court sustained the FCC's policy of refusing to compel broadcasters to accept editorial advertisements. It did so in the face of a strongly worded Brennan dissent that argued that the broadcasters' ban on such ads could "serve only to inhibit, rather than to further," robust public debate. Id at 172. In *Miami Herald Pub Co v Tornillo*, 418 US 241 (1974), the Court invalidated a Florida "right of reply" law that had been defended on the grounds that it furthered the "broad societal interest in the free flow of information to the public." Id at 245. Finally, in *Hudgens v NLRB*, 424 US 507 (1976), announcing that "the constitutional guarantee of free expression has no part to play in a case such as this," the Court squarely overruled *Amalgamated Food Employees v Logan Valley Plaza*, 391 US 308 (1968), which had treated a private shopping center as "the functional equivalent" of a downtown business district.

The second development involved the Court's repudiation of the concept that the First Amendment embodies a generally applicable right of press access to newsworthy governmental information. In *Pell v Procunier*, 417 US 817 (1974) and *Saxbe v Washington Post Co.*, 417 US 843 (1974), for example, the Court sustained prison regulations restricting press interviews with individual prisoners in the face of claims that the regulations interfered with the free public discussion of governmental affairs. While in *Richmond Newspapers, Inc., v Virginia*, 448 US 555 (1980), the Court granted a First Amendment right to the public and the press to attend criminal trials, it has not extended the right beyond the context of criminal adjudication.

The third development of note, which Geoffrey Stone called "the Burger Court's foremost contribution to first amendment analysis," Geoffrey R. Stone, *Content Regulation and the First Amendment*, 25 Wm & Mary L Rev 189 (1983), is the restriction on discrimination against speech based on its content. Justice Marshall summarized the restriction in *Police*

doctrinal detail to be worked out, Justice Blackmun's plurality opinion nevertheless sounded the death knell for a broad public forum access right. Before *Lehman*, it seemed that the "public forum" would become an expansive concept: the Court seemed on the verge of holding that "*wherever* citizens had a right to be" is a "public forum," and that citizens may always speak in a public forum *unless* the Court independently agreed with the judgment of the forum managers that "the manner of expression is basically incompatible with the normal activity of the particular place at the particular time."[34] In *Lehman*, however, the Court turned the public forum label into a vehicle for restricting First Amendment rights of access. As Ronald Cass perceptively noted:[35]

> [Rather than] providing an additional brake on governmental restriction of speech, Justice Blackmun's approach makes mandatory access a threshold test for protection: if a public forum is involved, substantial limits constrain governmental restrictions on speech use of that property, but absent involvement of a public forum, government need only be rational in restricting speech.

Justice Blackmun's plurality opinion in *Lehman* provided a few clues but almost no analytical explanation for the judgment that the car cards were not a "public forum." He implied that the absence of an historical practice of openness might be fatal to an access claim.[36] He asserted that "the nature of the forum and the conflicting interests involved have remained important in determining the degree of protection afforded by the Amendment to the speech in

---

Dept v Mosley, 408 US 92 (1972) (decided the same day as *Grayned*), when the Court struck down a local ordinance that exempted peaceful labor picketing from a ban on picketing within 100 feet of a school:

> [Above] all else, the First Amendment means that government has no power to restrict expression because of its message, its ideas, its subject matter, or its content.

Id at 95. As Stone's analysis suggests, the principal rationale for the prohibition of content-discriminatory laws is that, especially when they amount to prohibitions of particular ideas or viewpoints, they distort public debate in predictable and unacceptable ways.

[34] *Grayned*, 408 US at 116.

[35] Ronald A. Cass, *First Amendment Access to Government Facilities*, 65 Va L Rev 1287, 1301 (1979) (citation omitted).

[36] " '[T]he truth is that open spaces and public places differ very much in their character, and before you could say whether a certain thing could be done in a certain place you would have to know the history of the particular place.' " 418 US 298, 302 (1974) (citations omitted).

question,"[37] but he did not explicate the aspects of the nature of the forum that might be important. He stated the facts that had apparently dictated both his conclusion that the car card space was not a public forum and the very deferential standard of review that the nonpublic-forum conclusion entailed ("Here, we have no open spaces, no meeting hall, park, street corner, or other public thoroughfare. Instead the city is engaged in commerce."[38]), but he did not explain why these facts were controlling.

In dissent, Justice Brennan did not mount a frontal attack on the plurality's strategy of deciding access claims according to whether the property at issue was a "public forum." However, the criteria he proposed for deciding whether particular public property constituted a public forum were radically different from those that Justice Blackmun had found controlling. Neither historical practice nor the city's engagement in commerce was to the point for Justice Brennan. For him,[39]

> [t]he determination of whether a particular type of public property or facility constitutes a 'public forum' requires the Court to strike a balance between the competing interests of the government, on the one hand, and the speaker and his audience, on the other. Thus the Court must assess the importance of the primary use to which the public property or facility is committed and the extent to which that use will be disrupted if access for free expression is permitted.

The next important public forum case was *Greer v Spock*,[40] in which the Court sustained the authority of the military to exclude political candidates from entering the Fort Dix Military Reservation to engage in expressive activity. The Court in *Greer* had not yet firmly settled the question of how to approach the public forum issue. It seemed to affirm that access to at least some public places—"a municipality's open streets, sidewalks, and parks"[41]—is constitutionally guaranteed by virtue of a "long-established constitutional rule that there cannot be a blanket exclusion of first amend-

---

[37] Id at 302–3.

[38] Id at 303.

[39] Id at 312.

[40] 424 US 828 (1976).

[41] Id at 835.

ment activity."[42] It seemed also to affirm the negative implication of the public forum label, however, and rejected as having "never existed"[43] "the principle that whenever members of the public are permitted freely to visit a place owned or operated by the Government, then that place becomes a 'public forum' for purposes of the First Amendment."[44] Although the Court noted the absence of a historical tradition of openness on federal military reservations,[45] it also noted that "the business of a military installation like Fort Dix [is] to train soldiers, not to provide a public forum."[46] The Court thus left unclear whether denial of access was permissible because of the absence of a history of openness or because access would disrupt the primary use of the base. To complicate matters further, Justice Powell, who joined the majority opinion, also wrote a concurring opinion that proposed "basic incompatibility"[47] as the critical public forum issue.

Justice Brennan's dissenting opinion in *Greer* adopted an approach that was dissimilar to that taken either by the *Greer* majority or by his own dissent in *Lehman*. Justice Brennan clearly saw—and just as clearly spurned—the systemic implications of the categorical approach to access claims that the majority opinion foretold. Arguing that the Court's approach "only serves to answer a set of broad, falsely formulated issues and fails to provide the careful consideration of interests deserved by the first amendment,"[48] he urged the Court instead to adopt "a flexible approach . . . [in order to avert] the danger that certain forms of public speech at the locale may be suppressed, even though they are basically compatible with the activities otherwise occurring at the locale."[49]

Despite Justice Brennan's protestations, the Court moved inexorably toward a categorical approach, a movement culminating in the Court's 1983 decision in *Perry Educ Ass'n v Perry Local Educators'*

---

[42] Id.

[43] Id at 836.

[44] Id.

[45] Id at 838.

[46] Id.

[47] Id at 843.

[48] Id at 858.

[49] Id at 860.

Ass'n.[50] In *Perry*, the Perry Education Association (PEA), as the duly elected exclusive bargaining representative for the teachers of the Metropolitan School District of Perry Township, Indiana, had negotiated a collective-bargaining agreement with the Board of Education that gave the PEA exclusive access to the interschool mail system and teacher mailboxes in the Perry Township schools. Without challenging PEA's status or legitimacy as exclusive bargaining agent, a rival union, the Perry Local Educators' Association (PLEA), challenged PEA's exclusive access to—and its own exclusion from—the internal mail system.

In an opinion by Justice White, the Court rejected this claim. Announcing that the "existence of a right of access to public property and the standard by which limitations upon such a right must be evaluated differ depending on the character of the property at issue,"[51] the Court delineated three categories of public property and sketched the First Amendment standards by which it would evaluate exclusions from each. First, there are "quintessential public forums," which by long tradition or government fiat had been devoted to assembly and debate, and "immemorially held in trust" for expressive purposes, such as streets and parks. In such places, government may not ban all communicative activity: there is a First Amendment right of guaranteed access; "content-based regulations" of speech must be "narrowly drawn" to serve a compelling state interest, and content-neutral time, place, and manner restrictions are permissible only if they are narrowly tailored, and leave open ample alternative channels for communication.

Second, there are "designated public forums," which the state has opened for use for speech purposes, even though it was not constitutionally required to do so and could close entirely to communicative activity should it decide to do so. In such places, content-based regulations of speech must be narrowly drawn to meet a compelling state interest, and content-neutral regulations are permissible if they are "reasonable."

Third, there are "nonpublic forums," which have not by tradition or designation served as public forums. In such places, the state may impose reasonable time, place, and manner restrictions and can even engage in content and subject-matter regulation of

---

[50] 460 US 37 (1983).

[51] Id at 44.

speech, so long as the regulation is reasonable and is not an effort to suppress speech because of its viewpoint.

Justice White's opinion for the Court in *Perry* is striking in two respects. First, it offers no reasons of principle or policy for either the categories it establishes or the standards of review that accompany them. Although plausible arguments can in fact be made to support the Court's conclusions, *Perry* did not offer them. As a consequence, the Court's analysis and its categorical approach have been needlessly vulnerable to the claim that they are both arbitrary and insensitive to First Amendment values.

The second striking fact about *Perry* is the variation in the standards of review that the categories entail, and the assumption that the substantive content of First Amendment rights has a geographical dimension. Under the *Perry* framework, quintessential public forums contemplate review that differs little from that to which the Court subjects regulations of expressive conduct that does not involve public property at all. It has been argued that the dominant goal of the Court's review of regulations of speech should be to prevent government officials from engaging in deliberate discrimination against disfavored viewpoints. The relatively strict review of denials of access to quintessential public forums implies, however, that the substantive right at stake is the presumptive right of access, independent of any concern about censorship or viewpoint discrimination. Designated public forums evoke similarly strict standards of review, but only if the government "opts in" to strict review by voluntarily opening the property to expressive activity. This implicitly shifts the nature of the right from a positive claim *to* use public property to a negative claim of freedom *from* government manipulation of public debate. Finally, the standards of review applicable to property not "by tradition or designation a forum" are so deferential that the First Amendment hardly constrains government action in the absence of express viewpoint discrimination. The Court has never explained these variations in the levels of review, nor has it explored the potentially discordant messages about the substantive reach of the First Amendment that the variations imply. As a consequence, the Court has had a difficult time defending its approach in the face of continued challenge.

In *Clark v CCNV*,[52] decided in 1984, the Court made clear the

---

[52] 468 US 288 (1984).

institutional implications of its developing public forum doctrine. In *Clark*, the Court sustained a National Park Service regulation that proscribed camping in the national parks within Washington, D.C. The regulation was challenged as applied to prohibit demonstrators from sleeping in Lafayette Park and the Mall as a means of calling attention to the plight of the homeless. Although the regulation amounted to a prohibition on a particular manner of demonstrating within what all conceded to be a public forum, the Court nonetheless concluded that it was constitutional because it was content-neutral, it was "not being applied because of disagreement with the message presented,"[53] and "the plight of the homeless could not be communicated in other ways."[54] In the part of the opinion that has the most significant institutional implications, the Court made clear that, in its view, the regulation was a sensible, if possibly imperfect, means of achieving a legitimate government interest. The Court explained that it would not overturn such a regulation just because the demonstrators in a particular case could persuade a judge that their particular activities would not, taken by themselves, seriously erode the government's objectives. The Court held that "the validity of this regulation need not be judged solely by reference to the demonstration at hand."[55] Moreover, the Court explicitly rejected the notion that public forum doctrine assigns[56] "to the judiciary the authority to replace the Park Service as the manager of the Nation's parks or endows the judiciary with the competence to judge how much protection of park lands is wise and how that level of conservation is to be attained."

In *Cornelius v NAACP Legal Education and Defense Fund*,[57] the Court again signaled its commitment both to the categorical structure of public forum doctrine and to the substantial judicial deference to forum managers' decisions that the structure entailed. *Cornelius* held that the Federal Government did not violate the First Amendment by excluding legal defense and political advocacy organizations from participating in the Combined Federal Campaign

---

[53] Id at 295.

[54] Id.

[55] Id at 296–97.

[56] Id at 812.

[57] 473 US 788 (1985).

(CFC) charity drive directed at federal employees. The Court concluded that the CFC was a nonpublic forum and not a designated public forum, as plaintiffs had argued. Because the Court was satisfied that the government had reasonable grounds for limiting access, it held that the decision to exclude the claimants would stand unless on remand the plaintiffs could prove that their exclusion was motivated by the government's "desire to suppress a particular point of view."[58]

Cornelius is noteworthy because it is widely regarded as having substantially eviscerated the "designated public forum" category. Support for such a reading comes principally from the statement that "the government does not create a public forum by inaction or by permitting limited discourse but only by *intentionally* opening a nontraditional forum for public discourse."[59] The reading is bolstered by the fact that in *Cornelius* the Court seemed to insist on evidence of a "purposeful designation for public use"[60] or proof that "government was motivated by an affirmative desire to provide an open forum."[61] Critics argue that if the government can avoid a judicial finding that it has created a designated public forum simply by effectuating a policy of selective access, then access seekers are in a catch-22 situation, for the very selectivity they challenge will itself be the reason for the judicial deference they believe is unwarranted. The Court in *Cornelius* did not answer these concerns.

The final milestone on the road from *Hague* to *Lee* is *United States v Kokinda*,[62] in which the Court sustained a Postal Service regulation that prohibits soliciting alms and contributions on Postal Service property. The regulation had been applied to two political volunteers who had set up a table on a post-office-owned sidewalk near the entrance to the Bowie, Maryland, post office. Justice O'Connor's plurality opinion, joined by Chief Justice Rehnquist and Justices Scalia and White, concluded that the standards set forth for nonpublic fora were the appropriate ones by which to judge the regulation. Again, however, the criteria that guided the

---

[58] Id at 812.

[59] Id at 802 (emphasis supplied).

[60] Id at 804.

[61] Id.

[62] 497 US 720 (1990).

decision to categorize the post office sidewalk as a nonpublic forum were unexplained.[63]

Justice Kennedy's concurrence is the most interesting opinion in *Kokinda*, for it signals the discontent with the rigidity of the *Perry* categories that came to fruition in his opinion in *Lee*. Justice Kennedy hinted that he found "powerful" the argument that, because of the wide range of activities the government permitted on the postal sidewalk, "it is more than a nonpublic forum."[64] He suggested that, in the future, the Court might have to abandon the straitjacket of history and look to "certain [unspecified] objective characteristics"[65] to determine public forum status. But because he was persuaded that the regulation at issue was a reasonable time, place, and manner restriction, even if the postal sidewalk were "more than a nonpublic forum,"[66] Justice Kennedy joined the Court's judgment sustaining the regulation, and left the public forum issue for a later case.

E. LEE: THE CONSENSUS DISSOLVES

Chief Justice Rehnquist wrote two opinions in *Lee*, an opinion of the Court sustaining the solicitation ban and a dissent to the per curiam opinion that invalidated the leafleting ban.[67] Together, they approximate a faithful application of the *Perry* framework with its *Cornelius* gloss. The Chief Justice began with an unequivocal,

----

[63] Justice O'Connor's opinion was not a straightforward application of *Perry*, for she began her quest for the appropriate level of scrutiny with a reference to a

> long-settled principle that governmental actions are subject to a lower level of First Amendment scrutiny when "the governmental function operating . . . [is] not the power to regulate or license, as lawmaker, . . . but, rather, as proprietor, to manage [its] internal operation[s]. . . ."

497 US at 725. Long-standing the principle may be, and potentially useful in resolving access questions, but it had not been invoked to justify the Court's disposition of access issues since *Lehman*. Justice O'Connor herself proceeded at once to undermine the significance of this reference by noting that the "Government, even when acting in its proprietary capacity, does not enjoy absolute freedom from First Amendment constraints." Id. Then, without further explanation, she seemingly embraced and proceeded to apply the "tripartite framework" of *Perry*.

[64] Id at 737.

[65] Id.

[66] Id.

[67] 112 S Ct 2701, 2703; id at 2710.

though unexplained, assertion that "[w]here government is acting as a proprietor, managing its internal operations, rather than acting as lawmaker with the power to regulate or license, its action will not be subjected to the heightened review to which its actions as a lawmaker may be subject."[68] Then, without suggesting how the "government as proprietor" notion bore on the issue, and indeed seeming to emphasize the fact that the "cases reflect . . . a 'forum-based' approach,"[69] he turned to the question of whether the airport terminals are public or nonpublic fora. He found that the "tradition of airport activity does not demonstrate that airports have histori-cally been made available for speech activity."[70] Since airports are an artifact of modern times, he seemed to say, they cannot have been "immemorially . . . time out of mind"[71] dedicated to expres-sive purposes. Nor are airport terminals designated public forums, because they "have [not] been intentionally opened by their oper-ators . . . (except under the threat of court order)"[72] to solicitation and leafleting activity. Those who run airports consider "the pur-pose of the terminals to be the facilitation of passenger air travel, not the promotion of expression."[73] Because the terminals are thus by default nonpublic forums, the Chief Justice asked only whether the leafleting and soliciting bans were "reasonable."[74] In undertak-ing this inquiry, he explicitly eschewed any second-guessing of the motives of the airport managers or of the means they had chosen to effectuate their goals: "the restriction need only be reasonable; it need not be the most reasonable or the only reasonable limita-tion."[75] Rehnquist fully credited the Port Authority's judgment and even offered reasons of his own to support it.

Justice Kennedy rejected the Court's view that "the public forum status of public property depends on government's defined purpose for the property, or on an explicit decision by the government to

---

[68] 112 S Ct at 2705.

[69] Id.

[70] Id at 2706.

[71] Id at 2702.

[72] Id at 2706.

[73] Id at 2707.

[74] Id at 2708.

[75] Id.

dedicate the property to expressive activity."[76] He propounded a
very different test:[77]

> If the objective physical characteristics of the property at issue
> and the actual public access and uses which have been permit-
> ted by the government indicate that expressive activity would
> be appropriate and compatible with those uses, the property is
> a public forum. The most important considerations in this anal-
> ysis are whether the property shares physical similarities with
> more traditional public forums, whether the government has
> permitted or acquiesced in broad public access to the property,
> and whether expressive activity would tend to interfere in a
> significant way with the uses to which the government has as
> a factual matter dedicated the property.

On the issue of "interference," Justice Kennedy embraced a process
of classification rather than one of case-by-case evaluation, citing a
need to give guidance to the state.

Justice Kennedy concluded that airport terminals were public
forums under his criteria. He proceeded accordingly to subject the
solicitation and the leafleting bans to the more stringent review
that public forum status entails. Although he had "no difficulty
deciding"[78] that the leafleting regulation was invalid, he sustained
the solicitation ban because, in his view, in-person solicitation of
funds coupled with the immediate receipt of money raises unique
risks of fraud and duress. Thus, the Port Authority's judgment to
restrict such activity was "entitled to deference."[79]

Justice Kennedy's approach differs from Chief Justice Rehnquist's in more than its doctrinal choices. It adopts a more highly
embellished rhetorical tone, articulates a more generous view of the
purposes of the public forum doctrine, and exhibits a willingness to
elevate judicial judgments over those of forum managers. Justice
Kennedy expressed concern, for example, that the Court's "jurisprudence of categories"[80] would leave "almost no scope for the
development of new public forums"[81] and would thus lead to a

---

[76] Id at 2716.
[77] Id at 2718.
[78] Id at 2720.
[79] Id at 2722.
[80] Id at 2715.
[81] Id at 2716.

"serious curtailment of our expressive activity."[82] He asserted that the "Court's approach is contrary to the underlying purposes of the public forum doctrine," which ensures "citizens that their freedoms may be exercised . . . without fear of a censorial government, adding tangible reinforcement to the idea that we are a free people."[83] And in concluding that expressive activity is compatible with the uses of airport terminals, he was persuaded, not by the judgment of airport administrators, but by "the wide consensus among courts of appeals."[84]

Justice O'Connor offered a third approach. Although she professed agreement with Rehnquist's analytical framework, she subjected the regulations to a less deferential standard of review. For her, the "reasonableness" test required the Court to make its own evaluation of the need for the restriction "in light of the purpose of the forum and all the surrounding circumstances."[85] As she understood it, the reasonableness test imposed a significant burden of justification on forum managers. Indeed, to support her conclusion that the leafleting ban was invalid, she echoed the *Grayned* test: "it is difficult to point to any problems intrinsic to the act of leafleting that would make it naturally incompatible with a large multipurpose forum."[86] Moreover, she ascribed her inability to "see how peaceful pamphleteering is incompatible" with the airport not to her own lack of imagination but to the Port Authority's failure to offer satisfactory proof of incompatibility.

Justice Souter's opinion is the least deferential of all. Although purporting to agree with Justice Kennedy's statement of governing principles, he eschewed the categorical approach: "The inquiry may and must relate to the particular property at issue."[87] Moreover, even when seeming to speak in categorical terms, he brought the fact-specific *Grayned* test back to center stage. "We should classify as a public forum," he argued, "any piece of public property that is 'suitable for discourse' in its physical character, where ex-

---

[82] Id at 2717.

[83] Id at 2716–17.

[84] Id at 2719.

[85] Id at 2712.

[86] Id at 2713.

[87] Id at 2724.

pressive activity is 'compatible' with the use to which it has actually been put."[88]

Finally, in voting to invalidate even the solicitation ban, Justice Souter did not adjust the standard of review to take account of the fact that what was at stake was a localized regulation of expressive activity applicable only to particular public property. Instead, he made plain that he considered the government's burden of justification to be as heavy in this case as it would be if a generally applicable prohibition of speech were at issue, citing as authority, for example, many decisions outside the public forum context altogether.[89]

Thus, public forum doctrine is now riddled with uncertainty. First, it is unclear whether the categorical approach to the question of whether particular public property is a public forum retains vitality. Second, if it does, it is unlear what test the Court will use to determine whether particular property should be categorized as a traditional public forum. Will it be the narrow test articulated by Chief Justice Rehnquist or the expansive one offered by Justice Kennedy? Third, if the categorical approach survives, will the Court adopt a sliding scale of judicial scrutiny, as suggested by Chief Justice Rehnquist's approach, or will it move toward Justices Kennedy and O'Connor's preference for a more activist judicial review? Finally, will the Court eschew the categorical approach completely and embrace Justice Souter's case-by-case analysis instead? The answers to these questions will depend in large measure on how the Court resolves a fundamental issue about public forum doctrine, a question to which it has never given its focused attention: What is the underlying purpose of public forum doctrine? Or, put differently, what is judicial review of forum managers' decisions supposed to accomplish? In Part II, I consider this question.

---

[88] Id.

[89] Among the cases cited by Justice Souter were *Riley v National Federation of Blind of N.C., Inc.*, 487 US 781 (1988) (striking down licensing, disclosure, and fee limitations on professional fundraisers); *Virginia Pharmacy Bd. v Virginia Citizens Consumer Council, Inc.*, 425 US 748 (1976) (striking down a ban on price advertisement of prescription drugs); *NAACP v Claiborne Hardware Co.*, 458 US 886 (1982) (limiting the amount of damages recoverable for a black boycott of white merchants); *Organization for a Better Austin v Keefe*, 402 US 415 (1971) (striking down an injunction that prohibited a community organization from distributing literature critical of a suburban real estate broker).

II. Public Forum Theory

A. TWO MODELS

The cacophony of opinions in *Lee* testifies to deep division among the Justices about the underlying purpose of public forum doctrine. One way to understand the division is to see it as reflecting tension between two models of the First Amendment which have competed since *Hague* to supply the underlying premise of the public forum right.

First, there is the Enhancement model, which is concerned with how much speech takes place in society and with the overall quality of public debate. It is visionary in character. It envisions the First Amendment as embodying an ideal of democratic discourse in a self-governing society. The Enhancement model is committed to the view that First Amendment rules can and ought to be effective tools for augmenting both the quality and quantity of public debate, and accepts the corollary proposition that the Amendment sometimes imposes affirmative duties on government to maximize the opportunities for expression. It focuses almost exclusively on the substantive merits of particular claims. It takes as given that judicial review is an appropriate legal device for the realization of its ideals and seldom displays misgivings about the possibility that it might entail untoward institutional implications.

The Enhancement model derives in large part from the implications of Justice Brennan's opinion in *New York Times v Sullivan*.[90] In particular, it takes its cue from Brennan's affirmation of a "profound national commitment to the principle that debate on public issues should be uninhibited, robust and wide-open."[91] According to the Enhancement model, this commitment has both substantive and strategic dimensions. Substantively, it presupposes that the core mission of the First Amendment is to promote an idealized vision of the democratic process by promoting speech about public and, in particular, political issues.[92] Strategically, it presupposes a judicial mandate to interpret the First Amendment aggressively so

---

[90] 376 US 254 (1964).

[91] Id at 270.

[92] See generally Harry Kalven, Jr., *The New York Times Case: A Note on the "Central Meaning of the First Amendment*," 1964 Supreme Court Review 191.

as to promote and facilitate "uninhibited, robust and wide-open" debate. In its strategic dimension, this model assumes that ". . . the widest possible dissemination of information from diverse and antagonistic sources is essential to the welfare of the public,"[93] and that individuals have a constitutionally protected interest in *effective* self-expression.[94] It ascribes to the Court the responsibility of devising legal rules that will make these assumptions a reality.[95] The Enhancement model assumes that legal doctrine can transform public debate both qualitatively and quantitatively.[96]

On the other hand is the Distortion model. This model shares with the Enhancement model the premise that the central mission of the First Amendment is to protect speech about government and political issues, broadly defined. The Distortion model differs from the Enhancement model, however, in its strategic dimension and its much less idealized vision of public debate. The Distortion model sets a less ambitious agenda for First Amendment doctrine. Instead of conceiving the Amendment as authorizing the Court affirmatively to enhance the quality of public debate or to prime the pump of quantity, the Distortion model portrays the First Amendment as embodying nothing more than a set of constraints upon government actors. It adopts no norm or idealized vision of quality or quantity of public debate except that which results from a rigidly enforced official government neutrality. This model regards the First Amendment as a source of negative rights (freedoms from) rather than as a source of positive entitlements (freedoms to).[97] In contrast to the ambitious agenda of the Enhancement model, the Distortion model entails a modest notion of what First Amendment rules can and ought to do. According to the Distortion

---

[93] *Associated Press v United States*, 326 US 1, 20 (1944).

[94] Compare, for example, Geoffrey Stone, *Fora Americana: Speech in Public Places*, 1974 Supreme Court Review 233, 254; Note, *The Public Forum: Minimum Access, Equal Access and the First Amendment*, 28 Stan L Rev 117 (1975).

[95] For a critical analysis of what he terms a dominant consensus to the effect that adjudication can promote the level and quality of public debate, see Robert F. Nagel, *Constitutional Cultures: The Mentality and Consequences of Judicial Review* 27–59 (University of California Press, 1989).

[96] For elaborations of the Enhancement model in other contexts, see Jerome A. Barron, *Access to the Press: A New First Amendment Right*, 80 Harv L Rev 1641 (1967); Thomas I. Emerson, *The Affirmative Side of the First Amendment*, 15 Ga L Rev 795 (1981).

[97] For a general discussion of the differences between negative and positive rights, endorsing the view that the Constitution is principally a guarantor of negative rights, see David P. Currie, *Positive and Negative Constitutional Rights*, 53 U Chi L Rev 864 (1986).

model, the essential task of First Amendment rules is to restrain government from deliberately manipulating the content or outcome of public debate[98] and to prohibit it from censoring, punishing, or selectively denying speech opportunities to disfavored views.[99]

The Enhancement and Distortion models have strikingly different implications for judicial review. Under the Enhancement model, the Court's responsibility is to ensure that speech is not unduly curtailed and to devise rules that will maximize the opportunities for expression. Under the Distortion model, the Court's responsibility is only to determine whether the challenged government practice reflects deliberate governmental discrimination against disfavored viewpoints. When the Court adopts a categorical approach under this model, it does so, not with a view to promoting "more speech," but with a view to minimizing the risk of governmental abuse.

The opinions of Justice Kennedy and, to an even greater extent, of Justice Souter in *Lee* are premised on the assumptions inherent in the Enhancement model, whereas Chief Justice Rehnquist's opinions illustrate the Distortion model. The conflict between these models echoes the debates in *Lehman*, *Greer*, and *Kokinda*.

From *Lehman* to *Lee*, critics on and off the Court have assumed implicitly that public forum doctrine must make sense in terms of the Enhancement model. Much of their criticism, accordingly, faults the doctrine for being insufficiently alert to First Amendment values and hence insufficiently generous in sustaining access claims. Justice Kennedy in *Lee*, for example, chided the Court for

---

[98] Presenting a complete description of the underpinnings of the Distortion model is not my agenda in this article. Nevertheless, in the hope of forestalling one likely line of criticism, I believe it is necessary to point out that the Distortion model is not based on the naive premise that only deliberate government action affects the quality and quantity of public debate. The model does not, moreover, imply that the status quo is preferable to conceivable alternative states of the world. Nor does it seek to perpetuate powerlessness for any citizens who desire to participate in or affect the course of public debate. Instead, the Distortion model reflects a deep skepticism about the ability of the Supreme Court to identify—much less to rectify—all the untoward effects of government policy. It embodies a desire to match a conception of the task the Court has been assigned with the institutional capacity of the judiciary. Finally, it incorporates a commitment to the ideal that constitutional norms must be capable of sufficiently specific articulation that they can serve both to guide and constrain judicial judgment.

[99] For an endorsement of a somewhat analogous conception of the First Amendment, framed as a "negative theory," see Ronald A. Cass, *The Perils of Positive Thinking: Constitutional Interpretation and Negative First Amendment Theory*, 34 UCLA L Rev 1405, 1438–90 (1987).

ignoring "*the fact* that the purpose of the public forum doctrine is to give effect to the *broad command* of the First Amendment,"[100] and scolded it on the ground that its "failure to recognize the possibility that new types of government property may be appropriate forums for speech will lead to a serious curtailment of our expressive activity."[101] In fact, however, although the Enhancement model has powerful rhetorical appeal, it has little explanatory power either with reference to public forum doctrine or to any other body of First Amendment law.[102]

The Court itself has done little to rebut criticism like Justice Kennedy's or to join issue with its assumptions. To the contrary, beginning with *Lehman*, the opinions in public forum cases that rejected First Amendment claims have offered almost no theoretical justifications either for the doctrines they embraced or for the applications of those doctrines in particular cases. This has rendered the Court vulnerable to the kind of criticism so accurately summarized by Justice Brennan in *Kokinda*.[103] Close scrutiny, however, supports a more sympathetic rendering of the merits of the Court's public forum categories, for these decisions can be seen, not as a half-hearted commitment to the Enhancement model, but as a whole-hearted rejection of that model in favor of the Distortion model's more restrained vision of the First Amendment's central mission. Indeed, once understood as well-designed embodiments of the Distortion model, the rules and categories that comprise modern public forum doctrine make considerable sense.

---

[100] 112 S Ct at 2717.

[101] Id.

[102] See note 33 supra and cases cited therein. If First Amendment doctrine generally conformed to the Enhancement model, we would expect the Court to have granted instead of denying rights of speech access to privately owned resources such as shopping centers, newspapers, and broadcast networks. We would further expect the Court to have engaged in a steady expansion of rights of public access to government information, instead of limiting such access rights to the context of criminal trials. Finally, we would expect the Court to have devised doctrines to detect and monitor content-differential effects of content-neutral laws. The Court, however, has eschewed inquiries into effects, concentrating instead on developing doctrinal tools that can detect illicit governmental motives and deliberate distortions. See, e.g., Geoffrey R. Stone, *Restrictions on Speech Because of Its Content: The Peculiar Case of Subject-Matter Restrictions*, 82 U Chi L Rev 81 (1978).

[103] See note 6. See also Benjamin Kaplan, *The Great Civil Rights Case of Hague v. CIO: Notes of a Survivor*, 25 Suffolk L Rev 913, 939–46 (1991).

B. RECONCEIVING PUBLIC FORUM DOCTRINE: THE DISTORTION MODEL

Consider, first, that beginning with *Hague*, the Court's public forum decisions display the Distortion model's central concern of preventing forum managers from deliberately skewing public debate by denying access to citizens because they want to express disfavored views. The *Hague* dictum rejected the view that the Constitution grants government the same power to control public property that private owners can exert over private property. Although, read broadly, the *Hague* dictum seems consistent with the Enhancement model's notion that government has a duty to maximize speech opportunities by making publicly owned property generally available for expressive activity, the Court actually invalidated the ordinance in *Hague* not because it denied access, but because it established a discretionary permit system. Thus, while the rhetoric of the *Hague* dictum is consistent with the Enhancement model, the actual principle of decision is consistent with the Distortion model. The holding in *Hague* did not require government to facilitate speech. It merely prohibited it from abusing its power by engaging in purposeful distortion of public debate.

Consider, second, the vagueness doctrine and the prohibition on viewpoint discrimination. These doctrines are designed not to achieve the Enhancement model's objective of promoting the quantity or quality of speech, but to achieve the Distortion model's goal of limiting the use of illegitimate criteria of decision by government agents.

Consider, third, the public forum categories themselves. As Justice Kennedy pointed out when he proposed his more accommodating test, the boundaries of these categories have not been drawn to maximize speech consistent with the Enhancement model. Rather, the boundaries have been drawn to accomplish the goals of the Distortion model by adjusting the standards of review to address the different systematic possibilities for abuse that the various categories of property present. This conclusion, which is critical to my analysis, is evident from a close review of the categories themselves.

1. *The traditional public forum.* The principal difficulty in viewing public forum doctrine as a manifestation of the Distortion model is the existence of a category of places—traditional public fora—to which the Court has guaranteed citizens a First Amendment right of access. Would the Distortion model, which is de-

signed to forestall deliberate manipulation of public debate, prohibit even-handed government exclusion of speech from *any* publicly owned place?[104] A negative answer to this question would significantly undermine the explanatory power of the Distortion model. In fact, however, at least with respect to streets and parks (and, now, public sidewalks[105]), the Distortion model is consistent with such a rule. This is so because, as suggested by Justice Roberts in *Hague*, such places have historically been available for the public's exercise of the rights of speech and assembly. Historic openness supports a right of guaranteed access even under the Distortion model for a number of reasons. First, it forecloses any argument forum managers might make that expression is "incompatible" with the "primary use" of the property: these places have always, "time out of mind," accommodated not only a variety of uses, but a variety of uses *including speech and assembly*. Second, the long-standing availability of these places for First Amendment activity eliminates the need for courts to make their own assessment of compatibility. Third, because historic openness signals presumptive compatibility of speech and assembly with other uses of the property, it signals the possibility that illicit motives may lie behind the effort to exclude.[106]

It is also significant that the government has historically had an effective monopoly over the types of resources included within the traditional public forum category. As in other contexts, when the government "provides resources of which it is the sole supplier," it should be "limited . . . in the conditions it may impose on"[107] the users of the resources. The government's role as sole supplier

---

[104] Compare Currie, 53 U Chi L Rev at 878–80 (cited in note 97).

[105] Sidewalks have been included in the traditional public forum category at least since *Greer v Spock*, 424 US 828, 835 (1976).

[106] In *Cornelius*, and again in *Lee*, the Court suggested that historic openness is relevant to the analysis because it indicates that the accommodation of expression was a "principal purpose" of streets and parks. *Lee*, 112 S Ct at 2706 (quoting *Cornelius*, 473 US 788, 800 (1985)). Justice Kennedy persuasively rejected this suggestion: "[t]he notion that traditional public forums are property which have public discourse as their principal purpose is a most doubtful fiction." *Lee*, 112 S Ct at 2717. The more convincing argument for invoking historic openness as a determinant of traditional public forum status is that it permits the Court confidently to draw inferences about the compatibility of speech and signals the presence of systematic risks of deliberate political deck-stacking when government denies access altogether.

[107] Richard A. Epstein, *Unconstitutional Conditions, State Power, and the Limits of Consent*, 102 Harv L Rev 5, 22 (1988).

of property that has historically been available for speech uses arguably creates a heightened risk that denying access to such places
would be a manifestation of deliberate distortion. This is because,
by such denials, the government could effectively silence holders
of marginal viewpoints who would, by definition, have no place
else to go.

If government possession of monopoly power is part of the justification for guaranteed access under the Distortion model, the category of "streets and parks" is potentially overinclusive because satisfactory substitute places are often available in fact. The Court,
however, will not permit exclusions from the traditional public
forum to be justified by the availability of alternative locales for
expression.[108] This result can be explained in terms of administrative costs, for a different rule would jeopardize the benefits implicit
in the Court's strategy of pursuing a categorical approach. Presumably, the Court has determined to proceed categorically in part to
economize on its own decision-making resources and to provide
certainty for lower courts and forum administrators. If this is so,
the decision to include certain kinds of public property in the traditional public forum category must necessarily be framed in categorical terms. A perfect fit between the categorical boundaries and the
risk of monopoly is unrealistic. Rather, the question is whether the
error costs of the category's overinclusiveness are less than would
be the error costs of a different, less inclusive, category.

The argument to this point has been that recognition of a First
Amendment right of access to traditional public fora is consistent
with the Distortion model because the conjunction of historic access and government monopoly creates the risk that for the Court
to permit wholesale denials of access would invite deliberate governmental distortion of public debate. Accordingly, the decision
whether to expand the category to reach other kinds of places, such
as airport terminals, turns on whether these places present similar

---

108

    [T]he streets are natural and proper places for the dissemination of information
and opinion; and one is not to have the exercise of his liberty of expression in
appropriate places abridged on the plea that it may be exercised in some other
place.

Schneider v State, 308 US 147 (1939). Content-neutral time, place, and manner restrictions
will be sustained if they leave alternatives open. *Perry Ed. Assn. v Perry Local Educators' Assn*,
460 US 37 (1983).

opportunities for this particular form of distortion. Since *Perry*, the test the Court has used to determine whether public properties other than streets, parks, and sidewalks should be deemed traditional public forums has not focused explicitly on the risk of systemic abuse of government power. Nevertheless, the Court's approach conforms at least roughly to the Distortion model. The principal criterion for including property within the traditional public forum category has been historic access. As I have argued, this serves as a proxy for the possibility of systematic abuse. Moreover, the principal criterion of exclusion from the traditional public forum category has been the government's engagement in proprietary activity. This criterion also correlates with the Distortion model, for when the government acts in a proprietary capacity it is unlikely to be wielding monopoly power, thus reducing the risk of systemic abuse. This fact may explain why the Court has repeatedly seen "proprietary capacity" as a reason to exclude public property, such as airports, from the tradtional public forum category.

2. *The designated public forum.* The Court has held that designated public fora are those properties that the government has voluntarily made available for expression. The government is not constitutionally required to keep such property open for expression, as it is with traditional public forums. So long as it does keep them open, however, its speech regulations are subject to review according to "the same standards as apply in a traditional public forum."[109] Since *Cornelius*, the Court has effectively limited the designated public forum category to those properties that the government has intentionally, explicitly "opened for expressive activity by part or all of the public."[110] This limitation has evoked the kind of concern expressed by Justice Kennedy in *Lee:*[111]

> The requirements for such a designation are so stringent that I cannot be certain whether the category has any content left at all. In any event, it seem evident that . . . few if any types of property other than those already recognized as public forums will be accorded that status.

Justice Kennedy's assessment is probably close to the mark, and this would indeed be a matter of concern if the Court were at-

---

[109] *Perry*, 460 US at 46.

[110] *Lee*, 112 S Ct at 2705.

[111] Id at 2717.

tempting to achieve the goals implicit in the Enhancement model. According to the Distortion model, however, it is not a matter of concern that few if any additional public forums will be created: according to the Distortion model, the creation of more public forums is not a goal of the First Amendment.

As a descriptive matter, in defining the criteria for determining when public property constitutes a designated public forum, the Court has not been pursuing the Enhancement model's goal of facilitating or maximizing speech. Rather, it has been serving the more limited objective of preventing deliberate viewpoint discrimination. The designated public forum category serves this purpose by calling on government to justify selective exclusions from property that it has deliberately opened to expressive activity. When the government itself intentionally designates public property as a forum, it announces its own judgment that speech is compatible with the property's other uses. Thus, a policy of selective exclusion would be presumptively suspect as the product, not of a legitimate concern with disruption, but of an illicit concern with the speaker's viewpoint. In other words, it is the intentional decision to designate property as a public forum, and not the decision to close it altogether to speech uses, that heightens the risk that the government will engage in deliberate viewpoint discrimination and explains the designated public forum category. If there is no systematic risk that a decision by government not to open public property to expressive activity reflects covert viewpoint discrimination, the Distortion model would not require the Court to expand the designated public forum category beyond its present boundaries. Whether such systematic risks exist is the principal issue in the analysis of the nonpublic forum category.

3. *The nonpublic forum.* Between *Lehman* and *Lee*, the Court engaged in virtually no independent scrutiny of the access decisions of nonpublic forum managers, sustaining their content-neutral denials of access so long as they could be deemed "reasonable." Moreover, in making that determination, the Court accorded forum managers a very high level of deference. For this approach to be consistent with the Distortion model, such a level of deference must be justified in principle by the systematic absence in nonpublic fora of the kinds of First Amendment risks that the model is designed to prevent. The question, therefore, is whether decision making by the managers of nonpublic forum property presents

such minimal risks of deliberate viewpoint discrimination that the Court is warranted in adopting a highly deferential stance.

In addressing this question, a useful point of departure is Robert Post's reformulation of public forum doctrine, in which he suggested that a "line between governance and management corresponds to the distinction between the public and nonpublic forum."[112] As I shall demonstrate, this line also corresponds to the systematic presence or absence of the risk of deliberate government deck-stacking. Accordingly, a brief account of Post's analysis will be helpful.

At the outset, it is important to note that Post himself plainly ascribes to the Enhancement model. The First Amendment premises which he deems

> constitutionally congenial . . . [are] that the state should not suppress speech unless there is a good reason to do so, . . . [that the First Amendment] is designed to maximize the speech which the government is constitutionally required to tolerate . . . [and that] the first amendment's central objective . . . [is] ensuring "uninhibited, robust, and wide-open" public debate.[113]

His analysis recognized, however, that the Court's conception of the public forum doctrine could not be squared with these premises without considerable sacrifice of descriptive accuracy. In particular, he acknowledged that the Court used the nonpublic forum category to "demarcate a class of government property in which the first amendment claims of the public are radically devalued and immune from independent judicial scrutiny."[114] Accordingly, Post set himself the task of articulating a constitutional theory that could both explain and justify this unusual devaluation. Rather than attempting to forge a link between his First Amendment premises and the nonpublic forum category, however, he explained the nonpublic forum category and its concomitant judicial deference in terms of a complex "sociology of institutional authority, as well as a pervasive and important struggle between a public realm [where the

---

[112] Robert C. Post, *Between Governance and Management: The History and Theory of the Public Forum*, 34 UCLA L Rev 1713, 1833 (1987).

[113] Id at 1766 (quoting *New York Times v Sullivan*, 376 US 254, 270 (1964)).

[114] Id at 1766.

First Amendment applies with full force] and an organizational domain of instrumental rationality [where the First Amendment is of only marginal importance]."[115]

Some adherents of the Enhancement model argue that forum managers systematically undervalue speech and have significant incentives to overregulate it. They fear that deference permits forum managers to engage in gratuitous and unnecessary regulation.[116] Rather than attempting to allay that concern, Post insisted that it is the wrong way to think about the issue. For him, the appropriate question is not the Enhancement adherent's query whether judicial deference results in too little speech, but whether deference is necessary

> in order for a state organization to function effectively. If the government decision at issue entails a kind of authority which requires flexibility and discretion to function effectively, or which is part of the creation of a specific organizational culture for the management of the affected institution, there are strong justifications for judicial deference.[117]

Post's analysis provides the most convincing descriptive account of post-*Lehman* public forum doctrine. As he suggested, the distinction between governance and management corresponds quite closely to the Court's distinction between public and nonpublic fora. The explanation Post offered for deference to management decisions, however, runs parallel to his premises about the First Amendment. But it is neither correlated with, nor implied by, them. His analysis does not explain why the need for deference to achieve organizational ends is in itself sufficient to reconcile such deference with the First Amendment principles he himself embraces.

Despite this failure, Post's analysis supplies a crucial link in the effort to explain public forum doctrine in terms of the Distortion model. The line between government and management separates occasions where systematic First Amendment risks of deliberate

---

[115] Id at 1834–35.

[116] See generally David Goldberger, *Judicial Scrutiny in Public Forum Cases: Misplaced Trust in the Judgment of Public Officials*, 32 Buff L Rev 175 (1983). Ronald Cass, though not himself an adherent of the Output model, also suggested that forum managers might respond to perverse incentives. See Ronald A. Cass, *First Amendment Access to Government Facilities*, 65 Va L Rev 1287, 1329 n 207 (1979).

[117] Post, 34 UCLA L Rev at 1834 (cited in note 112) (emphasis supplied).

government deck-stacking are present from those where they are not. Oddly enough, this is true because of the factors Post himself uses to separate governance from management.

Post's central insight is that government actions can be divided conceptually between those taken within government organizations in pursuit of organizational goals taken as given—the domain of management—and those taken in the public realm outside organizational boundaries—the domain of governance where "common values are forged through public discussion and exchange."[118] When the state acts in the domain of governance, "the significance and force of all potential objectives are taken as a legitimate subject of inquiry."[119] Because this is so, government officials face the systematic temptation deliberately to skew the debate in favor of the outcomes they prefer. The risk that they will succumb to this temptation thus justifies stringent judicial oversight when the state is "governing."

When, however, "the state acts internally to manage speech within its own institutions, public ends are taken as given and as socially embodied within the forms and objectives of a government organization."[120] Within such government organizations, *precisely because public ends are taken as given*, the potential for deliberate government skewing of public debate is systematically irrelevant: by definition, the debate has run its course, its outcome is settled, and nothing remains to be skewed. Sometimes, the risk of deliberate skewing of public debate will in fact materialize even in a "management" context. Hence, the Court continues to prohibit deliberate viewpoint discrimination even in the nonpublic forum. The risk is not systematic, however, and judicial deference is therefore the appropriate norm in the absence of such deliberate discrimination. Indeed, as Post himself recognized, on the management side of the line, systematic risks of skewing debate inhere more in active judicial review than in judicial deference; for by dictating to public managers when they must accede to access claims, active judicial review disables them from achieving the settled public ends that they have been charged to effectuate.

---

[118] Id at 1788.

[119] Id at 1789.

[120] Id at 1833.

C. SOME INSTITUTIONAL QUESTIONS

A chasm separates the agenda of the Enhancement model from the more modest goals of the Distortion model. One way to characterize this chasm is as an artifact of the differing intensities of commitment of these models to core First Amendment values: adherents of the Enhancement model value expression more than adherents of the Distortion model, and they are less willing to tolerate regulation. Lapses from the ideal of "uninhibited, robust and wide-open" debate matter deeply to Enhancement adherents, but do not concern adherents of the Distortion model. If differing intensities of preference for speech in fact account for the principal disparities in the two models' doctrinal prescriptions, then the most significant normative question to ask about public forum doctrine is whether it accords sufficient weight to speech interests.

There may be a more complex explanation for this chasm, however, for it may be that it is due, not to differing intensities of preference for speech, but to differing (though unstated) assumptions about the practical limits of relying upon judicial review to transform the quality and quantity of public debate. The Enhancement model reflects, in addition to a preference for speech, an idealized conception of reality. The conception has an internal logic that, in its implicit faith in the transformative power of legal doctrine, may blind its adherents to real-world limitations that a practical perspective might require them to acknowledge. Adherents of the Distortion model, for example, might indeed share the Enhancement model's preference for speech, but might nonetheless entertain doubts, not shared by adherents of the Enhancement model, about the capacity of courts to make the kinds of comprehensive assessments of the effects of their decisions—on speakers, on forums, and on the quality and quantity of debate—that the Enhancement model contemplates. They may thus prefer bright-line rules, where outcomes turn on fewer relevant variables and where the variables themselves reflect systematic risks of government abuse, to more ad hoc decision making that attempts to account for a multiplicity of factors. Adherents of the Distortion model might also be skeptical about the ability of legal doctrine to create a desired reality. For this reason alone, they might favor a First Amendment regime of negative constraints on government rather than one of affirmative duties. Indeed, one way to describe the pre-*Lee* public forum doctrine applied by Chief Justice Rehnquist in *Lee* is in terms of the Distortion model's relatively modest set of assumptions about the appropriate boundaries of the judicial task and the transformative power of judicial review. From this perspective, the doctrine appears as a rejection of the more ambitious assumptions of the Enhancement model that were so earnestly put forth by the *Lee* dissenters.

Thoroughly to explore these possibilities is beyond the scope of the present inquiry, for they raise fundamental issues about how to conceptualize the role of the Court, of legal doctrine, and of the complex relationship between substantive norms and judicial methodology. Nevertheless, it may be useful to focus briefly on the institutional component of the public forum debate, if only to cast a more revealing light on the full implications of the choice between the Enhancement model of Justices Kennedy and Souter and the Distortion model of Chief Justice Rehnquist.

One of the most salient aspects of Chief Justice Rehnquist's approach in *Lee* is that it is rule-based and categorical. It reposes considerable trust in the good faith and managerial judgment of forum administrators and credits their capacity to give appropriate weight to First Amendment values in their management decisions. Justice Kennedy and Justice Souter, on the other hand, claim to accept a categorical approach in principle, but actually reject the judicial deference that is implicit in the categorical approach and evince a strong inclination for case-by-case analysis. They prefer the individual judgment of judges in particular cases to the collective judgment of forum administrators. Moreover, they adopt analyses that, because of the uncertainty of their categorical boundaries and their subjectivism, assure a continuing flow of litigation on public forum issues. Implicit in their analyses is thus a commitment to a decisional strategy that dilutes or, like Justice Brennan, abandons altogether the categorical approach in favor of one that explicitly attempts to achieve its substantive goals by considering a multiplicity of variables in every case. Their preferred methodology is one that Frank Michelman evoked when he referred, albeit in another context, to ". . . the judicial practice of situated judgment or practical reason. . . ."[121]

The Kennedy-Souter approach rests on the assumption that it

---

[121] Frank Michelman, *Takings, 1987*, 88 Colum L Rev 1600, 1629 (1988).

generates fewer errors in application than a more categorical approach.[122] It proceeds on the premise that, in the course of litigation, the Court can accurately and precisely identify and assess every relevant factor. The animating idea is that in each case the Court knows the value to place on the speech interest; the extent to which that value is compromised by the challenged restriction; how much disruption the speech will cause; and the effect of its decision on the quality and quantity of public debate. Though it is left implicit, this assumption that accurate judicial assessment of all relevant factors is possible offers the only conceivable underpinning to the claim that intensive case-by-case judicial scrutiny of the decisions of forum managers is preferable in principle to the greater deference implicit in the categorical approach.[123] In the public forum context, however, such an assumption is of questionable validity.

Moreover, even if the case-by-case approach could in fact yield the benefits that are claimed for it, a complete appraisal of its capacity to produce net gains must also consider the systemic costs it entails. It is worth asking, for example, whether the necessary implication of relatively intensive judicial scrutiny in public forum cases—that courts rather than forum managers ought routinely to have the last word—generates any negative side-effects that should be included in the social calculus.

1. *Accuracy.* Commentators typically assume that the choice between ad hoc judicial decision making and a categorical approach entails a straightforward trade-off between "precision of analysis and clarity of doctrine."[124] They also assume that the costs of an ad hoc approach are paid exclusively in the reduction in certainty, predictibility,[125] and the "feel of legality"[126] that a more categorical

---

[122] Consider, for example, the assumptions underlying the analysis in Daniel A. Farber & John E. Nowak, *The Misleading Nature of Public Forum Analysis: Content and Context in First Amendment Adjudication*, 70 Va L Rev 1219 (1984). See also C. Thomas Dienes, *The Trashing of the Public Forum: Problems in First Amendment Analysis*, 55 Geo Wash L Rev 109 (1986).

[123] See, for example, Note, *A Unitary Approach to Claims of First Amendment Access to Publicly Owned Property*, 36 Stan L Rev 121 (1982).

[124] Geoffrey R. Stone, *Content Regulation and the First Amendment*, 25 Wm & Mary L Rev 189, 251–52 (1983). Compare Nagel, *Constitutional Cultures* at 53 (cited in note 95).

[125] See, for example, Thomas Merrill, *Property Rules, Liability Rules, and Adverse Possession*, 79 Nw U L Rev 1122, 1137 (1985).

[126] Michelman, 88 Colum L Rev at 1628 (cited in note 121).

approach provides. Most important, they assume that precision of analysis is in fact enhanced by ad hoc analysis. They suggest that there is a high correlation between particularized judicial decision making and substantively correct decisions. This latter assumption is rarely challenged. It should be. The principal reasons to be dubious about the assumption arise from two sources. First, there is the unacknowledged complexity of the fact-finding that case-by-case decision making demands. Second, there is the problem of the indeterminate norm. The analytical tools offered by those who would have courts make case-by-case assessments of First Amendment claims of access to public property have an aura of formulaic determinacy.[127] On closer scrutiny, however, they seem incapable of seriously guiding or, ex post, of reflecting the actual decision-making process.[128]

Turning first to factual complexity, case-by-case decision making cannot be precise unless each of the factors considered, their relative weight, and the effects of alternative decisions can be specified, and a definite criterion of judgment can be articulated. Moreover, precision of analysis requires that the competing interests be commensurate:[129] only a distortion of results, rather than an accurate appraisal of the stakes, can emerge from a process that compares an individual claimant's interest in demonstrating at a particular time in a particular manner at a particular place against the whole of the public interest in orderly management of public places. Similarly, inaccurate results are inevitable if the entire First Amendment concern that "public debate be uninhibited, robust, and wide-open" is balanced against the governmental interest in excluding a particular demonstrator from a particular place at a particular time. And, especially if the process of review is undertaken in the service of the ambitious systemic objectives of the Enhancement model, precise analysis requires an ability accurately to predict and to assess the effects that a decision to grant or deny access will have on

---

[127] See generally Nagel, *Constitutional Cultures* at 121–55 (cited in note 95).

[128] Many of the points raised in the following paragraphs echo concerns that have been previously expressed by others in the context of more general critiques of Supreme Court decision making. See, for example, Nagel, *Constitutional Cultures* (cited in note 95). See also Alexander Aleinikoff, *Constitutional Law in the Age of Balancing*, 69 Yale L J 943, 972–83 (1987).

[129] See generally Charles Fried, *Two Concepts of Interests: Some Reflections on the Supreme Court's Balancing Test*, 76 Harv L Rev 755 (1963).

the overall quantity and quality of debate. A moment's reflection is sufficient to raise doubts whether a court can guage these effects except in a wholly impressionistic manner. Finally, even if a complete accounting of relevant factors is possible, and an accurate forecast of the decision's consequences for public debate is assayed, precision of analysis remains an illusion unless it is guided by, rather than serving as a formulaic substitute for, a shared vision of the competing First Amendment and governmental interests. This brings me to the indeterminacy of the Enhancement model's central norm.

An important difference between the Enhancement and the Distortion models is their resolution of the question of whether judicial review should have as its aim something more expansive than securing the negative right to be free from deliberate governmental distortion of public debate. Advocates of the Enhancement model, who advocate relatively rigorous judicial scrutiny of denials of access to all manner of public property, maintain that courts should do more than merely vindicate this negative right.[130] Even the most astute and thoughtful of commentators, however, do not specify exactly what that "more" might be or what overarching First Amendment vision might compel its vindication. Geoffrey Stone, for example, always a careful analyst, once praised the Court for having adopted in *Grayned*

> a comprehensive, intelligible approach to the problem. In each instance, the "crucial question" must be "whether the manner of expression is basically incompatible with the normal activity of a particular place at a particular time." The point, of course, is not that the individual has the right to speak, petition, or assemble whenever and wherever he chooses. It is, rather, that if we are to give content to the right to freedom of expression, we must seek a fair accommodation of the individual's interest in effective expression of that right, the public's interest in receiving the communication, and legitimate countervailing interests of the state. The Court's newly promulgated theory of the public forum embodies precisely that type of fair accommodation.[131]

---

[130] See, for example, Note, *The Public Forum: Minimum Access, Equal Access, and the Public Forum*, 28 Stan L Rev 117 (1975); Note, *A Unitary Approach to Claims of First Amendment Access to Publicly Owned Property*, 35 Stan L Rev 121 (1982).

[131] Geoffrey R. Stone, *Fora Americana: Speech in Public Places*, 1974 Supreme Court Review 233, 253–54.

For purposes of a critique of case-by-case analysis on the ground that it lacks precision, the approach that Stone endorses is problematic not because it seeks a "fair accommodation"—who could object to that on any ground?—or even because the First Amendment interests it purports to accommodate are necessarily inappropriate objects of judicial vindication. The problem rather is with the absence of specified—much less of specifiable—norms against which to measure the "effectiveness" of any particular exercise of an individual's right, the intensity of the public's interest in receiving the communication, or the relative weight of the countervailing interests of the state. Even the seemingly straightforward "basic incompatibility" test leaves much to be desired. As the cases reveal, the inquiry whether a particular means of expression is "basically incompatible" with a particular forum's normal activity is, to put it mildly, something about which reasonable justices differ.

More important, judges and justices routinely differ with forum administrators about "basic incompatibility," thus throwing into bold relief the fact that the real issue is not whether particular speech activities are incompatible with other activities that take place at particular locations but who gets to decide that question. *Lee* is only the most recent instance of such a dispute. Chief Justice Rehnquist thought it significant that many airport administrators consider it prudent to prohibit leafleting and solicitation activities in airport terminals.[132] Justice Kennedy, on the other hand, sustained the solicitation ban because of a combination of "our precedents as well as the actions of coordinate branches of government,"[133] but concluded that leafleting is not incompatible with normal airport activities because many courts had ordered airports to permit such activity without resulting in a single airport closure.

Laurence Tribe's analysis of the public forum cases offers a similarly multifaceted and complex inquiry.[134] Criticizing current doctrine as "manipulable and problematic,"[135] Tribe suggests that "it might be considerably more helpful if the Court were to focus more

---

[132] *Lee*, 112 S Ct at 2706–07.

[133] Id at 2721.

[134] Laurence H. Tribe, *American Constitutional Law* §§ 12–24 (Foundation Press, 2d ed 1988).

[135] Id at 987.

directly and explicitly on the degree to which the regulation at issue impinges on the first amendment interest in the free flow of information."[136] Further, he counsels that "the cloud of doctrine to which the public forum debate has led needs to be cleared away, the better to expose what is actually at stake in the restrictions and regulations at issue."[137]

But Tribe also fails to specify the baseline "flow of information" against which the effects of each particular regulation must be measured.[138] Moreover, "the degree to which the regulation impinges on" the flow of information will itself be a product of a multivariant, irreducibly indeterminate attempt to guage such factors as whether the speaker has ample (ample in whose judgment? by what criteria?) alternative channels of communication. Finally, Tribe fails to specify criteria for evaluating the relative importance of the competing interests that are "actually at stake" in any regulation.

2. *Systemic concerns: Uncounted costs, elusive gains.* The case-by-case approach to claims of access to public property implies that courts rather than forum managers should have the last word on whether particular access claims must be granted. In defense of this approach, it is often argued that managers of public property tend systematically both to undervalue speech and to overestimate its potential to disrupt,[139] and that the denial of access to public places distorts and unnecessarily contracts public debate because of the power necessarily implicit in state ownership and control of the relevant resources. The notion is that judicial oversight corrects this distortion because judges value speech more accurately than forum managers and are less susceptible to spurious fears of disruption. Careful review of the exclusionary decisions of public forum managers is therefore thought to produce net social gains.

Historically, of course, close judicial review has been highly correlated with vindication of First Amendment claims. Such review has been thought to produce more speech at little cost, on the assumption that the cost consists exclusively of manageable

---

[136] Id at 993.

[137] Id at 997.

[138] Specifying the constitutional norm entailed in the reference to the "free flow of information" is difficult indeed. See Lillian R. BeVier, *An Informed Public, An Informing Press: The Search for a Constitutional Principle*, 68 Calif L Rev 482, 506–12 (1980).

[139] See generally David Goldberger, *Judicial Scrutiny in the Public Forum Cases: Misplaced Trust in the Judgment of Public Officials*, 32 Buff L Rev 175 (1983).

increases in litigation[140] and modest inconvenience to the normal operation of the forum. In fact, however, the costs of case-by-case review of forum managers' decisions are more worrisome. First, as Robert Post has argued, constant vulnerability to judicial second-guessing may "diminish the authority at issue to such an extent as to impair the ability of the bureaucracy to attain its legitimate ends."[141] Second, although there is no evidence that this is so, the threat of judicial override may have the perverse effect of causing forum managers to decide that it is in their long-run strategic interest to make rules that are less rather than more accommodating to First Amendment activities, for a more restrictive posture might, by raising the cost, decrease the likelihood of access claims being made. Over time, such a strategy might require them to yield less of their managerial authority than a more permissive posture.

Third, the possibility of judicial intervention increases the risk that access claimants will engage in self-interested strategic behavior,[142] for it encourages them to characterize their claims in terms that systematically exaggerate the benefits of their behavior to themselves and trivialize its costs to others. Conceptualize public property as a commons—owned by all, thus owned by none. Like all commons, it is susceptible to overexploitation or abuse by anyone who can require others to absorb the costs of her use while enjoying most of the gain herself. It is possibly true, though it has never been empirically verified, that public forum managers undervalue speech.[143] Conversely, though, it is also plausible to argue that First Amendment claimants who have to internalize few of the costs of their activities at particular locales may tend both

---

[140] Id at 216–17.

[141] Robert C. Post, *Between Governance and Management: The History and Theory of the Public Forum*, 34 UCLA L Rev 1713, at 1772 (1987).

[142] Neither the risk that First Amendment claimants might engage in self-interested behavior, nor the possible appropriateness of tempering judicial generosity to individual rights claims as a means of reducing it, are often acknowledged, either by the Court or by commentators. Richard Epstein is the most notable exception to this rule. See, for example, Richard A. Epstein, *Unconstitutional Conditions, State Power, and the Limits of Consent*, 102 Harv L Rev 5, 25–26 (1988); compare generally Richard A. Epstein, *Takings: Private Property and the Power of Eminent Domain* (Harv Univ Press, 1985). For a quite different view of the implications that self-interested behavior ought to have for constitutional law generally, see Cass R. Sunstein, *Interest Groups in American Public Law*, 38 Stan L Rev 29 (1985); Cass R. Sunstein, *Naked Preferences and the Constitution*, 84 Colum L Rev 1689 (1984).

[143] The closest any commentator has come to offering empirical verification for the claim is Golberger, 32 Buff L Rev at 207, n 122 (cited in note 139).

to overvalue their need to exercise their First Amendment rights at particular places and to underestimate the adequacy of alternative sites. The prospect of getting a sympathetic judicial hearing if they can convince a court that the costs are trivial and the alternatives unsatisfactory seems likely to exacerbate this tendency.[144]

III. CONCLUSION

Not every instance of denial of access to publicly owned property signals an abuse of government power or carries a significant potential to distort public debate.[145] The role of categorical analysis in public forum jurisprudence is to generalize about the kinds of places where denials of access tend systematically to trigger well-founded concerns about deliberate governmental abuse and distortion. It thus conserves judicial resources for those circumstances in which the risks of abuse and distortion are high and there are thus likely to be important systemic gains from judicial intervention. It does not expend valuable judicial capital attempting to ferret out minimal risks for minimal systemic gains. The categorical approach implicitly recognizes that even when it comes to the First Amendment, judicial review is subject to the law of diminishing returns. As Richard Epstein has observed, "there comes a point at which the capacity to control governmental abuse diminishes, while the gains from controlling it are small. Then it is time to quit."[146] To reject the categorical approach in this context is to reject the idea that the risk of abuse varies systematically according to the nature of the place at issue and mistakenly implies that the systemic risk of abuse is not susceptible to useful generalization. It assumes, without foundation, that case-by-case judicial review in this setting is capable not only of constantly producing gains, but also of producing constant gains.

The concerns I have expressed in this article are "middle-level

---

[144] Compare, for example, Frank H. Easterbrook, *The Supreme Court—1983 Term: Foreward: The Court and the Economic System*, 98 Harv L Rev 4, 19–21 (1984).

[145] Compare generally Robert F. Nagel, *How Useful Is Judicial Review in Free Speech Cases*, 69 Cornell L Rev 302 (1984). See also Lee C. Bollinger, *The Tolerant Society: A Response to Critics*, 90 Colum L Rev 979, 997–1000 (1990).

[146] Epstein, 102 Harv L Rev at 57 (cited in note 142).

questions."[147] Because they focus on issues of "implementation and institutional context,"[148] they occupy an analytical tier between broad theory and narrow doctrine. Such questions have not of late generated much interest among First Amendment scholars, but this does not suggest that they are unimportant to a thoughtful understanding of the Court's work. Indeed, despite their lack of currency, such issues deserve the spotlight. If a reigning conception of the First Amendment requires judges to perform tasks that they cannot succeed in performing, First Amendment doctrine risks becoming no more than a rhetorical facade, shielding from view that its guarantee of an "uninhibited, robust and wide-open" public debate is an empty one. Aspirational rhetoric has an important role to play in First Amendment jurisprudence, but it should be used to make doctrine more transparent, not to disguise its emptiness.

---

[147] The term is Robert Ellickson's. See Robert Ellickson, *Cities and Homeowners Associations*, 130 U Pa L Rev 1519, 1521 (1982).

[148] Lillian R. BeVier, *Money and Politics: A Perspective on the First Amendment and Campaign Finance Reform*, 73 Cal L Rev 1045, 1047 (1985).

SUZANNA SHERRY

LEE v WEISMAN:
PARADOX REDUX

For more than two decades, the Supreme Court's Establishment Clause jurisprudence was "at war with" its Free Exercise jurisprudence.[1] In recent years, however, two major decisions—*Employment Division v Smith*[2] and *Lee v Weisman*[3] —have effected a significant shift in our religion clause jurisprudence. In this article I will suggest that, considered together, these two decisions have merely replaced one form of incoherence with another. In particular, I will suggest that either decision could be justified alone—and indeed, that either standing alone would be an improvement on the Court's previous religion clause doctrine—but that together they make little sense.

The twenty-year tension between the Court's interpretations of the two religion clauses was especially acute in the context of spe-

---

Suzanna Sherry is Earl R. Larson Professor of Civil Rights and Civil Liberties Law, University of Minnesota.

AUTHOR'S NOTE: I am very grateful to Daniel Farber, Douglas Laycock, Michael McConnell, and Michael Paulsen for their detailed critical comments on an earlier draft of this essay. They are among the most helpful critiques I have ever received, and the essay is a stronger piece as a result of their comments. As should be apparent from the text, however, their kindness in offering assistance should not be taken as agreement with any of my arguments.

[1] Jesse H. Choper, *The Free Exercise Clause: A Structural Overview and an Appraisal of Recent Developments*, 27 Wm & Mary L Rev 943, 947 (1986). See also Jesse H. Choper, *The Religion Clauses of the First Amendment: Reconciling the Conflict*, 41 U Pitt L Rev 673, 674 (1980); Michael W. McConnell, *Accommodation of Religion: An Update and a Response to the Critics*, 60 Geo Wash L Rev 685, 695 (1992); William P. Marshall, *In Defense of* Smith *and Free Exercise Revisionism*, 58 U Chi L Rev 308, 319–20 (1991); Mark Tushnet, "*Of Church and State and the Supreme Court*": *Kurland Revisited*, 1989 Supreme Court Review 373, 377.

[2] 494 US 872 (1990).

[3] 112 S Ct 2649 (1992).

cial exemptions for religiously motivated actions. Under the doctrine of *Lemon v Kurtzman*,[4] the Court construed the Establishment Clause to forbid the government from preferring religion to non-religion, or from subsidizing religious activities. Under the doctrine of *Sherbert v Verner*, however, the Court interpreted the Free Exercise Clause to require government to grant special exemptions to those who opposed general laws on religious grounds.[5]

The problem lay in the Court's attempt to enforce, simultaneously, broad interpretations of both clauses. When a broad reading of one clause directs the government not to promote religion and a broad reading of the other directs it not to hinder religion, it is not possible—especially in a state where government aid and government regulations are pervasive—to read both clauses as imperatives. If the government applies its laws neutrally, it will prohibit some people from practicing their religion. If the government exempts those with religious objections, it will discriminate against those with non-religious objections. Thus a broad interpretation of each clause is in direct conflict with a broad interpretation of the other.

Although commentators have suggested various ways to "reconcile" the two clauses, there are in fact only two solutions to the paradox: one clause or the other must be interpreted very narrowly. The result of a narrow interpretation, however, is to subordinate the core values of that clause to the core values of the other. Either Establishment Clause values must be subordinated to Free Exercise values, or Free Exercise values must be subordinated to Establishment Clause values.

For two short years, the Court resolved the religion clause paradox by adopting the latter of these alternatives, maintaining a broad interpretation of the Establishment Clause while narrowing its interpretation of the Free Exercise Clause.[6] The Court's most recent decision in this area, however, has undone this effort at reconciliation. In *Lee v Weisman* the Court abandoned the last vestiges of

---

[4] 403 US 602 (1971).

[5] 374 US 398 (1963). Sometimes these exemptions took the form of taxpayer supported subsidies and sometimes they constituted merely a discriminatory preference for religion over non-religion, but in either case the required exemptions seemed to run afoul of the Establishment Clause as interpreted by the Court.

[6] See *Employment Division v Smith*, 494 US 872 (1990), discussed at pp. 150–51.

Lemon's broad interpretation of the Establishment Clause, leaving little or no meaning to either of the religion clauses. Although this state of affairs may seem preferable to the incoherence of the prior two decades, it is in fact wholly unsatisfactory when evaluated in terms of its consistency with either the Constitution or political theory.

I. CLAUSES IN CONFLICT

In a series of decisions beginning in 1963, the Court held that where a neutral law of general applicability seriously compromised an individual's ability to follow his religious beliefs, the Free Exercise Clause required the government to grant an exemption unless there was a compelling reason not to do so. Although many claims for exemptions were rejected (especially in the waning years of the doctrine), either because the law was found not to impinge on religious beliefs or because the government's interest was found to be compelling, the Court required exemptions in at least four cases[7] and approved a legislatively granted exemption in another. Moreover, for more than a quarter century the Court never wavered in its commitment to the principle of the exemption doctrine, even if it applied it narrowly in fact.

In three decisions involving the denial of unemployment benefits,[8] the Court required states to pay benefits to individuals whose inability to find work stemmed from their refusal to work in otherwise ordinary situations that conflicted with their religious beliefs. In each case, the Court made clear that, although any non-religious refusal to work could result in a denial of benefits, the Free Exercise Clause required the government to grant an exemption to those whose objections derived from religious beliefs. Thus, for example, a refusal to work on Saturdays due to childcare responsibilities could result in a denial of benefits, whereas a refusal to work on Saturdays due to religious beliefs could not. Similarly, in *Wisconsin v Yoder*,[9] the Court held that the Free Exercise Clause required the

---

[7] In one other case, an equally divided Court affirmed a lower court decision mandating a religious exemption from a state law requiring photographs on drivers licenses. *Jensen v Quaring*, 472 US 478 (1985), affirming *Quaring v Peterson*, 728 F2d 1121 (8th Cir 1984).

[8] *Sherbert v Verner*, 374 US 398 (1963); *Thomas v Review Board*, 450 US 707 (1981); *Hobbie v Unemployment Appeals Comm'n*, 480 US 136 (1987).

[9] 406 US 205 (1972).

state to grant an exemption from its compulsory schooling laws to Amish parents who had religious objections to high school education. The Court noted that the state would not be required to grant such an exemption to a parent whose objection was "philosophical and personal," giving the example of an isolationism derived from Henry David Thoreau.[10]

Finally, in *Corporation of the Presiding Bishop v Amos*,[11] the Court upheld a legislatively granted exemption, embracing reasoning parallel to that of *Yoder*. In *Amos*, the Court upheld a provision of Title VII that exempted religious organizations—including their secular activities—from the general prohibition against religious discrimination. The Court held that the exemption was designed "to alleviate significant governmental interference with" religious organizations, rather than to foster religion. Although the Court did not reach the question of whether the Free Exercise Clause would have required the exemption of its own force, the *Yoder* doctrine strongly suggests that it would have.

Thus the Court construed the Free Exercise Clause, from 1963 until its 1990 decision in *Smith*, to require, in at least some circumstances, religious exemptions from neutral laws of general applicability. During most of this period, however, the Court simultaneously interpreted the Establishment Clause to prohibit such exemptions.

The Court first fully enunciated the interpretation of the Establishment Clause that guided its decisions for more than two decades in *Lemon v Kurtzman*.[12] The *Lemon* doctrine, which was announced in 1971 but derived from several earlier decisions,[13] prohibited any government support of religion (financial or otherwise) unless the government action had a secular purpose, had a primary effect that neither advanced nor inhibited religion, and avoided "excessive entanglement" with religion. Although inconsistently applied, especially in the area of aid to parochial schools,[14] the *Lemon* doctrine

---

[10] Id at 216.

[11] 483 US 327 (1987).

[12] 403 US 602 (1971).

[13] *Board of Education v Allen*, 392 US 236 (1968); *Walz v Tax Comm'n*, 397 US 664 (1970). See *Lemon*, 403 US at 612–13.

[14] For a list and description of the inconsistent cases, see, e.g., Michael A. Paulsen, *Religion, Equality, and the Constitution: An Equal Protection Approach to Establishment Clause Adjudication*, 61 Notre Dame L Rev 311, 315–17 (1986).

was uniformly acknowledged to be a broad interpretation of the Establishment Clause which invalidated a great deal of government support of religion.

Most important for present purposes, the *Lemon* doctrine logically rendered the exemptions granted in the *Yoder* line of cases unconstitutional.[15] This was so for several reasons. First, there is no secular purpose in discriminating between religious and non-religious reasons for individual action. The only purpose is to accommodate religious beliefs, which is not a secular purpose. Second, at its very core, *Lemon* prohibited the government from preferring religion to non-religion. The exemptions established in the Court's Free Exercise decisions mandated precisely that preference by permitting those with religious objections, but not those with philosophical or other non-religious objections, to avoid the general law. Third, an effect—arguably the primary effect—of mandating such exemptions only for those with religious claims is to advance religion, at least in the sense of encouraging or enabling adherents to practice their religion while denying to others the right to live by their own philosophical principles. Thus people are encouraged to base their lives on religious as opposed to non-religious principles. Fourth, to the extent that such exemptions require courts, legislatures, or administrators to determine which acts are religiously motivated, they result in significant entanglement of government with religion. Finally, at least in the unemployment benefits cases, nonadherent taxpayers were required to subsidize the religious beliefs of others. Indeed, it would seem that a religious exemption from a general law is no more secular—and thus no less a violation of the Establishment Clause—than an attempt to include parochial schools in a general program distributing educational maps to schoolchildren, which the Court struck down in *Meek v Pittenger*,[16] or a program allowing parochial and other private schools to use state school buses, which the Court invalidated in *Wolman v Walter*.[17]

In fact, the Court itself occasionally recognized that *Lemon* prohibited special exemptions for religious beliefs, and even invali-

---

[15] See generally id at 339–40.

[16] 421 US 349 (1975). See also *Wolman v Walter*, 433 US 229 (1977).

[17] 433 US 229 (1977).

dated two such exemptions. In *Estate of Thornton v Caldor*[18] the Court applied *Lemon* to strike down a state law requiring employers to give employees their Sabbath day off, and in *Texas Monthly, Inc v Bullock*[19] the Court struck down a state's attempt to exempt religious publications from its general sales tax. Thus from at least 1971 until 1990, the Court's analysis of religious exemptions from general laws was inconsistent in both theory and practice.

Moreover, the Court's broad readings of both religion clauses effectively enabled it to pick and choose among religions, requiring or approving exemptions for some religions while invalidating (or not requiring) exemptions for others. It is noteworthy that, in general, the religions favored by the Court were marginal Christian religions that posed little or no threat to mainstream American Christianity.[20] The Court required or approved exemptions for the Amish, Jehovah's Witnesses, Mormons, and Seventh-Day Adventists, all of which are long established Christian sects that have always remained relatively small in the United States. On the other hand, the Court consistently refused to require exemptions for Jews,[21] non-Christian Native American religions,[22] or fundamentalist Christian sects (which by their aggressive evangelical tactics and opposition to the secularization of mainstream Christianity threaten the established religious order).[23] Thus, in addition to its internal inconsistency, the Court's approach to the religion clauses tended in application to accord protection primarily to those religious minorities who least need it,[24] contrary to the usual conception of the role of the Court in protecting minorities from majoritarian abuse.

---

[18] 472 US 703 (1985).

[19] 489 US 1 (1988).

[20] See Frank Way & Barbara J. Burt, *Religious Marginality and the Free Exercise Clause*, 77 Am Pol Sci Rev 652, 664–65 (1983). Lower court decisions may show a somewhat different pattern.

[21] See, e.g., *McGowan v Maryland*, 366 US 420 (1961); *Braunfeld v Brown*, 366 US 699 (1961); *Goldman v Weinberger*, 475 US 503 (1986).

[22] See *Bowen v Roy*, 476 US 693 (1986); *Lyng v Northwest Indian Cemetery Prot. Ass'n*, 485 US 439 (1988).

[23] See *Bob Jones University v United States*, 461 US 574 (1983); *Tony & Susan Alamo Foundation v Secretary of Labor*, 471 US 290 (1985); *Jimmy Swaggart Ministries v Board of Equalization*, 493 US 378 (1990).

[24] Cf. Mark Tushnet, *The Constitution of Religion*, 18 Conn L Rev 701, 718 & n 90 (1986) (characterizing exemptions as occurring "in largely innocuous situations").

II. FALSE RECONCILIATIONS

Neither *Lemon* nor *Yoder* is necessarily correct, although each reflects the core values of the clause it interprets. The Free Exercise Clause is designed to protect the exercise of religion from government interference. The Establishment Clause is designed to prevent the government from putting its imprimatur behind any one religion or religion in general.[25] A broad reading of the free exercise principle of non-interference leads to *Yoder;* a broad reading of the establishment principle of no-imprimatur leads to *Lemon* (or some similar formula prohibiting the preferential treatment of religion). I will call these broad readings the "no interference" and "no discrimination" principles, respectively.[26]

There are four possible pairs of "pure" interpretations[27] of the religion clauses: (1) we might interpret both clauses broadly, as the Court did under *Yoder* and *Lemon;* (2) we might interpret both clauses narrowly; (3) we might subordinate core Establishment Clause values to the Free Exercise Clause by adopting only the no-interference principle; and (4) we might subordinate the core Free Exercise Clause values to the Establishment Clause by adopting only the no-discrimination principle. In order, the consequences of these pairings for the issue of exemptions would be: (1) exemptions are both required and prohibited; (2) exemptions are permitted but not required; (3) exemptions are required; and (4) exemptions are prohibited.

In adopting the first alternative, the Court created a paradox that justices and scholars have been trying to resolve ever since. It is

---

[25] I believe that almost all of the scholars I discuss in this essay would agree with these formulations in the abstract.

[26] I chose "no discrimination" instead of "no preference" because the latter is too close to "non-preferentialism," which has become a term of art for the argument that the Establishment Clause prohibits only preferential aid to some religions but does not bar aid to religion in general over non-religion.

[27] Of course, there are also what might be called "diluted" interpretations, or intermediate approaches that blend two or more of the core interpretation pairs. Thus one might combine a "quasi-broad" interpretation of the Establishment Clause with a "narrow but not toothless" interpretation of the Free Exercise Clause. This type of intermediate approach, however, still raises the same question: why should we allow one clause to trump the other in specific situations? Making each clause more flexible does not reconcile the conflict, but only reduces it to a conflict that is resolved differently in each individual case. This merely adds further unpredictability, and does not eliminate the core conflict that requires us to subordinate one clause to the other.

noteworthy that every proposed reconciliation of the tension between the two clauses has adopted one of the two subordinating
solutions. Despite repeated claims that it is possible to give full
value to the core principles of both clauses without creating a direct
conflict between them, every proposed reconciliation has either
recreated the paradox or devalued one of the two clauses. The
various attempts at reconciliation fall into two broad categories: (1)
attempts to distinguish among the various types of burdens that
exemptions or failures to exempt place on nonbelievers and believers, often discussed in terms of "coercion"; and (2) attempts to
determine whether exemptions or failures to exempt constitute religious discrimination, often discussed in terms of "neutrality."[28] I
will deal with each in turn.

A. COERCION

A common approach taken by some proponents of a strong Free
Exercise Clause is to interpret the Establishment Clause as prohibiting only government coercion of religion. This approach claims
to effect a reconciliation of the two clauses. In fact, however, it
"solves" the problem by devaluing the Establishment Clause and
rendering it essentially redundant and therefore unimportant.

Jesse Choper has suggested that the Establishment Clause should
be read to forbid only government action that has both a solely
religious purpose and the likely effect of "coercing, compromising,
or influencing religious beliefs."[29] It is therefore permissible to burden nonbelievers—even to impose "substantial costs"[30]—in order
to relieve the burden on believers unless the non-believers' religious
liberty is itself impaired, or tax funds are used to subsidize religious
beliefs.[31] Although he concludes that *Sherbert* was wrongly decided

---

[28] One scholar's attempt at reconciliation simply recreates the Court's own paradox by
urging "a strong position on both [clauses]." Kathleen M. Sullivan, *Religion and Liberal
Democracy*, 59 U Chi L Rev 195, 222 (1992).

[29] Jesse H. Choper, *The Free Exercise Clause: A Structural Overview and an Appraisal of Recent
Developments*, 27 Wm & Mary L Rev 943, 948 (1986) ("Structural Overview"); *accord*, Jesse
H. Choper, *The Religion Clauses of the First Amendment: Reconciling the Conflict*, 41 U Pitt L
Rev 673, 675 (1980) ("Religion Clauses").

[30] Choper, *Religion Clauses* at 694.

[31] Id at 677–80. He thus distinguishes, with little explanation, between "indirect social
costs" (permissible) and tax subsidies (impermissible), noting only that the latter, unlike the
former, "threaten the values undergirding the Establishment Clause." Id at 694.

because other taxpayers were required to subsidize Ms. Sherbert's religious refusal to work Saturdays,[32] he approves of most other types of exemptions as mere accommodations of religion that do not burden the religious liberty of nonbelievers.[33]

Michael McConnell appears similarly attracted to the notion of requiring coercion for a finding of an Establishment Clause violation.[34] In his most recent discussion of the issue, however, he suggests that even the presence of coercion may not make out a violation of the Establishment Clause because religious exemptions will always "involve government coercion of some sort."[35] Thus, in his view, exemptions may pass constitutional muster despite the presence of coercion.

A majority of Justices have also endorsed a coercion test, although they have not yet agreed on the details of its application. In 1989 in *County of Allegheny v ACLU*,[36] Justice Kennedy, joined by Chief Justice Rehnquist and Justices White and Scalia, would have made coercion the "sole touchstone" of Establishment Clause violations, "for it would be difficult indeed to establish a religion without some measure of more of less subtle coercion."[37] All four of these Justices agreed that placing a creche on public property did not constitute even subtle coercion and was therefore constitutional. This past term, in *Lee v Weisman*,[38] Justice Thomas also endorsed a coercion test, and only a technical dispute about the definition of coercion prevented a majority of the Court from officially adopting this standard.

Despite this lack of an explicit majority, *Lee v Weisman* clearly signals the death of *Lemon* and the adoption of a coercion test. In *Weisman*, Justice Kennedy wrote for a five-Justice majority inval-

---

[32] Id at 690–92; Choper, *Structural Overview* at 949.

[33] Choper, *Religion Clauses* at 685.

[34] In Michael W. McConnell, *Coercion: The Lost Element of Establishment*, 27 Wm & Mary L Rev 933 (1986), he argued that only coercive governmental action violates the Establishment Clause. More recently, however, he has suggested that a coercion test "could tend toward acquiescence in more subtle forms of governmental power." McConnell, *Religious Freedom at a Crossroads*, U Chi L Rev 115, 159 (1992) ("Crossroads"). I assume that he would approve of an Establishment Clause test that incorporated coercion broadly defined.

[35] McConnell, *Crossroads* at 165.

[36] 492 US 573 (1989).

[37] Id at 659, 660–61 (opinion of Kennedy).

[38] 112 S Ct 2649 (1992).

idating state-sponsored prayer at a public school graduation. Justice
Scalia dissented, along with Chief Justice Rehnquist and Justices
White and Thomas. The dissenters thought coercion was a necessary element of an Establishment Clause violation, and found none
on the facts of the case.

The dispute between the majority and the dissent centered on
whether the psychological coercion inherent in the graduation context was sufficient to violate the Establishment Clause. Justice Kennedy's majority opinion relied entirely on the coercive aspect of
the setting; he cobbled together a majority by studiously ignoring
Lemon[39] and by stating that "at a minimum, the Constitution guarantees that government may not coerce anyone to support or participate in religion or its exercise."[40]

Although joining Justice Kennedy's opinion, the other four justices in the majority recognized that Kennedy, building upon his
opinion in *Allegheny County*, was prepared to substitute a coercion
test for *Lemon*. They therefore found it necessary to add two separate concurring opinions emphasizing that the Establishment
Clause prohibited more than government coercion. In a concurring
opinion joined by Justices Stevens and O'Connor, Justice Blackmun explained that he joined the Court's opinion only "because
[he found] nothing in it inconsistent with the essential precepts of
the Establishment Clause," adding that "[a]lthough . . . proof of
government coercion is not necessary to prove an Establishment
Clause violation, it is sufficient."[41] Justice Souter, also joined by
Justices Stevens and O'Connor, wrote separately to address the
question "whether state coercion of religious conformity, over and
above state endorsement of religious exercise or belief, is a necessary element of an Establishment Clause violation."[42] He concluded

---

[39] He stated explicitly that the case did "not require [the Court] to revisit the difficult
questions dividing [it] in recent cases," and that the Court thus would "not accept the
invitation of petitioners and *amicus* the United States to reconsider our decision in *Lemon v.
Kurtzman*." Id at 2655.

[40] Id. He continued that government may not "otherwise act in a way which 'establishes
a [state] religion or religious faith, or tends to do so.'" Id. This formulation adds nothing
to the coercion test. It is a mere restatement of the Establishment Clause itself, and in
Allegheny County Kennedy conflated it with the coercion test by stating that "it would be
difficult indeed to establish a religion without some measure of more or less subtle coercion."
492 US at 659.

[41] 112 S Ct at 2664 (Blackmun, J, concurring).

[42] Id at 2667 (Souter, J, concurring).

it was not. Thus, although joining Justice Kennedy's opinion, each
of these Justices found it necessary to counter the clear implication
that government coercion is essential to a violation of the Establishment Clause. Indeed, even the dissenters read Justice Kennedy's
opinion as abandoning *Lemon* in favor of a coercion standard.[43]

The Court's new coercion test is similar to the approaches recommended by Choper and McConnell. In the exemption context, the
Court, after *Smith*, apparently will use the coercion standard to
test the constitutionality only of legislatively granted exemptions,
whereas the commentators would also use it to determine whether
exemptions that might be required by the Free Exercise Clause
are consistent with the Establishment Clause. The basic principles
urged by the commentators and adopted by the Court are similar,
however, and suffer from identical flaws.

The first flaw in the coercion test is the one identified—and put
aside—by McConnell. As long as nonbelievers are required either
to obey the offending law or, worse, to take on an additional burden to enable believers to disobey (as in *Amos* or cases where nonbeliever employees must work undesirable shifts to cover for Sabbath
observers), there will be some form of government coercion.

Choper attempts to avoid this problem by suggesting that the
Establishment Clause is violated only if *religious* beliefs are coerced.
He defines religious beliefs to exclude all beliefs about religion
which are not themselves religiously derived (atheism, for example).[44] Michael Paulsen—who combines the no-discrimination and
coercion arguments in favor of exemptions—makes a similar argument. He maintains that there is a difference between "religion"
and "religious belief or exercise," and that "[a] nonbeliever's objection [thus] arises only when [the costs of the exemption] actually
abridge or injuriously discriminate against his freedom of nonexer-
cise."[45] On this view, religious accommodation that burdens nonbe-

---

[43] Id at 2685 (Scalia, J, dissenting).

[44] Although that is implicit in his general discussion of the differences between ordinary
burdens and burdens on religious liberty, he makes it explicit when he states that *Epperson
v Arkansas*, 393 US 97 (1968), invalidating a law prohibiting the teaching of evolution, was
wrongly decided because the law did not coerce anyone's religious beliefs. Since the law
permitted the teaching of creationism, the beliefs that were compromised were scientific,
non-religious beliefs rejecting the religious doctrine.

[45] Michael A. Paulsen, *Religion, Equality, and the Constitution: An Equal Protection Approach
to Establishment Clause Adjudication*, 61 Notre Dame L Rev 311, 336–37 (1986) ("Religion and
Equality").

lievers, but does not curtail their freedom not to believe, does not violate the Establishment Clause.

This line of argument raises three parallel problems. First, under Choper's view, the anti-evolution statute invalidated in *Epperson v Arkansas*[46] is constitutional because it does not impair religious liberty.[47] This view fails to recognize that it may impair religious liberty for the government to suppress non-religiously derived beliefs that religious doctrine is erroneous—in other words, the freedom to believe carries with it the freedom not to believe.[48] Second, both Choper's and Paulsen's definitions of coercion are too narrow insofar as they fail to recognize that any government preference for religious over non-religious beliefs will necessarily influence religious beliefs, and thus subtly burden non-religious belief or exercise.[49] Finally, by arguing that the government may burden some people in order to support other people's religious beliefs, as long as it does not burden the first group's *religious* beliefs, the proponents of this position single out religious beliefs from other beliefs for special treatment. Unless they can demonstrate that religious beliefs are different from other beliefs, such a preference is antithetical to the core values of the Establishment Clause.[50] Thus, this "reconciliation" of the tension merely subordinates the Establishment Clause to the Free Exercise Clause.

The second problem with requiring coercion as an element of an Establishment Clause violation is that such an approach makes the Establishment Clause redundant. Any government action that coerces religious belief violates the Free Exercise Clause. Although

---

[46] 393 US 97 (1968).

[47] Choper, *Religion Clauses*, 41 U Pitt L Rev at 687–88 (cited in note 29).

[48] See Kathleen M. Sullivan, *Religion and Liberal Democracy*, 59 U Chi L Rev 195, 205 (1992). Paulsen, to his credit, does not fall into this trap.

[49] Of course, any preference for secular over religious beliefs will have the opposite effect, and might therefore undermine free exercise values. It is thus hard to see how *any* government action in which there are religiously based differences can fail to coerce, or at least influence, *someone's* religious beliefs. This is analogous to the problem with defining "neutrality" in this context. See pp. 135–46. Paulsen explicitly denies that coercion is implicit in government endorsement of religion. Although he would prohibit government coercion of religion, he notes that "[n]either a creche nor a legislative chaplaincy abridges the religious liberty of the nonadherent through either compulsion or inducement, and these symbolic uses of religion do not *themselves* communicate a message of disapproval of such nonadherence." Paulsen, *Religion & Equality* at 353.

[50] The possibility of differentiating between religious and non-religious beliefs is discussed more fully in the next section.

virtually all commentators (and the Court) agree that direct coercion of religious beliefs violates the Free Exercise Clause, the redundancy problem is especially acute for those who take an accommodationist approach, since they include even indirect coercion among Free Exercise violations. As Douglas Laycock has observed, "[c]oercion to observe someone else's religion is as much a free exercise violation as is coercion to abandon my own."[51] If all governmental coercion concerning religious beliefs violates the Free Exercise Clause, a coercion-based Establishment Clause does not prohibit anything that is not independently prohibited by the Free Exercise Clause.

The third and most obvious problem with the coercion requirement is that it conflicts with the plainest possible meaning of the Establishment Clause, for it would permit Congress to establish a church, as long as no one was required to join.[52]

Even if the Establishment Clause prohibits more than government coercion, however, there is significant dispute about the extent to which it prohibits government favoritism toward religion. This dispute takes the form of debate about discrimination and neutrality, to which I now turn.

B. NEUTRALITY

The central problem with the neutrality solution to the issue of religious exemptions is that, in this context, there is no such thing as neutrality. If an exemption is granted, then the government (whether the legislature or the Court) facially discriminates in favor of religion, as when it exempts the Amish but not the followers of Thoreau from compulsory schooling laws. If, on the other hand, no exemption is granted, then the government discriminates in effect against those with religious objections to the law, as when a compulsory schooling law fails to exempt the Amish. Thus, as one

---

[51] Douglas Laycock, *"NonPreferential" Aid to Religion: A False Claim About Original Intent*, 27 Wm & Mary L Rev 875, 922 (1986) ("A False Claim"). See also Douglas Laycock, *"Noncoercive" Support for Religion: Another False Claim About the Establishment Clause*, 26 Valp L Rev 37 (1991) ("Another False Claim"); Kathleen M. Sullivan, *Religion and Liberal Democracy*, 59 U Chi L Rev 195 (1992); Mark V. Tushnet, *Reflections on the Role of Purpose in the Jurisprudence of the Religion Clauses*, 27 Wm & Mary L Rev 997 (1986). Justice Souter's concurring opinion in *Weisman* makes the same point. 112 S Ct at 2672–73.

[52] See Laycock, *A False Claim* at 39.

scholar has noted, "the very concept of neutrality is inherently indeterminate."[53]

Most proponents of accommodation recognize this difficulty, and counter with a call for substantive rather than formal neutrality.[54] But unlike formal neutrality, which requires only that the government not single out religion for special treatment, the meaning of substantive neutrality is unclear in this context. The meaning assigned by those who favor accommodation, however, leads to an exceedingly narrow interpretation of the Establishment Clause.

The major modern proponent of accommodation and a broad Free Exercise Clause, at the expense of the Establishment Clause, is Michael McConnell. Although his theory of the religion clauses has developed over time—leading to several possible interpretations of his position—the core of his interpretation of the clauses is that together they protect religious liberty[55] against "government-induced homogeneity" or "uniformity."[56] McConnell argues that special exemptions for religion foster this goal because they enable citizens to follow their individual consciences. This echoes the Court's explanation that exemptions are permissible when (and only when) they "alleviate significant governmental interference with" religious beliefs and practices.[57]

Both McConnell and the Court explicitly deny that granting exemptions discriminates against the non-religious. McConnell suggests that secular objectors, who, under *Yoder*, are not granted an exemption, "suffer little or no consequence at all" in having to obey general laws because nonbelief "entails no obligations and no observances."[58] Religious beliefs are different, he argues, because

---

[53] Steven D. Smith, *Symbols, Perceptions, and Doctrinal Illusions: Establishment Neutrality and the "No Endorsement" Test*, 86 Mich L Rev 266, 315 (1987).

[54] See, e.g., Douglas Laycock, *Formal, Substantive, and Disaggregated Neutrality Toward Religion*, 39 DePaul L Rev 993 (1990) ("Neutrality"); Michael W. McConnell, *Accommodation of Religion: An Update and a Response to the Critics*, 60 Geo Wash L Rev 685, 729 (1992) ("Update"); Michael W. McConnell & Richard A. Posner, *An Economic Approach to Issues of Religious Freedom*, 56 U Chi L Rev 1, 10–12, 33 (1989).

[55] Michael W. McConnell, *Accommodation of Religion*, 1985 Supreme Court Review 1 ("Accommodation").

[56] McConnell, *Crossroads* at 168, 169.

[57] *Corporation of the Presiding Bishop v Amos*, 483 US 327, 335 (1987). See also *Texas Monthly, Inc. v Bullock*, 489 US 1, 18 & n 8 (1988).

[58] McConnell, *Accommodation*, at 9, 10–11; *see also* Michael W. McConnell, *Neutrality Under the Religion Clauses*, 81 Nw U L Rev 146, 152 (1986) (nonbelievers suffer only "slight inconvenience") ("Neutrality"). He does admit that non-religious moral convictions are entitled to "special respect," but not to the extent of granting exemptions. *Accommodation* at 11–12.

they are "matter[s] over which we have no control—the demands of a transcendent authority."[59] Thus there is no discrimination in granting religious exemptions because only the religious are harmed in this way by the law. The Court has similarly denied that exemptions are discriminatory, suggesting in *Sherbert* that the required exemption "reflects nothing more than the governmental obligation of neutrality in the face of religious differences."[60] Both the Court and McConnell therefore characterize the granting of exemptions as a form of neutrality that implements the values of the Free Exercise Clause without diminishing the Establishment Clause's prohibition of discrimination in favor of religion over non-religion.[61]

There are two problems with this explication of the religion clauses. First, McConnell's initial premise seems to be that nonbelievers do not suffer the same sort of harm as believers from having to obey a law. But as William Marshall has pointed out, the dilemma of conflicting duties arises "anytime one's beliefs conflict with those of the state, whether those beliefs are religious or not."[62] Secularly derived beliefs may be as deeply and sincerely held as religious beliefs. The parent who believes that it is her moral obligation as a parent to spend time with her children on the weekends because she must be away from them during the week suffers the same consequences from having to work on Saturdays as does the Seventh-Day Adventist who believes that her God commands her to refrain from working on Saturday. In both cases there is a deeply felt moral obligation imposed from without (from God or from principles of moral rightness) and not affected by the individual's

---

[59] McConnell, *Crossroads* at 172. It is interesting to compare this statement, which concludes with his comment that religious beliefs, unlike secular beliefs, are not "the product of free and voluntary choice," with his derogatory comment that the Justices tend to view religion as the result, not of "thoughtful consideration and experience" but of "conformity and indoctrination." Id at 122. If religious beliefs are entitled to special treatment specifically because they are commands that must be obeyed rather than voluntary choices, then perhaps the Justices are correct in their assessment of religion as implicating conformity and indoctrination.

[60] *Sherbert v Verner*, 374 US 398, 409 (1963). See also *Hobbie v Unemployment Appeals Comm'n*, 480 US 136, 145 n 11 (1987) (exemption "does not single out a particular class of . . . persons for favorable treatment").

[61] McConnell's latest scholarship explicitly notes that discrimination in favor of religion over non-religion is prohibited by the Establishment Clause, see McConnell, *Crossroads* at 175.

[62] William P. Marshall, *The Case Against Constitutionally Compelled Free Exercise Exemptions*, 40 Case W Res L Rev 357, 383 (1989–90) ("Case Against Exemptions").

own likes or dislikes. In both cases, the individual is placed in the difficult position of having to choose between sacred—to her—obligations and financial necessity.

I use the word "sacred" deliberately: it highlights the second problem with the McConnell position. McConnell's characterization of secular beliefs as not productive of the conflicts that result from religious beliefs is descriptively erroneous. However, he may instead be basing his argument—and the right to exemptions—on a normative notion that only religious beliefs should be treated as sacred by the government. To the extent that he is making that claim, however, he is urging overt government discrimination in favor of religious beliefs by "den[ying] religious and secular beliefs equal constitutional dignity."[63] This not only undermines the heart of the Establishment Clause by preferring religion to non-religion, it also runs afoul of the core principles of the Free Speech Clause, which suggest that "every idea is of equal dignity and status in the marketplace of ideas."[64]

McConnell's understanding of the core purposes of the religion clauses supports this normative reading of his argument, but also further demonstrates that under his version of neutrality the Free Exercise Clause will always trump the Establishment Clause. His interpretation makes the two clauses redundant: the Free Exercise Clause prohibits "inhibiting religious practice" and the Establishment Clause prohibits "forcing or inducing a contrary religious practice."[65] But anything that forces me to observe a contrary religious practice *necessarily* inhibits my own religious practices—whether by forcing me to do what violates my own religious precepts, such as praying to a God I do not believe in, or by reducing

---

[63] Id at 393. See generally id at 388–92.

[64] William P. Marshall, *In Defense of* Smith *and Free Exercise Revisionism*, 58 U Chi L Rev 308, 320 (1991). See also Marshall, *Case Against Exemptions*, at 394.

[65] McConnell, *Crossroads* at 169. To the extent that McConnell here appears to be endorsing coercion as a necessary element of an Establishment Clause violation, see my discussion at pp. 133–35. A similar formulation of the purposes of the religion clauses has been proposed by Mary Ann Glendon and Raul F. Yanes. They suggest that the "overarching purpose [of the clauses is] to protect freedom of religion." Again, however, their definitions make the Establishment Clause redundant: according to them, the clauses together "bar Congress from abridging religious freedom in one specific way [the Establishment Clause], and in general [the Free Exercise Clause]." Mary Ann Glendon & Raul F. Yanes, *Structural Free Exercise*, 90 Mich L Rev 477, 541 (1991). Moreover, unlike McConnell, they would not require neutrality between religion and non-religion, id at 539, and thus would further minimize the Establishment Clause.

the time and money I have available to support my own religion. Similarly, McConnell's understanding eliminates any independent meaning for the Establishment Clause: "Taken together, the Religion Clauses can be read most plausibly as warding off two equal and opposite threats to religious freedom—government action that promotes the majority's favored brand of religion and government action that impedes religious practices not favored by the majority."[66] McConnell obviously believes that these are two distinct threats, but it is not clear how any government action could promote one religion without simultaneously impeding others. This is especially problematic for those who, like McConnell, find that even indirect and unintentional inhibitions on religious practices violate the Free Exercise Clause. Thus every Establishment Clause violation is also a Free Exercise violation (although not vice versa), and the definitions render the Establishment Clause a nullity.

The crux of the problem with McConnell's interpretation of the religion clauses is that it fails to recognize the shades of meaning that might be comprehended by such terms as "inhibiting," "forcing," "promot[ing]," and "imped[ing]." Like "neutrality," these terms can refer either to government action that intentionally or facially favors or disfavors religious over non-religious practices, or it can refer to the actual or perceived effect of the government action. An atheist might reasonably believe that the government is forcing or promoting deism (or religion in general) when it accommodates those whose objection to obeying the law stems from religion but not those whose objection stems from secular beliefs, just as a believer is convinced that the government is inhibiting religion if it fails to grant an exemption. But McConnell's scheme leaves room only for the believer's objection and not for the atheist's; he does not consider accommodation as promoting religion.

McConnell's failure to recognize the atheist's claim as valid stems from his disparate treatment of religious and secular beliefs. McConnell accepts without question perceptions derived from religious beliefs, but rejects perceptions derived from contrary beliefs. For example, the eternal consequences of obeying a law in conflict with religious beliefs are all in the believer's mind (there are no tangible consequences that can be perceived by an objective observer). McConnell nevertheless counts as a cost the non-tangible

---

[66] McConnell, *Update* at 690.

harm that derives from ignoring those idiosyncratic and non-verifiable beliefs. On the other hand, McConnell "rules out of bounds costs consisting solely of aversions toward religion or particular faiths."[67] In other words, if I believe that I will be eternally damned if I work on Saturday, for the government to force me to do so imposes a cost on me. If, by contrast, I believe that religion condemns humanity to a stunted and uncreative future, for the government to foster religion by preferring your religious to my secular motivations in allocating benefits imposes no cost on me. In either case, however, there is neither a way to verify the belief—that I will be damned or that humanity will be stunted—nor any objective way to reckon the cost to me if the government acts in a way inconsistent with beliefs.[68]

The differentiation between religious and nonreligious beliefs thus plays a key role in McConnell's theories of accommodation. That distinction underlies the normative decision to treat only religious beliefs as worthy of special protection and also defines the sorts of non-tangible effects that will count for purposes of measuring discriminatory effects.

In order to explain and justify such differential treatment of religious and non-religious beliefs, McConnell must demonstrate that they are different in a relevant, if not compelling, way. Apart from the unsupported assertion that religious beliefs, unlike secular beliefs, are *commands*, and the oft-repeated observation that the Constitution singles out religion for special treatment,[69] no one has distinguished religious from non-religious beliefs in such a way as to justify the discrimination inherent in preferring religious beliefs. That the Constitution singles out religion is not itself persuasive, for it singles out religion for both preferential *and* disadvantageous

---

[67] McConnell & Posner, 56 U Chi L Rev at 35 (cited in note 54).

[68] One might try to label the costs to the religious believer as "Hohfeldian" and those to the nonbeliever as "non-Hohfeldian," but that characterization depends on a prior assumption that the nonbeliever's interest in humanity's future is different from the believer's interest in his own afterlife. Needless to say, that very distinction *also* depends on the beliefs of the two individuals, and may vary (some believers may be more concerned about humanity than about themselves, for example). Thus reckoning the cost, and differentiating between costs, ultimately depends on how one treats the individual's own beliefs.

[69] See, e.g., McConnell, *Update* at 717; Douglas Laycock, *The Remnants of Free Exercise*, 1990 Supreme Court Review 1, 16; Paulsen, 61 Notre Dame L Rev at 337 (cited in note 45).

treatment: the Establishment Clause and Free Exercise Clauses together bar the government not only from interfering with individual religious beliefs but also from favoring them.[70] This is unlike the Free Speech Clause, for example, which does not bar the government from speaking itself.[71] The most intriguing attempt to explain how religious beliefs are unique is John Garvey's. He suggests that "religion is a lot like insanity" in that true believers may be unable to perceive reality the way others do and may thus be unable to conform their conduct to the law in light of their perception that God commands them to do otherwise.[72] This hardly serves as a justification for requiring the government to cater to what would, in the insane, be called delusions. Thus, no attempt to distinguish religious from non-religious beliefs has successfully justified granting exemptions to religious objectors but not to secular objectors.

Thus McConnell—and the Court in its rare attempts to explain away the tension between its establishment and free exercise jurisprudence—achieves a resolution between the two clauses only by making the Establishment Clause virtually meaningless, at least in the context of exemptions that privilege religious objectors over secular objectors. In McConnell's view, the Establishment Clause prohibits the government from giving money to "religion *qua* reli-

---

[70] The argument that the Founders must have thought religion was different—otherwise they would not have adopted the religion clauses—does not get us very far. First, it is possible to read the Free Exercise Clause as a particularized version of the Free Speech Clause, guaranteeing only that the government could not suppress religious belief or expression any more than it could suppress political expression. For an elaboration of this argument, see Steven G. Gey, *Why Is Religion Special? Reconsidering the Accommodation of Religion Under the Religion Clauses of the First Amendment*, 52 U Pitt L Rev 75, 148 (1990). The Establishment Clause might then be read as a way of ensuring that religion would *not* be treated differently. Second, even if the founding generation believed that religion was different and therefore entitled to special consideration (and the best reading of the history, as with most such disputes, is probably that some did and some didn't), their intent might be incoherent in a modern regulated state. Finally, basing modern interpretations of the Constitution on the specific intent of the framers is controversial, to say the least.

[71] Justice Kennedy's majority opinion in *Weisman* recognized this difference in the context of government speech about religion. 112 S Ct at 2657–58. See also Sullivan, 59 U Chi L Rev at 206 (cited in note 51) ("there is no political establishment clause").

[72] John H. Garvey, *Free Exercise and the Values of Religious Liberty*, 18 Conn L Rev 779, 798–800 (1986). If that is in fact an accurate account of the difference between religious and non-religious beliefs, one should also note that the insane who commit crimes may not be punished but are nevertheless locked up until they give up their delusions. They are certainly not given carte blanche to disobey whatever law their delusions made them unable to obey.

gion,"[73] but does not prohibit the government from subsidizing Ms. Sherbert's religious beliefs or granting a sales tax exemption only to religious publications.[74] McConnell's Establishment Clause would prohibit little beyond direct discrimination among faiths or legislative declarations that everyone must tithe or attend church—rather remote legislative possibilities.[75] McConnell comments that the difference between substantive and formal neutrality "is the difference between a Free Exercise Clause that is a major restraining device on government action . . . and a Free Exercise Clause that will rarely have practical application."[76] That is true. But McConnell's position reduces the Establishment Clause to just such a practical nullity.

Other scholars similarly reconcile the two clauses—and label their reconciliation "neutrality"—by elevating the core values of the Free Exercise Clause over those of the Establishment Clause. Douglas Laycock advocates "substantive neutrality": the government should "minimize the extent to which it either encourages or discourages religious belief or disbelief, practice or nonpractice, observance or nonobservance."[77] According to Laycock, although no government act in this context can be wholly neutral, we can distinguish between the minor encouragement of religion that occurs when an exemption is granted and the severe discouragement of religion that occurs when an exemption is denied. He offers as illustration the question whether to grant an exemption from Prohibition for the religious use of wine.[78]

What Laycock, like McConnell, fails to appreciate is that whenever government attempts to remedy a de facto discrimination against religion by granting an exemption to religious objectors it

---

[73] McConnell, *Crossroads* at 185.

[74] He suggests that his approach would mandate a judicial return to the *Sherbert-Yoder* regime, "albeit with more vigorous and consistent enforcement," McConnell, *Crossroads* at 170, and nowhere suggests that any legislatively granted exemption is unconstitutional.

[75] McConnell does suggest that it might violate the Establishment Clause if the government influenced or subtly coerced a captive or vulnerable audience into conformity with government-preferred religious beliefs. See *Crossroads* at 158. Such coercion, however, would probably also violate the Free Exercise Clause since the coercion would operate to impede the audience's adherence to its own religious beliefs as well. The redundancy created by using a coercion test is discussed at pages 134–35.

[76] McConnell, *Update* at 689.

[77] Laycock, *Remnants*, 1990 Supreme Court Review at 16.

[78] Laycock, *Neutrality*, 39 DePaul L Rev at 1000–1003.

creates an equally noxious de jure discrimination against nonbelievers. For the government to grant only religious exemptions sends a message that religious belief is valued more than nonbelief (or non-religious belief)[79] and encourages religious belief. The fact that, as Laycock points out, it does not directly encourage religious belief[80] (most parents are not about to become Amish in order to avoid compulsory schooling laws) does not change the fact that the message is there. As Laycock himself observes, 83 percent of the American public claims to feel "close to God,"[81] and any government preference for religiously derived values over secularly derived values can only compound the pressure nonbelievers experience when they are reminded that America is a religious nation. How one evaluates the magnitude of the effect—whether it is minor or severe—depends on how one values the intangible, nonfalsifiable beliefs of both the religious and the non-religious. The harm done to believers who are prevented from practicing their religion is no different in kind or degree from the harm done to nonbelievers (in particular to atheists and others who subscribe to secular rather than religious worldviews) who are branded as unwelcome second-class citizens and implicitly informed that they will be welcome if only they will embrace the right beliefs. One's own perspective determines both which harm is considered greater and which principle—no-discrimination or no-interference—has priority. An unsympathetic atheist may scoff just as much at the believer's claim of religious compulsion as the believer may scoff at the atheist's sense of exclusion. Each may say, with equal justification, that the other suffers no real or tangible injury. Only by distinguishing religious beliefs from other beliefs (including non-religiously derived beliefs about religion) can Laycock distinguish the two harms.

Ira Lupu also champions a form of "neutrality," which he labels the pursuit of "equal religious liberty."[82] Under his scheme, how-

---

[79] Mark Tushnet, who has wavered between advocating formal neutrality and advocating substantive neutrality, has made the same observation. Mark Tushnet, *The Emerging Principle of Accommodation of Religion (Dubitante)*, 76 Geo L J 1691, 1703 (1988) ("Dubitante").

[80] Laycock, *Remnants* at 17.

[81] Douglas Laycock, *Vicious Stereotypes in Polite Society*, 8 Const Comm 395, 397 (1991).

[82] Ira C. Lupu, *Reconstructing the Establishment Clause: The Case Against Discretionary Accommodation of Religion*, 140 U Pa L Rev 555, 567–68 (1991) ("Reconstructing the Establishment Clause"); Ira C. Lupu, *Keeping the Faith: Religion, Equality and Speech in the U.S. Constitution*, 18 Conn L Rev 739 (1986) ("Keeping the Faith").

ever, the government is permitted to aid religion along with non-religion in some cases, and is required to aid religion alone in others.[83] Lupu, like McConnell and Laycock, recognizes the burden formal neutrality (no facial discrimination for or against religion) can place on religious believers, and rectifies it in the same way: by allowing facial discrimination in favor of religion where it is necessary to relieve the discriminatory effect on believers. Again, however, he fails to appreciate that this does not resolve the conflict, but simply shifts the burden of discriminatory effects from believers to nonbelievers. Moreover, to the extent that he interprets the Free Exercise Clause to protect religious liberty and the Establishment Clause to protect equal religious liberty,[84] the Establishment Clause appears to add nothing to what is already protected by the Equal Protection Clause of the Fourteenth Amendment.[85]

Mark Tushnet once suggested[86] a "reconciliation" that, while not explicitly couched in terms of "neutrality," suffers from the same flaws. He formulated a seemingly simple resolution of the tension between the two clauses, at least in the area of religious exemptions: "[o]ne could . . . interpret the establishment clause to prohibit all statutes that have a religious purpose, except for statutes with the purpose of accommodating religion in ways required by the free exercise clause."[87] Thus the breadth of the Free Exercise Clause is matched by a narrowing of the Establishment Clause. But there is no way to explain why this formulation is better than its opposite: interpret the Free Exercise Clause to require only those religions

[83] Lupu, *Reconstructing the Establishment Clause* at 588–89, 594–95. See also Paulsen, *Religion & Equality* at 314, 354–56 (cited in note 45). Paulsen, like Lupu, suggests that the religion clauses together protect "equality of religious freedom," mandating "neutrality." Id at 314, 332.

[84] Lupu, *Keeping the Faith* at 742.

[85] The fact that the Establishment Clause predates the Equal Protection Clause by more than half a century—and predates the modern interpretation of the Equal Protection Clause by which religious minorities are protected from discrimination by almost two centuries—might matter only to hardcore originalists. What most courts and scholars are struggling with today is not the original meaning of the Constitution, but the modern meaning. Moreover, as suggested at pp. 147–48, the founders' original intent may be incoherent in the context of today's activist state.

[86] He has apparently since abandoned that position and moved into the "formal neutrality" camp. See Tushnet, *Dubitante* (cited in note 76); Mark Tushnet, *"Of Church and State and the Supreme Court": Kurland Revisited*, 1989 Supreme Court Review 373.

[87] Mark V. Tushnet, *Reflections on the Role of Purpose in the Jurisprudence of the Religion Clauses*, 27 Wm & Mary L Rev 997, 1007 (1986). See also Geoffrey R. Stone, *Constitutionally Compelled Exemptions and the Free Exercise Clause*, 27 Wm & Mary L Rev 985, 994 (1986).

exemptions not prohibited by the Establishment Clause, and then interpret the Establishment Clause broadly. Similarly, Michael Paulsen suggests that "protecting the constitutional right to the free exercise of religion" should constitute a compelling governmental interest sufficient to withstand Establishment Clause scrutiny.[88] This formulation can also be reversed: protecting the values of the Establishment Clause should constitute a compelling government interest sufficient to justify the impact of neutral laws on religious exercise. Whichever clause serves as the compelling interest trumps the other. Which formulation one prefers depends solely on whether one places a higher priority on the values of the Establishment Clause or on those of the Free Exercise Clause.

If some alleged reconciliations of the religion clauses achieve their goal by subordinating the Establishment Clause, others make the opposite mistake. Those who oppose exemptions for believers often fail to see that neutral laws, rigidly applied, constitute a form of discrimination against believers, contrary to the values of the Free Exercise Clause. These scholars' "reconciliations" simply interpret the Free Exercise Clause narrowly, thus subordinating its core values to those of the Establishment Clause.

Philip Kurland is perhaps the strongest proponent of the rule against exemptions. Calling for neutrality, he suggests not only that courts should not grant religious exemptions (i.e., *Yoder* was wrongly decided), but also that legislatures should be prohibited from granting such exemptions (i.e., *Amos* was wrongly decided).[89] Although his scheme achieves formal neutrality, it effectively privileges Establishment Clause values over Free Exercise Clause values by upholding laws that have a severe discriminatory effect on religious believers. Just as one interpretation of the Establishment Clause prohibits the government from discriminating—facially or in effect—against nonbelievers, one interpretation of the Free Exercise Clause protects believers from the discriminatory effect of neutral laws. Kurland does not satisfactorily take into account this possible reading of the Free Exercise Clause. Thus just as McConnell and others undervalue the discrimination inflicted by exemp-

---

[88] Paulsen, *Religion & Equality* at 341–42 (cited in note 45).

[89] See Philip B. Kurland, *The Irrelevance of the Constitution: The Religion Clauses of the First Amendment and the Supreme Court*, 24 Vill L Rev 3 (1978–79); Philip B. Kurland, *Religion and the Law* (1962).

tions, Kurland undervalues the discrimination—eloquently described by McConnell and others[90]—inflicted by neutral laws.

William Marshall also opposes exemptions for religious objectors, but only those that have been imposed by judicial interpretation of the Free Exercise Clause. He apparently would uphold legislatively granted exemptions.[91] Because this is the approach that seems to command a majority of the current Court, I will engage in a fuller discussion of this position later.[92] For now, it is sufficient to note that although Marshall recognizes that a failure to grant exemptions may have a discriminatory impact on believers,[93] he nonetheless concludes that such de facto discrimination is preferable to the harm caused by granting exemptions.[94] Thus, unlike McConnell or Kurland, Marshall acknowledges that his solution requires at least some subordination of one religion clause to the other.

Scholars have also made parallel arguments on each side questioning the very framing of the question as one of "discrimination." McConnell has suggested that the Free Exercise Clause provides not only protection against religious discrimination, but also a substantive right to religious liberty.[95] He can therefore argue that the real evil of a generally applicable law is not its discriminatory effect

---

[90] Laycock's characterization of the Court's view of what it accomplished by not granting exemptions is perhaps the most telling. He notes that the Court believes that "religious minorities will give up their faith without a fuss if the law says they must." Laycock, *Remnants* at 29. In fact, as Laycock points out, for some believers this is incorrect. Although Laycock is surely right as far as he goes, it is probably also incorrect to assume that all secular objectors—especially those whose objections are principled and morally, politically, or philosophically based—will give up their beliefs easily. The many secular objectors to draft laws and Jim Crow laws who went to jail rather than obey are evidence that religious believers do not have a monopoly on martyrdom.

[91] Marshall, *In Defense of* Smith (cited in note 64).

[92] See Part III.

[93] Id at 318.

[94] Id at 318–19.

[95] Michael W. McConnell, *Free Exercise Revisionism and the* Smith *Decision*, 57 U Chi L Rev 1109, 1137 (1990). Even this formulation may not lead McConnell where he wants to go. It is not so clear that a law that unintentionally and indirectly infringes a constitutionally protected right is unconstitutional. For example, a law that indirectly (and purportedly unintentionally) infringes freedom of speech is not tested by strict scrutiny but by a less rigorous standard. See, e.g., *US v O'Brien*, 391 US 367 (1968). Similarly, refusing to fund abortion—analogous to refusing to exempt religious practices from general laws—does not violate the constitutional right to abortion, *Harris v McRae*, 448 US 297 (2980), even though it may have a detrimental effect on individual exercise of the underlying constitutional right.

on religious objectors but its infringement of their right to practice their religion. A similar gambit also can be made on the other side, however. Kathleen Sullivan has suggested that the Establishment Clause creates an analogous substantive right: the right to a "civil order for the resolution of public moral disputes."[96] Thus, whereas McConnell claims that religious adherents have a right to practice their religion, Sullivan claims that non-adherents have a right to a secular government. This merely reframes the discrimination issue in terms of conflicting substantive rights: any governmental accommodation of the right to practice one's religion necessarily infringes the right to a secular government (and vice versa).

These parallel recharacterizations yield an important observation. The gist of my argument is that it is not possible simultaneously to implement the core values of both religion clauses. By framing the question in terms of substantive rights, McConnell and Sullivan highlight an issue underlying the work of all the scholars I have discussed: what is the "true meaning" of the religion clauses? In response to my arguments, McConnell can claim that a narrow (or redundant) reading of the Establishment Clause is correct; Kurland, on the other hand, can claim that a narrow (or redundant) reading of the Free Exercise Clause is correct. Unfortunately, in their haste to reconcile the two clauses without subordinating either, neither they nor anyone else has seriously justified the choice of which clause to interpret narrowly and which to interpret broadly.

McConnell has argued that the founding generation intended a narrow reading of the Establishment Clause.[97] But beyond being subject to all the objections to originalism generally,[98] McConnell's history is itself controversial in its details.[99] Moreover, it is at least plausible that the founding generation intended broad readings of both clauses, without realizing that in our highly regulated and

---

[96] Kathleen M. Sullivan, *Religion and Liberal Democracy*, 59 U Chi L Rev 195, 197 (1992).

[97] Michael W. McConnell, *The Origins and Historical Understanding of Free Exercise of Religion*, 103 Harv L Rev 1409 (1990).

[98] See generally Daniel A. Farber, *The Originalism Debate: A Guide for the Perplexed*, 49 Ohio St L J 1085 (1989).

[99] Compare Michael W. McConnell, *Coercion: The Lost Element of Establishment*, 27 Wm & Mary L Rev 933 (1986), with Douglas Laycock, *"Noncoercive" Support for Religion: Another False Claim about the Establishment Clause*, 26 Valp U L Rev 37 (1991); and *Lee v Weisman*, 112 S Ct at 2672–76 (Souter, J, concurring).

subsidized society the two would often conflict.[100] Thus, religious believers in an era of truly limited government could quite reasonably press for the adoption of both clauses, in order to keep government from interfering with religious belief either positively or negatively, without foreseeing that one day a government policy that kept its distance from religion by not singling it out for special treatment in either direction might itself constitute an interference with religion.

Laycock has suggested an alternative justification for his preferred reading of the clauses. He says it would be "implausible" to adopt a reading of the Free Exercise Clause that would allow (or require) government to prohibit the religious use of wine if it prohibited alcohol consumption generally.[101] It is not implausible from a historical perspective, as the founding generation had no idea that government might be so involved in the lives of the people as to prohibit ordinary, everyday practices that affect religion. Advocates of the religion clauses feared deliberate persecution, not unforeseen general government growth with a negative impact on religion.[102] And it is only implausible from a practical perspective if one values religious celebrations more than non-religious ones—bringing us back to the issues of perspective and differentiation.

The main purpose of this essay is to suggest that what is needed is a *persuasive* justification for preferring one clause to the other. Rather than denying the subordinating effects of their "reconcilia-

---

[100] Robert Bork has made a similar observation about the Equal Protection Clause, suggesting that the Reconstruction architects' simultaneous desire for equality and for segregation made sense to them but cannot be implemented today. Robert Bork, *The Tempting of America: The Political Seduction of the Law* 74–84 (Macmillan 1990).

[101] Laycock, *Neutrality* at 1000–1001 (cited in note 54).

[102] McConnell bases his contrary historical conclusion on weak evidence. For example, he interprets Madison's original draft prohibiting the infringement of rights of conscience "on any pretext" as prohibiting infringement "for any reason," including unintentionally. McConnell, *Update* at 691 n 25 (cited in note 54). The more usual reading of "pretext," however, suggests an intentional act with a disguised motivation. Madison was guarding against intentional discrimination disguised as neutrality, not truly general laws enacted for nondiscriminatory reasons. The normal meaning of "pretext" is apparent in John Marshall's use of the term some years later in *McCulloch v Maryland*, 4 Wheaton 316, 423 (1819).

There is also some evidence that those who drafted the Bill of Rights specifically did not intend to require accommodation. Egbert Benson of New York, for example, moved to strike language requiring a military exemption for conscientious objectors on the ground that "[n]o man can claim this indulgence of right. It may be a religious persuasion, but it is no natural right, and therefore ought to be left to the discretion of the Government." 1 Annals of Cong. 751 (Joseph Gales ed., Washington, Gales & Seaton 1834) (Aug. 17, 1789).

tions," religion clause scholars might more constructively recognize the problem and attempt more forthrightly to justify their preferences for one clause over the other. What purposes does religion serve in a modern democracy, and how should we best foster those goals? Much of modern constitutional scholarship in other areas has focused on similar questions, but religion clause jurisprudence has been mired in attempts to reconcile the irreconcilable. The time has come to admit the conflict and to make an honest choice.[103]

Whether the issue is coercion or discrimination, we cannot escape the conclusion that anything we do with regard to exemptions harms someone in a constitutionally significant way. The scholars who subordinate the Free Exercise Clause recognize what McConnell and others overlook: that granting an exemption sends a message of endorsement of religious over secular beliefs and relegates nonbelievers to the status of outsiders. Ironically, those very same scholars fail to recognize that the failure to exempt religious believers from regulations that indirectly but severely burden religious practice has a similar effect on believers, relegating them to the status of outsiders whose fundamental beliefs are not respected by

---

[103] Justice Blackmun has suggested a different "reconciliation" that deserves brief comment. In Bullock, he suggested that while a special tax exemption for religious publications violated the Establishment Clause, failure to exempt such publications might violate the Free Exercise Clause. He proposed that perhaps the Court should therefore require the state to broaden its exemption to include secular literature devoted to similarly philosophical questions. 489 US at 27–28.

Blackmun's approach is similar to the approach taken in other discriminatory effect contexts. The usual rule under Title VII, for example, is that where a particular employment practice has a discriminatory effect on a protected group, the employer is prohibited from applying the practice either to that group *or* to any similarly situated non-minority employees.

Unfortunately, any attempt to implement such an approach in the religion context would be highly impractical. The Court has used this approach in determining the scope of conscientious objector status, concluding that such status must be granted to anyone whose objection to military service is equivalent to a religious objection. See *Welsh v United States*, 398 US 333 (1970); *United States v Seeger*, 380 US 163 (1965). The case-by-case determination required by that rule, however, severely reduced the efficiency of the selective service process, and the whole process ultimately favored primarily upper middle class whites. See, e.g., Lawrence M. Baskir & William A. Strauss, *Chance and Circumstance: The Draft, the War and the Vietnam Generation* 7–9, 41–42 (Knopf 1978). To extend such a process to every claim of objection to ordinary laws would be likely to affect both efficiency and neutrality in the same way but on a more massive scale.

Moreover, if any serious (non-frivolous) objection to a law led the courts to require a compelling interest in the law, either many laws would be invalidated or the compelling interest test would be drastically diluted. That dilution would in turn probably affect the application of strict scrutiny in other constitutional contexts.

the majority. The choice between these alternatives is not easy, but we cannot make it disappear by denying the hardship that each alternative causes.

III. The Court's Resolution: Paradox Redux

In 1990, the Court finally resolved the paradox in one of the two possible ways. In *Employment Division v Smith*,[104] it abandoned the *Yoder-Sherbert* line of cases (confining them to their facts) and announced that henceforth religious objectors had the same obligation to obey neutral laws as everyone else. Assuming that *Lemon* would still govern establishment cases, *Smith*'s repudiation of the exemption doctrine yielded a consistent jurisprudence that coupled a narrow interpretation of the Free Exercise Clause with a broad interpretation of the Establishment Clause. Although immediately attacked by most commentators,[105] *Smith* was the first glimmer of coherence in the Court's religion clause jurisprudence in twenty years.

As I have argued, there were only two ways for the Court to resolve the tension created by its broad interpretation of both the religion clauses—either to narrow its construction of the Establishment Clause or to narrow its view of the Free Exercise Clause. Although some might quarrel with the Court's decision to choose the latter course, one or the other was necessary. Which course one prefers depends on which clause one thinks more important,[106] but the burden of my argument has been to show that one of these two choices was essential. Despite the many failed efforts at "reconciliation," no one has yet persuasively justified choosing one

---

[104] 494 US 872 (1990). The result in *Smith* was presaged in a series of cases in which the Court seriously watered down the *Yoder* test in order to deny exemptions in a variety of situations, see, e.g., *Jimmy Swaggart Ministries v Board of Equalization*, 493 US 378 (1990); *Lyng v Northwest Indian Cemetery Prot. Ass'n*, 485 US 439 (1988); *Tony & Susan Alamo Foundation v Secretary of Labor*, 471 US 290 (1985), or interpreted legislatively granted exemptions so narrowly as to render them almost trivial, see, e.g., *Ansonia Board of Education v Philbrook*, 479 US 60 (1986).

[105] See, e.g., sources cited in Lupu, *Reconstructing the Establishment Clause*, 140 U Pa L Rev at 561 n 13.

[106] This is not to say that it is necessarily a matter of pure personal preference, of course. Different theoretical approaches to constitutional analysis would yield different answers to the question of which clause is more important. My point in the text is that since scholars seem to have concentrated largely on "reconciling" the two clauses, there is little or no scholarship considering why one clause or the other *ought* to be deemed superior.

clause over the other, and only such an argument could meaningfully defend or criticize *Smith* on its merits. In the absence of any
persuasive reason to prefer one clause over the other, *Smith* remains
defensible as one of two equally valid positions, and one that is
clearly more coherent than the hopelessly conflicted prior state of
affairs.

Although it resolved the paradox, however, *Smith* contained the
seeds of an equally problematic conflict, which came to fruition
only two years later in *Lee v Weisman*. Although the Court in *Smith*
held that exemptions for religious objectors are not constitutionally
required, it also suggested that such exemptions are not prohibited
if a legislature chooses to grant them. Thus, at the same time that
the Court narrowed its interpretation of the Free Exercise Clause,
it intimated that it was on the verge of narrowing its interpretation
of the Establishment Clause as well. In *Lee v Weisman* it did just
that, unofficially abandoning *Lemon* for its much narrower coercion
test.[107]

Thus, the brief but coherent reign of a narrow free exercise
jurisprudence and a broad establishment jurisprudence was almost
immediately replaced by narrow interpretations of both clauses. In
the context of exemptions, this means that exemptions are routinely
permitted, but never constitutionally required. In its own way,
this creates a paradox as puzzling as—and more troubling than—its
predecessor.

The problem with the Court's current interpretation is that it
leaves both clauses without substantive content, for no apparent
reason. No theory of the underlying values of the religion clauses—
whether neutrality, benevolence, or separationism—justifies a
scheme in which the government is permitted but not required to
grant exemptions.[108] Permitting the legislature broad leeway to
grant exemptions suggests that the purpose of the religion clauses

---

[107] In particular, it is clear that exemptions will be permitted even though they are not
required. Even Justice Souter, who with Justices Stevens and O'Connor rejected the coercion test in favor of an "endorsement" test, thought legislative accommodation of religious
practices would be permissible. *Lee v Weisman*, 112 S Ct at 2676–77 (Souter, J, concurring).

[108] Mark Tushnet has argued that the "disarray" of the religion clauses stems from our
abandonment of our republican heritage in favor of a purely liberal world. Mark V. Tushnet,
Red, White and Blue: A Critical Analysis of Constitutional Law 247–76 (Harvard 1988). Although
he wrote before either *Smith* or *Weisman*, his explanation could apply equally well to today's
religion clauses.

is, as McConnell suggests, to protect and nurture individual religious beliefs in the face of governmental pressure to conform, thus elevating free exercise values. But if that is the case, the clauses should also be read to require exemptions in circumstances where the pressure to conform is great and the need for conformity is minimal. Similarly, if—as the holding in *Smith* seems to suggest— the purpose of the religion clauses is to allow a secular government to operate independent of the varied religious beliefs of the citizenry, thus elevating Establishment Clause values, then accommodation of religion at the expense of non-religion must be forbidden in order to preserve that independence. For the Court generally to permit but not to require exemptions achieves no goal that can be explained by reference to any possible purpose of the religion clauses.

Moreover, the practical result of simultaneously narrow interpretations of both clauses is even worse than the result of the earlier conflict caused by the Court's broad interpretation of both clauses. Recall that under the *Yoder-Lemon* scheme the Court was effectively empowered to choose among religions, deciding which deserved exemptions and which did not. Under the current scheme, that same unfettered discretion is accorded the legislature. All religious accommodation is now "a matter of political discretion, rather than a matter of constitutional right."[109] The decision whether to grant or withhold exemptions will now reflect the religious preference of the majority, thus compounding the "bias in favor of mainstream over non-mainstream religions."[110] As a general rule, courts will be more evenhanded than legislatures, since they are "sworn to do equal justice to all . . . and to treat like cases alike." Legislatures, on the other hand, "are [constitutionally] free to reflect majority prejudices, to respond to the squeakiest wheel among minorities, to trade votes and make compromises, and to ignore problems that have no votes in them."[111]

This is the worst of all possible "solutions," for neither equal accommodation of religion nor equal indifference to religion is

---

[109] Lupu, *Reconstructing the Establishment Clause*, 140 U Pa L Rev at 573 (cited in note 82).

[110] McConnell, *Crossroads* at 139 (cited in note 34). See also Mark Tushnet, *"Of Church and State and the Supreme Court": Kurland Revisited*, 1989 Supreme Court Review 373, 386–87.

[111] Laycock, *Remnants*, 1990 Supreme Court Review at 15 (cited in note 69). *See also* Lupu, *Reconstructing the Establishment Clause*, 140 U Pa L Rev at 600–606 (cited in note 82).

mandated. Instead, an unrestrained majority is authorized to indulge its discriminatory preferences.[112] Despite the breadth of solutions offered by the various scholars discussed in this article, those scholars are almost unanimous in their condemnation of this particular scheme.[113] It is both tragic and ironic that the Court has moved toward a construction of the religion clauses that serves none of the possible underlying goals of First Amendment and that replaces a regime that encourages judicial incoherence with one that encourages legislative intolerance.

---

[112] Even McConnell appears to concede that *Smith*'s abandonment of required exemptions would be better paired with a broad Establishment Clause—which at least would strike down discriminatory accommodations by the legislature—than with a narrow one. McConnell, *Free Exercise Revisionism*, 57 U Chi L Rev at 1132 (cited in note 95). McConnell may have revised his position, as he has more recently suggested that legislatures are competent to make accommodation choices. McConnell, *Update* at 722–26 (cited in note 54).

[113] The only exception appears to be William Marshall, who applauds the Court's adoption of a rule of permissive but not required exemptions. See Marshall, *In Defense of* Smith, espec. p. 323 (cited in note 64). Marshall's main thrust in this short article, however, is to defend the more narrow holding of *Smith*—that exemptions are not required by the Free Exercise Clause—and his discussion of permissive exemptions focuses primarily on how they are constitutionally distinguishable from mandatory exemptions. Thus he offers no real defense of the general scheme of permitting but not requiring exemptions.

CHARLES FRIED

IMPUDENCE

. . . Hercules must expand his theory to include the idea that a justification of institutional history may display some part of the history as mistaken. But he cannot make impudent use of this device, because if he were free to take any incompatible piece of institutional history as a mistake, with no further consequences for his general theory, then the requirement of consistency would be no genuine requirement at all.[1]

* * *

Michael returned to his family, obtained steady employment, and repaid the victims of his crime. I thought no more about Michael until 1986, when the state supreme court . . . ordered me to resentence him to a minimum of five years in the state penitentiary. . . .

I was faced with a legal and moral dilemma. As a judge I had sworn to uphold the law, and I could find no legal grounds for violating an order of the supreme court. Yet five years' imprisonment was grossly disproportionate to the offense. . . . Given the choice between defying a court order or my con-

---

Charles Fried is Carter Professor of General Jurisprudence, Harvard Law School.

AUTHOR'S NOTE: I owe more than a usual debt of gratitude to my colleagues Richard Fallon, William Fisher, Daniel Meltzer, and David Shapiro for the time and attention they gave to reviewing earlier drafts. I am quite sure they continue to disagree with some of what I say and would still find errors, which are entirely my responsibility. Professor Shapiro's *In Defense of Judicial Candor*, 100 Harv L Rev 731 (1987), provides a harmonious counterpoint to the argument of this essay. Louis R. Hanoian, Deputy Attorney General of California, has generously provided comments and information that spared me from making a number of errors regarding the Harris case and related proceedings. I also thank Gail Brashes-Krug and C. Adrian Vermeule, students at the Harvard Law School, for their research assistance.

[1] Ronald Dworkin, *Taking Rights Seriously* 121 (Harvard University Press, rev ed 1978).

science, I decided to leave the bench where I had sat for 16
years.[2]

* * *

. . . [T]he Garrisonians would have agreed wholly with the
judiciary that, by external moral criteria, it would be improper
for a judge to use judical power in a manner contrary to agreed
rules. . . .

. . . It would, indeed, be impossible . . . to effectuate natural
law with respect to slavery while still playing by the rules that
Phillips acknowledged were and ought to be in force. Moreover, Phillips also agreed that the Constitution, which by those
limits had to be enforced, was in conflict with natural law on
the issue of slavery. Phillips did not shrink from the conclusion:
"Their only 'paramount obligation', as judges, is to do what
they agreed to do when they were made judges, or quit the
bench."[3]

I. Good Judging

The politics of the Bork hearings deprived the bench of a
high intelligence.[4] Bork would have added a distinctive and important voice to our judicial chorus. But that process had other, perhaps more pervasive ill effects. One of these was to create a near-
obsession with theories of constitutional interpretation and to invite
the attention of what is called serious journalism to this subject.
The categories and formulas that are now routinely deployed—
originalism, natural law, interpretivism and non-, to cite but the
most familiar—were certainly around well before 1986, but in the
media's subintellectual gaze they have taken on both a caricaturial
fixity and a prominence they never before enjoyed.

Not only has the ensuing debate been too shallow and abstract,
it has also focused too narrowly on constitutional interpretation,
when the real battle waged by the administrations, which nomi-
nated not only Judge Bork, but Warren Burger, William Rehnquist, Lewis Powell, Sandra O'Connor, Antonin Scalia, Anthony
Kennedy, David Souter, Clarence Thomas, and hundreds of lower

---

[2] Lois Forer, *Justice by Numbers*, Wash Monthly 12 (April, 1992).

[3] Robert M. Cover, *Justice Accused* 153 (Yale University Press, 1975) (footnotes omitted).

[4] For my disagreements with Judge Bork's legal philosophy, see Charles Fried, *Order and Law* ch 2, 3 (Simon & Schuster, 1991)

court judges, had to do with a very generalized attitude to law: to statutory interpretation, to precedent, to the role of courts and the federal courts, to the respect owed history, legislatures, the executive.[5] These nominees have not converged upon a single theory of law or government, nor do they offer a predictable alignment of opinions or results.[6] At most they tend to share an approach to law, to the task of judging. In this essay I consider the case of Robert Alton Harris, executed in the California gas chamber on April 21, 1992, after a night in which judges of the Ninth Circuit Court of Appeals issued and the Supreme Court lifted four stays of execution. Through the lens of that case I hope to get some perspective on the proper approach to the task of judging.

The conception of the task of judging that seems to me closest to the truth—closest to the right combination of institutional restraints, public expectations, professional discipline, and passion for justice—is described as well as I think it can be by Ronald Dworkin in his "Hard Cases."[7] His argument is at once too subtle and too well known to tempt me to summarize it here. It is enough to say that it enjoins the judge to make the best she can of the materials her legal culture offers for dealing with a case at hand, to respect not only those materials but the institutional priorities the society places on the different types and layers of materials, and while encouraging her to form these so far as possible into a morally satisfying whole, nonetheless to accept as her guide and constraint the morality implicit in them. This approach allows, indeed makes it inevitable that some of the materials be discarded, disregarded, or confined as mistakes, but—as noted in the passage which serves as one of the epigraphs to this essay—this is an operation intended to respect, not distort the body of materials as a whole. Dworkin calls such distortion impudent.

---

[5] May my hands fall off and my word processor crash if ever in this essay or anywhere else I use, other than in derision or refutation, the degraded epithet "judicial activism." Initially deployed, I suppose, by my team to designate the work of judges whose argumentation and even citation practice lacked integrity or even candor, it was then and certainly is now utterly devoid of meaning. Editorialists who dislike the work of the Reagan-Bush judiciary use it to designate any departure from precedents they cherish.

[6] See, for example, *Planned Parenthood v Casey*, 1992 US Lexis 4751; *Michael H. v Gerald D.*, 491 US 110, 127 n 6. See also Charles Fried, *The Once and Future Court*, New York Times Sec 4 at 11 (July 7, 1991); *The Conservatism of Justice Harlan*, 36 NY L Sch L Rev 33 (1991).

[7] Dworkin, *Taking Rights Seriously*, ch 4 (cited in note 1); Ronald Dworkin, *Hard Cases*, 88 Harv L Rev 1057 (1975).

Dworkin's is more an account than a theory. Indeed, knowing something of Dworkin's philosophical allegiances, one would be entitled to surmise that the very idea of a theory of judicial practice is misconceived. There is good and bad practice. Its general features may be shown and rigor is mainly available in the analysis and critique of particular instances of it. Impudence is the word I draw from him to describe judicial practice at its worst— combining arrogance, carelessness, and lack of candor. As I consider the case of Robert Alton Harris and the decisions of the many judges caught up in it over the last dozen years, I ask where, if anywhere, that damning sobriquet may justly be applied: to Justice Brennan, who began the whole process in 1963 in his decision in *Fay v Noia*,[8] to Judge Pregerson, who issued the last stay forty-five minutes after the Supreme Court had ruled on the matter in a brief but definitive *per curiam* opinion,[9] to the Supreme Court itself for issuing a remarkable order that "no further stays of . . . execution shall be entered by the federal courts except upon order of this Court,"[10] or to no one at all.

II. The Harris Case: What Happened

In 1978 Harris and his brother, Daniel, commandeered a car in which two boys, age fifteen and sixteen years, were sitting, eating hamburgers. Harris and his brother planned to use the car in a bank robbery. Harris ordered the boys to drive the car to a secluded spot, ordered them to leave, and then shot them several times. The killings did not show gratuitous cruelty so much as a complete lack of human feeling. After shooting one of the boys in the back Harris pursued the other, and finding him screaming and cowering in terror, shot him four times. The brothers returned to the stolen car, finished the boys' hamburgers, and laughed together about blowing one of the boy's arms off and splattering the other boy's brains. The Harrisses then proceeded to their planned bank robbery, shortly after which they were arrested. Daniel confessed to the bank robbery and to the abductions, placing the blame for

---

[8] 372 US 391 (1963).

[9] Judge Pregerson's stay, issued over the telephone at 3:51 A.M., followed the Court's opinion in *Gomez v United States District Court*, 112 S Ct 1653 (1992).

[10] *Vasquez v Harris*, USSC A-768, slip op at 1 (April 21, 1992).

the actual killings on Harris. Harris confessed to the killings and later repeated his confession in detail. He also admitted the killings to his sister, when she visited him in jail, and to a cellmate. At the penalty phase of his trial it was shown that Harris had pleaded guilty to a killing in 1975 and that the murders in this case had been committed while he was on parole from that earlier conviction. At the penalty hearing it also came out that while Harris had been in jail he had participated in a brutal rape of a fellow prisoner. The victim had complained to prison authorities, and when Harris openly threatened to kill him in reprisal, Harris's cell was searched and an improvised garrote was found hidden in his toilet. At the penalty stage Harris said he was sorry, admitted that he had lied at the guilt stage, and that he had killed the boys, though he said his brother had fired the first shot.

A psychiatrist employed by the state had examined Harris and concluded he was sane both at the time of trial and the time of the killings. Harris's court-appointed trial counsel engaged two psychiatrists at state expense. His trial counsel knew of a 1971 EEG report indicating organic brain damage attributed to chronic glue and solvent sniffing, but he decided not to introduce this evidence at the guilt phase because it was inconsistent with Harris's claim that it was his brother who had done the actual killing. His counsel also knew that a 1977 EEG had shown no abnormalities. Although Harris's counsel cross-examined the state's pyschiatrist extensively he did not produce any pychiatric testimony. He did, however, call Harris's mother and sister, who testified that as a child he had been severely abused by his father. Although a great deal more might have been made of the horrors of Harris's childhood[11] and so his trial counsel might be faulted for his judgment, tactics, and aggressiveness at the penalty stage, there was never a plausible claim that Harris was incompetently defended at trial. Perhaps it was an exaggeration to say, as did one federal court, that at trial and throughout subsequent proceedings Harris had been represented by "competent and outstanding" counsel.[12] But this was not one of the many death cases—usually coming from what is

---

[11] See Corwin, *Icy Killer's Life Steeped in Violence*, LA Times (May 16, 1982), p 1, col 1, reprinted in John Kaplan and Robert Weisberg, *Criminal Law: Cases and Materials* 29–31 (2d ed, 1991).

[12] *Harris v Vasquez*, USDC No 92-0588-T, slip op at 6 (SD Cal, April 18, 1992).

called the southern "death belt"—where defense counsel is ill-compensated, feckless, and inexperienced.[13]

At the conclusion of the trial in 1979 the jury sentenced Harris to death in the gas chamber.[14]

On appeal Harris urged numerous errors: failure to change venue because of prejudicial pretrial publicity, several trial errors, and improper admission of a confession (Harris's fourth) given during what was claimed to be an improper delay in arraignment. He also argued that the imposition of the death sentence would constitute cruel and unusual punishment under the federal Constitution, among other reasons because the California death penalty statute does not require that the reviewing court compare the sentence of death to sentences imposed in other capital cases in order to determine if the death sentence was disproportionately harsh. The Supreme Court of California, concentrating particularly on claims of prejudicial pretrial publicity, on the alleged trial errors, and on aspects of the psychiatric testimony, affirmed. Justice Tobriner in a concurring opinion stated that although he believed the state's death penalty statute to be unconstitutional, he was bound by a prior decision of the state supreme court to the contrary until the Supreme Court of the United States should overrule it, and agreed that Harris had received a fair trial. Chief Justice Rose Bird, joined by Justice Mosk, dissented on the ground that pretrial publicity made it "reasonably likely that appellant was not accorded a fair trial."[15] The United States Supreme Court denied certiorari.[16]

After that affirmance, Harris filed two habeas corpus petitions in state court[17] raising (among other points) the failure to provide proportionality review. The Superior Court denied both petitions, the California Supreme Court denied the petitions without opinion, and the Supreme Court denied certiorari on the second petition.[18] In March 1982, Harris filed his first federal habeas corpus petition in federal district court in San Diego, raising claims about

---

[13] See Stephen B. Bright, *Death by Lottery*, 92 W Va L Rev 679 (1990); see also *Death Penalty Representation in the 1990s*, ABA Annual Meeting (August 13, 1992).

[14] *People v Harris*, 28 Cal 3d 935, 623 P2d 240 (1981).

[15] Id at 965.

[16] *Harris v California*, 454 US 882 (1981).

[17] See *Harris v Pulley*, 852 F2d 1546 (9th Cir 1989) (recounting procedural history).

[18] *Harris v California*, 457 US 1111 (1982).

the administration of the death penalty in California and about both the adequacy of the *Miranda* warnings he received and the testimony of the state appointed psychiatrist. The district court denied that petition. While appeal from that denial was pending, Harris filed a second federal habeas petition in San Diego. The Court of Appeals for the Ninth Circuit heard the appeal in 1982 and concluded that the proportionality review Harris sought was constitutionally required and also that the district court should consider Harris's claims regarding prejudicial pretrial publicity and disproportionality in the imposition of the death penalty on defendants accused of murdering whites, on male defendants, and on younger defendants and defendants of lower economic status.[19] The Supreme Court granted certiorari on the question whether the state supreme court is required to engage in a proportionality review and reversed the Ninth Circuit on that point.[20] On remand the district court consolidated the unresolved issues in the two petitions. These included claims about ineffective assistance of counsel at the penalty stage of the trial and denial of due process, in that the state had failed to grant a postconviction request for a neurological examination—both issues that bore on claims that Harris would raise in subsequent proceedings. The district denied relief on all of Harris's claims.[21]

Harris appealed this denial in November 1984, drawing a new panel in the Court of Appeals, consisting of Judges Alarcon, Brunetti, and Noonan. The appeal was argued in November 1986. In July 1988, the Court of Appeals decided against Harris on all points,[22] but withheld its mandate until September 1989, when it amended its opinion (after five rounds of supplemental briefs) while denying Harris's petition for rehearing and suggestion of rehearing en banc.[23] Harris again brought his case to the U.S. Supreme Court, which in January 1990 denied certiorari.[24] Immediately

---

[19] *Harris v Pulley*, 692 F2d 1189 (1982) (per Choy, Anderson, Canby, JJ).

[20] *Pulley v Harris*, 465 US 37 (1984). Only Justices Brennan and Marshall, who believe the death penalty to be unconstitutional under all circumstances, dissented on the requirement of a proportionality review by the state supreme court. Justice Stevens concurred in the result. The case was argued for Harris by Professor Anthony Amsterdam.

[21] USDC No 82-1005-E, No 82-0249-E (July 26, 1984).

[22] *Harris v Pulley*, 852 F2d 1546.

[23] 885 F2d 1354.

[24] 493 US 1051.

after his petition was denied in the United States Supreme Court (his fourth time in that Court), Harris filed another petition in the state supreme court. This was denied in March 1990,[25] and a new execution date was set for April 3, 1990.

One week before that new date, on March 26, 1990, Harris filed his third federal habeas corpus petition in federal district court, complaining among other things that at the penalty stage of the trial he was not given competent psychiatric assistance in developing his claims regarding his mental condition. The petition was denied two days later, both on the merits and as an abuse of the writ. Judge Noonan of the Court of Appeals granted a stay of execution to allow that court to give "thoughtful examination" to the March 26 complaint, and the Supreme Court denied the state's application for an order vacating the stay.[26] On August 29, 1990, the Court of Appeals, again consisting of Judges Alarcon, Brunetti, and Noonan, affirmed the lower federal court's denial of Harris's petition,[27] but on November 19, 1990, while a petition for rehearing was pending, the court granted Harris's motion to remand to the district court for an evidentiary hearing on his claims that the cellmate to whom Harris had given one of several confessions was a state agent and thus the admission into evidence of the confession violated Harris's right to counsel. In May 1991, the district court found that the cellmate was not a state agent. The Court of Appeals, having requested additional briefing on whether any or all of Harris's claims constituted abuse of the writ under the Supreme Court's recently announced standard in *McCleskey v Zant*,[28] issued an amended opinion denying all relief on August 21, 1991,[29] and rehearing was denied on November 8, 1991. Judge Noonan dissented. He concluded that Harris should have been granted an

---

[25] *Harris v Pulley*, Cal No S013598, slip op (March 13, 1990).

[26] 901 F2d 724 (1990); *Vasquez v Harris*, 494 US 1064 (1990).

[27] *Harris v Vasquez*, 913 F2d 606.

[28] 111 S Ct 1454 (1991). A petitioner abuses the writ when he raises, in subsequent habeas corpus petitions, questions that he might have raised in his intitial petition, unless he can show both "cause"—a very exacting standard exemplified by constitutionally ineffective assistance of counsel or undiscoverable, willful concealment by the government—for having failed to do so, and actual prejudice. Only in the exceptional case where the petitioner can show that a "fundamental miscarriage of justice" will result may a federal court excuse a default. This last term was recently clarified by the Court in *Sawyer v Whitley*, 1992 US Lexis 3864.

[29] *Harris v Vasquez*, 943 F2d 930.

evidentiary hearing on his claim that he had been denied effective psychiatric assistance at the penalty stage of his trial. It will be recalled that Harris's trial counsel had had the assistance of two psychiatrists, paid for by the state. Harris had asserted this claim in various ways in most if not all of his posttrial pleadings. He now offered affidavits from several experts that the psychiatric assistance afforded him was ineffective, and that this ineffective failure violated his constitutional rights in light of a 1985 Supreme Court decision, *Ake v Oklahoma*,[30] which acknowledged a due process right to state-provided psychiatric assistance in a capital case where the accused's mental state is an issue. The majority in the Court of Appeals held that this claim was barred as an abuse of the writ under *McCleskey*, that it had been heard and rejected several times before, that in any event the substance of the *Ake* right had in fact been accorded, and that to grant an evidentiary hearing would allow each such case to become a battle of experts regarding the competency of psychiatric assistance that was in fact afforded. The court also pointed out that now, some twelve years after the trial, one of the two state-provided psychiatrists was dead and the other unavailable.[31] Over Judge Alarcon's dissent, the court then granted Harris a stay of execution to allow him to seek certiorari from the Supreme Court.[32] The Supreme Court denied certiorari on March 2, 1992.[33] The state trial court then set a fifth execution date for Tuesday, April 21, 1992 "in the manner and means prescribed by law."[34] On April 16, Harris filed another petition in the California Supreme Court, which was denied the next day, and on April 18, his lawyers filed his fourth federal petition in the federal district court in San Diego, claiming that Harris's brother had fired the first shot into one of the two victims, igniting Harris's shooting frenzy, and that the brother had been coerced and hypnotized into

---

[30] 470 US 68 (1985).

[31] Finally, the court got into a tangle about whether granting such a full-dress competency review at this stage would be to impose a new procedural requirement retroactively— something the Supreme Court in *Teague v Lane*, 489 US 289 (1989), had said should not ordinarily be done in federal postconviction proceedings. A purpose of *Teague* is to lend finality to completed state court proceedings and to avoid a new spate of federal postconviction proceedings every time the Supreme Court announces a new rule.

[32] 949 F2d 1497 (1991).

[33] *Harris v Vasquez*, 111 S Ct 1275.

[34] SD Super CR 44135 (March 13, 1992).

incriminating Harris. This petition, raising matters that, in large part, had been considered several times before, was denied as an abuse of the writ on the same day.[35]

We now come to the proceedings that directly led to the extraordinary events of the night of April 20 and the morning of April 21. In a different federal district court, the district court for the Northern District of California, sitting in San Francisco, and before a different federal judge (Judge Marilyn Hall Patel), Harris's lawyers filed a civil rights action under 42 USC section 1983, asking that all executions by cyanide gas in the California gas chamber be enjoined pending the court's disposition of their complaint that this method of execution violated the cruel and unusual punishment clause of the Eighth Amendment. On Saturday, April 18, Judge Patel issued the temporary restraining order, pending a hearing on that claim—a hearing that would involve a number of witnesses and much documentary evidence, and would certainly take many months to conclude. Given the pace of appeals in these matters in the Ninth Circuit, it is likely that even an outcome wholly unfavorable to the claim might have delayed Harris's execution for years. Furthermore, California law provides that a court order authorizing execution is good for only twenty-four hours, so that the necessity of the state court's setting a new execution date would certainly have meant a delay of at least one or two months.[36] Section 1983, which gives individuals a cause of action for money damages or injunctive relief for deprivations of constitutional rights by state authorities, has regularly been used to correct prison conditions found to be so oppressive as to constitute cruel and unusual punishment.[37] Judge Patel concluded that since Harris (as a member of the class of all prisoners under sentence of death in California) was challenging neither his conviction nor his death sentence (as he had in all his previous proceedings), Section 1983 was an appropriate alternative to habeas corpus.

The state, knowing that the death warrant was good for one day

---

[35] USDC No 92-0598-T (April 18, 1992).

[36] See Judge Stephen Reinhardt, *The Supreme Court, the Death Penalty and the Harris Case,* 102 Yale L J 205 (1992), criticizing this provision of California law. Four other states in the Ninth Circuit have identical provisions. See Idaho Code 19-2705; Mont Code Ann 46-19-103; Or Rev Stat 137.463; Wash Rev Code 10-95.160. The one-day warrant is used in at least five other death penalty states.

[37] See, e.g., *Rhodes v Chapman,* 452 US 337, 352 (1981) (Brennan concurring).

only and that it would have to get a new execution date from a state court if the delay caused by the TRO lasted longer than the day set for execution, went immediately to the Ninth Circuit for a writ of mandamus or prohibition to overturn Judge Patel's TRO. On Sunday evening, April 19, a panel of the Court of Appeals (consisting of Judges Alarcon, Brunetti, and Noonan) did just that. Judge Noonan dissented, accusing his fellow panel members of acting in haste where constitutional rights were in question. In overturning Judge Patel's TRO the court was exercising a rare and extraordinary but generally acknowledged power to interfere with ongoing proceedings in a lower court—a power that is used even more sparingly to interfere with TROs.[38] The court pointed out that Harris had never before raised the question of the constitutionality of the use of the gas chamber; that his last most recent logical time to do that was at the March 13, 1992 hearing when the state court had set his April 21 execution date "in the manner and means prescribed by law."

On Monday, April 20, several judges of the Ninth Circuit issued a stay of the execution so that the full bench could consider whether Judge Patel's restraining order had been proper and whether the appellate panel's reversal of that order had been proper. In fact various Ninth Circuit judges appear to have issued two stays of execution to allow full bench review of the rulings in the civil action under Section 1983, and a telephone poll of the judges of the circuit that evening gathered ten votes for such a stay.[39] The state sought to be relieved of this stay by the Supreme Court. But the Supreme Court had first to dispose of an earlier Ninth Circuit stay issued at 6:30 P.M. (Pacific time) in response to a call by Circuit Judge Betty Fletcher, to allow en banc review of a request for a

---

[38] Compare *Haitian Refugee Center, Inc. v Baker*, 950 F2d 685 (11th Cir 1991), which represented a struggle in many respects similar to that in this case: The injury to the government was systemic and the district judge determined to find a way to do what he thought was substantive justice, despite a previous decision of the court of appeals.

[39] By Ninth Circuit habeas rule 22-5 (c) (4) "any member of the panel [hearing the case] may enter an order granting the application [for a certificate of probable course and stay of execution]." Since the Alarcon, Brunetti, Noonan panel had presumably heard the appeal from Judge Patel's order under circuit rule 22-5 (b) as a "subsequent petition . . . [or a] matter[ ] pertaining to it," Judge Noonan and the other Ninth Circuit judges voting the stay might take the position that, though Judge Patel's case was not a habeas case, it should still be governed by the Circuit's habeas rules, with the result that Judge Noonan's certificate and stay would be sufficient, even if not concurred in by his two colleagues, to stay the execution pending an en banc vote.

habeas corpus hearing on the claim of newly discovered evidence that one of the victims had been shot not by Robert Harris but by his brother. This is a contention that Harris had made and recanted at various points. The same panel that had heard the state's motion to be relieved of Judge Patel's TRO had unanimously rejected this claim, and it was of that decision that Judge Fletcher sought en banc review. At 11:20 P.M. on Monday—2:20 A.M. in Washington, D.C.—the full bench of the Supreme Court dissolved that stay.[40]

Less than an hour later, the Supreme Court Justices received the two stays in the case raising the gas chamber issue and at 3 A.M. California time dissolved those stays as well, this time with a brief opinion. Saying that it did not matter whether the case was treated as a habeas corpus petition or a civil rights case, the Court ruled that Harris was not entitled to relief because of his "obvious attempt at manipulation. . . . This claim could have been brought more than a decade ago. There is no good reason for this abusive delay, which has been compounded by last-minute attempts to manipulate the judicial process." Justices Stevens and Blackmun dissented.

But that did not end the matter. Harris was already in the gas chamber when a single judge of the Ninth Circuit Court of Appeals, Judge Harry Pregerson, issued yet another stay of execution so that Harris could present his cruel and unusual punishment claim, this time in the form of a petition for habeas corpus, to the California Supreme Court. The state again sought relief in the U.S. Supreme Court, in a motion received at 7:05 A.M., Tuesday morning Washington time—4:05 A.M. California time. Within an hour, the Supreme Court (Justices Blackmun and Stevens again dissenting) vacated Judge Pregerson's stay of execution, adding that: "No further stays of Robert Alton Harris's execution shall be entered by the federal courts except upon the order of this Court."

---

[40] Ninth Circuit Rule 22-5 (f) allows "any active judge" to request a vote on a motion for en banc reconsideration and a stay of execution in a death case, even if the panel has voted unanimously to deny such a motion. The Circuit then has seven days to vote on the motion, and by Circuit Rule 22-59 (f) (3) the execution must be stayed pending the Circuit vote. This means, of course, that in a state with a one-day warrant the imposition of the death penalty can be postponed indefinitely, absent the kind of order the Supreme Court finally issued in this case. Although Judge Fletcher's name does not appear in the court papers, the *Los Angeles Times* reported that the stay was issued in response to her request. Richard C. Paddock and Harry Weinstein, *Appeal Judges Maneuvered Amid Chaos*, L A Times A-1 (April 22, 1992).

III. The Judge's Conscience

Capital punishment is seen by a wide array of persons as a
transcendent moral issue—and a transcendent moral wrong. I do
not know, but I would guess that Judge John Noonan shares a
moral disapproval of the death penalty with jurists who agree with
him on little else.[41] I admit that the thought that went into this
article, while not converting me, has given me a greater appreciation of a Kantian (which is my own general moral orientation)
objection to the death penalty—that the planned killing of a human
being, not as a measure of immediate defense, may be a strong
instance of treating a person as a means alone.[42] In California, the
death penalty is not just a ferociously contested moral issue but a
political metaphor: for some, the penalty is a sign of the repressive-
ness of the state, of the cruelty of all constituted authority, perhaps
even of man's overreaching, a kind of ultimate anti-ecological hu-
bris; for others, opposition to the penalty is the emblem of the lax,
indulgent, sentimental distaste for all authority, of the disposition
to lavish concern on those who break society's rules at the expense
of those who keep them, of a pseudoprofessionalism that finds
excuses for every delict and deviation—in sum a last vestige of the
dreadful sixties. This Manichaean opposition erupted into open
political warfare in the retention election of Chief Justice Rose
Bird. Her opposition to the death penalty was not in doubt, but
unlike Justices Brennan and Marshall, she did not preface her every
vote with a candid statement of that position. Rather, she managed
in every death case that came before her to find some more particular defect—as she did in this case. And since she was a jurist of
rather modest talents, the result was unconvincing, and in the end
I suspect far more provocative than frank and consistent opposition. And so the execution of Robert Alton Harris—the first execution in California in twenty-five years—was the denouement of a
struggle whose significance reached far beyond the life of one human being.

---

[41] The basis of my surmise is the deep veneration for the value of life which Judge Noonan
has shown in his writings on abortion. Noonan is not only a jurist of learning and eminence,
but one of the country's leading lay moral theologians. He has written major monographs
on usury, contraception, bribery, abortion, and the canon law of marriage and divorce.

[42] Of course Kant himself not only thought the death penalty permissible but morally
obligatory on a community lest it show disrespect to the murderer's victim. See *The Metaphys-
ics of Morals* (Tugendlehre) *334–35.

How should a judge who shares this moral disapproval of the death penalty respond? The question puts me in mind of the stories of judicial agony told by Robert Cover in *Justice Accused*.[43] The death penalty, even to its strongest opponents, can hardly be counted a greater evil than the lifelong enslavement of a totally innocent human being. Many state and federal judges were clear-eyed enough to look the evil of slavery in the face and see it for what it was, without any veil of temporizing justification or excuse. And in their work they were called upon to pronounce judgments that would return desperate men, women, and children—sometimes after years of anxious liberty—to bounty hunters and drivers of slaves; or to punish those who were brave and headstrong enough to assist the rescue of the runaways.

Cover tells of none who chose the path of total warfare and utter subversion—like the men and women described by Joseph Conrad in *Under Western Eyes*, whose lives were given over to plots, subterfuge, and the promise of violence. Even a judge who must decide the validity of a bill of sale or of a will transferring ownership in a fellow human being is implicated in the system of slavery—as were the bankers who financed the slave economy or the merchants who trafficked in its products. More deeply implicated was the judge who was asked to pronounce the judgment that returned the fugitive to service. His complicity was like that which must have been felt by Judge Lois Forer in the episode which supplies an epigraph to this essay. The state supreme court had ordered her to pronounce a sentence on a named person, a sentence that would take him from his family to the hell of prison—not only cruelly but, she felt, senselessly. She could not do it and left the bench. Hers was the response that the Garrisonians urged on the conscientious judge. They held that the Constitution, as it explicitly endorsed slavery, was "a pact with the devil" which allowed no room for accommodation to the person of conscience. In politics they urged dissolution of the Union. The holding of federal office was complicity in evil, and even state office in a non-slave state must be resigned if the Constitution's Supremacy Clause demanded cooperation with that evil, as it did in the case of the fugitive slave laws.

---

[43] Cover, *Justice Accused* (cited in note 3).

The more usual response of antislavery judges, the most prominent of whom were U.S. Supreme Court Justice Joseph Story and
Chief Justice Lemuel Shaw of Massachusetts,[44] was to treat laws
implementing the evils of slavery like any other and to enforce
them according to their intent to make the institution of slavery
secure and effective in the states where it was allowed. They did
this while openly proclaiming their opposition to slavery and working politically for its demise. In this they were like the judge described by Dworkin, and not disapproved by him, who enforces a
system of rules in the spirit of a background morality he cannot
deny, though he does not share it.[45]

Of greater interest are two intermediate strategies. One is the
strategy of defiance—that is, open refusal to comply with a for-
mally valid mandate. As the episode in *Abelman v Booth* described
below shows, defiance seemed to have its limits. As long as the
system was intact, the defiance was just a gesture, delaying but
not defeating the slave catchers. Or so it must have seemed to
many at the time—including some of the defiant ones. But this
defiance was followed by a civil war, emancipation, and radical
reconstruction. Would these have happened without defiance? We
have here again the antinomy of determinism: before, it looks as if
change will never come; after, it looks as if change was inevitable
and would have come no matter what. Vaclav Havel, writing about
individual responsibility in the face of overwhelming, pervasive
tyranny, analyzes and exemplifies the resolution to this antinomy.
Some lawyers but few judges took this way.

What is surprising, if Cover is right, is how few took another
way, what I would call the way of creative irony and meliorism.
It took an escaped slave, Frederick Douglass, to show this way
most forcefully. Douglass broke with his patrons, the Garrisonians,
in part because of his insistence that the Constitution can and
should be seen as an expression of humane and liberal (in the clas-

---

[44] Shaw, Cover tells us, was Herman Melville's father-in-law. Captain Vere in *Billy Budd*
was surely a metaphor for Shaw, or at least his situation. According to William Fisher,
Shaw and Story made more of an effort to move doctrine in an antislavery direction than
Cover suggests. See his *Ideology, Religion, and the Constitutional Protection of Private Property:
1760–1860*, 39 Emory L J 65, 121–31 (1990).

[45] Dworkin, *Taking Rights Seriously* (cited in note 1). Dworkin has written an important
review of Cover. See *The Law of the Slave-Catchers*, Times Literary Supplement 5 (December
1975), p 1437.

sic sense) commitments—in spite of the Fugitive Slave Clause, the Three-Fifths Clause, and the Importation Clause. To take one example, the Fugitive Slave Act of 1850 might quite plausibly have been declared unconstitutional in that it denied a jury trial to the supposed fugitive to determine his status. After all, the argument that the proceedings were a kind of summary *in rem* process to recover absconded property begs the question: if a person is presumed innocent until proven guilty, should he not also be presumed free? And why is the fugitive denied all the other devices of due process: compulsory process, confrontation, and the rest? To be sure, such procedural niceties would have made the Fugitive Slave Clause inoperable, given the strong antislavery sentiment in states like Pennsylvania, Ohio, and Massachusetts, which would have become sanctuaries for runaways. But what of it? Where does the Constitution provide that the clauses accepting the institution of slavery had to take precedence over the Due Process Clause? If there is a contradiction between the two, why must the slave catchers prevail?[46]

This line of argument was open until the Supreme Court's 1842 decision in *Prigg v Pennsylvania*.[47] In that case, a Maryland slave catcher had been denied the aid of summary process to remove an alleged slave by a Pennsylvania magistrate. He removed him forcibly anyway and was convicted of violating the state's kidnapping law. Justice Story, a strong opponent of slavery, voted with the majority to reverse the conviction, and in his opinion argued that Congress's power to implement the Fugitive Slave Clause included the authority to make that power effective, and thus to sweep aside devices and technicalities that would impede it—apparently even impediments derived from the Bill of Rights. As Cover tells the tale, what is striking is that after *Prigg* most antislavery judges just gave up. Rather than seizing on omissions or ambiguities in the seven opinions in the case, the reaction was to read Story's general message "faithfully" and to eschew limitations and distinctions: the Fugitive Slave Clause had been a compromise necessary to achieve union, and its intent to prevent the demise of slavery by hemor-

---

[46] My argument in these paragraphs is based on Cover, *Justice Accused* ch 10 (cited in note 3). For more on the views of black antislavery constitutionalists, see Randall Kennedy, *Comment on Rowan*, 47 Md L Rev 46 (1987).

[47] 16 Peters 539 (1842).

rhage could not be evaded. This faithfulness was amply demonstrated when *Prigg* was generally taken to resolve all arguments about the constitutionality of the later, far more draconian Fugitive Slave Law of 1850.

Considerations of federalism and states' rights also played an important role in this doctrinal struggle. Some state judges argued that, whatever the obligations of federal officials, they did not have to collaborate in the implementation of the fugitive slave laws, and Story's opinion in *Prigg* did suggest that there might be some limit to the extent that Congress could enlist state processes in the prosecution of a policy repugnant to that state.[48] Some antislavery state judges went further to assert a power to act affirmatively against the implementation of the 1850 law. This movement reached its dramatic and definitive denouement in the Sherman Booth affair. Here is Cover's account:

> . . . The slave Glover was apprehended in Racine by a federal marshal pursuant to a warrant. Upon Glover's arrest, the slaveowner, Garland, and the federal marshal were arrested by the sheriff for assault and battery upon Glover. While they went off to jail, Glover was rescued by a mob. The federal district court released the owner and marshal on a federal writ of habeas corpus. Sherman Booth and John Rycraft were then apprehended for prosecution [in federal court under the 1850 Fugitive Slave Act] as aiders and abettors in the rescue of Glover. They sought discharge on a writ of habeas corpus from the Wisconsin state courts. After apprehension, and before indictment, Booth was ordered discharged on the writ by Judge A.D. Smith of the Wisconsin Supreme Court, sitting alone during vacation. Smith upheld virtually all of the arguments that had been made against the Fugitive Slave Acts for the past two decades. He held the Act of 1850 unconstitutional on the ground that Article IV conferred on Congress no power to legislate with respect to fugitives; on the ground that the Act of 1850 denied to the fugitive a right to a trial by jury; and on the ground that the act denied the alleged fugitive due process of law. Smith considered *Prigg* an incorrect decision, and felt that he was bound to hold the Act of 1850 void in spite of that decision, even assuming it to be applicable.

> Upon reconvening, the full bench of the Wisconsin Supreme Court affirmed Smith's decision. After indictment, Booth was

---

[48] Compare *Testa v Katt*, 330 US 386 (1947); *New York v United States*, 112 S Ct (June 19, 1992); *FERC v Mississippi*, 456 US 742 (1982) (O'Connor concurring).

rearrested. Upon his application for a writ of habeas corpus, the Wisconsin court denied the writ. It held that the state court should defer to the federal court during the pendency of the criminal matter. However, after conviction both Booth and Rycraft again sought discharge from the Wisconsin court. This time, the State Supreme Court ordered their discharge, reaffirming their holding that the Act of 1850 was unconstitutional. The United States sought review in the Supreme Court of the United States. Upon instructions from the state judges, the clerk of the Wisconsin court refused to make any return to the writ of error from the United States Supreme Court. The high Court then held that such a refusal could not prevent the exercise of its appellate jurisdiction, and issued a direct order to the clerk to make a return. The return was never made. The Supreme Court proceeded to hear the case upon a certified copy of the record. The Supreme Court's decision was the last and greatest blow of the Taney court against antislavery.[49]

The Court's decision in *Abelman v Booth*[50] denied all power to the state courts to interfere with federal process and—more or less in passing—waved aside all of the constitutional objections to the fugitive slave laws that had been gathering over the years and were colleced in Judge Smith's opinion.

This history—like many similar, less edifying episodes in which state and lower federal courts responded defiantly to Reconstruction, the New Deal, and *Brown v Board*[51]—contains many of the elements that surfaced in the Harris imbroglio.

IV. Habeas Corpus and the Death Penalty

"On Saturday evening, April 18, a courageous Federal judge, Marilyn Hall Patel, refused to commit treason to the Constitution and . . . ordered a hearing on whether death by cyanide gas was cruel and unusual punishment . . . ." So wrote Judge John Noonan (who from 1984 onward sat on every appellate panel of the Ninth Circuit to consider any of Harris's claims) in an op-ed piece shortly after the Supreme Court forbade any further stays without its permission.[52] The clear implication was that the Su-

---

[49] Cover, *Justice Accused* at 186–87 (cited in note 3) (footnotes omitted).

[50] 21 Howard 506 (1859).

[51] 349 US 294 (1955).

[52] Noonan, *Should State Executions Run on Schedule?*, New York Times A 17 (April 27, 1992).

preme Court's order, by contrast, was an act of treason. Treason is one word; I have chosen impudence. Noonan implies the Court was impudent. The Court implies that impudence lay elsewhere. There are injustices: punishment imposed where objective truth shows it cannot be deserved, as on an innocent person;[53] and injustices of a more controversial sort, as in the Harris affair, because a punishment (death, or death by cyanide gas) is imposed that some think cannot be justified irrespective of guilt, or because there is something wrong about the way in which guilt was determined. Is it impudent for one who has the authority—a judge, a juror, perhaps a witness at the trial—to save an accused from unjust punishment, even if it means defying authority? Are our categories of thought so befuddled and our belief in reason so degraded that we do not believe we can ever judge what the terms of authority are? Is such confidence warranted anywhere in this affair, so that we must move to the harder, deeper question? Certainly Judge Noonan's charge of treason to the Constitution suggests no such pervasive skepticism.

Harris committed murder in violation of state law and was convicted in a state court. Why may Judge Patel, or any federal judge, presume to interfere in a process of another jurisdiction—why should a federal judge order relief for the victim of an unjust judgment of a California court any more than of a court in China or Cuba? The reason, of course, established in *Martin v Hunter's Lessee*[54] and *Cohens v Virginia* (the first criminal case to make the point),[55] and quite clearly expressed in the Federalist Papers,[56] is not simply the (undoubted) supremacy of federal law but also the supremacy of federal court judgments in respect to matters of federal law in a particular case. In both *Martin* and *Cohens* the Supreme Court held that, having been granted appellate jurisdiction in cases arising under the Constitution and laws of the United States, the Court could hear a federal question raised in a state court case, and if the resolution of that question should determine the outcome, enter a judgment that might contradict the determination of the state court system. So while we had two court systems, in respect

---

[53] I have nothing to say to those who object that there are no objective truths.

[54] 1 Wheaton 304 (US 1816).

[55] 6 Wheaton 264 (US 1821).

[56] Federalist 80, 82 (Hamilton); see also Akhil Amar, *A Neo-Federalist View of Article III: Separating the Two Tiers of Federal Jurisdiction*, 65 BU L Rev 205 (1985).

to federal questions the Supreme Court sat as the court of last resort in both.[57] But that power was never in play in the Harris affair. As we have seen, after Harris was convicted in California, the Supreme Court declined to hear his appeal, and so in any but a criminal case that would have been the end of the matter: with the denial of certiorari the processes of law are complete and conclusive on all, including federal, grounds.[58] It is habeas corpus that gives the federal courts, and particularly the lower federal courts, an additional role to play.

In its origins both in England and in this country, habeas corpus was by no means a device allowing courts to question the correctness of judgments reached in other courts. Rather it tested the power, the jurisdiction it was said, of any authority—whether a court, a government official, or a private person—to restrain another's liberty. If a court had authority over the person and the subject matter, then factual or legal errors committed in the course of proceedings where it exercised that authority could only be challenged if at all by appellate process. A person tried and convicted by such a court was by hypothesis deprived of his liberty by the law of the land, by due process of law.[59] Due process, one might say, included whatever appellate process the state makes available for testing errors, and when appellate process had run its course, no further objection on that score could exist. This is how Chief Justice Marshall put it in 1830:

> An imprisonment under a judgment cannot be unlawful, unless that judgment be an absolute nullity; and it is not a nullity if the Court has general jurisdiction of the subject, although it should be erroneous.[60]

So the federal postconviction proceedings in Harris's and thousands of other cases show a considerable enlargement of this origi-

---

[57] The authorities in the preceding note support the proposition that the Constitution would permit giving lower federal courts appellate jurisdiction over state court judgments implicating federal questions.

[58] There is an issue regarding the extent that a court of another jurisdiction is required under the Full Faith and Credit Clause and 28 USC § 1738 to take that judgment into its own system, and enforce it there, but whatever else its effect any such consideration elsewhere certainly does not invalidate the judgment in the jurisdiction where it was originally rendered. It is generally said that this obligation is limited to matters where there has been a "full and fair" adjudication. See *Kremer v Chemical Const Corp*, 456 US 461 (1982).

[59] See *Brown v Allen*, 344 US 443, 533 (1953) (Jackson concurring).

[60] *Ex Parte Watkins*, 3 Peters 193, 202, quoted in *Wainwright v Sykes*, 483 US 72, 78 (1977).

nal conception.[61] Anything one might say to explain that enlargement is bound to be controversial.[62] Indeed, history has been pressed (squeezed?) as much in the service of controverted policy here as in any topic in the law.[63] What I shall offer is not yet another historical brief, but an account of the principal conceptual poles between which the cases (and the theories for them) have oscillated. For the purposes of setting the scene for the judgments in Harris's various actions, that should be sufficient.

Until the Habeas Corpus Act of the Reconstruction Congress of 1867,[64] federal courts had no general power to inquire into the legality of detention under state authority. Indeed, it should be recalled, until the adoption of the Fourteenth Amendment in 1868 the very grounds with which we had become most familiar for saying that a person was held "in violation of the Constitution, or laws, or treaties of the United States" did not exist. All conceptions agree that this statute, as revised in 1966[65] and supplemented by the habeas rules in 1977,[66] are the source of federal court authority to review state court judgments in habeas. One pole, which I shall call the process pole,[67] is grounded not just in the early history of the writ but in a conception—a conception whose attractions for me I had better admit at once. The process conception, harking back to the early history of the writ, asserts that a person is never held in violation of law if he is held pursuant to a court having jurisdiction over him, which has "fully and fairly"[68] adjudicated any claims that might be raised against that custody. Illegal custody, then, is a conclusion internal to the legal process, and if that

---

[61] 372 US 391, 450–61 (1963).

[62] Indeed, I recognize that even my statement of the early English conception and its understanding in Chief Justice Marshall's time is controverted. See, e.g., Peller, *In Defense of Federal Habeas Corpus Relitigation*, 16 Harv CR-CL L Rev 579, 604–5 (1982).

[63] Compare id with Bator, *Finality in Criminal Law and Federal Habeas Corpus for State Prisoners*, 76 Harv L Rev 441 (1963) and Mayers, *The Habeas Corpus Act of 1867: The Supreme Court as Legal Historian*, 33 U Chi L Rev 31 (1965); or compare Justice Brennan's opinion for the Court with Justice Harlan's dissent in *Fay v Noia*, 372 US 391 (1963).

[64] 14 Stat 385.

[65] 14 Pub L 89–711, 80 Stat 1104–5 (1966).

[66] Cited in note 88.

[67] Following Peller, 16 Harv CR-CL L Rev 579 (cited in note 62).

[68] The phrase is drawn from the law governing when a judgment of one jurisdiction must be given full faith and credit in another under 28 USC 1738. It is invoked in this context to designate those state law adjudications that should be deemed to preclude habeas review. See, e.g., *Stone v Powell*, 428 US 465 (1976) and S 1241, 102d Cong, 1st Sess (1991).

process has itself accorded with constitutional and other norms, then its decrees are for purposes of the law conclusive. The process conception, therefore, treats as a solecism the question which motivates the opposing polar conception, which I shall call the "correct" outcome or relitigation conception. The relitigation conception asks whether the prisoner is *really* in custody in accordance with the law; and that question is not concluded by full and fair adjudcation in a competent court system. Just as the process conception leaves us uneasy that a real injustice may remain uncorrected for reasons that seem formalistic and bureaucratic, the relitigation conception implies a fallacy that was never more pithily exposed than by Justice Jackson:

> Conflict with state courts is the inevitable result of giving the convict a virtual new trial before a federal court sitting without a jury. Whenever decisions of one court are reviewed by another, a percentage of them are reversed. That reflects a difference in outlook normally found between personnel comprising different courts. However, reversal by a higher court is not proof that justice is thereby better done. There is no doubt that if there were a super–Supreme Court, a substantial proportion of our reversals of state courts would also be reversed. We are not final because we are infallible, but we are infallible only because we are final.[69]

The process conception is hard, so hard that it generated counter pressures; perhaps these illustrate a truth—a truth evident in the Harris case—that in the end a court with power will not forever deny itself the use of it in the face of what seems gross injustice.

The first such pressure was on the concept of full and fair adjudication. In 1915, in Leo Frank's case, *Frank v Magnum*,[70] Justice Holmes wrote that it was a premise for this preclusive rule that Frank had had the opportunity to raise and have determined somewhere his claim that his murder trial had been so dominated by a threatening mob that it could not count as a legal proceeding at all. In 1935, in *Mooney v Holohan*,[71] the Court applied this notion of a vitiated proceeding to a conviction procured by the knowing use of perjured testimony. There was pressure, but in both these cases·

---

[69] *Brown v Allen*, 344 US 443, 540 (Jackson concurring). See also Bator, 76 Harv L Rev at 447–53 (cited in note 63).

[70] 237 US 309, 347 (Holmes dissenting).

[71] 294 US 103.

the Supreme Court denied the availability of the writ, because "corrective process" had indeed been available in state courts—in Frank's case because he had had an opportunity to raise his claim on appeal to the state supreme court. This was not seen as a way of punishing the petitioner for his (or his lawyer's) neglect to avail himself of a state's corrective process, but rather as a conception of the writ itself: that an opportunity to raise the issue in state court saved the state court proceedings from the taint of the initial flaw, so that the process below could no longer be claimed to be so deficient as to count as no process at all.

But for all that, it must be acknowledged that Holmes's dissent in *Frank*, by conceding the possibility that federal courts may use habeas corpus to inquire into any aspect of the correctness of a judgment of a state court—a court that no one doubts had authority to try and, but for the error, condemn this man for this crime—had admitted a principle that could not be easily contained. One might ask whether Holmes's statement in *Frank* was perhaps the initial instance of impudence in this history. Was he not asserting a kind of residual authority in the Supreme Court, or in federal courts, or in any court that might get its hands on the matter, that some injustices are so gross that the power to correct them justified its exercise? I do not believe Justice Harlan entirely disposes of Justice Brennan's argument in *Fay* that neither the Supreme Court nor earlier English practice always attempted or even were able to draw a rigorous line between jurisdictional and substantive defects. And so the history displays not so much instances of impudence as what Harlan himself refers to as "stage[s] of development."[72]

A similar question might be asked about *Brown v Allen*,[73] in which the Supreme Court considered claims of another gross injustice: a death sentence upon a conviction of rape, by a jury from which blacks had been systematically excluded and which had been procured as result of a coerced confession. Although the Supreme Court rejected Brown's claims on the merits, it acknowledged his right to have them heard in a federal court habeas proceeding even after a full and procedurally correct hearing in the state court system and after denial of certiorari by the Supreme Court. It is

---

[72] 372 US 391, 450–63 (Harlan dissenting).
[73] 344 US 443 (1953).

not possible to avoid the conclusion that *Brown* established the proposition that a state prisoner had the right to present to a federal court every well-preserved federal constitutional objection to his conviction. *Brown* was radical in that it declined to treat denial of certiorari by the Supreme Court as satisfying that right—a pragmatic conclusion that recognized that the Court's formal ability to review federal constitutional claims raised in all criminal cases on appeal was practically limited, and it was more sensible to have lower federal courts sort them out at least in the first instance. But this solution, which provoked the words of Justice Jackson above, admitted (or enacted) the premise that there exists a right to *plenary* federal court consideration of state court judgments outside the usual appellate route. More important, it was seen, not by Jackson alone, as a large step in the direction of the relitigation conception.[74]

But only a step. Brown's codefendant was denied the right to a federal court hearing on the same claims because his lawyer had filed his appeal one day late. Since the state had offered "an adequate and easily-complied-with method of appeal," the Court held that the federal statute conferring habeas corpus jurisdiction, which requires exhaustion of state remedies, had not been complied with.[75] Another way to put it was that the state court judgment rested *not* on an incorrect proposition of federal law—for instance about what constituted a proper jury or a voluntary confession—but on the ground that even in a death case the state may insist on compliance with filing deadlines, at least if the prisoner has counsel or is not prevented from complying.[76] This reasoning extends to lower federal courts in habeas the rationale of the established doctrine that the Supreme Court has not been granted power by Congress to exercise appellate jurisdiction where the question of federal law is not the basis for the judgment appealed from—the so-called-independent-and-adequate-state-ground doctrine.[77] As applied to habeas review, that doctrine swings back to the process conception

---

[74] The Bush Administration's proposal to reform habeas corpus takes explicit aim at *Brown v Allen*. See S 1241, 102d Cong, 1st Sess (1991).

[75] *Daniels v Allen*, 344 US 443, 485 (1953).

[76] For a recent example of this same phenomenon, see *Coleman v Thompson*, 111 S Ct 2546 (1991) (appeal filed three days late is defaulted).

[77] See *Murdock v City of Memphis*, 20 Wall. 590 (1875); *Fay v Noia*, 372 US 391, 448 (1963) (Harlan dissenting).

pole: the prisoner is not held in violation of federal law (because of
the claimed underlying violation) but rather because of a fair rule
of state law, a rule about how to go about obtaining the appellate
review or other state corrective process that *Frank* said could cure
the earlier defect in state judgment.

The next and greatest step toward a full embrace of the relitigation conception was Justice Brennan's opinion for the Court in *Fay
v Noia*,[78] which embraced the expansive premise of *Brown* while
rejecting the limitation of its companion case. Justice Black, in his
dissent in *Daniels*, had put the proposition bluntly: ". . . it is never
too late for courts in habeas corpus proceedings to look straight
through procedural screens in order to prevent forfeiture of life or
liberty in flagrant defiance of the Constitution."[79] The only difference was that Justice Black had added the soothing caveat that he
was "willing to agree that [this power] should not be exercised . . .
except under special circumstances or in extraordinary situations,"
while Justice Brennan made access to federal courts a matter of
course.[80]

Was this impudence? It would be harsh to say so: Justice Brennan argued that the independent state ground limitation applied
only to the Supreme Court's appellate jurisdiction, while here the
federal court (in the first instance a lower federal court) was not
exercising appellate jurisdiction at all, but rather an independent
head of authority under the habeas corpus statute to inquire into
the legality of the detention or punishment. Just as the argument
Justice Brennan had used to get around the Congressional requirement that state remedies be exhausted,[81] this argument is brittle,
to say the least. The independent-state-ground doctrine denies appellate jurisdiction to the Supreme Court because the federal claim
is not the basis of the judgment. By the same reasoning a federal

---

[78] 372 US 391 (1963).

[79] 344 US 443, 554 (1953).

[80] For a full survey of these issues, one sympathetic but not uncritically so to Brennan's
view of forfeiture, see Meltzer, *State Court Forfeitures of Federal Rights*, 99 Harv L Rev 1128,
1200–02 (1986).

[81] The Court disposed of the exhaustion requirement, a requirement imposed on federal
habeas corpus by Congress, by arguing that there were no longer any state remedies to
exhaust. Of course this begs the question: is Congress's exhaustion requirement properly
respected by failing to take advantage of available state remedies, thus causing them to
become unavailable?

court exercising original jurisdiction in habeas would be precluded from concluding that the petitioner's imprisonment is constitutionally defective. To be sure, if there had not been constitutional error at the trial, there might never have been a conviction, but that is true in both instances. Yet such brittleness of reasoning is common. More to the point is the fact that Justice Brennan in *Fay v Noia* was continuing a trend giving federal courts a final reviewing authority over state criminal processes, a trend that began in *Frank* and gained considerable impetus in *Brown*.

Closer to impudence was Justice Brennan's account of when a petitioner would be foreclosed from raising a claim in habeas: when the *accused* (not just his lawyer) can be said to have deliberately bypassed state procedure, saving his claim to raise later in federal court. This was all that was left of the notion that federal court review—and lower federal court review especially—was reserved for exceptional and outrageous cases. By acknowledging a category of "deliberate bypass" Justice Brennan created the impression of continuity with the past, but his application of that notion in *Fay* itself showed what a meager bone he was throwing. Justice Brennan held there was no deliberate bypass because Fay, who had been sentenced to life imprisonment for his part in a felony murder, had declined to appeal his conviction to avoid the risk of a death sentence on retrial. This argument displayed contempt for the very considerations of federalistic comity it was supposed to honor.[82] Perhaps the opinion hides a deeper solecism: that no lawyer's maneuver may be condemned as too manipulative when carried out under the shadow of the death penalty, to which Justice Brennan later displayed unalterable hostility. But in the end, even here one might acquit of impudence, since Justice Brennan's Court exercised a power that in some sense it undoubtedly enjoyed, extending—though perhaps disingenuously—a doctrine that had long been gathering momentum. Disingenuousness is infuriating, but it is not quite what I have in mind by impudence.

In any event, whatever instability inheres in the process conception is matched at the other pole: for if a claim (a federal claim at least) is never settled until it is settled right, in practical effect that

---

[82] For another example of Justice Brennan's willingness to play fast and loose with such comity "while flying banners of federalism," 379 US at 457 (Harlan dissenting), see *Henry v Mississippi*, 379 US 443 (1965).

means it is never settled. That logic is hard enough to bear when
its entailment is endless process in the federal courts, but at least
the prisoner remains in prison the while; applied to capital cases,
however, the entailment promises the frustration of the state's right
to punish altogether—for if process is not final, death is. That is
why, with the decision in *Gregg v Georgia*,[83] once more making the
death penalty available, *Fay* was bound to be repudiated. Indeed,
Fay was part of the sense of a Supreme Court run off the rails
against which candidate Nixon (and Reagan and Bush after him)
explicitly inveighed. In 1977, in *Wainwright v Sykes*,[84] a recon-
structed Supreme Court held, with only Justices Brennan and Marshall dissenting, that any claim not raised in state court was unavailable in habeas corpus unless there was cause for the omission,
and "cause" (it became increasingly clear) meant a major impedi-
ment to raising the claim at trial such as constitutionally ineffective
assistance of counsel or misconduct by the government—the kinds
of defects exhibited in *Frank v Magnum* and *Mooney v Holohan*.
Lawyer's tactics, error of judgment, or even negligence would no
longer do. In its 1991 decision in *Coleman v Thompson*,[85] the Rehnquist Court definitively restated the *Brown v Daniels* line of forfeiture endorsed by Justice Harlan in his dissent in *Fay*,[86] and explicitly overruled the last vestige of *Fay*. Failure to invoke a fairly
available and reasonable rule of state corrective process cut off
further federal review. Since the Court left a loophole for manifest
miscarriages of justice going to guilt or innocence,[87] one cannot
say, however, that it completely adopted Harlan's view in *Fay* that
in such cases the independent-and-adequate-state-ground doctrine
foreclosed federal court intervention as a matter of constitutional
law.

Finally, the Court has been embroidering a parallel doctrine—
the abuse of the writ—to deal with second and successive petitions
for habeas corpus. The habeas statute provides that a federal court

---

[83] 428 US 153 (1976).

[84] 433 US 72. Was *Wainwright* impudent in its treatment of *Fay*, as protected by the
doctrine of *stare decisis?* No more so than *Fay* itself, of which it had a considerable advantage
in terms of candor.

[85] 111 S Ct 2546 (1991)

[86] 372 US 391 (1963).

[87] See note 28.

may refuse to entertain subsequent petitions if "satisfied that the applicant on the earlier application deliberately withheld the asserted ground or otherwise abused the writ."[88] One approach would treat this as a response to a problem on the extreme—the prisoner who files repetitive, harassing petitions—and would respond along the lines of Justice Brannan's doctrine of "deliberate bypass" in *Fay*. But the same Justices who closed in on exhaustion in *Wainwright* pursued a similar project in respect to successive petitions: a prisoner should bring all his constitutional complaints in one proceeding, not dribble them out one by one over the years, clogging the courts and in death cases postponing execution until he dies of old age. In a series of cases a plurality of Justices proposed that a prisoner should be barred from bringing up in a later petition any claim he could have brought on his first trip to federal court.[89] In 1991 in *McCleskey v Zant*[90] the Court closed the loop and imposed the same condition of "cause" to excuse forfeiture for failure to raise a claim in an earlier federal proceeding as *Wainwright* imposed on failures to raise a claim in state court.

This regime may seem draconian, I suggest, for a jumble of good and bad reasons. Certainly in a number of death penalty states the quality of representation is unacceptably low. This has accustomed us to tales of bungling and neglect, in the face of which the Court nevertheless measures whether a claim has been defaulted by the very permissive standard of what makes for constitutionally ineffective assistance of counsel in criminal cases generally.[91] Unfortunately for the poor wretches caught up in these cases, those absolutely opposed to the death penalty have seized on this phenomenon to distort doctrines that might have done proper service there into devices that can be used to upset any death sentence at all.[92] Thus we have become accustomed to, even besotted by a

---

[88] 28 USC 2255 (b); see also Rule 9 (b) of the 1977 Rules Governing Section 2255 Proceedings in the United States District Courts.

[89] *Kuhlmann v Wilson*, 477 US 436, 444–55 (1986) (Powell's plurality opinion); *Rose v Lundy*, 455 US 509, 520–21 (O'Connor's plurality opinion).

[90] 111 S Ct 1454 (1991).

[91] See, e.g., *Coleman v Thompson*, 112 S Ct 1845 (1992).

[92] I am dubious about the validity of statistics that show a 40 to 60 percent reversal rate in death cases on habeas. See note 13. The statistics do, of course, in part reflect the failures of appointed counsel in some death states. But they reflect as well the very phenomenon of disingenuous overscrupulousness that the Court is seeking to discipline.

regime unfamilar to and unenvied anywhere else in the world—
though it must be acknowledged that few other nations must accommodate procedural finality with the other kind of finality
brought by the penalty of death. This confusion feeds then into
our profound ambivalence about capital punishment, causing us as
a society to shrink from doing what we are not willing to reject
outright.

V. Whose Impudence?

The doctrines the Supreme Court has been elaborating over
the past decade and a half, particularly the doctrines of exhaustion,
forfeiture, and abuse, move our system firmly in the direction of
greater finality. There are lawyers and judges who think this trend
is wrong, and have inveighed against it at every step. Justice Brennan dissented bitterly in *Wainwright*. But it is also the case that the
Supreme Court has not been backing off.[93] On the contrary, any
lawyer and judge will tell you that they are tightened every year,
blocking off lines of evasion. The Supreme Court has sent its
strongest signal that it takes the second rule very seriously, the rule
against successive petitions in *McCleskey v Zant*.

There are some who do not like it,[94] but none who do not recognize what there is not to like. Among those who like it the least
are many of the judges of the Ninth Circuit. So much so that only
three months earlier the Supreme Court had issued a clear rebuke
to a panel of the Ninth Circuit.[95] The panel had heard argument in
March 1989 on a second federal habeas corpus petition by Charles
Rodman Campbell, sentenced to death in the state of Washington
in 1982 for the murder of two women and an eight-year-old girl.
By January 1992 the panel—in spite of repeated requests by the
Washington Attorney General—had not issued its ruling.

It is not hard to acquit the first habeas panel in *Harris* (Choy,
Anderson, Canby, JJ) of impudence in their 1984 ruling that the

---

[93] *Wright v West*, 1992 US Lexis 3689 may be seen as an indication of reluctance to undo
Brown v Allen to block habeas review in an important class of cases—those involving the
application of law to facts—in the absence of abuse or other grounds of forfeiture. Justice
O'Connor wrote in her separate opinion that Congress's restatement of the habeas statute
in 1966 precluded this further step.

[94] See Reinhardt, 102 Yale L J 205 (cited in note 36).

[95] *In re James Blodgett*, 112 S Ct 674 (1992).

California Supreme Court had been wrong not to make a proportionality determination about the death sentence in Harris's case. I must admit to some lurking doubts: the concept of proportionality is indeterminate and biased against capital sentences,[96] so that a less benign spirit than my own might see here the offer of a device that state judges might use to indulge a predilection against the death penalty if they had it, and a federal court might use to keep the ball in play indefinitely if the state judges did not. It is striking that the Supreme Court's 1984 reversal of the panel garnered only two dissents, Justices Brennan and Marshall, who have stated their opposition to the death penalty in all circumstances.

Nor is there much to complain about the second panel (Alarcon, Brunetti, and Noonan) that received this case from the district court in 1984—except perhaps that this time it took five years to dispose of the case. And it is worth remembering that Judge Noonan did not dissent from this disposition.

Judge Noonan's primary intervention on Harris's behalf was in his 1990 dissent from the same panel's denial of relief on what I count as Harris's third federal habeas petition. Here again, I would acquit of impudence; one might in good faith say, as Noonan does, that Harris's *Ake*[97] claim is neither close enough to issues Harris had already raised several times before, nor barred by the doctrine of abuse of the writ. The rules about what constitutes justification for not having brought a claim earlier, even after *McCleskey v Zant*,[98] leave enough play for unexpected developments in the law that one might conclude that these rules had been satisfied here. Perhaps the question comes down to how far may one stretch a point when a man's life is at stake, when all you are doing is asking for an evidentiary hearing on whether there had been a serious denial of effective assistance at the penalty stage.

This indulgence is tested when we read that Judge Noonan characterized as "courageous" Judge Patel's April 18 stay. Have we reached the point where good faith judicial pressure on an avenue

---

[96] After twenty-five years with no executions, the skew would be strongly against the death penalty, and the concept of proportionality is inhospitable to a fundamental change in public values.

[97] See notes 30–35 and accompanying text.

[98] 111 S Ct 1454 (1991). See note 28 and accompanying text.

of doubt passes into sheer manipulation (the Supreme Court's word[99]), crossing the threshhold to impudence? If Judge Patel can fairly be convicted of impudence, then Judge Noonan's celebration of her order and opinion of April 18 makes him her accomplice and suggests something about the criteria that led to his earlier opinion regarding Harris's *Ake* claim.

Would such a judgment on Judge Patel be too harsh? Certainly a habeas petition complaining not of the death sentence but of the method of its imposition would have been barred as an abuse of the writ: Harris had had many opportunities to raise it earlier, starting with his initial appeal through the several proceedings in which the California court had set his date of execution "in the manner prescribed by law"[100]—that is, by cyanide gas. The latest of these was on March 13, 1992. At none of these had the objection been raised. Nor is there the slightest plausibility to the argument that newly discovered evidence or a change in the legal standard had precluded an earlier claim. True, the ACLU lawyers bringing the class action on behalf of Harris and others included affidavit accounts of the execution by cyanide gas in Arizona of Donald Harding on April 6 to support their claim that this method of execution entailed "unnecessary suffering" in violation of the Supreme Court's rule in *Louisiana ex rel Francis v Resweber*.[101] In any event the Arizona affidavits simply repeated the equally grizzly materials adduced from the California records of earlier executions at San Quentin, the last of which had occurred some quarter of a century earlier. The thinnest argument might be made that the Arizona legislature's decision just eight days earlier to propose a state constitutional amendment substituting execution by lethal injection for cyanide gas in reaction to the Donald Harding execution represented the kind of changing moral consensus that would in turn justify a change in the meaning of cruel and unusual punishment.[102]

---

[99] *Gomez v United States District Court*, 112 S Ct 1653, 1653 (1992).

[100] *People v Harris*, 28 Cal3d 935 (1981).

[101] 329 US 459 (1947).

[102] On August 28, 1992, Governor Wilson of California signed a bill, to take effect on January 1, 1993, giving persons condemned to death the choice of execution by lethal injection as an alternative to the gas chamber. New York Times (August 30, 1992), section 1, page 28, column 3.

Judge Patel[103] did not rest her TRO on the escape clauses in *McCleskey*, but rather on the argument that this was not a habeas case at all, but rather a claim for an injunction under Section 1983 to put an end to an unconstitutional governmental practice. Such injunctions have often been issued to reform inhumane conditions of confinement.[104] And although the Supreme Court had made clear in *Preiser v Rodriguez*[105] that this route could not be used to evade the strictures of habeas corpus, there is some plausibility to the argument that the *Preiser* doctrine did not apply in this case since only the method, not the fact of execution, was in issue. Nor had the Supreme Court ever passed on the application of *Preiser* to a 1983 challenge to a method of execution claimed to be unconstitutional. The Supreme Court, when Judge Patel's order reached it, ruled that since the ACLU was asking for the equitable remedy of an injunction, the notion of abuse of the writ was reflected in the similar doctrine barring equitable relief when a claimant has abused the process by unjustifiably waiting until the last minute to bring his claim. But this doctrine of want of equity is sufficiently porous that a judge might have concluded in good faith that its strictures are overcome by the enormity of a gruesome and agonizing death. So I must allow that there is enough room for argument about the correctness of Judge Patel's stay—and therefore Judge Noonan's dissent from the panel's mandamus dissolving that stay, and even the stay issued by two sets of Ninth Circuit judges to allow en banc consideration of this proceeding—that the question whether these were acts of impudence depends on the subjective motivations of the judges: did they believe in good faith they were pursuing avenues left open to them by the rules and principles they were institutionally bound to respect?

Judge Patel (and her colleagues) might have predicted that the Supreme Court would reject her invocation of Section 1983. Judge Noonan might have predicted similarly in respect to the substance and availability of the *Ake* claim. Indeed, the first habeas panel

---

[103] I do not fault the ACLU lawyers for advancing such arguments when a client's life is at stake. The systemic justification for such aggressive maneuvers on the part of advocates is the counterweight of faithful and disciplined responses on the part of judges, a counterweight that was sometimes missing in this case.

[104] See, e.g., *Rhodes v Chapman*, 452 US 337, 352 (1981) (Brennan concurring).

[105] 411 US 475 (1973).

which granted relief on the proportionality ground in *Harris v Pulley*[106] might have predicted the Supreme Court's eventual 7–2 reversal. But I do not believe that a conscientious judge fulfills her role in a hierarchy of courts by seeking to predict how a superior court will rule. Her task is to interpret the superior courts' opinions, and that means taking their text—not the subjective intentions of their authors[107]—and fitting it into the whole body of controlling legal materials, including materials bearing on her subordinate role. It is possible, even likely, sometimes that a superior court's immediately preceding judgment states less than that court's members hope and wish lower courts to do, but the superior judges' own sense of restraint may keep them from putting that wish into words. The lower court judge may predict that her hierarchical superiors will do what she thinks is the wrong thing, but she need not rule as if they had already done it. This conception, of course, makes the system a hostage to the judge's good faith, modesty, restraint, and good judgment. But that is what makes impudence so much more grievous a defalcation, when it occurs.

Finally, it might be said in Judge Patel's defense that after all she only issued a TRO, which prevented the issue from becoming moot as to Harris while she considered it further. If California's provision limiting its death warrants to twenty-four hours created a difficulty, this is a difficulty that should not in general suffice to prevent even preliminary consideration of a constitutional claim, however meritorious. But this generality leaves out of account the whole history of this case. There are two sides to the question whether the state's interest in having an execution proceed on schedule raises the kind of equity that makes the issuance of a TRO an abuse of discretion, such as would occasion extraordinary intervention by the court of appeals. After these many years of delay, even a state where the death warrant remained valid for, say, thirty days might have a claim that the spectacle of continued postponements imposed an intolerable burden on the state officials involved in carrying out the execution, on the family of the victims, on the public, and even on the defendant himself—perhaps even

---

[106] See supra note 19 and accompanying text.

[107] See Fried, *Sonnet LXV and the "Black Ink" of the Framers' Intention*, 100 Harv L Rev 751 (1987).

allowing the defendant to raise a cruel and unusual punishment issue on account of the delay itself.

I am willing to leave this question open to each reader's own conclusion and to rest on an admittedly vague and subjective criterion of good faith, because events close in on the question (and the judges). First, very little can be said to justify the stay issued at about the same time at Judge Fletcher's instance in response to her call for an en banc.[108] Her call responded to yet another denial of a district habeas corpus petition brought in federal district court in San Diego raising the claim that not Harris but his brother Daniel had fired the fatal shots. The question of Daniel's role had been raised numerous times before, and so this stay was appropriately swept aside by the Supreme Court. Yet what Ninth Circuit afficionados call the "Danny case" did depend on a factual claim and went to factual innocence, and so here too in the end one comes down to Judge Fletcher's subjective state of mind—was she acting on a good faith concern or was this a pretext to interfere with, postpone, and perhaps allow time for a change in the political climate regarding the imposition of the death penalty? One argument will not do: that a judge cannot ever be wrong to insist on at least an evidentiary hearing on a claim of newly discovered evidence relating to guilt or innocence. Since such claims can and are regularly made repeatedly just on the eve of execution, if they can never be disposed of on the affidavits, papers, and arguments, but always justify an evidentiary hearing, it is obvious executions can be delayed indefinitely.[109]

Whether or not the threshold of impudence has been crossed so far, there can be no justification in law for Ninth Circuit Judge Harry Pregerson's stay, the last in this case, issued after Harris was already in the gas chamber. Judge Pregerson stayed the execution to allow Harris to present "unexhausted claims . . . to the California Supreme Court."[110] These were the cruel and unusual

---

[108] See note 40 and accompanying text.

[109] It would be the worst of all solutions to rely solely on the lawyer's duty to certify the bona fides of the factual claim. First, it is inconceivable that a lawyer could not be found to forward such claims in a death case, and in any event the defendant has a right to proceed pro se in federal court.

[110] It is hard to understand why a federal judge has authority to issue a stay to allow a state court to be presented with a claim which that state court has no federal obligation to hear. To be sure, the California Supreme Court might choose to hear the claim, but then the stay petition should have been directed to the state, not the federal court.

punishment claims in the Section 1983 proceeding brought before
Judge Patel, which (according to Judge Pregerson) Harris now
asked to be treated as a habeas corpus petition. Judge Pregerson's
action differed from Judge Fletcher's in one salient respect: as Judge
Pregerson knew,[111] the Supreme Court had less than an hour earlier
issued an opinion explicitly calling Harris's claim "an obvious attempt to avoid the application of *McCleskey v Zant . . .* to bar this
successive claim for relief. Harris has now filed four prior federal
habeas petitions. He has made no convincing showing of cause for
his failure to raise this claim in his prior petitions." The Court went
on to say that "whether his claim is framed as a habeas petition or
a sec. 1983 action, . . . there is no good reason for this abusive
delay, which has been compounded by last minute attempts to
manipulate the judicial process. . . ." Nor could the Supreme
Court's opinion be understood as only an explanation of why it
would not exercise its own equitable jurisdiction to stay execution,
since stays had been granted below not to preserve the Supreme
Court's jurisdiction on certiorari, but rather to preserve the Ninth
Circuit's ability to rehear en banc the Alarcon, Brunetti, and Noonan panel's order that the execution could proceed on schedule. It
was these stays that the Supreme Court was going out of its way
to vacate as improper. In other words, this was inescapably a definitive judgment that Harris was not entitled to a stay of execution
in federal court on the basis of his Eighth Amendment claim. And
it was precisely such a stay that Judge Pregerson issued less than
an hour later.

The Supreme Court has the hierarchical authority to set the law
for lower courts. There are famous instances in which Presidents,
state officials, and state courts have asserted the right to reach
independent conclusions about matters of federal law. Abraham
Lincoln, among other Presidents, famously asserted such a right
in respect to the *Dred Scott* decision. Southern governors asserted

---

[111] Judge Reinhardt suggests that Judge Pregerson may not have been fully aware of the
import of the Supreme Court's order at the time he ruled. Reinhardt, 102 Yale L J at 212–13
(cited in note 36). California Attorney General Daniel E. Lungren and Deputy Attorney
General Louis R. Hanoian wrote me on July 24, 1992: "while our office was verifying Judge
Pregerson's identity and the validity of the stay, Deputy Attorney General Dane Gillette
was speaking to Judge Pregerson and asked him if he was aware that the Supreme Court
had vacated the earlier stays issued in the case. When Judge Pregerson replied in the affirmative, Gillette asked why he was granting the stay? Judge Pregerson replied, 'Because the
ACLU asked me to.' " Letter on file with the author.

such a right in resisting implementation of *Brown v Board*. And *Martin v Hunter's Lessee* and *Cohens v Virginia* raised and determined the issue in respect to state courts' subordination to the Supreme Court in matters of federal law. In each of these bitterly controverted matters, the final authority of the Supreme Court to settle the very claim before it had either been acknowledged or at least acquiesced in. And this is what has made the claim a claim within the legal system, acknowledging the last-word authority of the Supreme Court in general, while questioning it in the particular case. Analogous challenges from the lower federal courts, which after all the Constitution calls "Tribunals inferior to the Supreme Court," have been rare. There are the shenanigans of Judge Cox in resisting the implementation of *Brown*. There was Judge Brevard Hand's decision purporting to overrule (disregard?) the Supreme Court's school prayer jurisprudence as wrongly decided. In both examples, a rhetoric similar to that invoked to justify Judge Pregerson's order was deployed: that the oath taken is not to the Court but to the Constitution, faithful service to which means independent judgment. But in these cases too the authority of the Supreme Court to pronounce the last word *in the particular case* was not put in question.

Judge Pregerson defied an explicit ruling of the Supreme Court in the very case at hand. No argument was available about whether a statement in an earlier case was dictum or holding, or whether it truly extended to this case. This *was* this case, and so the challenge was the one even Lincoln declined to make: to the authority of the Supreme Court to dispose finally of a particular case. As such, it moves into a different domain of discourse altogether—not what is the best and most moral interpretation of a demand made on me by an institution to which I owe loyalty, but when does a transcendent duty supersede and excuse such loyalty? When the Wisconsin supreme court refused to make return on the Supreme Court's writ of error in *Abelman v Booth* it acted as Judge Pregerson did— perhaps somewhat less defiantly, since a refusal to act is less an affront to authority. But Judge Pregerson had put us on notice. During his confirmation hearings in 1979 the following colloquy occurred:

> *Senator Simpson*. . . . If a decision in a particular case was required by case law or statute as interpreted according to the intent that you would perceive as legislative intent, and yet

that offended your own conscience, what might you do in that situation?

Mr. Pregerson. Well, of course it's a hypothetical question and life does not present situations that are that clear cut, but I think all of us judges and lawyers, would be very pleased if the congressional intent was clearly discernible. I have to be honest with you. If I was faced with a situation like that and it ran against my conscience, I would follow my conscience.

Senator Simpson. I didn't hear, sir.

Mr. Pregerson. I said, if I were faced with a situation like that that ran against my conscience, disturbed my conscience, I would try to find a way to follow my conscience and do what I perceived to be right and just. Not that, I would hope not, it would mean I would act arbitrarily. I was born and raised in this country, and I am steeped in its traditions, its mores, its beliefs, and its philosophies; and if I felt strongly in a situation like that, I feel it would be the product of my very being and upbringing. I would follow my conscience.

Senator Simpson. So that would be a tough one for you in that situation?

Senator Pregerson. Yes, sir.

Senator Simpson. Let's say a decision in a particular case seemed to require, by case law or statute, and yet was inconsistent with what you believed might be the values of contemporary society; what might you do?

Senator Pregerson. I would seek to distinguish that case.

. . .

Senator Simpson. Thank you very much. I appreciate it. I have nothing further.

Senator Leahy. Thank you. I have nothing further, Judge.

I can't help but think, in your answer to Senator Simpson's question, that I expect a great number of Federal judges feel as you do, but I suspect only a small percentage would be as candid as you were in your response. I appreciate the candor and directness of your answer.[112]

Ronald Dworkin in *Hard Cases* acknowledges that some regimes or parts of regimes are so iniquitous that it would be appropriate for a judge to lie and cheat in order to circumvent or undermine

---

[112] Hearings Before the Committee on the Judiciary, 96th Cong, 1st Sess. Serial No 96-21, part 4, pp 450–51.

their evils.[113] This is different from interpretation, which at its best has a creative and ameliorative aspect: the judge, who is part of the legal and political community, interprets its materials in a way that affirms and perhaps extends what is best in its traditions. Where the community's values deserve not respect but enmity, the judge serves humanity by disserving them. Defiance is a version of this stance, where the judge wages not secret but open warfare. The appropriateness of one or the other stance depends on the circumstances and the chances of success. Impudence is neither of these. The impudent judge does not admit his alienation from the system he claims to serve. He admits that his moral title to exercise authority over his fellow citizens derives from the authority of that system—and yet he will not act according to its terms.

Finally we come to the Supreme Court's order that "no further stays of Robert Alton Harris's execution shall be entered by the federal courts except upon order of this Court."[114] I have dwelt at such length on Judge Pregerson's indefensible divagation because some commentators, with an Orwellian rhetorical twist, have urged that the Supreme Court's order responding to Judge Pregerson was itself the only instance of impudence in this whole unedifying story. The argument that the Supreme Court's order broke faith with the system granting the Court its authority is an argument that would allow the Court to exercise its judgment, but would leave to others the final authority to interpret and execute that judgment. Surely this is wrong: courts at every level have claimed the power to issue orders and to insist on compliance with them. Might it be said that the Supreme Court, however, in its appellate function, in its relation that is to other courts, must adopt this important stance? The Supreme Court's situation at the apex of the court system is due, this argument would have it, not to its greater wisdom—its judgments are not divinely inspired—but only to a structural need which is quite consistent with final authority to interpret and execute its judgments in whatever lower court has original jurisdiction over a matter. Just as this system assumes no inherent wisdom, only authority and good faith in the Supreme Court, it assumes an equal portion of good faith in the courts below.

---

[113] Dworkin, *Taking Rights Seriously* at 327 (cited in note 1).

[114] *Vasquez v Harris*, USSC No A-768, slip op at 1 (April 21, 1992).

This conception is bolstered by the sense that judges like Judges Patel, Fletcher, and Pregerson, being closer to the scene, can evaluate and respond to the claims of concrete, immediate circumstances. After the Supreme Court put the Ninth Circuit into a sort of receivership on the Harris matter, what would happen if there had been some genuine last minute demonstration of innocence and the Supreme Court was unavailable to hear it? Nonetheless, the power of appellate over inferior courts has always included the power to take over and enforce a mandate in the face of obduracy. The system up and down the line is not so starry-eyed as to assume conclusively that lower courts always act in good faith. Superior courts have always enjoyed the authority to issue not only propositions of law but executive decrees to courts below, and to supervise them to make sure they are properly executed. The Supreme Court prefers to reverse and remand, but sometimes—especially when faced with obduracy—it will issue a direct decree. So just last Term, when the supreme court of Georgia had repeatedly found some new reason to reinstate a death sentence the Court had reversed and remanded to them, the Supreme Court finally just reversed and ordered a new trial without remand.[115] The grant of authority to issue writs of mandamus and prohibition is clearly available to compel a state court "to conform its decision to the Supreme Court's previous mandate."[116] Indeed, *Marbury v Madison*, while denying the Court original jurisdiction to issue a writ of mandamus to an executive officer, proceeded from the premise that the coercive writ may be issued "to enable them to exercise appellate jurisdiction."[117]

There is, of course, not the slightest reason why an authority the Supreme Court enjoys over state courts is lacking to control misbehavior (though it is not called that) by lower federal courts. On the contrary, added to the authority just cited is the general supervisory authority every superior court exercises over courts inferior to it in the same system.[118] The Court's language authoriz-

---

[115] *Ford v Georgia*, 111 S Ct 850 (1991).

[116] See 28 USC 1651; Hart & Wechsler, *The Federal Court and the Federal System* 354 (3rd ed Bator, Mishkin, Meltzer and Shapiro, 1988). See generally, *Note on Enforcement of the Mandate*, id at 518–21.

[117] 5 US 137, 175 (1803); 28 USC 1651.

[118] See authorities cited in Stern, Gressman & Shapiro, *Supreme Court Practice* 500–507 (6th ed 1986).

ing this rare exercise of power, while redolent of reluctance, is peremptory: mandamus is available when a lower court "does not proceed to execute the mandate, or disobeys and mistakes its meaning."[119] Or in another context: "While the courts have never confined themselves to an arbitrary and technical definition of 'jurisdiction,' it is clear that only exceptional circumstances amounting to a judicial 'usurpation of power' will justify the invocation of this extraordinary remedy."[120] These words recognize and show a readiness to meet a harsh reality: that there are judges who may "disobey" or "usurp[ ] power." The authority is there, implicit in the structure of hierarchy and the statutes conferring power, to deal with these breaches of faith, even if that authority too, in its turn, like all authority, may be abused and usurped.

The path of impudence does not travel full circle.[121]

---

[119] *United States v Fossat*, 20 How. 445, 446 (1858).

[120] *Will v United States*, 389 US 90, 95 (1967), quoting *DeBeers Consolidated Mines, Ltd. v United States*, 325 US 212, 2176 (1945). See authorities cited in Stern, Gressman & Shapiro, *Supreme Court Practice* at 500–507 (cited in note 118).

[121] Judge Pregerson's conduct was egregious, but the Court's harsh response may have been evoked as well by other actions of the Ninth Circuit, in this and other cases. See note 95 supra and accompanying texts. Of particular concern is the Ninth Circuit's rule allowing any active judge to trigger a seven day stay of execution by calling for an en banc vote, a rule Judge Fletcher had used in respect to the "Danny claim," a claim both the district court and the panel—unanimously, including Judge Noonan—had rejected. Although the Ninth Circuit rule itself may not constitute institutional impudence, it certainly gives scope and cover (the call being anonymous) to individual impudence. For the sake of completeness, it must be said that the two stays by the en banc court in respect to Judge Patel's order may be seen not as seeking to support Judge Patel so much as vindicating the circuit's own rules, see note 39 supra, which Judges Alarcon and Brunetti may on one interpretation of those rules be seen as disregarding. The Supreme Court, however, was entitled to dissolve the circuit's stays on the merits, whether or not it had been issued to protect the Ninth Circuit's en banc procedures.

ROCHELLE COOPER DREYFUSS

A *WISEGUY*'S APPROACH TO INFORMATION PRODUCTS: MUSCLING COPYRIGHT AND PATENT INTO A UNITARY THEORY OF INTELLECTUAL PROPERTY

For a time, it was fashionable for copyright scholars to make their mark by questioning the relationship between the First Amendment and the Copyright Clause.[1] They began by pointing out the inherent inconsistency between these two provisions, the constitutional clause granting Congress power to create law suppressing expression; the amendment barring Congress from creating law suppressing expression. The authors then argued that although the latter could be read as overriding the former, history indicates that this was not the intent, and that there are indeed principles within copyright providing for enough access to expression to make the two provisions work compatibly. Typically cited were a series of limits on the ability to acquire exclusive rights in information and other necessities of speech, including the dichotomy between ideas

Rochelle Cooper Dreyfuss is Professor of Law, New York University Law School.

AUTHOR'S NOTE: I wish to thank Roberta Kwall and Diane Zimmerman for their perceptive comments. They are in no way responsible for any errors. I am especially grateful for the wonderful research assistance provided by Michael Finn. Research for this article was supported by the Filomen D'Agostino and Max E. Greenberg Research Fund of the New York University Law School.

[1] US Const, Art I, § 8, cl 8. The phrase "Copyright and Patent Clause" has been shortened to "Copyright Clause" for expository convenience.

and facts on the one hand and expression on the other, and the merger doctrine.[2] All these authors thus shared the view that the First Amendment and copyright are in fundamental conflict, and that whenever the two meet, it is the free speech guarantees of the First Amendment that triumph; that the First Amendment means that sometimes, creators must donate their work to the public.[3]

As of last Term, this position seemed to have more than won over the Supreme Court. In two recent cases, the Court addressed the question of intellectual property protection for works arguably near the core of First Amendment concern: so-called "information products," whose content is so closely tied to the facts and laws of life and nature that there is little room for creative variation.[4] Each time, the Court found reasons to deny intellectual property protection. *Bonito Boats, Inc. v Thunder Craft Boats, Inc.*[5] concerned the constitutionality of a Florida statute prohibiting boat hull manufacturers from copying their competitors' designs by directly fabricating fiberglass molds from new hulls. The Court found that this prohibition was a form of intellectual property protection because it required competitors to use more expensive methods of copying, thereby raising the costs of copying to the point where the copyist could not undercut the selling price of the initial developer. As such, the statute was preempted by federal patent powers because

---

[2] These doctrines are defined in text at notes 52–53. In addition, some authors claimed that even where works are protectable, the First Amendment sometimes requires that infringement be excused through devices like fair use, 17 USC § 107, which creates royalty-free licenses for limited uses of copyrighted works, when such uses promote important social purposes. Some authors also advocated a distinct First Amendment defense.

[3] See, for example, Melville B. Nimmer, *Does Copyright Abridge the First Amendment Guarantees of Free Speech and Press*, 17 UCLA L Rev 1180 (1970); Paul Goldstein, *Copyright and the First Amendment*, 70 Colum L Rev 983 (1970); Lionel S. Sobel, *Copyright and the First Amendment: A Gathering Storm*, 19 ASCAP Copyright Law Symposium 43 (1971); Robert C. Denicola, *Copyright and Free Speech: Constitutional Limitations on the Protection of Expression*, 67 Cal L Rev 283 (1979).

[4] Examples of such products include historical and biographical works, as well as software programs, computerized databases, maps, directories, industrial designs, semiconductor chips, and informational molecules (such as gene sequences and genetically engineered products). See Rochelle C. Dreyfuss, *Information Products: A Challenge to Intellectual Property Theory*, 20 J Intl L & Pol 897 (1988). Some of these products fall into Jane Ginsburg's concept of works of "low authorship." See Jane C. Ginsburg, *Creation and Commerical Value: Copyright Protection of Works of Information*, 90 Colum L Rev 1865 (1990); Jane C. Ginsburg, *No "Sweat"? Copyright and Other Protection of Works of Information After Feist v. Rural Telephone*, 92 Colum L Rev 338 (1992).

[5] 489 US 141 (1989).

the state had, in effect, created exclusive rights to a functional product insufficiently innovative to merit a patent.

Feist Publications, Inc. v Rural Telephone Services Co.[6] bolstered *Bonito Boats* in an important way. *Feist* considered whether an alphabetical arrangement of telephone subscribers' names and numbers was copyrightable. The Court held that it was not. Information consisting solely of facts arranged in a straightforward manner are not "original works of authorship" within the meaning of the Copyright Act. Indeed, they are not "writings" in the constitutional sense.[7] They are, accordingly, beyond Congress's power to protect.

Read in conjunction with each other, these cases clearly support the views of the fashionable, for their apparent effect is to put information products into the public domain, protected by neither federal nor state law.[8] The consequence, however, is curious. Because the demand for accuracy usually makes the cost of producing information works high while modern technology tends to make the effort in copying them low, the profits of first-movers are at considerable risk, absent some form of legal protection. Thus, by stripping the nation of the power to enact statutes creating economic incentives, these decisions endanger the vitality of our information industries. To a nation that counts information as an important asset and a principal export, the outcome is (or should be) extremely worrisome.[9]

Enter that wiseguy, Henry Hill. Armed with a lifetime of experiences in organized crime and willing—for a price—to share his insights with the public, Hill encountered New York's "Son of Sam" law.[10] To prevent criminals from profiting from their crimes and to compensate victims, New York had enacted a statute that

---

[6] 111 S Ct 1282 (1991).

[7] 111 S Ct at 1288–90.

[8] See Paul J. Heald, *The Vices of Originality*, 1991 Supreme Court Review 31.

[9] This has been the view of the Office of Technological Assessment. See OTA, *Intellectual Products in an Age of Electronics and Information* 9 (US Gov't Printing Office, 1986). Significantly, the European Community has recently perceived the need to fashion a species of intellectual property law to provide incentives to compilers of information. See Comm'n of the European Community, Proposal for a Council Directive on the legal protection of databases (Com (92) 24 final) (Brussels, 13 May 1992).

[10] NY Exec Law § 632-a (McKinney 1982 & Supp 1991).

differed from the *Feist* rule in intent, but not in result: it too barred certain creators from enjoying the profits generated by certain of their labors. By presenting the effect of the law on Hill, *Simon & Schuster v New York State Crime Victims Board*[11] enabled the Court to see graphically how a loss of financial incentives can decrease the stock of whole classes of intellectual efforts. The Court was thus confronted with a facet of the First Amendment that the fashionable had largely ignored. The First Amendment is not only a guarantee of an individual's ability to speak; it also protects the mix of information that the public receives. The content-based disincentive of the Son of Sam law was so disruptive of that mix that the Court found that even New York's strong interest in the law could not save its constitutionality.

Under *Simon & Schuster* those aspects of intellectual property law, validated in *Bonito Boats* and *Feist*, that withhold protection from whole categories of intellectual efforts create (rather than resolve) First Amendment problems. Because they destroy economic incentives for targeted classes of works, they too have the systematic effect on the storehouse of knowledge that the Court found objectionable in the Son of Sam law. To accommodate the national interest in providing incentives to information producers while protecting the access interests of the public, a richer theory of intellectual property protection is therefore required. This article explores a theory that unifies copyright and patent and reconceives intellectual property as a broad continuum containing an array of techniques for maximizing public welfare in the products of human ingenuity. If intellectual property law is understood in this way, congressional power to act across the full spectrum of intellectual endeavor becomes apparent.

I. Simon & Schuster

Had information producers constructed a case to illustrate the problems posed by *Feist* and *Bonito Boats*, they could hardly have done a better job than *Simon & Schuster*. Nicholas Pileggi's *Wiseguy* purports to be a factual portrayal of the life of Henry Hill, a minor figure in organized crime and, as of the writing of the book, a participant in the Federal Witness Protection Program.

---

[11] 112 S Ct 501 (1991).

The origins of the work are somewhat obscure,[12] but it is clear that the publisher had agreed that, in exchange for cooperating with Pileggi, Hill would be entitled to a portion of the profits generated by *Wiseguy*.[13]

Because the work's subject matter included descriptions of crimes for which Hill had been convicted, the agreement between Hill and Simon & Schuster fit squarely within the provisions of a New York law enacted in the aftermath of the notorious "Son of Sam" (David Berkowitz) case.[14] This statute required a legal entity contracting with a person accused or convicted of crime in New York for works involving "the expression of such accused or convicted person's thoughts, feelings, opinions or emotions regarding such crime" to submit a copy of its contract to New York's Crime Victims Board and to pay over to the Board any money owing to the person so accused or convicted. If the person was indeed convicted of the described crime, this fund was to be held in escrow for five years and made available to the person's creditors, with claims of attorneys and victims having first and second priority, respectively. After five years, unallocated funds were to be distributed according to the contract's terms.

Wiseguy was published to good reviews and considerable commercial success. Warner Brothers later made it into the movie *Good-Fellas*. When Simon & Schuster failed to comply with the Son of Sam law, the Crime Victims Board initiated an investigation and ultimately ordered that royalties allocated to Hill should be held in escrow pursuant to the statute. Simon & Schuster brought a federal action challenging the order on First and Fourteenth Amendment grounds. The District Court, reasoning that the stat-

---

[12] The parties claimed in court that officials at Simon & Schuster conceived the idea of the book and engaged Sterling Lord, a literary agent, to find someone to write it. *Simon & Schuster v Fischetti*, 916 F2d 777, 779 (2d Cir 1990). In the book, however, Pileggi (as sole author) states: "A year after Henry Hill's arrest, I was approached by his attorney, who said that Hill was looking for someone to write his story." Nicholas Pileggi, *Wiseguy: Life in a Mafia Family* 3 (Pocket Books, 1990).

[13] *Simon & Schuster*, Joint Appendix at 56. These included profits from the book itself and from the subsidiary rights to create plays, movies, educational materials, radio or television shows. It also included profits from periodical and commercial rights, foreign language and British commonwealth rights.

[14] For a description of the legislative history of the statute, see Note, *Simon & Schuster, Inc. v. Fischetti: Can New York's Son of Sam Law Survive First Amendment Challenge*, 66 Notre Dame L Rev 1075 (1991).

ute was not intended to affect expressive conduct, applied an intermediate level of scrutiny and found the statute constitutional.[15]

The Court of Appeals for the Second Circuit applied a different standard but also upheld the law. The Court of Appeals stated that "[w]ithout a financial incentive to relate their criminal activities, most would-be story tellers will decline to speak or write" and that "[t]he possibility of a payday five years or more down the road . . . can hardly be seen as providing an adequate incentive."[16] The Court then applied the strict scrutiny standard formulated to test content-based regulations that directly burden speech. Over a dissent arguing that the statute was underinclusive, the majority found the statute constitutional, concluding that it was narrowly drawn to accomplish the state's compelling interest in punishing criminals and preventing their unjust enrichment, while compensating victims and satisfying their sense of justice.

The Supreme Court reversed. Noting that "the statute plainly imposes a financial disincentive only on speech of a particular content," the Court also subjected the statute to strict scrutiny.[17] While it too agreed that New York's interest was compelling, it was especially concerned that the regulation reached every work mentioning an author's crime, no matter how tangentially related to the principal subject matter of the work. Citing several well known works, and referring to the hundreds of books listed in the Association of American Publishers' amicus brief,[18] the Court concluded from the fact that "the Son of Sam law can produce such an outcome" that "the statute is, to say the least, not narrowly tailored to achieve the State's objective. . . ."[19]

The standard that the Court applied is not of particular interest; good arguments can be made for each of the formulations pro-

---

[15] *Simon & Schuster v Fischetti*, 724 F Supp 170 (SDNY 1989), citing *United States v O'Brien*, 391 US 367 (1968).

[16] *Simon & Schuster v Fischetti*, 916 F2d 777, 781 (2d Cir 1990), comparing the law with *Perry Educ. Assn. v Perry Local Educators' Assn.*, 460 US 37 (1983) (content-based regulations) and *Arkansas Writers' Project, Inc. v Ragland*, 481 US 221 (1987) (media-targeted regulations).

[17] *Simon & Schuster v New York Crime Victims Board*, 112 S Ct 501, 508, 509 (1991).

[18] Id at 511.

[19] Id at 512. Two concurring opinions were filed. Justice Blackmun agreed that the statute was overinclusive, but would have held it underinclusive as well. Id at 512 (Blackmun concurring). Justice Kennedy would have abandoned the compelling interest/narrow tailoring analysis in favor of a categorization approach. Id at 513–14 (Kennedy concurring).

posed.[20] Rather, given recent opinions in the intellectual property area, what is especially notable here is the ease with which the Supreme Court accepted the logical predicates to that issue: first, that depriving authors of royalties influences the kinds of information produced; and second, that the effect is enough of a burden on speech to raise a First Amendment question.

A. INFLUENCE

The *Simon & Schuster* Court treated the relationship between profit and production as almost self-evident, as ordinary common sense suggests it is. Nonetheless, the significance of this finding cannot be overstated, for in each of the last two Terms, the Court was confronted with cases in which this relationship appeared crucial, yet each time, it managed to omit discussion of it. In *Bonito Boats*, where the question was whether a Florida statute prohibiting the direct molding of boat hulls was preempted by federal patent law, the argument for preemption was that hull designs not sufficiently innovative to merit patent protection should be in the public domain, free for anyone to copy. The argument against preemption was that boat hull designers confront a special problem. So long as boat hulls are copied by traditional methods—measuring dimensions, constructing the shape in hardwood, covering the hardwood with fiberglass, and then removing the wood when the fiberglass solidified—copyists and developers compete on a fairly level playing field. On such a field, the developer can probably capture enough of a market to recoup the costs of innovation. But it is much cheaper to copy a hull by directly molding fiberglass to an embodiment of the first mover's boat. Since copyists using this method do not face expenses equivalent to those of developers, they can charge less for their hulls, capture the developers' markets, and prevent developers from recouping their investments. Statutes

---

[20] See, for example, Garrett Epps, *Wising Up: "Son of Sam" Laws and the Speech and Press Clauses*, 70 NC L Rev 493 (1992); Note, 66 Notre Dame L Rev 1075 (cited in note 14); Note, *Have Courts Intruded on First Amendment Guarantees in Their Zeal to Insure that Crime Does Not Pay*, 11 Loyola Entertainment L J 505 (1991); Note, *Crime Doesn't Pay—Or Does It? Simon & Schuster v. Fischetti*, 65 St John's L Rev 981 (1991). The due process argument that the Court never reached is considered in Note, *Compensating the Victim from the Proceeds of the Criminal's Story—The Constitutionality of the New York Approach*, 14 Colum J L & Soc Probs 93 (1978); Note, *Criminals Turned Authors: Victims Rights v. Freedom of Speech*, 54 Ind L J 443 (1978).

such as Florida's, that prohibit direct molding but not traditional methods of copying, therefore strike a nice balance between public and private interests. They allow the public to copy new hull designs, but not by a method that puts copyists in an economically advantageous position relative to developers.

On this reasoning, the Court of Appeals for the Federal Circuit had upheld the constitutionality of a similar law from California.[21] But the Supreme Court gave that case, and the economic argument it presented, extremely short shrift. Reasoning that federal policy depends on "substantially free trade in publicly known, unpatented design and utilitarian conceptions,"[22] the Court declared the Federal Circuit opinion "defective," "troubl[ing]," and "puzzling."[23] In its rush to invalidate this modest attempt to spur innovation by assuring developers a profit from their work, the Court left unexplained why the economic argument was wrong, or how adequate incentives could be provided for this industry in the future.

Feist was to the same effect. That case raised the question whether copying a telephone subscriber directory was actionable infringement under the Copyright Act. Because the evidence of wholesale copying was uncontrovertible, the case came down to deciding whether the directory was copyrightable. The Court held it was not. Although the Act protects compilations,[24] the white pages did not meet the definitional test of an "original work of authorship."[25] The data included in the directory were facts and therefore not original to the compiler, and the alphabetical arrangement was not creative enough to qualify as authorship. And, perhaps to avoid an attempt by Congress to alter the statute to encompass these works, the Court made clear that the facts and arrangement were also not the "writings" of "authors" under the Copyright Clause,[26] implying that the Constitution requires that fact works arranged along standard organizational principles must remain in the public domain.

Absent from the opinion, once again, was any consideration of the implications of this holding for future production of fact works.

---

[21] *Interpart Corp. v Italia,* 777 F2d 678 (Fed Cir 1985).

[22] *Bonito Boats,* 489 US at 156.

[23] Id at 163, 164, 165.

[24] 17 USC § 103.

[25] See *Feist,* 111 S Ct at 1293–94; 17 USC § 101.

[26] 111 S Ct at 1288–90.

The plaintiff had, of course, made the argument that compiling accurate factual directories was an expensive proposition and sunk costs would not be recoverable if free riders could outcompete developers in the marketplace.[27] Indeed, the Association of American Publishers, whose amicus brief was specifically cited in *Simon & Schuster*, had presented the incentives argument in *Feist* as well.[28] The Court, however, firmly rejected the "sweat of the brow" and "industrious collection" doctrines, which considered investment as an important reason to recognize copyright protection.[29] Equating attempts to protect "sweat" with attempts to monopolize the underlying facts,[30] the Court easily reached the conclusion that "sweat" works could not, as a constitutional matter, be copyrighted.

Admittedly, the Court's omission of any discussion of incentives in *Feist* and *Bonito Boats* was not entirely implausible. In a very influential article, Stephen Breyer had questioned the value of copyright (and, by extension, other intellectual property protection), suggesting that the market system contained other mechanisms to assure adequate levels of investment in innovation.[31]

---

[27] *Feist*, Brief for Respondent at 37–38.

[28] *Feist*, Brief of the Association of American Publishers on behalf of Rural Telephone at 5. This claim was also forcefully presented in an amicus brief filed in support of neither party by the Information Industry Association and ADAPSO. This group, which includes manufacturers of copying technology, made the novel argument that innovation in *reproductive technology* is also inhibited by the failure to protect developers against copyists. The experience of DAT technology supports this position. See, for example, Stephen Levine, *The Digital Duel Could Be Ending; Manufacturers, Music Industry Reach Pact*, Wash Post B8 (July 11, 1991).

[29] The term "sweat of the brow" has been in use at least since *Amsterdam v Triangle Publications, Inc.*, 189 F2d 104 (3d Cir 1951), usually as a ground for *recognizing* the protectability of fact works. See, for example, *Schroeder v William Morrow & Co.*, 566 F2d 3 (7th Cir 1977). Interestingly, the Supreme Court seemed to have juxtaposed "sweat" (and its mate, "industry") against "creativity" and "imagination" as a means for *denying* protection.

[30] 111 S Ct at 1291. The Court did, however, acknowledge that it "may seem unfair" to fail to compensate the compiler. Id at 1289–90.

[31] Stephen Breyer, *The Uneasy Case for Copyright: A Study of Copyright in Books, Photocopies, and Computer Programs*, 84 Harv L Rev 281 (1970); Stephen Breyer, *Copyright: A Rejoinder*, 20 UCLA L Rev 75 (1975). It should be noted that the subsequent literature suggests the extent of other incentives is overstated, see, for example, Barry Tyerman, *The Economic Rationale for Copyright Protection for Published Books: A Reply to Professor Breyer*, 18 UCLA L Rev 1100 (1971), unlikely to be right across the full range of fields that rely on intellectual property rights, compare Robert P. Merges and Richard R. Nelson, *On the Complex Economics of Patent Scope*, 90 Colum L Rev 839, 880 (1990), or untrue now that the technology of copying has improved, see, for example, William M. Landes and Richard A. Posner, *An Economic Analysis of Copyright Law*, 18 J Legal Stud 325 (1989). My argument, however, is that even if Breyer is generally correct, production at the margin remains a key concern. So long as exclusive rights are used to motivate the creation of some works, excluding targeted classes of material raises problems.

Breyer argued that costs can often be recouped before the copyist enters the market, or captured through enduring first-mover advantages. He also thought private arrangements, including consortia to produce needed works and retributive measures to punish free riders, protected incentives. And in truth, the facts of *Bonito Boats* and *Feist* bear out his views. Since copyists want only those innovative hull designs that prove to be commercially successful, boat designers probably do have some lead time. Significantly, the boat hull at issue in *Bonito Boats* was developed before the Florida statute went into effect.[32] In *Feist*, the subscriber lists were actually by-products of the plaintiff's telephone service business, making the costs of development so low that it is difficult to believe they could not be recouped, even in a competitive market. In addition, because state law required all telephone companies to publish directories, *Feist* was actually evidence that consortia (in this case, subscribers) can, in fact, organize to induce the right level of production.[33]

At first blush, then, it may seem possible to reconcile these three cases—*Bonito Boats*, *Feist*, and *Simon & Schuster*—on the theory that profit protection is important only in the absence of other indicia of sufficient motivation. But in fact, that position is untenable, for precisely the same claims about incentives could have been (and were) made about *Wiseguy*. People write for a variety of reasons, many of which are unrelated to financial considerations. They may wish to contribute to the cultural heritage, to forge links to others, to satisfy their own aesthetic sense, to establish their reputation, or provoke others.[34] Criminals also have special motivations. Public apology and acceptance of responsibilty may expiate guilt. Alternatively, writers can reventilate claims of innocence, urge others to help find the true perpetrator, and alert the public to problems within the criminal justice system.[35] Some may simply wish to brag or kill time. Certainly, the Supreme Court is no stranger to

---

[32] *Bonito Boats*, 489 US at 144. Compare Constance Holden, *MIT Techies Help Keep the America's Cup*, 256 Science 1277 (1992) (discussing noneconomic incentives).

[33] *Feist*, 111 S Ct at 1286.

[34] Rochelle C. Dreyfuss, *The Creative Employee and the Copyright Act of 1976*, 54 U Chi L Rev 590, 606–10 (1987); Thomas I. Emerson, *Toward a General Theory of the First Amendment*, 72 Yale L J 877 (1963).

[35] See H. Bruce Franklin, *Prison Literature in America* (Oxford University Press, 1989); Jack Henry Abbott, *American Prison Writing and the Experience of Punishment*, 10 Crim Just & Behav 441 (1983); *Feist*, Brief for Respondent Crime Victims Board at 30–33.

the concept of the voluntary confession; such scenarios are regular features of the Fifth Amendment docket.[36]

Notwithstanding Simon & Schuster's claims to the contrary,[37] *Wiseguy* seems a prime example of a book that might have been written anyway. Hill apparently approached Pileggi with the idea, perhaps to revive his days of quasi-celebrity.[38] Apparently, he was willing to invest his efforts well before he received, or could be sure of, any compensation at all.[39] And, since the statute did not run to Pileggi's royalties or Simon & Schuster's returns, it posed no barrier to recapturing the costs of creating, manufacturing, and disseminating the work. Furthermore, the statute did not really strip Hill of any financial incentives. It created no new cause of action.[40] It would have done no more with his earnings than *any* honest writer would do: it would have distributed them to his creditors. Granted, the regulation imposed its own priority, but Hill's attorneys had first preference and after five years, Hill would have gained full control over undistributed funds.[41]

Simon & Schuster must, therefore, be read as holding that even if there is reason to believe that innovation will occur in the absence of royalties, profit-stripping regulations are nonetheless problematic; that the residuum of creators who may be deterred from producing are a source of concern. The question, then, is why does this effect on production at the margin amount to an unconstitutional burden?

---

[36] See, for example, *Illinois v Perkins*, 496 US 292 (1990); *Moran v Burbine*, 474 US 412 (1986); *Hoffa v United States*, 385 US 436 (1986).

[37] *Feist*, Brief for Petitioner at 7.

[38] See note 12; Pileggi, *Wiseguy* at 13, 15, 24, 36, 42, 68, 167, 283, 289 (cited in note 12).

[39] According to the contract, no funds were owed until the manuscript was accepted for publication. *Simon & Schuster*, Joint Appendix at 56. While advances are customary in the industry, Hill apparently received his first distribution 3 years after the contract was signed. Id.

[40] An interesting comparison is provided by the substitute legislation New York is currently considering. This statute would not reach the profits from a criminal's work. Instead, it would lengthen the statute of limitation on victims' claims. See Bruce Webber, *Lawyer in Shooting Case Offers Girl's Story for Bail*, NY Times B4 col 5 (June 9, 1992).

[41] Some state laws struck down by *Simon & Schuster* even provided for the support of the criminal's dependants. See, for example, Fla Stat Ann § 944.512(2)(a) (West, 1992); Note, *Criminals Selling Their Stories: The First Amendment Requires Legislative Re-examination*, 72 Cornell L Rev 1331 (1978). See generally Sue S. Okuda, *Criminal Antiprofits Laws: Some Thoughts in Favor of Their Constitutionality*, 76 Cal L Rev 1353 (1989).

B. BURDEN

In some ways, the most surprising aspect of *Simon & Schuster* is the jump from recognizing the (apparently elusive) relationship between profits and production to finding a burden on speech. Although the Supreme Court labeled the Son of Sam law content-based discrimination,[42] the statute did not, as the District Court recognized, bear any of the traditional indicia of this First Amendment problem. It betrayed no hostility to speech, nor did it attempt to reduce its impact. Unlike, for example, a taxing statute that levies on activities indispensible to printing information, or a labor law that interferes with dissemination activities, this provision did not in any way diminish a criminal author's capacity to deliver a message.[43] Because it protected the profits of agents, publishers, and ghost writers, the statute affected none of the elements that criminal authors might require in order to move along the publication pipeline; any manuscript submitted would have the same chance of being disseminated and publicized as any other work.[44] Indeed, the legislature appears to have taken great care to make sure that books written by criminals would be successful, perhaps in the hope that profits would then be available to compensate victims and creditors.

Nor was the statute aimed at suppressing particular viewpoints. It applied to material celebrating a life of crime as well as to tracts demonstrating how little crime pays and how much criminals suffer; to works advocating civil disobedience as well as violent revolution. It applied to the hardcore offender and the reformed criminal; as the Supreme Court noted, it could have reached Henry Hill,

---

[42] *Simon & Schuster*, 113 S Ct at 508.

[43] A few comparisons may be useful here. One is *Minneapolis Star v Minnesota Commr. of Rev.*, 460 US 575 (1983), which invalidated a use tax on paper and ink. Since that statute changed the costs of producing printed matter, it posed the danger of reducing the total amount of material that a publisher would print, and thereby decreased the chances that any particular work would be published. In contrast, the Son of Sam law made no changes in the costs facing the *publisher*. Similarly, in *Meyer v Grant*, 486 US 414 (1988), and *Buckley v Valeo*, 424 US 1 (1979), attempts were made to control the funds available in the dissemination phase. Since the Son of Sam law had no effect on distribution or advertising expenditures, it could not affect the impact that a published work would have on the public.

[44] It should be noted that Simon & Schuster claimed that the idea to write *Wiseguy* was its own, and that the statute undermined its ability to have it written because it became impossible to adequately compensate Hill. But this is a claim that the law affected Simon & Schuster in its role as author, not in its role as publisher. Furthermore, the accuracy of this scenario can be questioned. See note 12.

David Berkowitz, Jean Harris, Mark David Chapman, R. Foster Winans, Malcolm X, Saint Augustine, Henry David Thoreau, Emma Goldman, Martin Luther King, Jr., Sir Walter Raleigh, Jesse Jackson, and Bertrand Russell.[45]

Since the statute was not the product of an improper motive, such as hostility to the genre of criminal writing, or to a particular viewpoint within that genre, and did not affect the impact of the expression of criminals, then the free speech problem must arise from some other source. The Supreme Court never specified the nature of its concern, but presumably it was the problem that Geoffrey Stone has labeled distortion.[46] Unlike laws of general applicability, which affect a wide swath of works in essentially unpredictable ways, this statute changed the incentive structure for a particular category, giving rise to the probability that a gap in the domain of knowledge would result. As Judge Newman noted in his Second Circuit dissent, if nothing else, the statute might lead publishers of books tangentially related to crime to "purge manuscripts of all material arguably within the scope of the statute."[47] Possibly, the effect would be much greater. Faced with a choice of what to write (or which opportunity to take up), some people subject to the statute might choose to write on themes other than their crimes.[48]

To be sure, the lacuna created by Son of Sam would not be a gap in viewpoint. Thus, *Simon & Schuster* must be understood as deeming problematic a mere alteration in the mix of works reaching the marketplace. The content of the storehouse of knowledge—the proportion of works dedicated to particular topics—must itself be considered a message. The problem in the Son of Sam law is that,

---

[45] *Simon & Schuster*, 112 S Ct at 506, 511. For comparison, consider the statute at issue in *Texas v Johnson*, 109 S Ct 2533 (1989), which was aimed at suppressing flag burning—symbolic speech antagonistic to the United States. See also *Leathers v Medlock*, 111 S Ct 1438, 1443–45 (1991) (distinguishing between regulations that target on the basis of viewpoint and those that do not).

[46] Geoffrey R. Stone, *Restrictions on Speech Because of Its Content: The Peculiar Case of Subject-Matter Restrictions*, 46 U Chi L Rev 81, 101 (1978); Geoffrey R. Stone, *Content-Neutral Restrictions*, 54 U Chi L Rev 46, 55 (1987).

[47] *Simon & Schuster*, 916 F2d at 787 (Newman dissenting).

[48] Again, it is instructive to compare this legislation to the substitute provision currently pending in New York, see note 40, which would subject all a criminal's assets to claims by a victim. While this law might persuade some people to do nothing after conviction, it would not affect the motivation of anyone who does decide to work. Accordingly, it does not have the same distortive impact.

in effect, the statute turns this message into a lie. Furthermore, because the problem is so subtle, it may be difficult to discern the point at which the disincentives begin actually to deprive the marketplace of particular viewpoints.[49] Whether the First Amendment is conceived as principally protection for a democratic system of self-government,[50] or a broader-based assurance of autonomy for individuals,[51] its values are compromised by any rule that distorts the storehouse of knowledge by reducing the economic incentives to write targeted classes of works.

Under this analysis, *Feist* and *Bonito Boats* are quite puzzling. While *Feist* concerned only the question whether compilations of facts were "writings" and *Bonito Boats* was directed at the protection of a functional object clearly outside the ambit of the First Amendment, collectively these cases constitutionalize a series of doctrines that limit the capacity of government to create profit-incentives in information products. For example, the fact/expression dichotomy doctrine, which states that copyright protects only expression, not the facts expressed, diminishes the ability of government to protect profits in factual works wholly lacking an expressive dimension.[52] The merger doctrine takes this one step further by deeming even expressive works unprotectable if the underlying facts can be expressed in only a limited number of ways.[53] It is true that these doctrines safeguard access to materials needed to speak, and thus can be said to be in aid of the First Amendment. But as soon as *Simon & Schuster* shifts the focus of the First Amendment from the speaker to the audience, they become problematic. Factual works such as biographies and directories, and functional products, such as computer programs, are surely as important to First Amendment

---

[49] Or, as Stone put it, viewpoint-neutral restrictions can have viewpoint-differential effects. Stone, 46 U Chi L Rev at 110 (cited in note 46), citing *First Natl. Bank v Bellotti*, 435 US 765, 784–86 (1978).

[50] Alexander Meiklejohn, *The First Amendment Is an Absolute*, 1961 Supreme Court Review 245; Harry Kalven, Jr., *The New York Times Case: A Note on the "Central Meaning of the First Amendment,"* 1964 Supreme Court Review 191.

[51] David A. Strauss, *Persuasion, Autonomy and Freedom of Expression*, 91 Colum L Rev 334 (1991).

[52] See 17 USC § 102. Compare *Zacchini v Scripps-Howard Broadcasting Co.*, 433 US 562 (1977) (explaining the First Amendment significance of honoring proprietary interest in expression while permitting public use of the material expressed).

[53] See, for example, 17 USC § 101 (pictorial, graphic, and sculptural works can be protected "only if, and only to the extent that, such design incorporates . . . features that can be identified separately from, and are capable of existing independently of, the utilitarian aspects of the article"); *Baker v Selden*, 101 US 99 (1879).

values as books about crime, yet *Feist* (combined with *Bonito Boats*) seems to leave little room for motivating people to produce them. Thus, *Feist* and *Bonito Boats* generate the same kind of gaps in the storehouse of knowledge that *Simon & Schuster* found to be constitutionally suspect.

II. FEIST AND BONITO BOATS REVISITED

Simon & Schuster, in short, puts the question of incentives back on the table, raising the question why, if gaps in the storehouse of knowledge are an important concern and evenhandedness a significant value, the legal system would take such a firm position against protecting fact and functional works. The justifications usually cited can be divided (rather roughly) into two categories: the first is that these works are of too little value to merit protection; the second is that they are of too much value to be protected. Aside from the unattractiveness of building law on inconsistent theories, both sets of arguments tend to fail when tested against the interests recognized in *Simon & Schuster*.

A. TOO VALUELESS

The "too little" justification can be traced to what Jessica Litman and Peter Jaczi call the "romantic" vision of authorship.[54] This is the idea that the operative word in the phrase "intellectual property" is "intellectual." Protected works are those that are the product of deep thought and inspiration; each must, in constitutional language, contribute to the "progress of science and useful arts." Patent law and copyright are hierarchically related through the degree of creativity required for protection. Patent law, with its requirement of nonobviousness,[55] is at the top end, where it provides the highest level of protection—a right to exclude all others, including independent inventors, from making, using, or selling the invention.[56] Copyright protects only against copyists and derivative users[57] because it demands mere originality.[58]

---

[54] Jessica Litman, *Copyright as Myth*, 53 U Pitt L Rev 235 (1991); Peter Jaszi, *Toward a Theory of Copyright: The Metamorphoses of "Authorship,"* 1991 Duke L J 455.

[55] 35 USC § 103.

[56] 35 USC § 271(a).

[57] 17 USC § 106.

[58] 17 USC § 102(a).

Under this approach, fact works and functional products do not qualify for protection because they fall beneath copyrightable works in this hierarchy. Facts are "already out there," and so require no work to create; functional products are dictated by the laws of nature, not the creative input of their producers. Because they are so grounded in the stuff of the real world, producing these works cannot count as "progress." The *Feist* Court's repeated references to "sweat of the brow" make creating such works seem no different from plumbing a sink. Since no one would call a plumber an "author," the legal system should not provide intellectual property protection for the work of a compiler.

There are several problems with this conclusion. Foremost is the fact that many information products are simply not "already out there." Facts, for example, do not always lie around like pipe fittings, waiting to be connected. Determining what the market wants and fashioning a method for conveying the information clearly can require a very high level of ingenuity.[59] Such products can make as significant a contribution to the storehouse of knowledge as any other work, and so merit the evenhanded treatment *Simon & Schuster* requires.

Granted, *Feist* can be read as recognizing the copyrightability of innovatively selected and arranged material.[60] But the level of protection made available is haphazard. The more accurate and comprehensive the work, the more likely it is to run afoul of the spirit of *Feist* (because it is "merely" a compilation), the fact/expression dichotomy (because it lacks an imaginative dimension), or the merger doctrine (because a similarly accurate and comprehensive product could not be expressed much differently). Paradoxically, there is a sense in which the more valuable the work, the less protection the final product will receive.[61] Moreover, in the modern

---

[59] See, for example, Jessica Litman, *The Public Domain*, 39 Emory L J 965, 997 (1990). Exactly this type of creativity is protected by patent law. See, for example, *Eibel Process Co. v Minnesota & Ontario Paper Co.*, 261 US 45, 67–68 (1923) ("The invention was not the mere use of a high or substantial pitch to remedy a known source of trouble. It was the discovery of the source not before known. . . ."); *United States v Adams*, 383 US 39, 51–52 (1966) ("Despite the fact that each of the elements of Adams battery was well known in the prior art, to combine them as did Adams required that a person reasonably skilled in the prior art must ignore . . . long accepted factors. . . .").

[60] *Feist*, 111 S Ct at 1289.

[61] An example is furnished by *Kregos v Associated Press*, 937 F2d 700 (2d Cir 1991), which concerned the application of *Feist* to a newspaper pitching form. The form used information such as starting pitchers' seasonal won/lost record, seasonal earned run average, record

age of computers, the particulars of arrangement do not always matter; copyists who avoid the arrangement and use only the facts may escape infringement.[62] Protection that is so unpredictable, that fails to reflect the value of what is produced or the effort expended in producing it, that actually increases the level of protection as the work becomes less comprehensive, accurate, and usable, cannot be providing the right incentives.

Furthermore, the truth is that even plumbers get paid. Especially in cases in which the fundamentals—conceptualizing the field, creating user-friendly classifications—are well understood, information products lack the intellectual challenges that produce psychic benefits. Pecuniary gain is therefore fairly unambiguously the major source of motivation. Derogatory labels, such as "industrious collection" and "sweat," do not make it any easier for those who have sunk considerable costs into information products to compete with cheap copyists, recoup costs, or earn profits.[63]

More important, putting certain works down to "sweat" and "industry" proves too much. For the most part, the only thing of financial value that copyright protects is labor. Ideas are rather cheaply conceived; what takes time is articulating and arranging them.[64] And, ideas are not what is protected; copyright subsists only in expression.[65] Thus, for even the most artistic, creative, and

---

against the opposing team, and record on-site, to calculate the odds on daily games. The district court found the variation in statistics that could be used for predictive purposes limited, and held the forms unprotectable. It was only because the Court of Appeals did not believe these choices to be the universal, comprehensive bases for predicting outcomes that it reversed the decision and found the forms copyrightable. The court emphasized that protection would not be available "[w]here a selection of data is the first step in an analysis that yields a precise result or even a better-than-average probability of some result." Id at 707.

[62] See, for example, *Warren Publishing, Inc. v Microdos Data Corp.*, 1992 WL 235745 (ND Ga 1992). Jane Ginsburg notes that producers may be tempted to be less comprehensive, less efficient, and less accurate in order to raise the level of protection they receive. See Ginsburg, 92 Colum L Rev at 347 (cited in note 4).

[63] If a comparison is useful, consider *Boston Professional Hockey Assn. v Dallas Cap & Emblem Mfrg.*, 510 F2d 1004 (5th Cir), cert denied, 423 US 868 (1975), and *Midler v Ford Motor Co.*, 849 F2d 460 (9th Cir 1988), which involve attempts to capture consumer surplus (in logos and singing styles). Since these quasi-trademark and publicity claims do not rely on theories about incentives or cost recoupment (which are provided by the principal businesses of the plaintiffs), nothing said here applies. For reasons stated in Rochelle C. Dreyfuss, *Expressive Genericity: Trademarks as Language in the Pepsi Generation*, 65 Notre Dame L Rev 397 (1990), any clash between the First Amendment and these claims should be resolved in favor of denying protection.

[64] Landes and Posner, 18 J Legal Stud at 348 (cited in note 31).

[65] 17 USC § 102(b).

imaginative work, copyright protection extends only to that portion of the work that is the product of the industriously sweating brow. This is especially evident with regard to copyright in derivative works, such as translations. The intellectual challenge will often lie in creating the material on which the derivative work is based, yet copyright is nonetheless available to protect that which the derivative user contributes.[66]

Perhaps because the laborious aspect of the work is always the part that is copyrightable, many courts, before *Feist*, had little trouble bringing information products into the scope of intellectual property protection.[67] And perhaps because it is so clear that there is still a need to provide this incentive to labor, even after *Feist*, the lower courts have, with a few exceptions,[68] stretched to find some way to offer a modicum of protection to information products.[69]

---

[66] See Landes and Posner, 18 J Legal Stud at 353–57 (cited in note 31). An example of concern for the industrious labor of middlemen is *Mills Music, Inc. v Snyder*, 469 US 153 (1985). Much the same can be said of patent law, for protection requires not only conception, but also the far sweatier activity of reducing the invention to practice. See 35 USC § 102(g). See also 35 USC §§ 200–12, which create patent rights in inventions discovered with federal funds on the theory that exclusivity is needed to encourage the (sweaty) activities required for commercialization. See 132 Cong Rec S11100-02 (August 9, 1986). A discussion of this issue is provided by Edward Samuels, *The Idea-Expression Dichotomy in Copyright Law*, 56 Tenn L Rev 321, 435 (1989).

[67] See, for example, *Emerson v Davies*, 8 F Cas 615 (CCD Mass 1845) (No 4436); *International News Service v Associated Press*, 248 US 215 (1918); *Jeweler's Circular Publishing Co. v Keystone Publishing Co.*, 274 Fed 932 (2d Cir 1921) (Learned Hand), cert denied, 259 US 581 (1922). See also Eaton S. Drone, *A Treatise on the Law of Property and Intellectual Productions in Great Britain and the United States* 210 (Little, Brown, 1879); Ginsburg, 90 Colum L Rev at 1873–93 (cited in note 4). Compare Richard A. Epstein, *International News Service v. Associated Press: Custom and Law as Sources of Proprietary Rights in News*, 78 Va L Rev 85 (1992) (using customs in the newspaper industry as a basis for arguing that factual information requires some level of protection).

[68] *Illinois Bell v Hanes & Co.*, 932 F2d 610 (7th Cir 1991) posed precisely the same factual scenario as *Feist* and was decided the same way. See also *Victor Lalli v Big Red Apple*, 936 F2d 671 (2d Cir 1991) (racing forms); *Sem-Torg, Inc. v K Mart Corp.*, 936 F2d 851 (6th Cir 1991) (sets of road signs); *Project Development Group v O.H. Materials Corp.*, 766 F Supp 1348 (WD Pa 1991) (bid proposal); *NADA v CCC Info.*, 1991 WL 287961 (ND Ill) (used car guide). With the exception of *NADA*, which was decided only with respect to preliminary relief, even here, there were other reasons to deny protection: the racing form in *Victor Lalli* was of a format used by all publishers within the industry, and thus was not an original compilation of the plaintiff; the bid proposal in *Project Development* was provided by the contractor, not the plaintiff/bidder; the signs in *Sem-Torg* were not packaged or sold as compilations.

[69] See *Kregos*, 937 F2d 800, and *Warren Publishing*, 1992 WL 235745, discussed in notes 61–62; *Atari Games Corp. v Oman*, 979 F2d 242 (D.C. Cir 1992) ("Breakout" game copyrightable despite use of standard shapes and colors). *Key Publications v Chinatown Today Publ. Ent.*, 945 F2d 509 (2d Cir 1991) (distinguishing *Feist* to find sufficient originality in yellow

Nor is it insignificant that the Supreme Court has twice before gone down the road of making extravagant pronouncements on the level of ingenuity required for intellectual property protection and each time there was a return to the status quo ante. In *Cuno Engineering Corp. v Automatic Devices Corp.*, the Court announced that inventions were patentable only if they revealed a "flash of creative genius."[70] The decision caused substantial disarray in the lower courts and made patent protection so unpredictable it was considered not useful.[71] The Patent Act was then recodified with a new section returning the law to the pre-*Cuno* standard,[72] and eventually the Supreme Court retreated as well.[73] Similarly, in *Sears Roebuck & Co. v Stiffel Co.*[74] and *Compco Corp. v Day Brite Lighting, Inc.*,[75] the Court ruled that works that did not measure up to the level of protection required by patent and copyright law could not be protected by the states. Those decisions led to cries of anguish from industry,[76] were narrowed extensively by the lower courts,[77] and until revived by *Bonito Boats*, seemed to have been implicitly overruled.[78]

Cuno, *Sears*, and *Compco* were apparently motivated by the perception that works of "too little" value were being accorded intellec-

---

page directories to support copyright); *Corsearch, Inc. v Thomson & Thomson*, 792 F Supp 305 (SDNY 1992) (trademark data base); *Penelope v Brown*, 792 F Supp 132 (D Mass) (examples of syntax copyrightable but fair used); *Armond Budish v Harley Gordon*, 784 F Supp 1320 (ND Ohio 1992) (medicaid tables); *Lipton v Nature Co.*, 781 F Supp 1032 (SDNY 1992) (chart of venery terms); *Allen-Myland v IBM*, 770 F Supp 1004 (ED Pa 1991) (computer code); *Apple v Microsoft + Hewlett Packard*, 779 F Supp 133 (ND Cal 1991) (computer program). Congress has been active in this area as well. See note 105.

[70] 314 US 84, 91 (1941).

[71] Edmund W. Kitch, *Graham v. John Deere Co.: New Standards for Patents*, 1966 Supreme Court Review 293.

[72] See 35 USC § 103.

[73] *Graham v John Deere Co.*, 383 US 1 (1966).

[74] 376 US 225 (1964).

[75] 376 US 234 (1964).

[76] See, for example, *Product Simulation: A Right or a Wrong?*, 64 Colum L Rev 1178 (1964).

[77] See, for example, *Application of World's Finest Chocolate, Inc.*, 474 F2d 1012 (CCPA 1973); *Fotomat Corp. v Photo Drive-Thru, Inc.*, 425 F Supp 693 (DNJ 1977); *Fotomat v Cochran*, 437 F Supp 1231 (D Kan 1977).

[78] See *Goldstein v California*, 412 US 546 (1973) (upholding California law protecting sound recordings from copying prior to their coverage within federal copyright); *Kewanee Oil Co. v Bicron Corp.*, 416 US 470 (1974) (enforcing trade secret claim on invention falling within the scope of patent law). See generally Rochelle C. Dreyfuss, *Dethroning Lear: Licensee Estoppel and the Incentive to Innovate*, 72 Va L Rev 677 (1986).

tual property protection; that "progress" requires more.[79] Their abandonment recognized that "progress" is sometimes made in small jumps and sometimes in large leaps, that it is difficult to assess the value of any particular contribution at the time that it is made, and that even if individual works contribute little, the Constitution is satisfied so long as the regime *as a whole* moves knowledge further. The advantages of a system that creates predictable promises of remuneration is evident as soon as the nexus between incentives and production is fully appreciated.[80]

B. TOO VALUABLE

The "too much" view stems from a more prosaic perspective that puts its emphasis on the "property" part of "intellectual property."[81] Under this approach, there is no such thing as originality: everything is an amalgam of what went before; creation is a synonym for infringement. However, some contributions are more important than others. Fact and functional material, like principles of nature, are the building blocks upon which the "progress of science and useful arts" depends. As such, this material belongs in the public domain. Again, patent and copyright can be thought of as hierarchically related, but this time information products are at the top. If protectable at all, they must pass through the examination procedure required by the Patent Act[82] and be disclosed pursuant to its specification provisions.[83] That way, the public is sure to get its money's worth from the monopoly provided and the Patent Office guarantees that works of the highest importance remain unprotected.

As applied to raw ideas, this theory actually works well. So long as they are not enshrouded in the costly process of articulation and arrangement, ideas do not require heavy financial investments.

---

[79] See also *Great Atlantic & Pacific Tea Co. v Supermarket Equip. Corp.*, 340 US 147, 154 (1950) (Douglas dissenting) ("The invention, to justify a patent, has to . . . push back the frontiers of chemistry, physics, and the like; to make a distinctive contribution to scientific knowledge.").

[80] See also Robert A. Gorman, *Copyright Protection for the Collection and Representation of Facts*, 76 Harv L Rev 1569 (1963).

[81] This view is also nicely presented in Litman, 39 Emory L J at 1004–12 (cited in note 59).

[82] 35 USC §§ 131–54.

[83] 35 USC §§ 112–15.

Whatever sunk costs there are will be captured when the producer markets an application. When ideas are left free, the losses associated with rent seeking are avoided, as is the tracing problem that would be created if appropriating nonarticulated and unarranged ideas were actionable.[84] Most important, unfettered access to ideas lowers the costs of producing downstream works. Although in theory, multiple uses of the same idea represent a waste of creative resources, good ideas can be exploited in ways that appeal to different markets. It is doubtful, for example, that anyone would consider *West Side Story* a social loss because it relies on the same theme as *Romeo and Juliet*. And since different markets are involved, there is little danger that competition will weaken incentives.

But fact and functional works do not fit this mold at all. Facts are expensive to collect, arrange, and disseminate. That they are more valuable to the "progress of science" than other works is no reason to stop worrying about incentives and cost recoupment. It may be true that protecting works that involve more labor than intellectual prowess stimulates rent seeking, but the problem does not seem different in magnitude from the experience in patent law.[85] And somewhat surprisingly, because of practices such as seeding—intentionally adding irrelevant material—tracing[86] is

---

[84] One explanation for the requirements of concreteness and novelty in the law of ideas is that they create an evidentiary trail to the originator. See, for example, *Lueddecke v Chevrolet Motor Co.*, 70 F2d 345 (8th Cir 1934).

[85] In patent law, the nonobviousness requirement theoretically protects against supraoptimal efforts by ordinary artisans. But patentability is not "negatived by the manner in which the invention [is] made," 35 USC § 103; inventions made through trial and error—in other words, sweat—are therefore patentable, so long as the end product is not too obvious. See, for example, *In re Dillon*, 919 F2d 688 (Fed Cir 1990) (en banc) (discussing the standard for deciding what constitutes motivation to try).

[86] For example, in *Feist*, the defendant had duplicated four of the fictitious listings plaintiff had introduced to detect copying. 111 S Ct at 1287. For a software example, see *Apple Computer v Franklin Computer Corp.*, 714 F2d 1240 (3d Cir 1983), cert denied, 464 US 1033 (1984), where the defendant had duplicated two words intentionally embedded in Apple's computer code. See also *Hassenfeld Bros., Inc. v Mego Corp.*, 150 USPQ 786 (SDNY 1966) (defendant's toy soldier was demonstrably not based on a genuine soldier because it reproduced the same misplaced thumbnail as plaintiff's doll).

Despite the prevalence of these practices, some of the cases hostile to finding fact-based works copyrightable appear to have been motivated by concern that an independent will not be able to disprove copying. For example, in *Gracen v Bradford Exchange*, 698 F2d 300, 304 (7th Cir 1983), the court stated:

Suppose Artist A produces a reproduction of the Mona Lisa . . . which differs slightly from the original. B also makes a reproduction of the Mona Lisa. A, who has copyrighted his derivative work, sues B for infringement. . . . [I]f the difference between the original and A's reproduction is slight, the difference between A's

rarely an issue. In fact, in most information product cases, copying is apparently conceded.[87]

The main argument for putting original information products into the public domain is therefore to lower the costs of producing downstream works. In its noneconomic guise, this is the claim that the First Amendment requires free access to facts and to the realities of nature; that without free access, speakers would be barred (or deterred) from discussing the world around them. The *Feist* Court, for example, spoke of copyright in fact compilations as extending protection "to the facts themselves,"[88] and *Bonito Boats* referred often to the "public's ability to exploit."[89]

But this perception is a fallacy. The issue in these cases was copying, not using. Even if these materials had been protected, the information itself would have remained in the public domain; anyone could have retrieved it in exactly the way that the first mover did, and even ridden free on the first mover's method of using it.[90] True, it is always cheaper to take information than to find it anew, but the guarantee of "free" speech means only free of government interference; it does not mean costless.[91] Under an anti-copying regime, the public is no worse off than it is if the first use and its associated intellectual property right did not exist.[92] In fact, the

---

and B's reproductions will also be slight, so that if B had access to A's reproductions the trier of fact will be hard-pressed to decide whether B was copying A or copying the Mona Lisa itself.

Actually, the burden of proof is on A. Absent testimony that B had copied, if B did not reproduce a palpable variation introduced by A, A's case would be dismissed. Although it might appear silly to require B to figure out what was wrong with A's picture, the rule makes economic sense because so long as A is clever, the costs of finding the error will be comparable to the cost of creating anew. A and B will compete on a level playing field, which is all A can ask. (And if A wants that much, A should know to be that clever.)

[87] Examples include *Corsearch*, 792 F Supp 305; *Penelope*, 792 F Supp 132; *Armond Budish*, 784 F Supp 1320; and *NADA*, 1991 WL 287961. These cases are discussed in notes 68–69.

[88] *Feist*, 111 S Ct at 1291.

[89] *Bonito Boats*, 489 US at 167; see also id at 153, 156, 158, 159–60, 163.

[90] For example, even if direct molding were prohibited, anyone could measure the dimensions of a new boat hull and build a copy by traditional methods. That person would have full use of the new design, but at a price comparable to that of the original designer. See John Shepard Wiley, Jr., *Bonito Boats: Uninformed but Mandatory Innovation Policy*, 1989 Supreme Court Review 283.

[91] See, for example, *Cohen v Cowles Media Co.*, 111 S Ct 2513, 2519 (1991) (First Amendment does not allow reporters to breach contracts with informers).

[92] See Bruce W. Bugbee, *Genesis of American Patent and Copyright Law* 7 (Pubic Affairs Press, 1967).

public is likely to be better off because the property right is a relatively cheap mechanism for spreading the costs of production among all potential users. And to the extent that the first person discovers a niche—a database no one ever considered assembling, for example—the public is much better off for the effort.[93]

For a noneconomist, refuting the economic version of this argument is somewhat more difficult. Landes and Posner's work on copyright conceives of works as combinations of existing and original materials.[94] Since the cost of producing new works increases as the level of property rights associated with the existing material is raised, there is a limit to how much increasing protection will increase output. That is, there is an optimal level of protection that balances the benefit of improving incentives upstream against the burden of raising costs downstream.[95] Protection should be denied to ideas and facts because these are the elements that are most needed by subsequent creators.[96]

As noted above, this analysis works well with ideas, but it needs refinement with respect to facts. Thus, Landes and Posner's model treats a new work and a copy as distinct entities. When the works are imaginative, this distinction is clear. Because copyright protects expression, to be noninfringing, a work constructed on the same idea will necessarily be expressed differently. Going back to *Romeo and Juliet: West Side Story* used its plot, and since plots are considered ideas,[97] it was freely appropriable even if the play were copyright-protected. The musical was therefore somewhat cheaper to

---

[93] The emergence of data bases of tenants who have sued their landlords is a good example. See *Tenant Screening Program Offered*, Chi Trib E1 (Nov. 20, 1988); Simson L. Garfinkel, *From Database to Blacklist*, Christian Science Monitor 12 (August 1, 1990). Prior to the development of these bases, it is doubtful that many landlords perceived the advantage of knowing whether potential tenants had ever been to housing court. Even if one had, it is not likely that the benefit that person could realize would outweigh the costs of compiling the data. Absent some form of intellectual property protection, the transaction costs of identifying, contacting, and negotiating with other landlords would be too high to make such a project feasible. It is therefore the promise of copyright (or some other mechanism for protecting profits) that makes the possibility of such a compilation a reality. But note that under an anti-copying regime, every landlord would remain free to use the *idea* of considering the litigation activity of applicants, and could avoid paying tribute to the compiler by investigating filings independently.

[94] Landes and Posner, 18 J Legal Stud at 332 (cited in note 31).

[95] Id at 335.

[96] Id at 347–53.

[97] See, for example, *Nichols v Universal Pictures Corp.*, 45 F2d 119 (2d Cir 1930), cert denied, 282 US 902 (1931).

create. Output increased, so denying protection to the plot made sense.

But what happens when the works are factual? Now consider a book containing tables of Medicaid requirements in each of the fifty states.[98] The facts and arrangements are available for free and a second compiler appropriates them to create a second book containing tables of Medicaid requirements in each of the fifty states. There are two different authors, so each book apparently counts as a "new work" for Landes and Posner. But because there is no expressive element to differentiate these books, the public has not received the benefit of two distinct works. What has happened by denying protection to facts is that incentives are lost with no offsetting increase in output. Worse, the increased availability of fact works relative to expressive material may entice producers to recreate old works rather than devote their resources to producing new ones. Not only are current efforts misdirected, future resources will also be wasted because thorough researchers (of, say, Medicaid practices in the 1990s) will need to review both works. Indeed, the rise in abstracting services and full-text computer searching techniques can be thought of as demonstrating that in some respects, production of information works may be supra-optimal and that a complete analysis of exclusive rights should take into account a pruning function.[99]

Equally important, the crux of *Simon & Schuster* is that society cares about the *mix* of works that is produced. Landes and Posner developed their theory with a model that sums across the entire domain of knowledge. But that is not sufficient. Determining the optimum level of protection requires that output and incentive effects be balanced for every category of work and then normalized across categories. Given that there is no baseline for measuring the ideal mix, this is obviously an impossible task. Nonetheless, it does seem clear that denying protection to some classes of works while making it available to others will create a different mix from a system that offers equivalent protection to all intellectual products.

---

[98] Compare *Armond Budish v Harley Gordon*, 784 F Supp 1320 (ND Ohio 1992).

[99] Compare John J. O'Connor, *TV Weekend; Blythe Danner's Turn as the Troubled Mother*, NY Times C38 col 5 (May 15, 1992) (discussing the propensity of television producers to make docudramas about precisely the same events).

Several counterarguments can be made. First, a system that protects fact and functional works wastes resources because those who choose not to deal with the first mover duplicate earlier efforts. Second, the previous discussion ignores the transaction costs involved in negotiating rights to reuse protected materials. Third, it can be argued that the Medicaid illustration works only because it posits wholesale copying. Actually, works can be reused in a variety of ways. Most downstream uses of information products are "productive"—they create new works that incorporate only selected material. A book on elder care in New York might use the Medicaid tables for New York and combine that information with material about nursing homes and senior citizen programs to create a wholly different book. In that case, leaving the first work unprotected does lower the cost of producing a second, distinct, work.

Most important, despite the right of independents to recreate fact and functional works, the Supreme Court's concern about monopolization is sometimes real. *Feist*, in fact, is an example. That case began when the plaintiff refused to license its directory to the defendant.[100] Since, in the usual case, all independent creators face similar costs, such a refusal generally does no more than force the would-be copyist to start from scratch and compete on a level playing field with the first mover. In *Feist*, however, plaintiff's costs were close to zero because the directory was essentially the same as the plaintiff's billing record. But the costs involved in recreating these facts was extraordinarily high; too high to permit effective competition. Thus, refusing to deal produced a genuine holdup and gave the first mover something quite close to a monopoly.[101]

Nor is this as unusual a problem as might be thought, for there

---

[100] *Feist*, 111 S Ct at 1286.

[101] This concern was echoed in the *Feist* Court's repeated references to Ray Patterson's and Craig Joyce's article on (among other things) *West Publishing Co. v Mead Data Central, Inc.*, 799 F2d 1219 (8th Cir 1986), cert denied, 479 US 1070 (1987). See *Feist*, 111 S Ct at 1288, 1289, 1291, 1296, citing L. Ray Patterson and Craig Joyce, *Monopolizing the Law: The Scope of Copyright Protection for Law Reports and Statutory Compilations*, 36 UCLA L Rev 719 (1989). That case, which involved the copyrightability of the page numbers on which case material appears in West's reporters, potentially presented the same kind of holdup because the numbers were a by-product of West's manufacturing process and would have been extraordinarily costly for Mead Data to recreate. However, in *Feist* the antitrust claims were separately litigated and rejected, *Feist Publications Inc. v Rural Telephone Service Co.*, 957 F2d 765 (10th Cir 1992), cert denied, 113 S Ct 490 (1992).

are productive uses that are in the nature of "comment." That is, second comers use the first work as part of their own reality.[102] A book advocating national health insurance might point to—and quote extensively from—the original work on Medicaid to demonstrate the inadequacies of the current health care system. Or a computer programmer may need some information from an earlier work in order to produce compatible software. Recreation is not an option in these cases, and so protecting the original work could allow the first mover to censor others.[103]

But why is the choice posed as purely bilateral, as between absorbing these costs (in order to provide incentives to the production of fact and functional works) or adversely influencing the mix of works produced (by failing to offer any protection)? A richer theory of intellectual property could easily expand upon these options by viewing the scope of the subject matter qualifying for exclusivity as one parameter among others for mediating between the needs of producers and users. Under this approach, issues such as the scope of infringement, the duration of the right, the contours of defenses, and the availability of remedies would all be regarded as tools for achieving the appropriate balance between up- and downstream users. A wider variety of works could then be protected, and the gaps worrying the *Simon & Schuster* Court filled. In the final analysis, *Feist* may have been correct in rejecting the current copyright statute as the means for protecting information works. But it was nonetheless wrong, and *Bonito Boats* was wrong, to see intellectual property as so impoverished as to require that the nation deny itself all capacity to use exclusive rights to motivate production.[104]

---

[102] A useful way to discuss these concepts was recently proposed by Wendy Gordon, who calls the facts of the actual world Facts$_1$; human depiction of these facts, Facts$_2$; and facts that enter another's reality, "art/facts" or Facts$_{1a}$. Wendy J. Gordon, *Reality as Artifact: From Feist to Fair Use*, 55 L & Contemp Probs 93 (1992).

[103] See, for example, *Sega Enterprises Ltd. v Accolade, Inc.*, 977 F2d 1510, 24 USPQ 2d 1561 (9th Cir 1992); *Maxtone-Graham v Burtchaell*, 803 F2d 1253 (2d Cir 1986), cert denied, 481 US 1059 (1987).

[104] See also Robert A. Gorman, *Fact or Fancy: The Implications for Copyright*, 29 J Copyright Soc 560 (1982); Robert C. Denicola, *Copyright in Collections of Facts: A Theory for the Protection of Nonfiction Literary Works*, 81 Colum L Rev 516 (1981). An interesting example of an attempt to bring a fuller array of tools to the protection of factual works is provided by Leo Raskind, *The Continuing Process of Refining and Adapting Copyright Principles*, 14 Colum-VLA J L & Arts 125 (1990).

III. Protecting Information Products

The difficulty in locating information products on the copyright-patent hierarchy can be grouped with a series of phenomena betraying unease with the traditional dichotomy between copyright and patent, between writings and discoveries, between expressiveness and functionality. Included here are sui generis federal laws creating intermediate levels of protection for new (and some old) technologies,[105] the willingness of courts and scholars to apply principles developed in one branch of the law to problems arising within the other sphere,[106] as well as the rejection of certain rules of thumb of protectability like the blank-form doctrine in copyright and the printed-matter doctrine of patent law.[107] Simply put, advances in production and reproduction make it increasingly clear that the distinctions that seemed to be inherent in the terms "pat-

---

[105] See, for example, Orphan Drug Act, 21 USC §§ 360aa–360ee (creating exclusive rights in known drugs found useful in treating ailments afflicting fewer than 200,000 people); Plant Variety Protection Act, 7 USC §§ 2231–2583 (creating exclusive rights in new sexually reproduced plants); Semiconductor Chip Act, 17 USC §§ 901–14 (creating exclusive rights in original mask works); Amateur Sports Act, 36 USC § 380 (creating private rights in the olympic symbols); 17 USC §§ 102(a)(8), 120 (creating limited copyright in architectural works). Congress is currently considering special protection for industrial designs. See, for example, The Design Innovation and Technology Act of 1991, HR 1790, 102d Cong, 1st Sess (1991). See also Pamela Samuelson, *CONTU Revisited: The Case against Copyright Protection for Computer Programs in Machine-Readable Form*, 1984 Duke L J 663 (suggesting special legislation); Kevin W. O'Connor, *Patenting Animals and Other Living Things*, 65 S Cal L Rev 597 (1991) (discussing protection for animals).

The constitutionality of several of these measures has been questioned post-*Feist*. See, for example, John J. Flynn, *The Orphan Drug Act: An Unconstitutional Exercise of the Patent Power*, 1992 Utah L Rev 389.

[106] For cases, see *Lasercomb America, Inc. v Reynolds*, 911 F2d 970 (4th Cir 1990) (adopting the doctrine of patent misuse to deal with holdup problems in copyright); *United Telephone Co. v Johnson Publishing Co.*, 855 F2d 604 (8th Cir 1988) (same); *United States v General Electric Co.*, 115 F Supp 835 (DNJ 1953) (creating a compulsory license as a remedy in a patent/antitrust case); *Charles Pfizer & Co. v FTC*, 401 F2d 574 (6th Cir 1968) (same), cert denied, 394 US 920 (1969). See also Clean Air Act, 42 USC § 7608 (creating a compulsory license for patented inventions necessary to protect the environment). For articles, see John Shepard Wiley, Jr., *Copyright at the School of Patent*, 58 U Chi L Rev 119 (1991); P. McCoy Smith, *Copyright, Suppression, and the Problem of Unpublished Work: Lessons from the Patent Law*, 10 AIPLA Q J 309 (1991). Compare Rebecca S. Eisenberg, *Patents and the Progress of Science: Exclusive Rights and Experimental Use*, 56 U Chi L Rev 1017 (1989) (proposing an experimental use defense to patent infringement similar to copyright's fair use defense).

[107] The blank-forms doctrine denies copyright protection to works that are thought not to convey information, but to instead create a method for ordering it. See 37 CFR § 202.1; *Kregos v Associated Press*, 937 F2d 700 (2d Cir 1991). The printed-matter doctrine denies patent protection to writings. See, for example, *Flood v Coe*, 31 F Supp 348 (1940) (finding that certain arrangements of printed matter can be physical structures).

ent" and "copyright" are in fact illusory because they fail to capture anything that is significant about the products of human intellect. It may be that a degree of judicial sympathy for labor once allowed the traditional hierarchy to function acceptably, but it is now becoming evident that it is not going to be easy to continue this fiction into the next century.

The time has therefore come to rethink the old structure, to examine patent and copyright functionally and as a part of the larger legal order that includes unfair competition, trademark law, and the sui generis legislation mentioned above. Although separately named, these legal constructs share common insights, objectives, methods, and concerns. Each looks to profits to motivate original intellectual endeavors, each uses exclusive rights to protect profits, and each seeks to maximize public welfare with a series of doctrines that balance the interests of creators against the needs of those who use the materials that they create.

Thus, patent is different from copyright, but not because it covers different subject matter or requires a different level of inventiveness. Rather, patent is the coverage provided to spur creativity in one group of endeavors having particular characteristics; the "copyright industries" are structured differently, and therefore require another sort of coverage. It would be comforting to believe that there is method to the existing regime—that, for instance, patents are of short duration and large scope relative to copyrights because, relative to the copyright industries, patent industries require a more rapid payback or quicker release from exclusivity. More likely, however, classifications developed fortuitously. The emphasis on "writing" and "object" placed certain products into copyright and others into patent even though a different categorization might have worked better. In any event, hybrid enterprises, such as the information product industries, demonstrate that in many fields, neither classification works well.

For the future, then, two conceptual tasks are in order. First, it is necessary to understand the structure of innovative industries and to identify the characteristics within each that are responsive to intellectual property rules. These would include such matters as the time-value of a typical innovation; the extent to which the industry can protect profits through relational rights; the degree to which new works are tied to earlier innovations; the relationship between technological advances and developments within basic science; the feasibility and desirability of library research; the maturity of the industry; and the identification of industrial participants with the culture—and the noneconomic incentive structure—of the allied basic scientists, academicians, and researchers.[108]

Second, the economic significance of intellectual property doctrine needs to be abstracted from the details of individual protective regimes. When viewed as a whole, dissimilarities in nomenclature and history recede and it becomes evident that there is a continuum here: a continuous array of techniques that can be deployed to tailor protection closely to the individual needs of particular intellectual property industries.[109]

As the *Feist* and *Bonito Boats* Courts suspected, the scope of infringement is indeed a key concern, for it most explicitly determines how robustly an innovation can be used downstream. A broad definition that reaches even independent producers should be reserved to those industries where innovation can be practiced in secret (and therefore more is needed to induce disclosure) and to industries where downstream requirements are so extensive that duration must be short, but where the high cost of innovation makes broad coverage necessary to assure adequate payback. For information products, there is little evidence that costs are so high that such extensive protection is necessary.[110] Moreover, the rapidity with which information depreciates makes unfeasible the rigorous examination, disclosure, and claiming procedures necessary to

---

[108] Some of these parameters have been mentioned by others. See Merges and Nelson, 90 Colum L Rev at 880 (cited in note 31); Wiley, 58 U Chi L Rev at 144–145 (cited in note 106); Landes and Posner, 18 J Legal Stud at 345 (cited in note 31); Rebecca S. Eisenberg, *Proprietary Rights and the Norms of Science in Biotechnology Research*, 97 Yale L J 177 (1987).

[109] This task has begun only in relation to the duration variable. See, for example, William D. Nordhaus, *Invention, Growth and Economic Welfare* (MIT Press, 1969); Frederic M. Scherer, *Nordhaus's Theory of Optimal Patent Life: A Geometric Reinterpretation*, 62 Am Econ Rev 422 (1972); Merges and Nelson, 90 Colum L Rev 839 (cited in note 31). To the extent that any of these seminal pieces can be said to be in error, it is that their focus on one particular variable obscures the capacity of the system to minimize costs by altering other parameters.

The idea of thinking of these rules as comprising a continuum was suggested in Wendy J. Gordon, *An Inquiry into the Merits of Copyright: The Challenges of Consistency, Consent, and Encouragement Theory*, 41 Stan L Rev 1343, 1369–70 (1989).

[110] For example, boat hull designers were apparently content with the direct molding statute, and semiconductor chip manufacturers with protection against copying, 17 USC § 905. Compare *Feist*, Amicus Brief of the Association of American Publishers on behalf of Rural Telephone at 7 (arguing that protection against wholesale copying strikes the appropriate balance).

build a record for deciding whether an independent inventor has infringed. What would work better is some form of anti-copying rule. Since the protected work would act as a benchmark for determining infringement, there would be no need for the formalized claiming system of patent law. And without the need for examining claims, coverage could begin as soon as the work was completed. Such a regime would also reduce some of the fears of monopolization. Because independent creation would not be infringing, the first mover's price would be capped at the expense involved in recreation.

Infringement can be even more finely calibrated, for the continuum contains a series of definitions ranging from trademark's ban on confusingly similar uses at one end to the direct molding statute's prohibition of a single method of copying on the other. In many information product industries, works cannot be exploited in secret, and the prevalence of commentors and productive users means that advances are characterized by a high degree of interrelatedness. Accordingly, a definition narrower than that used in copyright is desirable. Just as trademark law modifies the anti-use regime of patent law to reach only those uses that intrude on the core needs of the trademark owner, protection for original information products could narrow the anti-copy regime to target only those copyists who interfere with the core interests of the first mover: the ability to recoup costs and earn a reasonable profit. As in trademark, the issue in a typical case would then be to decide whether the harm is a competitive injury or whether the second user has instead adapted the information to another market.[111] Trademark law may also offer insights into solving the difficult problem of delineating the first mover's rights to potential ancillary markets.

For fact works, for example, the result may be that only whole-

---

[111] Compare *Mead Data Central, Inc. v Toyota Motor Sales*, 875 F2d 1026 (2d Cir 1989) ("lexis" and "lexus" marks are used in different markets). The fair use defense of copyright, 17 USC § 107, can also be analyzed in this functional way. Even First Amendment scholars generally unsympathetic to rights in information concede that there may be a limited role for well-delimited market incentives. See, for example, Diane Leenheer Zimmerman, *Information as Speech, Information as Goods: Some Thoughts on Marketplaces and the Bill of Rights*, 33 Wm & Mary L Rev 665, 732 (1992). This is the approach under consideration in the European Community, Proposal for a Council Directive, Art. 2(5) (cited in note 9) (protecting databases from unauthorized extraction, "in whole or in substantial part, for commercial purposes.").

sale copying is actually prohibited. After all, the original contribution of the compiler subsists in the totality of the presentation rather than in individual facts, so it is only the wholesale copyist who takes the essence of the effort. Furthermore, it is only the wholesale copyist who outcompetes the first mover solely by saving the costs of development and who produces works that should not be considered distinct in the Landes and Posner model. Obviously, the line here will not always be clear.[112] However, there is a standard to guide the decision, giving the courts one leg up on the fact-and-idea/expression dichotomy currently in place.[113] And if easy evasion by downstream users becomes a problem, other templates within the continuum could be adapted. These include the doctrine of equivalents in patent law, confusing similarity in trademark law, and substantial similarity in copyright.[114]

The balance can be adjusted further through the definition of

---

[112] *Simon & Schuster* furnishes an excellent example. Consider what would have happened if Warner Brothers had refused to pay for the right to base *GoodFellas* on *Wiseguy*. Under current copyright law, it is fairly clear that if Warner Brothers was willing to avoid putting Pileggi's words into the mouths of the actors, paying for the story was not necessary. After all, if facts are not copyrightable, then appropriating the facts of Henry Hill's life is not actionable. See, for example, *Narell v Freeman*, 872 F2d 907 (9th Cir 1989); *Walker v Time Life Films*, 784 F2d 44 (2d Cir 1986); *Miller v Universal City Studios*, 650 F2d 1365 (5th Cir 1981); *Hoehling v Universal City Studios*, 618 F2d 972 (2d Cir 1980); *Rosemont Enterprises, Inc. v Random House*, 366 F2d 303 (2d Cir 1966). And since *GoodFellas* is clearly a distinct work from *Wiseguy*, and appeals to a somewhat different audience, under the test proposed here, it is possible to argue that the same result should obtain: the movie is not wholesale copying of the book and therefore does not infringe it. Yet apparently, Hill's motivation included the profits of both book and movie. See note 13; *Simon & Schuster*, Motion Picture Association Amicus Brief at 21. Since both works appeal mainly to those interested in being entertained by true crime stories, it is likely that some people who see the movie will forgo reading the book. Thus, a court could not decide the infringement issue without reviewing both works to determine the extent to which the movie substitutes for the book by comprehensively tracking its facts.

It is worth noting that as with other factual materials, some courts have strained to protect the profits of researchers under circumstances such as the one hypothesized. See, for example, *Toksvig v Bruce Pub. Co.*, 181 F2d 664 (7th Cir 1950); *Burgess v Chase-Riboud*, 765 F Supp 233 (ED Pa 1991); *Craft v Kobler*, 667 F Supp 120 (SDNY 1987). Compare *Nash v CBS*, 899 F2d 1537 (7th Cir 1990) (allowing reuse of notion that John Dillinger survived shootout at Biograph theater, but criticizing *Hoehling*).

[113] See, for example, *Whelan Associates, Inc. v Jaslow Dental Laboratory, Inc.*, 797 F2d 1222, 1233 (3d Cir 1986); *Lotus Development Corp. v Paperback Software Intern.*, 740 F Supp 37, 42, 58 (D Mass 1990); *Engineering Dynamics v Structural Software*, 785 F Supp 576 (ED La 1991) (illustrating the difficulty in applying the idea/expression dichotomy).

[114] Each of these doctrines expands the scope of infringement to include minor variants. See, for example, *Graver Tank & Mfg. Co. v Linde Air Products Co.*, 339 US 605 (1950) (patent law); *Northam Warren Corp. v Universal Cosmetic Co.*, 18 F2d 774 (7th Cir 1927) (trademark); *Steinberg v Columbia Pictures Indus.*, 663 F Supp 706 (SDNY 1987) (copyright).

what is encompassed by purchase, and by defenses and privileges that raise or lower the cost of downstream use. The first mechanism is illustrated by the first sale doctrine of copyright law and the exhaustion principle in patent law. These could be applied to information products to excuse from infringement those downstream uses most clearly contemplated by the first mover—the right to "copy" a telephone number by dialing it, or the right to use the Medicaid tables to determine elder care options in New York.[115]

The notion that downstream use can be safeguarded by ensuring high downstream costs may seem paradoxical, but it makes economic sense. Provisions of this type include the Semiconductor Chip Act's right to analyze and improve,[116] and (arguably) patent law's reverse doctrine of equivalents.[117] In each case, productive uses are so expensive that second users compete on a level playing field with the first mover, or are in an advantageous position by reason of their own contributions and not solely their free ride on development costs. As applied to fact works, this strategy would argue for a "slipping privilege" permitting the subsequent user to refer to the first work "for the purpose of directing him where to call."[118] The second comer saves because there is no need to start from scratch, but being directed where to call still requires calling. Costs are not so low that the first mover is driven out of the market.

Mechanisms that lower downstream costs are more common. The fair use doctrines of copyright and trademark law safeguard

---

[115] See 17 USC § 109(a) & (e) (copyright); *Adams v Burke*, 84 US 453 (1873); *Aro Mfg. Co. v Convertible Top Replacement Co.*, 365 US 338 (1961) (patent). See also 17 USC § 117(1) (allowing purchasers of software to copy the program into computer memory); Pamela Samuelson, *Modifying Copyrighted Software: Adjusting Copyright Doctrine to Accommodate Technology*, 28 Jurimetrics 179 (1988).

[116] 17 USC §§ 906(a)(1) and (2) allow downstream users of new chip designs to escape infringement if they, in turn, create works original enough to qualify for protection.

[117] Under the reverse doctrine of equivalents, an invention that performs the same functions as a patented invention in a "substantially different way" escapes infringement. See Merges and Nelson, 90 Colum L Rev at 864–68 (cited in note 31), citing *SRI International v Matsushita Electric Corp. of America*, 775 F2d 1107 (Fed Cir 1985) (en banc). See also note 86.

[118] *Morris v Wright* (1870) LR 5 Ch 279, 286. This privilege was recognized in early cases involving fact works, see, for example, *Edward Thompson Co. v American Law Book Co.*, 122 Fed 922 (2d Cir 1903), and continues to be relied on in England, where fact works remain protected, see Thomas P. Arden, *The Conflicting Treatments of Compilations of Facts under the United States and British Copyright Laws*, 10 AIPLA 267 (1991). See also Gorman, 76 Harv L Rev at 1585–89 (cited in note 80).

the interest of commentors by allowing them free use of material that is indispensible to their work.[119] Special privileges also exist in both copyright and trademark to remove from the scope of protection those forms of expression that have special significance to the user or extraordinary resonance to the public—"scenes à faire" in copyright, geographic and personal names in trademark.[120] The Semiconductor Chip Act mirrors this mechanism with the concept of the unprotectable "staple, commonplace, or familiar" design, and this idea could be easily adapted to other information products.[121] If these rules are insufficient to deal with holdups, they can be augmented with doctrines modeled on patent misuse.[122] An alternative is to create a march-in right permitting the government to claim rights in under-exploited works.[123] In egregious cases, antitrust law will apply.[124]

Furthermore, it is always possible to balance upstream and downstream needs by controlling price more directly. Copyright law contains a long series of compulsory licensing provisions that rely on a variety of devices such as mandatory fees, compulsory arbitration, and duties to bargain.[125] Alternatively, a liability rather than a pure property rule could be created. Instead of allowing first movers to enjoin copyists, holders could be limited to compen-

---

[119] 17 USC § 107; 15 USC § 1115(b)(4). See, for example, *Columbia Pictures Corp. v NBC*, 137 F Supp 348 (SD Cal 1955).

[120] See, for example, *Alexander v Haley*, 460 F Supp 40, 45 (SDNY 1978).

[121] 17 USC § 902(b)(2).

[122] These doctrines render intellectual property rights unenforceable if they are used to restrain competition in material not covered by the right. For patent misuse, see, for example, *Dawson Chem. Co. v Rohm & Haas Co.*, 448 US 176 (1980). For copyright misuse, see cases cited in note 106.

[123] See, for example, 35 USC § 203. In such cases, the government then usually grants nonexclusive licenses to others.

[124] See, for example, *Charles Pfizer & Co. v FTC*, 401 F2d 574 (6th Cir 1968) (requiring licensing at a reasonable royalty), cert denied, 394 US 920 (1979). Compare *Corsearch, Inc. v Thomson & Thomson*, 792 F Supp 305 (SDNY 1992) (rejecting claim that refusal to deal is a violation of § 2 of the Sherman Act, 15 USC § 16, on the ground that defendant lacked sufficient market power).

[125] See, for example, 17 USC § 115(c)(2) (specified fee); id §§ 111(d), 119(c)(3) (creating tribunal to determine fees in certain cases); id § 116A (duty to bargain in good faith). See also 7 USC § 136a(c)(1)(D)(ii); *Thomas v Union Carbide Agr. Products*, 473 US 568 (1985); *Ruckelshaus v Monsanto Co.*, 467 US 986 (1984) (permitting Environmental Protection Agency to use data submitted by one producer in deciding whether to approve competitors' product; to equalize costs, parties who wish to have the data used must bargain with the first submitter. In the absence of agreement, arbitration is required.).

sation—to recovery of a portion of their sunk costs plus a reasonable profit on their investment.

A few words should also be said about wasteful duplication and transaction and enforcement costs. Several of the mechanisms mentioned above lower the cost of downstream use and release users from the need to negotiate with the right holder. This reduces the temptation to start from scratch, eliminating both waste and transactions.[126] The search portion of the transaction costs can also be reduced by building on trademark's registration requirement[127] to make recovery contingent on keeping registration current. Adopting a liability rule (coupled with a ban on punitive damages) would lower costs even more because subsequent users could wait for the right holder to step forward. By the same token, the continuum includes a series of devices to minimize enforcement costs. Reevaluation procedures divert cases from courtrooms into cheaper administrative tribunals.[128] Baseless cases can be filtered out quickly through proper distribution of burdens of proof,[129] the availability of sanctions against frivolous lawsuits,[130] and lowering standards for summary judgment.[131] As a final calibration, there is the question of how long the right should last.[132]

---

[126] See generally Wendy G. Gordon, *Fair Use as Market Failure: A Structural and Economic Analysis of the Betamax Case and Its Predecessors*, 82 Colum L Rev 1600 (1982); Landes and Posner, 18 J Legal Stud at 357–61 (cited in note 31).

[127] See, for example, 15 USC §§ 1051–59 (including continuing duties to keep registration current).

[128] See, for example, 35 USC §§ 251–52 (permitting patentee to have defective patent reissued); id §§ 301–07 (permitting the Commissioner of Patents and other parties to have certain issues of patentability reexamined).

[129] See, for example, 35 USC § 282 (burden of proving invalidity on challenger); 17 USC § 504(b) (allocating the burden of proving damages). In all regimes, the burden of proving infringement is on the right holder, which encourages practices such as seeding. See note 86. The second comer is not always helpless. In the computer industry, for example, clean room procedures have emerged which allow the defendant to demonstrate independent development despite similarities caused by external factors. See, for example, *NEC Corp. v Intel Corp.*, 10 USPQ2d 1177, 1188 (ND Cal 1989).

[130] See, for example, *Business Guides, Inc. v Chromatic Commns. Enterprises*, 111 S Ct 922 (1991), where a litigant was sanctioned under FRCP 11 for basing an allegation of copyright infringement on the reproduction of 10 "seeds" which turned out to be legitimate entries.

[131] *Arnstein v Porter*, 154 F2d 464 (2d Cir 1946), was often cited for the proposition that copyright cases cannot be decided on summary judgment because the substantiality of similarity virtually always raised a triable issue. But that decision has been undercut by the trio of *Matsushita Electrical Industrial Co. v Zenith Radio Corp.*, 475 US 574 (1986), *Anderson v Liberty Lobby Inc.*, 477 US 242 (1986), and *Celotex Corp. v Catrett*, 477 US 317 (1986).

[132] In most cases of sui generis statutory protection for information products, the term is short. Under the Semiconductor Chip Act, it is ten years, 17 USC § 904(a), and under the Orphan Drug Act, it is seven years, 21 USC § 360cc(a).

It is also important to keep in mind that these costs are relative. There is little reason to believe that the transaction and enforcement costs of a rights-based scheme will differ substantially from those produced in the relational regime envisioned by Breyer and apparently endorsed by *Bonito Boats*.[133] It is not even clear that duplication is wasteful. Repeaters verify accuracy, correct mistakes, and refine presentation.[134] Fresh talent may begin with the idea of simply recreating, but once they see the field, they may discern other possibilities it. The result could be the same product, or something entirely new.[135]

It would, of course, have been nicer at this point to have unveiled a comprehensive Intellectual Property Law, or at least a theory about industrial categorization that would facilitate matching the level of protection to the characteristics of the industries protected.[136] Unfortunately, the empirical research required to undertake this sort of analysis is not likely to be conducted until the advantages of reconceptualization are well understood. Thus, what should be recognized at this point is the advantages of systematically rethinking the field. If the pattern of innovation within industries is understood and the economic significance of individual rules is abstracted from the standard hierarchical convention in which they are embedded, it will be possible to achieve the evenhandedness required by *Simon & Schuster* while minimizing the costs that led the *Feist* and *Bonito Boats* Courts, along with free speech and economic theorists, to deny the possibility of protecting certain categories of intellectual effort.

IV. Constitutional Authority After Feist and Bonito Boats

That said, there is still the question of finding legislative authority to institute a new order. The post-*Feist* and *Bonito Boats*

---

[133] Relational claims apparently survive because *Bonito Boats* cited with approval both *Aronson v Quick Point Pencil Co.*, 440 US 257 (1979), and *Kewanee Oil Co. v Bicron Corp.*, 416 US 470 (1974). *Bonito Boats*, 111 S Ct at 150, 155–56. *Aronson* enforced a royalties contract for an invention on which patent protection was denied, and *Kewanee* enforced a trade secret.

[134] Compare Robert K. Merton, *The Normative Structure of Science* 267, 276 (Chicago, 1973) (arguing that fraud and mistakes in science are avoided through the replication of experiments). See also Eisenberg, 56 U Chi L Rev at 1064 (cited in note 106).

[135] Compare Merges and Nelson, 90 Colum L Rev at 873–74 (cited in note 31).

[136] For reasons stated in Dreyfuss, 20 J Intl L & Pol 897 (cited in note 4), a single legal regime articulating general principles is preferable to a series of discrete laws. The latter may, however, be more practical.

literature amply demonstrates why this is a problem.[137] To sum it up, the constitutional portion of the *Feist* decision puts information products beyond the reach of the Copyright Clause because nothing in the real world is original enough to protect, no matter how difficult it might be to retrieve. Although Congress solved a defect in its legislative authority to enact trademark law by passing the Lanham Act under its commerce powers, that strategy is not feasible here.[138] Restrictions on constitutional grants of legislative power, such as the Copyright Clause, would be meaningless if Congress could evade them simply by announcing that it was acting under some broader authority.[139]

Nor is it possible to argue that residual power resides in the states, for that position is blocked by *Bonito Boats*. Described as creating a kind of dormant Copyright Clause,[140] that decision stands for the proposition that the national interest in encouraging the progress of science and useful arts is exhausted by conferring upon Congress the limited right to act with respect to writings and discoveries, authors and inventors. There is no residual interest, and therefore no residual power, in the states. If *Bonito Boats* is read broadly, even state common law rules, such as the misappropriation doctrine, which might otherwise operate to protect profits in information products, are—apparently—preempted.[141]

In some ways, it is easy to defend *Feist*. Its reliance on the bipolarity of the "protect" choice, which led it to classify the directory as functional (and therefore not copyrightable) and obvious (and therefore not patentable), accords with the history of intellec-

---

[137] See Heald, 1991 Supreme Court Review 31 (cited in note 8); Ginsburg, 92 Colum L Rev 338 (cited in note 4).

[138] The Lanham Act, 15 USC §§ 1051 et seq, was enacted after the Supreme Court held its predecessor, 19 Stat 141 (1876), an unconstitutional exercise of congressional authority under the Copyright Clause. *The Trademark Cases*, 100 US 82 (1879).

[139] Compare *Railway Executors Assn. v Gibbons*, 455 US 457 (1982) (nonuniform bankruptcy laws cannot be enacted pursuant to the commerce power).

[140] Flynn, 1992 Utah L Rev at 418 (cited in note 105).

[141] Actually, the Supreme Court created the misappropriation doctrine to create a vehicle for protecting profits in news reports that were not copyrightable, *International News Service v Associated Press*, 248 US 215 (1918). After *Erie Railroad Co. v Tompkins*, 304 US 64 (1938), eliminated general federal common law, the doctrine was adopted by many states as a matter of state common law, see, for example, *Board of Trade of Chicago v Dow Jones Co.*, 98 Ill 109, 456 NE2d 84 (S Ct Ill 1983). See generally, Dennis S. Karjala, *Copyright and Misappropriation*, 17 U Dayton L Rev 885 (1992).

tual property[142] and the literary form of the Copyright Clause.[143] What is not easy to defend, however, is the notion of a constitutional clause that is so porous that whole categories of work slip through. These holes disappear if copyright and patent are reconceived as a general theory of intellectual property. Viewed as a continuum of protective regimes, the "intellectual property clause" gives Congress plenary authority to create private rights across the entire spectrum of human intellectual endeavors.

As to *Bonito Boats*, it is hard to find an explanation that is even worth refuting. The case seems to read the Copyright Clause as so hostile to intellectual property rights that it bars all of *government* from creating them, not merely Congress. Yet there is nothing in our constitutional history that reveals a reason to impute to the Framers this level of suspicion. At the time of the Constitutional Convention, exclusive rights were not conflated with the notion of monopoly because theorists understood monopolies as privatizing matter already in use by the public while exclusive rights were for newly developed material.[144] Indeed, at the time of the Convention, most states had intellectual property laws; the principal argument for empowering Congress was that state-by-state protection would be ineffectual.[145] Moreover, it is difficult to believe that a Constitution so firmly rooted in capitalism would put products of such great

---

[142] See Frank D. Prager, *A History of Intellectual Property from 1545 to 1787*, 26 J Pat Off Socy 711 (1944); Frank D. Prager, *The Early Growth and Influence of Intellectual Property*, 34 J Pat Off Socy 106 (1952).

[143] One part of the provision directs Congress to promote science (i.e., knowledge) by securing to authors exclusive rights in writings; the other empowers Congress to promote useful arts by securing to inventors exclusive rights in discoveries. See *In re Bergy*, 596 F2d 952 (CCPA 1979); *Baker v Selden*, 101 US 99, 102 (1879).

[144] See Bruce W. Bugbee, *Genesis* at 6–7 (cited in note 92), citing Edward Coke, *Institutes of the Laws of England*, III, 181 (c 85) (London, 1797); *Charles River Bridge v Warren Bridge*, 11 Peters 420, 607 (1837). Compare Prager, 34 J Pat Off Socy at 122–26 (cited in note 142) (similar understanding animated even earlier theorists). Indeed, the Supreme Court invalidated the enactment of trademark legislation under the Copyright Clause because it recognized as important the distinction between material in the public domain and original contributions. *The Trademark Cases*, 100 US 82, 94 (1879).

[145] See Bugbee, *Genesis* at 130 (cited in note 92), citing Federalist 43 (Alexander Hamilton, John Jay, and James Madison) in Paul Leicester Ford, ed, The Federalist 281 (New York, 1898). Interestingly, the first two petitions asking Congress to exercise its intellectual property powers involved fact works: David Ramsay's *The History of the Revolution of South Carolina from a British Province to an Independent State*, and the maps, globes, and tables prepared pursuant to John Chruchman's new navigational methods. After private bills were enacted to protect these works, Congress took up the question of enacting a general patent and copyright law. Id at 131–33.

potential economic significance, both domestically and internationally, beyond the reach of the market mechanism.

It could be argued that the Clause arises from the same fear of Balkanization that led to the enactment of the Commerce Clause. Under this view, the states cannot create exclusive rights because if there were different rights in different trade areas, sellers could not operate across the entire United States. Since exclusivity would fragment markets as surely as tariffs, the constitutional scheme is equally hostile to them.[146]

It is not, however, clear that this view correctly captures the Commerce Clause. As Donald Regan has pointed out, the United States was never the European Community: the Framers were not trying to avoid war by making the states economically interdependent, nor were they seeking to enhance the nation's competitive position in world markets by creating economies of scale. Their notion of free movement of goods was limited to the idea that no one should be excluded from a market by reason of being a nonlocal. Exclusion caused by regulations imposed for nondiscriminatory purposes was not a concern at that time, and it is not prominent in modern Commerce Clause jurisprudence.[147] Since the statute at issue in *Bonito Boats* prohibited the sale of any directly molded boat hull, irrespective of whether the designer, buyer, or seller was foreign or local, it contained no hint of the kind of protectionism at which the Commerce Clause is aimed.

In any event, the dormant Commerce Clause is not a national rule outlawing disuniformity or even a national rule outlawing state activity in the commerce area. In fact, states regularly enact legislation affecting commerce; for the most part, only discriminatory legislation is set aside.[148] *Bonito Boats* goes further because it reads the dormancy of the Copyright Clause as comprehensively preempting its field. And, there is no indication in *Bonito Boats* that

---

[146] The *Bonito Boat* Court's reference to the possibility of fifty different protective regimes, 489 US at 161 and 162, suggests this concern may have partially animated the decision.

[147] Donald H. Regan, *The Supreme Court and State Protectionism, Making Sense of the Dormant Commerce Clause*, 84 Mich L Rev 1091 (1986). Compare, for example, *Hunt v Washington State Apples Advertising Commn.*, 432 US 333, 353 (1977), with *Pike v Bruce Church, Inc.*, 397 US 137, 142 (1970).

[148] Even theories of the Commerce Clause that recognize interests other than antiprotectionism envision some level of legitimate state activity in the area. See, for example, Julian Eule, *Laying the Dormant Commerce Clause to Rest*, 91 Yale L J 425 (1982).

Congress could step in to authorize state legislation otherwise forbidden by the "dormant" Copyright Clause, as it can with legislation forbidden by the dormant Commerce Clause.[149] Indeed, *Feist* seems to make that position untenable.

Simon & Schuster bolsters these arguments in an important way. By linking the dynamics of creativity and the significance of protecting profits to the First Amendment, it finds in the constitutional scheme an affirmative reason to create exclusivity.[150] This is not to say that an argument for according protection to information products could be based solely on the First Amendment. *Simon & Schuster*'s concern appears to be with evenhandedness. Thus, it is agnostic to the decision whether *any* intellectual property protection should exist. However, the Court's focus on the quality of the product reaching the audience and the danger of distortion requires that if the decision is made to protect some works, *Feist* and *Bonito Boats* must be read narrowly so that the nation retains the capacity to protect all works. *Feist* should be confined to a decision about the viability of one particular mechanism on the intellectual property continuum; *Bonito Boats* should be limited to the protectability of products already in the public domain.

V. Conclusion

The law has long had difficulties accommodating information products within the copyright-patent regime. Because of the public's strong interest in access to reality-based material, the poor match between these works and conventional notions of patentable and copyrightable subject matter was traditionally exploited to render these works unprotectable. It is possible that this system functioned well in earlier times, when lead time was significant and first mover advantages endured. Even if incentives suffered, the damage was alleviated by the lowered costs of downstream use. So long as trade was mainly domestic, national wealth was unaffected, as losses experienced by developers were balanced by savings by those who appropriated their work.

But however well things worked out in the past, modern devel-

---

[149] See, for example, *Quill Corp. v North Dakota*, 112 S Ct 1904, 1916 (1992).

[150] Significantly, Simon & Schuster's brief relied on copyright cases. See *Simon & Schuster*, Brief for Petitioner at 20.

opments make this regime unsuitable for the the future. Lead time has vanished because of modern reproductive technologies, such as telecommunication techniques and digital recording methods. Internationalization of the marketplace means that the failure to adopt legislation protecting significant industries will negatively affect the nation's balance of payments. More important, the products of human ingenuity have changed. As the demand grows for advances like informational molecules, genetic maps, hypertexts, and computerized databases, providing appropriate incentives becomes an increasing concern. *Simon & Schuster* underscores this concern, for it teaches the importance of thinking not only of the individual user but also the receiving public. Its emphasis on the evenhandedness of profit protection makes the deficiencies in the earlier regime impossible to ignore.

The time has therefore come to rethink copyright and patent, to unify the theory of intellectual property in order to create a system of law that is capable of providing the right incentives across the entire domain of human intellectual endeavor. It is, in short, time to stop thinking of "patents" and "copyright" as about particular subject matter. Rather, they should be conceived as constellations of doctrines, offering a series of choices about the scope of subject matter certainly, but also about infringement, duration, remedies, and defenses; choices that should be carefully tailored to the characteristics of the industries seeking protection. The products of the modern age are imaginative hybrids of the technologies that preceded them; no less imagination is required of the law.

BARRY CUSHMAN

DOCTRINAL SYNERGIES AND LIBERAL DILEMMAS: THE CASE OF THE YELLOW-DOG CONTRACT

The three decades spanning the years 1908 to 1937 saw a remarkable transformation of the Supreme Court's jurisprudence concerning the rights of workers to organize. In 1908, the court held that a federal law prohibiting employers from discharging an employee because of his membership in a labor union violated the liberty of contract secured to the employer by the Fifth Amendment.[1] In 1915, the Court similarly declared a state statute prohibiting the use of "yellow-dog" contracts unconstitutional.[2] In 1937, by contrast, the Court upheld provisions of the Wagner Act prohibiting both discharges for union membership and the use of yellow-dog contracts.[3] Thus, the doctrine of "liberty of contract" no longer operated as a bar to legislation protecting the rights of workers to organize for purposes of collective bargaining.

Barry Cushman is Assistant Professor of Law, St. Louis University School of Law.

AUTHOR'S NOTE: The author gratefully acknowledges the valuable criticisms of Patrice Cushman, Chris Eisgruber, Daniel Ernst, Roger Goldman, John Griesbach, Michael Klarman, Charles McCurdy, William Nelson, John Phillip Reid, Reuel Schiller, Doug Williams, and the members of the Legal History Colloquium at the New York University School of Law.

[1] *Adair v United States*, 208 US 161 (1908).

[2] *Coppage v Kansas*, 236 US 1 (1915). A "yellow-dog" contract was a contract of employment in which the employee would agree, as a condition of his employment, not to join a labor union.

[3] *NLRB v Jones & Laughlin Steel Corp.*, 301 US 1 (1937); *NLRB v Fruehauf Trailer Co.*, 301 US 49 (1937); *NLRB v Friedman–Harry Marks Clothing Co.*, 301 US 58 (1937); *Associated Press Co. v NLRB*, 301 US 103 (1937); *Washington, Virginia & Maryland Coach Co. v NLRB*, 301 US 142 (1937).

Remarkably, the intellectual history of this transformation has not been written. Historians writing about the Wagner Act cases, preoccupied by the more dramatic commerce clause issues, have tended to give only cursory treatment to the due process dimensions of the decisions.[4] The outcome of the cases has been seen as an essentially political response to the external political pressure brought to bear by the Court-packing plan and the 1936 election.[5] This explanation has apparently been seen as obviating any sustained conceptual or doctrinal analysis.[6]

The tale of the yellow-dog contract is naturally of interest because of its centrality to the development of American labor law and the decline of substantive due process. Beyond this, however, the story can be seen as a critical chapter in the development of American liberal legalism. The yellow-dog contract provoked something of a crisis in liberal discourse, because it brought into conflict two time-honored liberal values: liberty of contract and freedom of association. Recent scholarship has shown how "liberty of contract" was forged from such diverse liberal resources as Adam Smith's liberal political economy, Jacksonian liberalism, and the Northern "free labor" ideology that animated the abolitionist movement.[7] Freedom of association enjoyed no less venerable liberal

---

[4] See, e.g., Peter Irons, *The New Deal Lawyers* 287–88 (Princeton Univ, 1982); Kelly & Harbison, *The American Constitution: Its Origins and Development* 766–77 (Norton, 4th ed 1970); Mason & Beaney, *The Supreme Court in a Free Society* 182–84 (Norton, 1968); Robert McCloskey, *The American Supreme Court* 176 (Univ of Chicago, 1960); Paul Murphy, *The Constitution in Crisis Times, 1918–1969*, 157–58 (Harper & Row, 1972); Fred Rodell, *Nine Men* 249–250 (Vintage, 1955); Bernard Schwartz, *The Supreme Court: Constitutional Revolution in Retrospect* 21–22, 34–36 (Ronald Press, 1957); William Swindler, 2 *Court and Constitution in the Twentieth Century: The New Legality, 1932–1968*, 99–100 (Bobbs-Merrill, 1968); Benjamin Wright, *The Growth of American Constitutional Law* 204–5 (H Holt, 1942).

[5] See, e.g., Edward Corwin, *Court Over Constitution* 127 (Princeton Univ, 1938); Robert McCloskey, supra at 224; Paul Murphy, supra at 115; Walter Murphy, *Congress and the Court: A Case Study in the American Political Process* 65 (Univ of Chicago, 1962); William Swindler, supra at 81; Benjamin F. Wright, *The Growth of American Constitutional Law* 205, 222 (Univ of Chicago, 1967).

[6] For a critique of the political response theory, see Cushman, *"Rethinking the New Deal Court: The "Switch-in-Time" Reconsidered* (forthcoming); Michael J. Klarman, *Constitutional Fact/Constitutional Fiction*, 44 Stan L Rev 759, 771 n 76, 774–75 n .98 (1992).

[7] See Eric Foner, *Free Soil, Free Labor, Free Men: The Ideology of the Republican Party Before the Civil War* (Oxford Univ, 1970); William Forbath, *The Ambiguities of Free Labor: Labor and the Law in the Gilded Age*, 1985 Wis L Rev 767, 772–800 (1985); Charles McCurdy, *The Roots of "Liberty of Contract" Reconsidered: Major Premises in the Law of Employment, 1867–1937*, in *1984 Yearbook of the Supreme Court Historical Society* 20 (1984); William Nelson, *The Impact of the Antislavery Movement upon Styles of Judicial Reasoning in Nineteenth Century America*, 87 Harv L Rev 513 (1974).

pedigree. Its protection against government infringement en-
shrined in the First Amendment,[8] the freedom to affiliate with the
lawful organizations of one's choice, had been a widely embraced
feature of American culture since well before the Civil War.[9] Indeed, the passion of the American people for voluntary associations
had attracted the fascination of Alexis de Tocqueville during his
journey to the United States in the 1830s.[10]

The yellow-dog contract exposed a tension between these two
values of American liberalism. Opponents of the yellow-dog contract contended that the employer was using his constitutionally
protected liberty of contract as a means to inhibit his employee's
freedom to associate with his fellow workingmen. In characteristi-
cally liberal terms, the answer to this charge would turn on
whether the employee was seen as having surrendered his freedom
of association voluntarily, or as a product of coercion. The answer
to this question would in turn depend upon assumptions about the
structure of the labor market—assumptions that would change over
time. Beneath this discourse, I believe, lay concerns about whether
labor unions were properly analogized to the other sorts of voluntary associations celebrated by American liberalism. As those concerns became increasingly allayed over time, labor's advocates
could more successfully appropriate the liberal rhetoric of associational freedom.

Yet the story of the yellow dog's demise cannot be adequately
understood by looking at cultural context alone. In order to understand the voting patterns of the various Justices and the views they
expressed in their opinions, one must pay close attention to the
development of doctrine. A study of the doctrine pertaining to the
yellow-dog contract reveals to us the poverty of the notion that
substantive due process and dual federalism were merely convenient weapons in the arsenal of a reactionary Court devoted to the
maintenance of financial and industrial elites.[11] Instead, we may
see the weblike, interconnected structure of laissez-faire constitu-

---

[8] See Nowak, Rotunda & Young, *Constitutional Law* § XII, at 958–59 (West, 2d ed 1983).

[9] See Gross, *The Minutemen and Their World* 173–75 (Hill & Wang, 1976); Ryan, *Cradle of the Middle Class*, ch 3 (Cambridge Univ, 1981); Walters, *American Reformers, 1815–1860* 29–35 (Hill & Wang, 1978).

[10] See Alexis de Tocqueville, 2 *Democracy in America* 128–33, 138–44 (New York, 1972).

[11] See, e.g., Corwin, *Twilight of the Supreme Court* (Yale Univ, 1934).

tionalism.[12] The doctrinal manifestations of commerce clause and due process jurisprudence were not simply free-floating rules that could be changed or abandoned without consequences extending beyond the particular doctrine involved. These areas of doctrine were developmentally intra- and interdependent. Modifications of one substantive due process doctrine entailed changes in another; developments in due process and commerce clause doctrine produced mutual, synergistic ramifications. In short, doctrinal commitments made by Justices in one area of doctrine entailed corresponding commitments in another area. In order to follow the trail of the yellow dog, we must trace these ripple effects across structurally related areas of doctrine.

I. ORIGINS: THE ERDMAN ACT, ADAIR v UNITED STATES, AND COPPAGE v KANSAS

The idea of "liberty of contract" is generally thought to have first appeared in a Supreme Court decision in *Allgeyer v Louisiana*,[13] decided in 1897; to have entered American constitutional jurisprudence in 1886 with *Godcharles v Wigeman;*[14] and to have emerged in American social thought well before the Civil War.[15] It is curious, then, to note that when Congress enacted the Erdman Act in 1898, no one in either House suggested that its Section 10 was unconstitutional.[16] That section prohibited interstate carriers from, inter alia, (1) requiring "any employee, or any person seeking employment, as a condition of such employment, to enter" into a so-called "yellow-dog" contract ("an agreement, either written or verbal, not to become or remain a member of any labor corporation, association, or organization"), and (2) "threaten[ing] any employee with

---

[12] See Cushman, *A Stream of Legal Consciousness: The Current of Commerce Doctrine from* Swift *to* Jones & Laughlin, 61 Fordham L Rev 105 (1992); McCurdy, *Justice Field and the Jurisprudence of Government-Business Relations: Some Parameters of Laissez Faire Constitutionalism, 1863–1897*, 61 J Am Hist 970 (1975).

[13] 165 US 578 (1897).

[14] 133 Pa 431 (1886).

[15] Eric Foner, note 7; William Forbath, *The Ambiguities of Free Labor* (cited in note 7); Charles McCurdy, note 7; William Nelson, note 7.

[16] See legislative histories of HR 4372, S 3653, and S 3662, 31 Cong Rec 74-5566 (55-2); S Rep 591 (55-2); HR Rep 454 (55-2). For background on the enactment of the Erdman Act, see Gerald Eggert, *Railroad Labor Disputes* (Univ Michigan, 1967).

loss of employment" or "unjustly discriminat[ing] against any employee" because of his union membership.[17] Why, in an era in which constitutional debate on the floor of both Houses of Congress flourished,[18] did these legislators believe that such abrogations of an employer's common law contractual prerogatives were constitutional?

The opinion of the district court in *United States v Adair*[19] suggests the unarticulated rationale on which many in Congress may have relied. The indictment charged that William Adair, master mechanic of the Louisville & Nashville Railroad Company, had discharged locomotive fireman O. B. Coppage because of the latter's membership in the Order of Locomotive Firemen. Adair's demurrer contended, inter alia, that Section 10 of the Erdman Act violated the liberty of contract secured to him under the Fifth Amendment.

District Judge Andrew M. Cochran conceded that the Fifth Amendment constituted an independent limitation on the federal power to regulate interstate commerce.[20] The liberty of contract secured to a lawful private business, however, was greater than that secured to a common carrier engaged in interstate commerce.[21] Because the latter "exercises a public function,"[22] held the Court, "[t]he only possible ground for holding that [Section 10] is in violation of the fifth amendment is that it has no real and substantial relation to the free course of interstate commerce."[23] Because Section 10's "tendency" was "to prevent an interruption to interstate commerce by reason of strikes, lockouts and boycotts,"[24] it constituted a legitimate regulation of the contractual relations of a business affected with a public interest. In other words, the common carrier's status as a business affected with a public interest rendered it subject to regulations to which a purely private business could

---

[17] 30 Stat 424, 428, ch 370 (55-2).

[18] See Donald G. Morgan, *Congress and the Constitution: A Study of Responsibility*, ch 7 (Belknap, 1966).

[19] 152 F 737 (ED Ky 1907).

[20] Id at 754–55.

[21] Id at 755–56.

[22] Id at 756.

[23] Id at 759.

[24] Id at 752.

not constitutionally be subjected; and the relationship between the company's contractual relations with its employees and the free flow of interstate commerce provided the rationale supporting the instant regulation.

A majority of the justices of the United States Supreme Court disagreed with Judge Cochran. The majority opinion, written by Justice John Marshall Harlan, took no notice of the fact that the company was a business traditionally regarded as affected with a public interest, and stated the parties' contractual rights in absolutist terms.[25]

> While, as already suggested, the rights of liberty and property guaranteed by the Constitution against deprivation without due process of law, is [sic] subject to such reasonable restraints as the common good or general welfare may require, it is not within the functions of government—at least in the absence of contract between the parties—to compel any person in the course of his business and against his will to accept or retain the personal services of another, or to compel any person, against his will, to perform personal services for another.

The common law prerogative of the employer to discharge his employee at will for any or no reason, Justice Harlan appeared to be saying, was insulated from government regulation by the Due Process Clause of the Fifth Amendment.

Yet despite having held that the statute violated the Fifth Amendment, Harlan went on to entertain at length the suggestion that, the Fifth Amendment notwithstanding, Section 10 might be a legitimate exercise of the federal power to regulate commerce among the states.

At first blush, this seems a curious mode of analysis. The commerce power, after all, was conferred in Article I, Section 8 of the original Constitution of 1787. The Fifth Amendment is an amendment to that document, and accordingly trumps the commerce clause to the extent the two are in conflict. If the Fifth Amendment rendered Section 10 of the Erdman Act unconstitutional, one is led to inquire, how could the statute have been independently sustained under the commerce power? It would seem that Harlan's Fifth Amendment analysis should have ended the inquiry into the statute's constitutionality.

---

[25] *Adair v United States*, 208 US 161, 174 (1908).

The solution to this puzzle lies in recognizing that Harlan and his colleagues were, like Judge Cochran, reasoning by analogy to Fourteenth Amendment due process cases. The Court had recognized in *Holden v Hardy*[26] and *Lochner v New York*[27] that the Fourteenth Amendment's Due Process Clause did not prohibit the state from regulating the labor contract if such regulation was reasonably related to the protection of public health, safety, or morals. Conventionally termed "police powers," these powers to protect public health, safety, and morals were held to be inherent in the sovereignty of the several States; and with these residuary police powers, the Court had held, "the Fourteenth Amendment was not designed to interfere."[28]

The federal government, as a government of enumerated powers, did not have residuary police powers. However, Congress did possess a power analogous to the police powers of the state legislatures. Just as the states were empowered to legislate to protect public health, safety, and morals, the federal government was empowered to legislate to protect the free flow of interstate commerce.[29] Harlan's mode of analysis thus suggests that a majority of the Court believed that the impact of employer-employee relations on interstate commerce might have provided a "commercial police power" rationale for the regulation of rights otherwise secured by the Fifth Amendment.

Yet unlike Judge Cochran, the majority could find no "real and substantial relation" between interstate commerce and the acts proscribed by Section 10. "[W]hat possible legal or logical connection is there between an employee's membership in a labor organization and the carrying on of interstate commerce?" queried Justice Harlan. "Such relation to a labor organization cannot have, *in itself* and in the eye of the law, any bearing upon the commerce with which the employee is connected by his labor and services."[30]

> One who engages in the service of an interstate carrier will, it must be assumed, faithfully perform his duty, whether he be a member or not a member of a labor organization. His fitness

---

[26] 169 US 366 (1898).

[27] 198 US 45 (1905).

[28] Id at 53.

[29] See, e.g., *Swift & Co. v United States*, 196 US 375 (1905).

[30] *Adair v United States*, 208 US 161, 178 (1908) (emphasis in original).

for the position in which he labors and his diligence in the discharge of his duties cannot in law or sound reason depend in any degree upon his being or not being a member of a labor organization. It cannot be assumed that his fitness is assured, or his diligence increased, by such membership, or that he is less fit or less diligent because of his not being a member of such an organization. It is the employee as a man and not as a member of a labor organization who labors in the service of an interstate carrier. Will it be said that the provision in question had its origin in the apprehension, on the part of Congress, that if it did not show more consideration for members of labor organizations than for wage-earners who were not members of such organizations, or if it did not insert in the statute some such provision as the one here in question, members of labor organizations would, by illegal or violent measures, interrupt or impair the freedom of commerce among the States? We will not indulge in any such conjectures. . . .[31]

Justice Joseph McKenna, writing in dissent, thought the majority was simply being dense. "[I]t is not necessary to suppose that labor organizations will violate the law," wrote the dissenting Justice. "Their power may be effectively exercised without violence or illegality. . . ."[32] The Senate Committee had opined, McKenna noted, that "this bill, should it become law, would reduce to a minimum labor strikes which affect interstate commerce. . . ."[33] "A provision of law which will prevent or tend to prevent the stoppage of every wheel in every car of an entire railroad system," wrote McKenna, certainly concerned practices having a "direct influence on interstate commerce."[34]

Yet McKenna was careful to note the limits of his disagreement with the majority.[35]

I would not be misunderstood. I grant that there are rights which can have no material measure. There are rights which, when exercised in a private business, may not be disturbed or limited. With them we are not concerned. We are dealing with rights exercised in a *quasi*-public business and therefore subject to control in the interest of the public.

---

[31] Id at 178–79.

[32] Id at 187.

[33] Id.

[34] Id at 189.

[35] Id at 190 (emphasis in original).

McKenna was thus thinking about Section 10 in much the same way that Judge Cochran had. The common law contractual prerogatives of the employer were regulable at all only because the business concerned was affected with a public interest; the impact that the employer's exercise of those prerogatives exerted on interstate commerce provided the commercial police power rationale for their regulation.[36]

Despite the fact that the majority had disagreed with McKenna about the impact of an employer's labor policies on interstate commerce, both majority and minority had embraced a common analytical model. Though Harlan and his colleagues in the majority were almost willfully agnostic about the relationship between railroad labor relations and interstate commerce, they had forged an important connection between commerce clause jurisprudence and due process jurisprudence. The sphere of liberty of contract protected by the Fifth Amendment was now defined in terms of the impact that employer-employee relations exerted on interstate commerce. If the Court ever came to view those relations as exerting a direct effect on interstate commerce, the Fifth Amendment would no longer serve to insulate those relations from congressional regulation. Moreover, though the majority had expressed no opinion on the issue, McKenna had suggested that the employer's common law contractual prerogatives could be regulated only if his business was affected with a public interest. So as the category of businesses affected with a public interest expanded, the sphere of liberty protected by the Fifth Amendment would accordingly contract. Three areas of constitutional jurisprudence—liberty of contract, the concept of a business affected with a public interest, and the notion of what constituted a direct effect on interstate commerce—had thus become developmentally interdependent.[37]

An issue similar to that presented in *Adair* came before the Court in 1915. *Coppage v Kansas*[38] concerned the constitutionality of a Kansas statute prohibiting employers from requiring their employees, as a condition of employment, to sign yellow-dog contracts.

---

[36] Justice Holmes wrote a separate dissent, in which he argued, typically, that it was not unreasonable for Congress to assume that the provisions of Section 10 would advance the policy of preventing strikes tending to interrupt interstate commerce. 208 US at 190–92.

[37] On the consequences of interdoctrinal synergy for commerce clause doctrine, see Cushman, note 12.

[38] 236 US 1 (1915).

A Mr. Hedges, a switchman for the St. Louis & San Francisco Railway Company and a member of the Switchmen's Union of North America, had refused to sign a yellow-dog contract presented to him by his employer. Mr. T. B. Coppage, superintendent of the company (and apparently no relation to the O. B. Coppage of *Adair*), had accordingly discharged Mr. Hedges. Mr. Coppage was indicted and convicted under the Kansas statute, and appealed his conviction to the Supreme Court.

Justice Mahlon Pitney, who had voted for the Erdman Act in 1898 while a Congressman from Morristown, New Jersey,[39] wrote the opinion of the Court declaring the statute unconstitutional. The Kansas statute, the Court held, was not distinguishable in principle from the federal statute reviewed in *Adair*. "Under constitutional freedom of contract," wrote Pitney, "whatever either party has the right to treat as sufficient ground for terminating the employment, where there is no stipulation on the subject, he has the right to provide against by insisting that a stipulation respecting it shall be a *sine qua non* of the inception of the employment, or of its continuance if it be terminable at will."[40]

Because *Coppage* concerned a state statute, the commerce power could not be invoked to provide a police power rationale. The regulatory justification would accordingly have to be found within the conventional categories of the state's police power. "[W]hat possible relation," asked Pitney, did the statute have "to the public health, safety, morals or general welfare? None is suggested, and we are unable to conceive of any."[41] The primary object of the statute was that of "leveling inequalities of fortune,"[42] and this was not a recognized police power rationale.

Justice McKenna, who had dissented in *Adair*, demonstrated his fidelity to *Adair*'s analytical model by joining the *Coppage* majority. Both cases had involved regulations of a business affected with a public interest. But in *Coppage*, unlike in *Adair*, there had been no police power rationale on which to justify the regulation of the employment contract.

---

[39] 31 Cong Rec 5053 (55-2).

[40] 236 US at 13 (emphasis in original).

[41] Id at 16.

[42] Id at 18.

Dissenting for himself and Justice Hughes,[43] Justice Day chided the majority for not taking the associative rights of the workers seriously. "Would it be beyond the legitimate exercise of the police power," asked the dissenters, "to provide that an employee should not be required to agree, as a condition of employment, to forego affiliation with a particular political party, or the support of a particular candidate for office?"[44] Might not the State prohibit an employer from requiring its employee to join or not to join a particular church?[45] "It seems to me," wrote Justice Day, "that these questions answer themselves."[46] "The law should be as zealous to protect the constitutional liberty of the employee as it is to guard that of the employer. A principal object of this statute is to protect the liberty of the citizen to make such lawful affiliations as he may desire with organizations of his choice. It should not be necessary to the protection of the liberty of one citizen that the same right in another citizen be abridged or destroyed."[47]

A defense of the right to join a union cast in the rhetoric of freedom of association was not novel in 1915. In *Commonwealth v Hunt*,[48] decided in 1842, Chief Justice Lemuel Shaw of the Massachusetts Supreme Judicial Court had deployed similar associational language in his landmark opinion holding that labor unions were not per se criminal conspiracies.[49] In upholding the right of the Boston Journeymen Bootmakers' Society to organize, Shaw sought to analogize unions to other common societies formed for purposes of mutual aid and protection. "Such an association," he wrote, "might be used to afford each other assistance in times of poverty,

---

[43] Holmes again dissented separately, arguing that *Adair* and *Lochner* ought to be overruled. 236 US at 26–27.

[44] 236 US at 37.

[45] Id at 39.

[46] Id at 37.

[47] Id at 40.

[48] 4 Met 111 (1842).

[49] Id at 129–31, 134. See Leon Fink, *Labor, Liberty and the Law: Trade Unionism and the Problem of the American Constitutional Order*, 74 J Am Hist 904, 910 (1987); A. Konefsky, *"As Best to Subserve Their Own Interests": Lemuel Shaw, Labor Conspiracy, and Fellow Servants*, 7 Law & Hist Rev 219 (1989); Levy, *The Law of the Commonwealth and Chief Justice Shaw* 203 (Harvard Univ, 1957); Tomlins, *The State and the Unions: Labor Relations, Law, and the Organized Labor Movement, 1880–1960*, 42–44 (Cambridge Univ, 1985); Woodiwiss, *Rights v. Conspiracy: A Sociological Essay on the History of Labour Law in the United States* 58–61 (St. Martin's, 1990).

sickness and distress; or to raise their intellectual, moral or social condition; or to make improvement in their art; or for other proper purposes."[50] The association's objective of recruiting all bootmakers into the society was not unlawful, Shaw held, for it would give to the union "a power which might be exerted for [such] useful and honorable purposes. . . ."[51]

Following Shaw's opinion in *Hunt*, American courts generally adhered to the view that the formation of labor associations for mutual aid and protection was perfectly legal.[52] Indeed, throughout the balance of the nineteenth and twentieth centuries, American judges generally agreed that strikes to obtain higher wages, shorter hours, or better working conditions were lawful.[53] Shaw's view that strikes to obtain a closed shop were legal, however, was not so readily accepted by the American bench. Throughout the late nineteenth and early twentieth centuries, state and federal courts repeatedly held that strikes and boycotts designed to secure the employment of only union workers were unlawful.[54] Such union actions were enjoinable, the courts held, for two reasons: first, they constituted coercive interferences with the right of the employer to run his business as he saw fit; and second, they aimed to require the non-union workingman to surrender a portion of his associational liberty as the price of plying his lawful trade.

---

[50] 4 Met at 129.

[51] Id.

[52] Indeed, some courts occasionally expressed the view that the formation of such associations was not only not criminal, but positively laudable. See, e.g., *Coeur D'Alene Consolidated & Mining Co. v Miners' Union*, 51 F 260, 263 (CCD Idaho 1892); *State v Stewart*, 9 A 559, 566 (Vt 1887).

[53] Arnold Paul, *Conservative Crisis and the Rule of Law* 106 (P Smith, 1976); Herbert Hovenkamp, *Enterprise and American Law, 1836–1937* 216, 226 (Harvard Univ, 1991).

[54] Id. Hovenkamp, supra at 233. See *Coeur D'Alene Consolidated & Mining Co. v Miners' Union of Wardner*, 51 F 260 (CCD Idaho 1892); *Casey v Cincinnati Typographical Union No. 3*, 45 F 135 (SD Ohio 1891); *Old Dominion Steamship Co. v McKenna*, 30 F 48 (SDNY 1887); *Bausch Machine Tool Co. v Hill*, 231 Mass 30 (1918); *Snow Iron Works v Chadwick*, 227 Mass 382, 116 NE 801 (1917); *Martin v Francke*, 227 Mass 272, 116 NE 404 (1917); *Folsom v Lewis*, 208 Mass 336, 94 NE 316 (1911); *Plant v Woods*, 176 Mass 492 (1900); *Erdman v Mitchell*, 207 Pa 79 (1903); *State v Dyer*, 67 Vt 690, 32 A 814 (1895); *State v Stewart*, 59 Vt 273, 9 A 559 (1887); *State v Glidden*, 55 Conn 46 (1887); *State v Donaldson*, 32 NJL 151 (1867). See also *Kayser v Fitzgerald*, 178 NYS 130 (1919); *Kealey v Faulkner*, 7 Ohio NP 49 (1907); *Lucke v Clothing Cutters' Assembly*, 77 Md 396, 26 A 505 (1893); Ernst, *The Closed Shop, the Proprietary Capitalist, and the Law, 1897–1915* in S. Jacoby, ed, *Masters to Managers* (1989). See also Commons & Andrews, *Principles of Labor Legislation* 112–15 (Harper & Bros, 1927), and cases there cited.

In *Plant v Woods*,[55] the Supreme Judicial Court of Massachusetts condemned the defendant union's threats to strike and boycott employers employing certain non-union plaintiffs. "The purpose of these defendants," the court found, "was to force the plaintiffs to join the defendant association, and to that end they injured the plaintiffs in their business, and molested and disturbed them in their efforts to work at their trade."[56] The union men "had no right to force other persons to join them."[57] The attempt by the defendants "to compel the [non-union men] against their will to join the association" was, the court held, "intolerable, and inconsistent with the spirit of our laws."[58]

Erdman v Mitchell[59] involved one closed-shop strike in a larger campaign "to drive every plumber in Philadelphia into the United Association of Journeyman Plumbers."[60] In *Erdman*, the court found that the defendant union members, through a perfectly peaceful strike, "undertook, by intimidation of plaintiffs and their employers to coerce the plaintiffs into joining their organization."[61] "By this conduct of defendants," the court noted, "plaintiffs have been unable to secure any steady employment at their trade, and will have to enter one of defendants' unions or leave the city."[62] Condemning the union's actions, the court accepted the plaintiff's contention that "an agreement by a number of persons that they will by threats of a strike deprive a mechanic of the right to work for others merely because he does not choose to join a particular union, is a conspiracy to commit an unlawful act, which conspiracy may be restrained."[63] *Erdman* is of particular interest, because it was not a case of a court protecting the right of workers to remain non-union men. The plaintiffs in the case were actually members of another union, who wished to remain loyal to the association with which they had voluntarily affiliated.

---

[55] 176 Mass 492 (1900).

[56] Id at 502.

[57] Id.

[58] Id.

[59] 207 Pa 79 (1903).

[60] Id at 89.

[61] Id.

[62] Id.

[63] Id.

In *Casey v Cincinnati Typographical Union*, the court decried the boycott of a non-union newspaper as "an organized effort to force printers to come into the union, or be driven from their calling for want of employment."[64] The court in *Old Dominion Steamship Co. v McKenna* stated the rule succinctly: "All combinations and associations designed to coerce workmen to become members, or to interfere with, obstruct, vex, or annoy them in working, or in obtaining work, because they are not members . . . are *pro tanto* illegal combinations or associations."[65]

As these cases made clear, the rights of workers to associate together, even to strike, were legally protected; these rights simply could not be used as a means to coerce workers in the exercise of their right to freedom of association. In deploying associational rhetoric in the *Coppage* dissent, Day and Hughes were simply calling for symmetry in the protection of associational liberty. Granted that the employer's liberty of contract was generally constitutionally protected, the dissenters would have held, the state could constitutionally prohibit him from using his freedom of contract to coerce the employee into forgoing his associational liberty. "While this court should, within the limitations of the constitutional guaranty, protect the free right of contract, it is not less important that the State be given the right to exert its legislative authority, if it deems best to do so, for the protection of rights which inhere in the privileges of the citizen of every free country."[66]

At the core of the disagreement between the majority and the dissent lay a difference over whether the employee's agreement not to join a union was the product of coercion. The majority was able to resolve the tension between liberty of contract and freedom of association by finding simply that the employee had voluntarily contracted away this associational right. To the majority justices, there was no coercion involved.[67] The dissenters could not accept this voluntary waiver theory; indeed, they seemed prepared to take judicial notice that such a waiver would always be the product of coercion. Day and Hughes saw the inequality of bargaining power between employer and employee as rendering the employment re-

---

[64] 45 F 135, 143 (SD Ohio 1891).

[65] 30 F 48, 50 (SDNY 1887) (emphasis in original).

[66] *Coppage v Kansas*, 236 US 1, 40 (1915).

[67] Id at 8–9, 14–16, 20–21.

lationship inherently subject to coercive abuse. The yellow-dog contract was for them coercive per se.[68]

Yet the majority was not taking the position that economic pressure exerted in the employment context could not constitute coercion. Less than three years following the *Coppage* decision, the Court would enjoin an effort by the United Mine Workers to unionize a non-union mine.[69] All of the employees of the Hitchman Coal & Coke Company had signed yellow-dog contracts. An agent of the U.M.W. proceeded secretly to persuade employees of the company to agree to join the union. The plan was that, once a sufficient number of employees had agreed to do so, they would quit in a body, join the union, and refuse to return to work unless the company consented to a closed-shop agreement with the U.M.W.

The Court enjoined the U.M.W.'s actions as an unlawful attempt to induce the employees to breach their contracts with the company. The Court further made it clear that it was troubled by "misrepresentations, deceptive statements, and threats of pecuniary loss" made by the union representative to the company's employees, as well as by the history of violence associated with coal strikes.[70] But the Court also repeatedly condemned threats to strike for a closed-shop agreement as "coercive" of the employer and of the employees who had chosen not to join the union.[71] The objective of such a strike, the Court stated, would be "to coerce the employer and the remaining miners to 'organize the mine,' that is, to make an agreement that none but members of the Union should be employed. . . ."[72] "The same liberty which enables men to form unions, and through the union to enter into agreements with employers willing to agree, entitles other men to remain independent of the union. . . ."[73]

In dissent, Justice Brandeis criticized the asymmetry presented by the *Coppage* and *Hitchman* decisions. "If it is coercion to threaten to strike unless [the employer] consents to a closed union shop, it

---

[68] Id at 32, 35, 38–42.

[69] *Hitchman Coal & Coke Co. v Mitchell*, 245 US 229 (1917).

[70] Id at 258–59.

[71] Id at 248, 250–51, 253, 255, 258–59, 261.

[72] Id at 255.

[73] Id at 251.

is coercion also to threaten not to give one employment unless the [employee] will consent to a closed non-union shop. The employer may sign the union agreement for fear that *labor* may not be otherwise available; the workman may sign the individual agreement for fear that *employment* may not otherwise be obtainable."[74] As Brandeis was not-so-obliquely suggesting, the fact that the Court (and the American judiciary generally) simultaneously embraced the view that a strike for a closed shop was coercive while the exaction of a yellow-dog contract was not[75] seemed the rankest anti-union hypocrisy.

Perhaps it was. The majority may have remained troubled by the reputation for violence and syndicalism that had become associated with unionism as a result of the events of Haymarket Square, Homestead, the "Debs Rebellion," and other similar instances.[76] Yet the majority's view that yellow-dog contracts were not coercive may not have seemed as preposterous in 1915 as it appears from the vantage point of the late twentieth century. As Herbert Hovenkamp has recently noted, America suffered throughout the nineteenth century from severe shortages of labor. In part as results of such shortages, slavery persisted in the United States long after it had disappeared in other Western nations; American entrepreneurs led the world in the development of labor-saving technology; America maintained virtually an open immigration policy; and the United States experienced significantly less labor unrest than contemporary England. Wages in the United States rose steadily throughout the nineteenth and early twentieth centuries, and wages and working conditions for American laborers were generally far better than those obtained by European workers.[77]

---

[74] Id at 271 (emphasis in original). Justice Brandeis actually concluded that neither the strike to obtain a closed-shop nor a yellow-dog contract implied "coercion in a legal sense." Id.

[75] For a discussion of the near-unanimity of state court decisions holding anti-yellow-dog contract statutes unconstitutional, see *Coppage v Kansas*, 236 US at 21–26. It should be noted that not all states condemned strikes to obtain a closed shop. In those states, of course, the asymmetry criticized by Brandeis was not present. See Sayre, *Criminal Conspiracy*, 35 Harv L Rev 393, 407–8, n 49 (1922).

[76] See Paul, *Conservative Crisis and the Rule of Law* (cited in note 53). The stronger claim that the Court was anti-worker would be harder to sustain. For example, in 1917, the year *Hitchman* was decided, the Court upheld an Oregon law limiting the working day for men to ten hours. *Bunting v Oregon*, 243 US 426 (1917).

[77] Hovenkamp, *Labor Conspiracies in American Law, 1880–1930*, 66 Tex L Rev 919, 930 (1988).

In light of these historical consequences of the labor shortage, argues Hovenkamp, political economists writing in the early twentieth century "perceived the bargaining positions of capital and labor as more or less equal. Indeed, they felt that the advantage, if any, lay with labor. . . . They argued that it was labor and not employers that could make take-it-or-leave-it offers."[78]

Illustrative of the view that laborers could avail themselves of a veritable smorgasbord of employment options was the opinion of the Georgia Supreme Court in *Western & Atlantic R.R. Co. v Bishop.*[79] In *Bishop*, an employee of the railroad had in his employment contract waived his statutory right to recover against the company for injuries occasioned by the negligence of his fellow servant. Subsequently injured by a fellow employee, Bishop sought to have the waiver set aside on the grounds that it violated public policy. Bishop relied heavily on the U.S. Supreme Court decision in *Railroad Company v Lockwood*,[80] which had held void as against public policy a contract exempting a common carrier from liability for damage to freight or passengers caused by the negligence of the carrier or its servants. Distinguishing *Lockwood*, the Georgia court held that the carrier stood in a monopolistic relation to the passenger or shipper, and its contractual prerogatives could be regulated for that reason. In relation to its employee, however, the railroad held no such monopoly. Upholding the contractual waiver, the court held that the railroad was "only one of a million of employers with whom [Bishop] might have sought employment."[81]

The massive waves of immigration to the United States in the late nineteenth and early twentieth centuries may have helped somewhat to ameliorate the perception of labor shortage that undoubtedly lay behind the Georgia court's seemingly hyperbolic remarks. Between 1886 and 1916, nearly 19 million immigrants arrived in the United States.[82] Yet wage rates continued to rise significantly, especially in the years leading up to the *Coppage* decision. Despite nearly flat growth in the 1890s, real wages in the

---

[78] Id at 930–31. Hovenkamp offers this observation as a means of explaining why early-twentieth-century courts and political economists were inclined to treat labor combinations as analogous to, rather than different from, business combinations.

[79] 50 Ga 465 (1874).

[80] 17 Wall 375 (1873).

[81] 50 Ga at 472.

[82] Ellis Hawley, *The Great War and the Search for a Modern Order* 11–12 (New York, 1979).

United States rose 37 percent between 1890 and 1914.[83] This occurred despite the fact that not even 8 percent of the American
labor force was unionized at any time before 1914.[84] The productive capacity of the American economy appeared to be more than
adequate to absorb the flood of new immigrants.[85] Indeed, the lot
of the American worker seemed to be getting consistently better
rather than worse.[86] The existence of some unemployment was
acknowledged, but was frequently attributed to laziness or other
defects of character.[87] In 1907, the year in which the *Hitchman*
case was commenced, the nationwide unemployment rate was 2.8
percent;[88] in 1917, the year of the Court's decision, the national
rate was only 4.6 percent.[89] There was little reason to think that
the remote panhandle of West Virginia harbored a large untapped
reservoir of labor. As Justice Pitney wrote for the majority, "[i]t
was one thing for [the company] to find, from time to time, compar-
atively small numbers of men to take vacant places in a going mine,
another and a much more difficult thing to find a complete gang
of new men to start up a mine shut down by a strike. . . ."[90]

Though the Court probably did not have access to some of these

---

[83] Stuart Bruchey, *The Wealth of the Nation* 138 (Harper & Row, 1988).

[84] Id at 137.

[85] Between 1901 and 1913 the nationwide unemployment rate in the manufacturing and
transportation sectors rose above 7 percent only twice, in the recession years of 1904 and
1908. In all other years, the rate was below 6 percent; in seven of those thirteen years, the
rate was 4 percent or lower. Commons et al, 3 *History of Labor in the United States* 128
(Macmillan, 1935). The nationwide unemployment rate for the entire civilian workforce
during those years rose above 6 percent only twice, in 1908 and 1911. In all other years,
the rate was below 6 percent; in five of those thirteen years, the rate was 4 percent or lower.
Stanley Lebergott, *Manpower in Economic Growth: The American Record Since 1800* 43–47, 512
(New York, 1964). The average national unemployment rate for all civilian workers in the
decade 1900–1909 was 4 percent; for the decade 1910–1919, the figure was 5 percent. Id at
189.

[86] Dubofsky, *Industrialism and the American Worker, 1865–1920*, 119 (H. Davidson, 1985).

[87] Commons et al, note 85, at 115; John Garraty, *Unemployment in History* 113–18 (Harper
& Row, 1979); Lebergott, note 85, at 166; Roy Lubove, *The Struggle for Social Security* 147
(Harvard Univ, 1968).

[88] Lebergott, note 85, at 512.

[89] Id. The rate for the manufacturing and transportation sectors in each of those years
was 3.5 percent. Commons et al, note 85, at 128. Moreover, at least some of this unemployment was probably attributable to factors having little to do with the size of the labor
supply: inability to work during certain months of the year due to weather conditions,
which particularly afflicted the nation's large population of agricultural workers; a lack of
paid vacations to absorb seasonal declines in demand; and perhaps in some regions a higher
incidence of worker illness than we experience today. Lebergott, note 85, at 165–71.

[90] *Hitchman Coal & Coke Co. v Mitchell*, 245 US 229, 258 (1917).

specific statistics on wages and employment, the Justices undoubtedly entertained at least an impressionistic understanding of their
import. In his opinion striking down the District of Columbia minimum wage law in *Adkins v Children's Hospital*,[91] Justice Sutherland
remarked: "[w]e cannot close our eyes to the notorious fact that
earnings everywhere in all occupations have increased—not alone
in States where the minimum wage law obtains but in the country
generally. . . ."[92] Reasoning in the idiom of Adam Smith, many
legal minds must have continued to believe that the growth in
demand for labor had exceeded the growth in supply. A judge who
had grown to maturity in the labor-short nineteenth century might
well have thought that the American laborer in 1915 was actually
bargaining from a position of some strength.[93] To be sure, individual laborers and employers often did not bargain from equal positions of strength—even in times of low unemployment—and the
Coppage majority recognized this.[94] But these disparities in bargaining power were not in the majority's view so great as to render
the labor contract the product of coercion. As they saw it, the
laborer wishing to retain his freedom to associate with a union
could always find another employer to bargain with. Recognizing
the structure of the labor market and the perceived ease of employee mobility,[95] an employer in a labor-hungry market was in
no position to "coerce" his employee into contracting away his
associational freedom. But an employer struck for a closed shop
was frequently in no position to bargain with a non-union man.

If such a view was problematic in 1915, it was to become increasingly implausible. The demobilization of the armed forces following World War I, coupled with the tremendous influx of European
immigrants in 1919 and 1920, caused fears of widespread unemployment.[96] Indeed, 1921's unemployment rates of 21.2 percent in
the manufacturing and transportation sectors marked the highest
rate in decades.[97] President Harding brought together a Commis-

---

[91] 261 US 525 (1923).

[92] Id at 560.

[93] Hovenkamp, note 77, at 931.

[94] *Coppage v Kansas* 236 US 1, 17 (1915).

[95] Hovenkamp, note 77, at 931.

[96] Parmet, *Labor and Immigration in Industrial America* 169–90 (Twayne, 1981).

[97] Commons et al, note 85, at 128. The nationwide civilian unemployment rate of 11.7
percent was the highest since 1898. Lebergott, note 85, at 43, 512.

sion on Unemployment in 1921, and attempts to alleviate the problem through state unemployment insurance programs began in earnest.[98] The AFL again renewed its long-standing campaign for immigration restriction. Some business interests predictably contended that there was a labor shortage, but few were persuaded. In 1921 and again in 1924, a Republican-controlled Congress and White House enacted and signed legislation placing substantial restrictions on immigration.[99] Despite this contrived contraction of the labor market, the subsequent onset of the Great Depression brought sustained unemployment in numbers previously unimaginable.[100]

The cases condemning strikes for a closed shop demonstrated that the courts were prepared to see coercion in economic pressure exerted by one of the parties to the employment relationship. As the *Hitchman* case illustrated, the meaning of the term "coercion" was not so constricted that the Court could not have found that an employee was coerced into signing a yellow-dog contract. There was no need for the Court to expand its notion of coercion to include pressure brought to bear from a superior bargaining position. In order to arrive at the conclusion that yellow-dog contracts were coercive, however, the Court would have to change its assumptions about the relative bargaining strengths of employers and employees. Changes in the structure of the labor market between 1915 and the 1930s would prompt a re-examination of those assumptions.

Yet in 1915 Day and Hughes were not contending that the employment relationship was inherently coercive and therefore regulable in all its aspects.[101] The dissenters were instead suggesting that there were certain valuable rights of association to which liberty of contract ought to give way. Indeed, it was the nature of the right compromised that appears to have led them to the conclu-

---

[98] Lubove, note 87, at ch 7.

[99] Parmet, note 96, at 169–90.

[100] In 1932, more than 13 million adult men were unemployed. Leuchtenburg, *Franklin D. Roosevelt and the New Deal* 1 (Harper & Row, 1963). In 1933, fully 25 percent of the labor force was unemployed. Bruchey, note 83, at 157–58. In the decade of 1930–1939, the average national unemployment rate was 18 percent. Lebergott, note 85, at 189.

[101] For an early analysis of the concept of coercion in the employment relationship and other contexts, see Hale, *Coercion and Distribution in a Supposedly Non-Coercive State*, 38 Pol Sci Q 470 (1923).

sion that the bargain was coerced. Day's analogies between yellow-dog contracts and contracts promising not to join a particular church, political party, or other "such lawful affiliations" were of course designed to reduce the majority's position to absurdity. But by implying that the majority would have decided cases involving such hypothetical contracts differently, the dissenters were also accusing the majority of according labor unions second-class status as voluntary associations. As one historian has put it, "American labor organizations lived in a legal twilight zone, expressions of an associational impulse growing in society at large, yet differentiated from other expressions of that impulse by society's law. . . ."[102]

In 1915, only Day, Holmes, and Hughes were prepared to reach across that twilight zone to assimilate unionism to liberalism's traditional solicitude for voluntary association. In 1930, however, Hughes would return from a fourteen-year hiatus in his judicial career to lead a reconstituted Court. During his tenure as Chief Justice, the accommodation between contractual and associational liberty for which he and Justice Day had contended would be struck.

II. WARTIME LESSONS AND A NEW PROFILE FOR ORGANIZED LABOR

As the country confronted the exigencies of domestic production, communication, and transportation brought on by World War I, it became clear that the *Adair* majority's professed agnosticism on the relationship between union-management relations and interstate commerce was no longer tenable. It was now "essential to the national safety that the volume of production be maintained at the highest possible level, and that the avenues of communication and transportation remain always open."[103] It was recognized that industrial strife would tend to frustrate the implementation of these critical objectives. Accordingly, the National War Labor Board was established in April of 1918 for the purpose of ensuring the peaceful and prompt settlement of labor disputes in vital war industries.[104]

---

[102] Tomlins, note 49, at 33.

[103] Joel Seidman, *The Yellow Dog Contract* 25 (Johns Hopkins, 1932).

[104] Id; Valerie Jean Conner, *The National War Labor Board*, ch 2 (Univ North Carolina, 1983); Pringle, *The Life and Times of William Howard Taft* 915 (Farrar & Rinehart, 1939).

President Wilson appointed to the co-chairmanship of the Board former President William Howard Taft. Taft, a former judge on the United States Court of Appeals, a professor at Yale Law School, and a future Chief Justice of the United States, was perhaps the most prominent conservative lawyer of the day, and was widely expected to be a pro-employer member of the Board. But, as Taft's biographer reports, the future Chief Justice found his experience on the Board to be personally transformative. An extended trip to the munitions and textile mills of the South convinced Taft of the need for the establishment of minimum wages. This conviction was duly reflected in the orders of the Board, and subsequently in Taft's dissent in *Adkins v Children's Hospital*.[105]

Taft and his fellow Board members also recognized that industrial peace was necessary to the uninterrupted production and transportation of the goods needed for the successful prosecution of the war. To this end the Board announced that (1) "The right of workers to organize in trade unions and to bargain collectively, through chosen representatives, is recognized. This right shall not be denied, abridged, or interfered with by the employers in any manner whatsoever"; and (2) "Employers shall not discharge workers for membership in trade unions, nor for legitimate trade union activities."[106] The Board ordered numerous reinstatements with back pay for employees discharged for engaging in legitimate union activities; prohibited employers from requiring employees to sign yellow-dog contracts; and forbade employers to require their employees to join company unions.[107] Indeed, the Board ordered employers to discontinue the use of yellow-dog contracts in cases involving General Electric, Smith & Wesson, and the Omaha and Council Bluffs Street Railway Company.[108] The war had temporarily transformed businesses that were ordinarily purely private into businesses affected with a national public interest and consequently

---

[105] Conner, supra; Pringle, supra, at 916, 918.

[106] US Bureau of Labor Statistics, *National War Labor Board*, Bulletin No 287, 30–34 (1922), quoted in Philip Taft, *Collective Bargaining Before the New Deal*, in Harry A. Millis, ed, *How Collective Bargaining Works* 901–2 (New York, 1942); Presidential proclamation, April 8, 1918, cited in Pringle, *The Life and Times of William Howard Taft* at 917–18 (cited in note 104).

[107] Conner, *The National War Labor Board* (cited in note 104); Philip Taft, supra, at 902.

[108] Conner, note 104, at ch 7; Daniel Ernst, *The Yellow Dog Contract and Liberal Reform, 1917–1932*, 30 Labor History 251, 254 (1989); Pringle, note 104, at 921; Seidman, note 103, at 25; Edwin Witte, *The Government in Labor Disputes* 222 (McGraw-Hill, 1932).

subject to a greater degree of regulation.[109] And the National War Labor Board, headed up by a leading conservative and the next Chief Justice, had taken judicial notice of the fact that an employer's interference with his employees' legitimate associational activities could impede the capacity of such a business to perform its crucial public function.[110]

The years following World War I also brought increasing solicitude for the associational rights of the nation's workers. This may well have been a by-product of changing perceptions about the nature of labor unions. At the turn of the century, Christopher Tomlins has noted, the leadership of the American labor movement had embraced trade unionism as a means to achieve larger, radical political goals. Through association, Samuel Gompers had explained, "the workers would come to know that 'the state is by rights theirs' and would thereupon take over the functions of government 'in the interests of all.' "[111] Collective bargaining was "an entering wedge toward industrial democracy and abolition of the profit system," the end result of which would be "full labor control" of industry.[112]

Over the course of the next twenty years, however, the AFL sloughed off "its old associational ideology for a redefined voluntarism which drastically downplayed the radical political connotations of associationalism."[113] Instead of a means to "accomplish the transformation of prevailing political and social institutions," "[v]oluntary association and collective bargaining became mechanisms for the improvement of material conditions within the political and industrial framework of the new corporate economy."[114] By World War I, Tomlins argues, "this ideology was manifest

---

[109] See *Block v Hirsh*, 256 US 135, 155 (1921).

[110] See David Brody, *The American Worker in the Progressive Age: A Comprehensive Analysis*, in Brody, *Workers in Industrial America* 42 (Oxford Univ, 1980); Brody, *The Emergence of Mass Production Unionism*, in Braeman et al, eds, *Change and Continuity in Twentieth Century America* 243 (Ohio Univ, 1964).

[111] Tomlins, note 49, at 74; see also id at 54–59.

[112] Id, quoting Robert F. Hoxie in *Trade Unionism in the United States* 274–75 (D. Appleton, 1923); Forbath, note 7, at 800–817.

[113] Tomlins, note 49, at 77.

[114] Id at 74–75; see David Brody, *The Expansion of the American Labor Movement: Institutional Sources of Stimulus and Restraint*, in Brody, ed, *The American Labor Movement* 121 (Harper & Row, 1971); Samuel Gompers, *Labor and the Employer* 286 (Arno, 1920).

in virtually all of the AFL leadership's actions."[115] Rather than conceptualizing themselves as corporative bodies seeking to absorb the functions of the state, AFL unions now saw themselves as individual entities pursuing their own legitimate self-interests within the state's common law contractualist paradigm. "Organized workers, they argued, were freely associating citizens who ought to enjoy the same freedoms of action and expression that individual workers and citizens enjoyed. . . . In Gompers's hands, the AFL model was a labor version of the kind of business-based association-alism that elite reformers like Herbert Hoover and organizations like the National Civic Federation advocated during the first decades of the new century."[116] In addition, the AFL sought to refurbish its public image "by providing a model of the good worker/citizen that was essentially the same as that to be found in the literature of the middle-class, Progressive movement. The worker was intelligent, responsible, civic-minded, thrifty, self-reliant, tolerant of other people's religions, and patriotic. . . ."[117]

The liberalization of the AFL was accompanied by two other major developments in the history of labor unions. First, as the result of a wave of prosecutions initiated during and in the wake of World War I, the syndicalist Industrial Workers of the World was virtually defunct by the early 1920s.[118] Second, the years following World War I also saw the relationship between the Socialist Party and the nation's workers grow increasingly attenuated. By 1921, membership in the Party had dwindled to 13,000.[119] By 1928, membership had fallen to under 8,000, and the party had become "increasingly an organization of ministers and intellectuals rather than industrial workers."[120] "The labor movement of the 1920's," Tomlins concludes, "was a loose and disaggregated combination of individual organizations, not the quasi-syndicalist associa-

---

[115] Tomlins, note 49, at 77.

[116] William Forbath, *Law and the Shaping of the American Labor Movement* 147 (Harvard Univ, 1991).

[117] Anthony Woodiwiss, *Rights v. Conspiracy*, note 49, at 139; see Sweeney, *The A.F.L.'s Good Citizen, 1920–1940*, 13 Labor History (1972).

[118] Joseph Rayback, *A History of American Labor* 282, 289–90 (Macmillan, 1968); see Conlin, *Bread and Roses, Too* (Greenwood, 1969); Melvyn Dubofsky, *We Shall be All: A History of the Industrial Workers of the World* (Quadrangle, 1969).

[119] Hawley, note 82, at 130.

[120] Id at 131.

tion of self-governing trades established in 1886. As such, its reconciliation to the prevailing common law tradition was no longer
problematic."[121] In other words, unions had come increasingly to
be seen as liberal institutions.

These changes in the complexion of the labor movement made
defenses of unions cast in the rhetoric of liberal rights discourse
increasingly resonant. Indeed, the growing recognition of the associational legitimacy of unions was widely expressed in the critique
of yellow-dog contracts that flourished in the 1920s. Opponents
of the contract "repeatedly depicted the agreement as an illiberal
institution, which snatched from workers their rights of free association, speech, and thought."[122] The yellow-dog contract, argued
one Illinois labor leader, violated the workers' rights of free association, "the essential difference between the free man and the
slave."[123] Such contracts were "a plain denial of the right of association," wrote Felix Frankfurter and Nathan Greene.[124] Echoing Justice Day's *Coppage* dissent, Edwin Witte wrote: "would anyone
tolerate for a moment aid by the courts to employers in the enforcement . . . of promises which they may exact from their employees not to join the Methodist Church or the Masons, or any
other religious or fraternal organization?"[125] Cornelius Cochrane, a
persistent critic of the contract for the *American Labor Legislation
Review*, likewise echoed Justice Day's critique. "Union labor," he
wrote, "is convinced that if employers insisted upon employees
signing a contract that they would not vote the Republican or
Democratic ticket, or attend the Protestant or Catholic Church, or
join the Knights of Columbus or the Masons, there would be an
immediate public outcry against this invasion of the right of voluntary association."[126] "[U]nless we are permanently to overthrow the
American principle that organization into voluntary societies is to
be encouraged rather than strangled," Cochrane contended, "the

---

[121] Tomlins, note 49, at 91; see William Forbath, note 116, at 128–35.

[122] Ernst, note 108, at 263.

[123] Id.

[124] Frankfurter and Greene, *Congressional Power Over the Labor Injunction*, 31 Colo L Rev
385, 396 (1931).

[125] Edwin Witte, *"Yellow Dog" Contracts*, 6 Wis L Rev 21, 31 (1930).

[126] Cochrane, *Why Organized Labor is Fighting "Yellow Dog" Contracts*, 15 Am Lab Legis
Rev 227, 232 (1925).

'yellow dog' contract must be declared illegal."[127] A study of labor relations in the coal industry undertaken by the United States Coal Commission in 1922 and 1923 resulted in a scathing denunciation of the contract. "A manager," stated the Commission's report, "who can mine coal only with the use of spies, intimidation, and forced contracts, which aim to destroy the freedom of will of his workers, is not much of a manager and less of a man."[128]

By the late 1920s the New York courts were refusing to enforce yellow-dog contracts on the grounds that they were void for lack of mutuality.[129] Emboldened by the trend, Wisconsin passed a statute in 1929 declaring yellow-dog contracts void and unenforceable as opposed to public policy; Arizona, Colorado, Ohio, and Oregon followed suit two years later.[130] And in 1930 the Senate rejected the nomination of John J. Parker to the Supreme Court largely because Parker had upheld the validity of yellow-dog contracts in the *Red Jacket Coal* case.[131] Even Parker's Senate supporters vigorously denounced the yellow-dog contract, and called for its statutory abolition.[132] Of the ten Senators who spoke in defense of Parker's nomination, only one suggested that the contract was legitimate.[133]

---

[127] Cochrane, *"Yellow Dog" Abolished in Wisconsin*, 19 Am Lab Legis Rev 315, 316 (1929).

[128] Seidman, note 103, at 31–32.

[129] See *Interborough Rapid Transit Co. v Lavin*, 247 NY 65, 159 NE 863 (1928); *Exchange Bakery and Restaurant, Inc. v Rifkin*, 245 NY 260, 157 NE 130 (1927); *Interborough Rapid Transit Co. v Green*, 131 Misc 682, 227 NYS 258 (1928); Carey and Oliphant, *The Present Status of the* Hitchman Case, 29 Colum L Rev 441 (1929); Cochrane, *Branding "Yellow Dog" Contracts*, 18 Am Lab Legis Rev 115 (1928); Witte, *"Yellow Dog" Contracts* (cited in note 125).

[130] Irving Bernstein, *The Lean Years* 394, 411 (Houghton Mifflin, 1960); Cochrane, *"Yellow Dog" Abolished in Wisconsin* (cited in note 127); Witte, note 108, at 228; Seidman, note 103, at 35. The proliferation of state anti-yellow-dog statutes continued throughout the 1930s. See Fraenkel, *Recent Statutes Affecting Labor Injunctions and "Yellow Dog" Contracts*, 30 Ill L Rev 854, 858–59 (1936). Many of these statutes sought to preserve associational liberty by prohibiting not only yellow-dog contracts, but agreements requiring the employee to *join* a union as well. Id at 859, n 29.

[131] *United Mine Workers v Red Jacket Consolidated Coal & Coke Co.*, 18 F2d 839 (CCA 4th, 1927), cert denied, 275 US 536 (1927); Irving Bernstein, note 130, at 406–9; Cochrane, *Public Opinion Flays Judicial Approval of "Yellow Dog" Contracts*, 20 Am Lab Legis Rev 181 (1930).

[132] Irving Bernstein, note 130, at 407.

[133] Ernst, note 108, at 255; Seidman, note 103, at 36; see Peter Graham Fish, *Red Jacket Revisited: The Case That Unraveled John J. Parker's Supreme Court Appointment*, 5 Law & History Rev 51–104 (1987).

III. THE RAILWAY LABOR ACT AND TEXAS & NEW ORLEANS RAILROAD CO. V BROTHERHOOD OF RAILWAY CLERKS

The Court was not again confronted with the kinds of constitutional issues presented in *Adair* and *Coppage* until Hughes had returned to lead the Court in 1930, when *Texas & New Orleans Railroad Co. v Brotherhood of Railway and Steamship Clerks*[134] presented the constitutionality of Section 2 of the Railway Labor Act of 1926.[135] The pertinent provision stated: "Representatives, for the purposes of this Act, shall be designated by the respective parties . . . without interference, influence or coercion exercised by either party over the self-organization or designation of representatives by the other."[136] The Railroad had previously recognized the Brotherhood, but had, in the wake of a dispute over wages, sought to organize its own company union of railway clerks, and "endeavored to intimidate members of the Brotherhood and to coerce them to withdraw from it and to make [the company union] their representative in dealing with the Railroad Company."[137] The district court issued a temporary injunction ordering the Railroad and its agents to cease "interfering with, influencing, intimidating, or coercing" any of the clerks in their "free and untrammeled right of self-organization."[138] The Railroad nevertheless proceeded to recognize the company union, and not the Brotherhood, as the legitimate representative of its clerical employees. The district court subsequently found the Railroad in contempt of its earlier order. The Court directed the Railroad to purge itself of contempt by (1) disestablishing the company union, (2) reinstating the Brotherhood as the representative of its clerical employees, and (3) reinstating certain employees who had been discharged by the Railroad for participating in lawful union activities.[139] The temporary injunction was subsequently made permanent, and a motion to vacate

---

[134] 281 US 548 (1930).

[135] 44 Stat 577, ch 347.

[136] Id.

[137] 281 US at 555.

[138] The text of the temporary injunction is reproduced at 281 US at 555–56, n 1.

[139] 281 US at 557.

the order in the contempt proceedings was denied.[140] The Circuit Court of Appeals affirmed the decree, and the Supreme Court granted a writ of certiorari.[141]

In the congressional debates over the Railway Labor Act, which had set up a system for the voluntary arbitration of disputes between the railroads and their employees, Section 2 had been uncontroversial. Members of both Houses of Congress had repeatedly justified the provisions of the bill by observing that railroads were businesses affected with a public interest and that the public had an interest in the continuous and uninterrupted flow of commerce.[142] *Adair* and *Coppage* had twice been cited in the context of a debate over whether the ICC could constitutionally set aside a wage agreement between a railroad and a union.[143] No one, however, had suggested that those cases rendered Section 2 constitutionally infirm.

Predictably, the brief for the Texas and New Orleans Railroad did. The Railroad contended that all of its actions, including the discharge of its employees, were constitutionally protected. Relying principally on *Adair* and *Coppage*, the Railroad asserted that its agents[144]

> had an inherent constitutional right even *to make membership in [the company union] a condition to the continuation of employment.* Certainly this includes the lesser right to peaceably, without threats, influence employees to join [the company union], and to recognize [the company union] as the only organization through which they would confer and negotiate with their employees. . . . [T]he defendants had the constitutional right to refuse to confer or negotiate with any organization at all, which includes the right to confer and negotiate only in a particular manner.

---

[140] *Brotherhood of Railway and Steamship Clerks, et al. v Texas & N.O.R. Co. et al.*, 25 F2d 873 (SD Texas 1928); *Brotherhood of Railway and Steamship Clerks, et al. v Texas & N.O.R. Co. et al.*, 25 F2d 876 (SD Texas 1928).

[141] *Texas & N.O.R. Co. et al. v Brotherhood of Railway and Steamship Clerks et al.*, 33 F2d 13 (5th Cir 1929); *Texas & N.O.R. Co. et al. v Brotherhood of Railway and Steamship Clerks et al.*, 280 US 550 (1929).

[142] 67 Cong Rec 4507, 4519, 4648, 4669, 8815, 9048; S Rep 606 (69-1) at 2–3; H Rep 328 (69-1) at 6.

[143] 67 Cong Rec 8817, 8893.

[144] Brief for the Petitioner at 86, *Texas & N.O.R. Co.*, 281 US 548 (emphasis in original).

The federal government, the Railroad contended, could not constitutionally require an employer "to retain in his service an unwanted employee, or . . . to deal or not to deal with certain groups of his employees."[145] Nor could the commerce power supply the police power rationale for regulating the employer's constitutional prerogatives. Railway labor organizations were not in 1930, any more than they had been when *Adair* was decided, "so definitely connected with interstate commerce that Congress may require the employer to deal or not to deal with them in certain ways."[146] "If the evils existing in 1898 [the year of the Erdman Act's enactment] after the great strike [the Pullman strike of 1894] were not sufficient to authorize a much milder interference with the relations of employer and employee," argued the Railroad, "it is difficult to see how conditions have so changed as to authorize an even greater interference when conditions have changed, if at all, for the better."[147]

On the brief for the Brotherhood was the Chicago-based attorney for the Railway Employees' Department of the AFL, Donald Richberg. Richberg, who would one day replace Hugh Johnson as the head of the National Recovery Administration, was a co-author of what would become the Norris-LaGuardia Act, and the principal architect of the Railway Labor Act.[148] Richberg's extensive experience dealing with the constitutional dimensions of labor law made him singularly qualified to defend the Act before the Court.[149]

Richberg's principal task was to provide the analytic link that the majority had found missing in *Adair*—the connection between membership in a labor organization and interstate commerce. Richberg's strategy was to recount the lessons learned during and in the wake of World War I. In *Wilson v New*,[150] decided in 1917, the Court had held that it was within the emergency war power

---

[145] Id at 93.

[146] Id.

[147] Id at 93–94.

[148] Ernst, note 108, at 267, 271–73; Peter Irons, note 4, at 29.

[149] See Thomas E. Vadney, *The Wayward Liberal: A Political Biography of Donald Richberg* (Univ Kentucky, 1970).

[150] 243 US 332 (1917).

of the federal government to prescribe wages for railway employees in a case in which a railroad and its employees' union could not reach an agreement concerning wages. The Court had held that the government might "exert the legislative will for the purpose of settling the disputes, and bind both parties to the duty of acceptance and compliance, to the end that no individual dispute or difference might bring ruin to the vast interests concerned in the movement of interstate commerce." The government must have, the Court had held, the "power to remedy a situation created by a dispute between employers and employees as to rate of wages, which, if not remedied, would leave the public helpless." The extreme step of wage fixing had admittedly been taken in a time of emergency which no longer obtained; but the Court had nevertheless recognized the impact that a dispute between management and organized labor might exert on interstate commerce.[151]

In the wake of World War I, Richberg noted, Congress had enacted Title III of the Transportation Act of 1920. The Act had created the Railroad Labor Board, which was designed to settle labor-management disputes that threatened to interrupt interstate commerce. The railway employees were to be represented before the Board by representatives of their various labor organizations. Therefore, argued Richberg, the Act had "created an imperative legal recognition of a very definite legal connection between membership in a labor organization and the carrying on of interstate commerce."[152]

The Railway Labor Act similarly "expressed a public policy to adopt as the means of preventing interruptions of interstate commerce, and therefore, as the means of a most necessary regulation of interstate commerce, the encouragement of collective bargaining between carriers and their employees. . . ." "Thus," concluded Richberg, "the questioning of the majority opinion in the *Adair* case—as to the 'legal or logical connection * * * between an employee's membership in a labor organization and the carrying on of interstate commerce'—is completely answered. The connection is now both legal and logical."[153]

---

[151] Brief for the Respondent at 93–94, *Texas & N.O.R. Co.*, 281 US 548.

[152] Brief for the Respondent at 86–87, *Texas & N.O.R. Co.*, 281 US 548. On the politics and legislative history of the Transportation Act of 1920, see K. Austin Kerr, *American Railroad Politics, 1914–1920* (Univ Pittsburgh, 1968).

[153] Brief for the Respondent at 92–93, *Texas & N.O.R. Co.*, 280 US 550.

Having offered up the commercial police power rationale for the regulation, Richberg next sought to minimize the law's intrusion on the employer's liberty of contract, to emphasize its protection of the employees' freedom of association, and to note the public nature of the railroad's business. In making his argument, Richberg glossed over the fact that the Railroad had been found in contempt for discharging some of its union employees, and that in order to have purged itself of contempt it would have been required to reinstate them. Richberg rather contended that the Railway Labor Act, unlike the Erdman Act, did not "make it a crime for an employer to hire whom he pleases, or discharge whom he pleases. The Act does not attempt to limit his power of hiring or discharge. The Act provides only that those who *are* his employees shall have the right to designate their own representatives to negotiate with him concerning terms and conditions of employment. . . . It must be apparent that there is not in issue in the present case the basis of the decision in the *Adair* case, that is, the right of the employer to hire whom he pleases."[154]

The "minor restraint here sought upon the employer's liberty of contract,"[155] Richberg contended, ought to be indulged in order to protect the fundamental rights of its employees. "[T]he right of employees to associate themselves together (which is, of course, an inherent right under our form of government), should be protected as a 'legitimate object for the exercise of the police power.' "[156] And why were the associational rights of these employees a fit subject for the protection of the police power? Because "[r]ailway employees are 'charged by law' with public duties, and by Act of Congress their *organizations* have been charged with most important public duties."[157]

Richberg had now pressed all of the requisite analytic buttons. The common law prerogatives of the employer were subject to police power regulation because the business in which he was engaged was affected with a public interest. The wartime experience had made clear that the connection between labor-management relations and interstate commerce was sufficiently close to provide

---

[154] Id at 89–90 (emphasis in original).

[155] Id at 101–2.

[156] Id at 93.

[157] Id (emphasis in original).

the rationale for invocation of the commercial police power. And with respect to such businesses affected with a public interest, the legislature could constitutionally truncate the employer's common law prerogatives in order to protect employees in their exercise of legitimate rights of association.

A unanimous Supreme Court (Justice McReynolds did not participate) thought that the constitutionality of the Act was not even a close question.[158] "We entertain no doubt of the constitutional authority of Congress to enact the prohibition," wrote Chief Justice Charles Evans Hughes. Hughes gave short shrift to arguments that had carried the day in *Adair*. Indeed, the dismissal of *Adair*'s contention that there was no nexus between membership in a labor organization and the free flow of interstate commerce merited no more than two sentences. "Congress," the Court held, "may facilitate the amicable settlement of disputes which threaten the service of the necessary agencies of interstate transportation. In shaping its legislation to this end, Congress was entitled to take cognizance of actual conditions and to address itself to practicable measures."[159]

The Court likewise demonstrated its willingness to take cognizance of actual conditions. The Railroad's promotion and subsidy of the company union and its discharge of the Brotherhood's leaders, the Court found, constituted "interference, influence or coercion" of its employees with respect to their rights to self-organization.[160] Such terms were now held to mean "pressure, the use of the authority or power of either party to induce action by the other . . . the abuse of relation or opportunity so as to corrupt or override the will. . . ."[161] Because the threat of lost employment coerced the employees in their freedom to determine which (if any) labor association they might wish to join, their decision to join the company union could not be seen as a voluntary waiver of their right to associate with some other organization. The Railroad was

---

[158] The unanimity of the Court was readily obtained. Justice Van Devanter, who had voted with the majority in *Coppage*, wrote Chief Justice Hughes that he considered the opinion "as near perfect as is humanly possible." Pusey, 2 *Charles Evans Hughes* 713 (Macmillan, 1951).

[159] *Texas & N.O.R. Co. et al. v Brotherhood of Railway and Steamship Clerks et al.*, 281 US 548, 570 (1930).

[160] Id at 560.

[161] Id at 568.

using its contractual prerogatives as a means of depriving its employees of their freedom of association. Because the decision to join the company union was recharacterized as coerced rather than voluntary, the resolution of the conflict between liberty of contract and freedom of association effected by the *Coppage* majority was no longer available. Having abandoned Pitney's voluntary waiver theory, the Court would have to find some other reconciliation of the conflict between contractual and associational liberty.

For the first time, the Court resolved the conflict in favor of associational freedom. When these two competing liberal ideals of liberalism came into conflict, the Court held, liberty of contract would have to be recede so that freedom of association might be preserved. Accordingly, the Court held, Section 2 of the Railway Labor Act constituted a legitimate protection of employees' right of free association.[162]

> The legality of collective action on the part of the employees in order to safeguard their proper interests is not to be disputed. It has long been recognized that employees are entitled to organize for the purpose of securing the redress of grievances and to promote agreements with employers relating to rates of pay and conditions of work. Congress was not required to ignore this right of the employees but could safeguard it. . . . Thus the prohibition by Congress of interference with the selection of representatives for the purpose of negotiation and conference between employers and employees, instead of being an invasion of the constitutional right of either, was based on the recognition of the rights of both.

Such a characterization of the Court's reconciliation of the conflict of rights was less than forthcoming; and Hughes's prestidigital performance was far from over. Glossing over, as had Richberg, the fact that the district court's orders enforcing the Act had required the Railroad to reinstate employees it had discharged, Hughes dismissed *Adair* and *Coppage* as "inapplicable."[163]

> The Railway Labor Act of 1926 does not interfere with the normal exercise of the right of the carrier to select its employees or to discharge them. The statute is not aimed at this right of the employers but at the interference with the right of employees to have representatives of their own choosing. As the carri-

---

[162] Id.

[163] Id at 571.

ers subject to the Act have no constitutional right to interfere
with the freedom of the employees in making their selections,
they cannot complain of the statute on constitutional grounds.

This was a distinction that could be remembered just long enough
to be stated once;[164] and there were at the time and have been since
several commentators who wondered whether, after 1930, there
was anything left of *Adair* and *Coppage*.[165] Just how much of those
cases was left, to which of the Justices, and for what reasons, would
not be clear until 1937.

IV. The Luxuriation of the Associational Rationale

Congress was quickly alert to the possibilities offered by the
Texas & New Orleans case, and was sensitive to the associational
language employed in Hughes's opinion.[166] Section 3 of the Norris-
LaGuardia Act, enacted in 1932, declared that yellow-dog contracts were contrary to the public policy of the United States and
would henceforth be unenforceable in the federal courts.[167] Members of both Houses repeatedly invoked the authority of the *Texas
& New Orleans* case in support of this provision, and persistently
declared that yellow-dog contracts deprived employees of their
freedom of association.[168] "It would not be tolerated for a moment,"
argued Wisconsin Senator Blaine, echoing the words of Justice

---

[164] Paul Freund, *Charles Evans Hughes as Chief Justice*, 81 Harv L Rev 4, 35 (1967).

[165] Seidman, note 103, at 35, n 109; Berman, *The Supreme Court Interprets the Railway Labor
Act*, 20 Am Econ Rev 619 (1930); Richard Cortner, *The Jones & Laughlin Case* 22 (Knopf,
1970); B. C. Gavit, *The Commerce Clause of the United States Constitution* 231–33 (Principia,
1932); Thomas R. Fisher, *Industrial Disputes and Federal Legislation* 170, n 21 (New York,
1940); Comment, 37 W Va L Q 101 (1930); Comment, 40 Yale L J 92 (1930); Comment,
25 Ill L Rev 307 (1930); Samuel Hendel, *Charles Evans Hughes and the Supreme Court* 228, 260
(Kings Crown, 1951); see Fraenkel, *Recent Statutes Affecting Labor Injunctions and Yellow Dog
Contracts*, 30 Ill L Rev 854, 862, n 46 (1936). One commentator opined that the Texas &
New Orleans decision "would seem to bring [the Court] still closer to complete realization
that 'liberty to contract' may mean a liberty to join voluntary associations of workmen
unhindered by the 'yellow dog' contract." Comment, 81 U Pa L Rev 68, 73 (1932). For a
perceptive contemporary understanding of the limited implications of the Texas & New
Orleans decision, see Johns, *The Validity of Federal Labor Legislation with Special Emphasis Upon
the National Labor Relations Act*, 20 Marq L Rev 57, 70–71 (1936).

[166] See Comment, 30 Ill L Rev 884, 904 (1936) (*Texas & New Orleans* decision "recognize[d]
the power of Congress to preserve the right of freedom of association of employees").

[167] 47 Stat 70, ch 90 (72-1).

[168] 75 Cong Rec 4503, 4504, 4626–28, 4677, 4762, 4917, 5463, 5469; S Rep 163 (72-1) at
11–14; H Rep 669 (72-1) at 7. See Witte, *The Federal Anti-Injunction Act*, 16 Minn L Rev
638, 655 (1932).

Day's *Coppage* dissent, "if employers compelled all their employees to sign contracts that they would not belong to some lodge or to some particular church, or that they will vote the Republican ticket. . . ."[169] But if employers could require employees to sign yellow-dog contracts, argued Blaine, they could prevent their employees from "doing anything, either in or out of working hours, that they do not like."[170]

The seriousness with which this associational rationale was taken was reflected in a disagreement between the House and Senate over the bill's declaration of policy. The version of the bill passed by the House provided in part[171]

> Sec. 2. . . . Whereas . . . the individual unorganized worker is commonly helpless to exercise actual liberty of contract and to protect his freedom of labor . . . wherefore it is necessary that he have full freedom of association [to organize and select representatives, etc.]"

The Senate version of the bill's declaration of policy inserted, between "wherefore" and "it is necessary," the phrase, "though he should be free to decline to associate with his fellows."[172] The House initially balked at the Senate's amendment;[173] but the Senate, whose members nearly unanimously supported the anti-yellow-dog provision, insisted on its pristine formulation of the worker's associational liberty.[174] In the final version of the bill, the Senate's amendment prevailed.[175] As one commentator noted, "[t]he freedom of association of workers and of employers alike is held to be a necessity in order to foster freedom of contract."[176]

Senator Norris scored another victory for associational liberty the following year when Congress enacted the Bankruptcy Act of 1933.[177] Shortly before the close of the legislative session, Norris

---

[169] 75 Cong Rec 4628 (72-1).

[170] Id.

[171] 75 Cong Rec 5469 (72-1).

[172] H Rep 821 (72-1) at 6.

[173] 75 Cong Rec 5720.

[174] 75 Cong Rec 5551.

[175] 47 Stat 70, ch 90 (72-1).

[176] Comment, *An Advance in Labor Legislation—The Anti-Injunction Act*, 21 Geo L J 344, 345 (1933).

[177] 47 Stat 1467 (72-2), ch 204.

succeeded in persuading the Senate to amend the House version of the bill, adding what were to become Sections 77 (p) and (q).[178] Section 77 (p) provided:[179]

> No judge or trustee acting under this Act shall deny or in any way question the right of employees on the property under his jurisdiction to join the labor organization of their choice, and it shall be unlawful for any judge, trustee or receiver to interfere in any way with the organizations of employees, or to use the funds of the railroad under his jurisdiction, in maintaining so-called company unions, or to influence or coerce employees in an effort to induce them to join or remain members of such company unions.

Section 77 (q) provided: "No judge, trustee, or receiver acting under this Act shall require any person seeking employment on the property under his jurisdiction to sign any contract or agreement promising to join or to refuse to join a labor organization," and required the judge, trustee, or receiver in question to discard any such contract in force before the subject property came under his jurisdiction.[180]

Defending his amendment on the Senate floor, Norris emphasized the fact that the worker's associational liberty would be thereby preserved. "It [the amendment] permits rather than compels men to join a so-called company union, to join whatever union they want to that they shall be free men, and that they shall not have that freedom taken away from them by any action of the receiver or by any order of the court."[181] As Irving Bernstein noted, Norris's amendment "outlawed both the yellow-dog contract and the closed shop."[182] This symmetrical protection of workers' associational liberty was again embraced by the Emergency Railroad Transportation Act of 1933, whose Section 7 (e) incorporated by reference Sections 77 (p) and (q) of the Bankruptcy Act.[183]

---

[178] 76 Cong Rec 5118–22 (72-2). The House agreed to the amendment at 76 Cong Rec 5360 (72-2).

[179] 47 Stat 1467, 1481 (72-2).

[180] 47 Stat 1467, 1481.

[181] 76 Cong Rec 5119 (72-2).

[182] Bernstein, *The New Deal Collective Bargaining Policy* 44 (Univ California, 1950).

[183] 48 Stat 211, 214 (73-1), ch 91. See Bernstein, note 182, at 44–46. Norris and his colleagues contemporaneously sought to protect workers' freedom of association through Section 7(a) of the National Industrial Recovery Act ("NIRA"), the precursor of the Wagner Act. Donald Richberg was again the principal author. R. W. Fleming, *The Significance of the*

Similarly revealing were the debates over the 1934 amendments to the Railway Labor Act. The amendments created a new Section 2, which set out the "general purposes" of the Act. Among these purposes was "to forbid any limitation upon freedom of association among employees or any denial, as a condition of employment or otherwise, of the right of employees to join a labor organization."[184] And indeed, the backers of the bill mobilized associational rhetoric in its support.[185] But the House and Senate differed on the form these associational protections should take. The original House bill prohibited employers from influencing, coercing, or requiring their employees to join company unions.[186] The Senate version prohibited employers from influencing, coercing, or requiring their employees to join any labor organization whatsoever.[187] The Senate again insisted on its symmetrical formulation, and the House, adequately assured that the Senate's version prohibited company unions, again capitulated.[188] Once again, Congress had sought to safeguard workers' associational liberty by outlawing both the yellow-dog contract and the closed shop.[189]

Thus in four major pieces of legislation enacted in the early 1930s, Congress had evinced a preoccupation with symmetrical protections for the worker's freedom of association. The employer could not require the employee to agree not to join a union, nor could he discharge him for joining one. Neither could the employer seek to influence or coerce the employee into joining a company union. Finally, the employer could not, at his employee's union's

---

Wagner Act, in Derber & Young, eds, *Labor and the New Deal* 126 (Da Capo, 1972). Section 7(a) required that every code of fair competition propounded pursuant to the NIRA provide: (1) that employees be free to organize to bargain collectively free from employer interference or coercion; and (2) "that no employee and no one seeking employment shall be required as a condition of employment to join any company union or to refrain from joining, organizing, or assisting a labor organization of his own choosing." 48 Stat 195, 198–99, ch 90 (73-1). The Act's aberrationally permissive posture regarding the closed shop was in large measure the quid pro quo for the AFL's acceptance of the trade association provisions sponsored by the Chamber of Commerce. Irving Bernstein, *The Turbulent Years* 32 (Houghton Mifflin, 1969). With both business and organized labor happy to have more room to maneuver than conventional antitrust law might have permitted, the freedom of non-union workers not to associate with a labor organization got lost in the shuffle.

[184] H Rep 1944 (73-2) at 5.

[185] H Rep 1944 (73-2) at 1–2; 78 Cong Rec 11717, 11720, 12553–12555.

[186] H Rep 1194 (73-2) at 6.

[187] 78 Cong Rec 12550.

[188] 78 Cong Rec 12553–12555.

[189] Irving Bernstein, *The Turbulent Years* at 212 (cited in note 183).

behest or otherwise, seek to influence or coerce any of his employees into joining a noncompany union. In the discrete areas of industry covered by these acts, the asymmetry of the *Coppage* era appeared to be rectified. With the passage of the Wagner Act the next year, however, this preoccupation with symmetry would be abandoned, and the asymmetry of the yellow-dog period would be turned on its head.

V. Virginian Railway Co. v System Federation, No. 40

The constitutionality of the amended Railway Labor Act was attacked before the Court in 1937. The dispute arose over attempts by the Railway to avoid collective bargaining with the Federation, which was the duly accredited representative of the Railway's mechanical department ("back-shop") employees. The district court's decree had directed the Railway (1) to "treat with" the Federation and to "exert every reasonable effort to make and maintain agreements concerning rates of pay, rules and working conditions . . ."; (2) not to enter into "any contract, undertaking, or agreement of whatsoever kind concerning rules, rates of pay or working conditions affecting its Mechanical Department employees, . . . except . . . with the Federation"; and (3) not to interfere with, influence, or coerce its employees with respect to their free choice of representatives, nor, for such purposes, to organize or foster any company union.[190] As the Court's opinion noted, the Railway did not argue that the third part of the district court's order was unconstitutional. In view of the decision in the *Texas & New Orleans* case, noted the Court, "[t]hat contention is not open to it."[191]

The Railway did, however, challenge the other two portions of the lower court's order, and it did so on two fronts. The Railway clearly could not claim that it was not a business affected with a public interest—the business in which it was engaged was paradigmatically public. But the *Adair* case had also involved a business affected with a public interest, and the Railway could rely on the absolutist language in which Justice Harlan had described the employer's liberty of contract. Glossing over the fact that the Railway

---

[190] *Virginian Railway Co. v System Federation, No. 40*, 300 US 515, 538–41 (1937).

[191] Id at 543–44.

was engaged in a public business, attorney for the Railway James
Piper told the Court that "the freedom of contract argument is that
it is our right to refuse business negotiations with anyone."[192] The
Railway further argued that the back-shop employees were engaged in the purely intrastate activities of repair and manufacture,
neither of which was sufficiently related to the interstate activities
of the Railway to admit of federal regulation. Because the activities
of the back-shop employees were beyond the reach of the federal
commerce power, the impact of those activities on interstate commerce could not supply the commercial police power rationale for
regulating the Railway's liberty of contract.[193]

The Act and the lower court's decree were defended by the
Federation and by the United States, which filed a brief as amicus
curiae. "The Railway Labor Act," argued the brief for the Federation, "does not require a carrier to enter into any contract, but
merely that it shall negotiate with regard to the matter. . . . Negotiations are not contracts, and in and of themselves cannot have the
effect of bringing into existence contractual rights or duties."[194]
"The petitioner is *not* placed under a duty to enter into a particular
agreement, to agree upon particular terms, or to make any contract
whatsoever," argued the brief for the United States.[195] "One who
confers, unlike one who contracts, is not bound as to any future
conduct. His future freedom is not thereby restrained."[196]

This much was true. But the defenders of the Act also had to
justify that portion of the lower court's order that had restrained
the Railway from entering into any contract concerning rates of
pay, rules, and conditions with anyone other that the Federation.
That portion of the decree, noted the brief for the United States,
did not restrain the Railway "in the normal exercise of its right to
select or discharge its employees."[197] But to the extent that the
decree did impose limitations on the Railway's liberty of contract,
observed the Federation's brief, it was important to bear in mind

---

[192] *Arguments in Cases Arising Under Labor Acts Before the Supreme Court*, Sen Doc 52 (75-1),
at 13–14 [hereinafter *cited* as *Arguments*].

[193] Brief for the Petitioner at 38–47, *Virginian Railway Co.*, 300 US 515.

[194] Brief for the Respondent at 48–49, *Virginian Railway Co.*, 300 US 515.

[195] Brief for the United States at 82, *Virginian Railway Co.*, 300 US 515 (emphasis in
original).

[196] Id at 84.

[197] Id at 89.

that the Railway was "a common carrier, a public utility, the opera-
tor of a business peculiarly charged with the public interest. Its
business may, therefore, be regulated to a greater extend [sic] than
is the case with other industries without infringing upon the constitutional guarantee of freedom of contract."[198]

There remained only the task of articulating the police power
rationale for the regulation. The congressional power to regulate
commerce could reach the activities of back-shop employees, argued the brief for the United States, even though such employees
were not themselves engaged in interstate commerce. The *Texas &
New Orleans* case had upheld the validity of the Act as applied to
clerks, whose work was clearly intrastate in nature. A strike by the
Railway's back-shop employees would "both endanger the safety
of interstate transportation and directly obstruct its movement."
Moreover, any dispute between the Railway and its back-shop employees would likely be communicated to Railway employees engaged in interstate commerce, thereby further threatening the continuity of interstate transportation.[199] The purpose of the Act,
argued the Federation, was "to aid and encourage the railroads and
their employees to make and maintain agreements to the end that
labor strife and discontent be allayed and labor harmony and good
morale prevail; all to the end that there be no interruption of commerce in the public interest."[200] The means employed by the Act
were, the Federation contended, reasonably related to that legitimate end.[201]

The litigants were given a foreshadowing of the Court's decision
when Justice Sutherland interrupted the Railway counsel's freedom of contract argument to inquire, "[d]o you attach any importance to the fact that the railroad company is engaged in a business
charged with the public interest?"[202] Piper's reply was a convoluted
"no," and counsel for both the Federation and the United States
were sure to emphasize the Railway's public nature in their presen-
tations.[203] "Does the Fifth Amendment," asked counsel for the

---

[198] Brief for the Respondent at 55–56, *Virginian Railway Co.*, 300 US 515; see also id at 57, 63.

[199] Brief for the United States at 7, *Virginian Railway Co.*, 300 US 515.

[200] Brief for the Respondent at 52, *Virginian Railway Co.*, 300 US 515.

[201] Id.

[202] *Arguments*, note 192, at 13.

[203] Id at 32, 39–40.

United States, "prevent the Congress from infringing somewhat upon the absolute right to be perfectly free in the operation of your business and in your dealings with your employees in order to assure continuous operation of the railroad systems—a great public necessity . . . ?"[204] Citing *Nebbia v New York*[205] for the proposition that due process requires "only that the law shall not be unreasonable, arbitrary, or capricious, and that the means selected shall have a real and substantial relation to the object sought to be obtained," counsel concluded that "the slight interference [here involved] with the personal liberty of the railroad management . . . seems a very minimum that they could be asked to relinquish in order that we may bring about industrial peace."[206]

The opinion of the Court, delivered March 29, was unanimous. Employing again the analytical model initially embraced in *Adair*, the Court noted that each of the doctrinal prerequisites to regulation of the employment relationship had been satisfied. First, the court noted, the business of the railroad was clearly affected with a public interest. "More is involved," wrote Justice Stone, "than the settlement of a private controversy without appreciable consequences to the public. The peaceable settlement of labor controversies, especially where they may impair the ability of an interstate carrier to perform its service to the public, is a matter of public concern."[207]

The Court nevertheless sought to minimize the extent of the intrusion on the employer's common law prerogatives. Neither the Act nor the decree required the Railway to enter into any agreement, held the Court—the Railway was merely required to "treat with" the Federation, not to contract with it.[208] Moreover, the portion of the decree restraining the Railway from entering into a collective agreement with anyone other than the Federation did not prevent the Railway from refusing to enter into any collective contract and instead negotiating contracts with its employees on an individual basis.[209] Because the provisions of the Act did not "'interfere with the normal exercise of the right of the carrier to

---

[204] Id at 39.

[205] 291 US 502 (1934).

[206] *Arguments*, note 192, at 39–40.

[207] *Virginian Railway Co. v System Federation, No. 40*, 300 US 515, 552 (1937).

[208] Id at 557, 559.

[209] Id at 548–49, 557, 559.

select its employees or to discharge them,'" *Adair* and *Coppage* had "no present application."[210]

Finally, Justice Stone articulated the commercial police power rationale undergirding the instant application of the Act. A strike by the Railway's employees, he wrote, "if more than temporary, would seriously cripple [the Railway's] interstate transportation."[211] The means prescribed by the Act were reasonably related to the legitimate end of preventing such interruptions of commerce. The Act was therefore a legitimate exercise of the federal government's commercial police power.[212]

VI. The Impact of Nebbia v New York

Early in 1934, before the enactment of either the Wagner Act or the amendments to the Railway Labor Act, the Supreme Court handed down a decision that would have profound repercussions for liberty of contract jurisprudence. Yet *Nebbia v New York*[213] did not concern any regulation of the employment relationship. Instead, it involved a New York State Control Board regulation of retail milk prices. The regulation was an attempt to ameliorate the effects of cutthroat competition in the retail milk business, where price-cutting had reduced the income of dairy farmers to a level below the cost of production. Leo Nebbia, a retailer convicted of selling milk below the price prescribed by State regulation, argued that the regulation deprived him of property without due process of law in violation of the Fourteenth Amendment. Price regulation, Nebbia contended, was constitutional only as applied to a business affected with a public interest. For a business to be affected with a public interest, he argued, it had to be either a public utility or a natural monopoly. Because neither Nebbia's business itself nor the milk industry as a whole belonged to either of these categories, Nebbia contended, his business was not affected with a public interest and therefore was not subject to price regulation.[214]

The Court, by a vote of five to four (the Four Horsemen—

---

[210] Id at 559.

[211] Id at 556.

[212] Id at 553–57.

[213] 291 US 502 (1934).

[214] Id at 531.

McReynolds, Sutherland, Van Devanter, and Butler—dissenting), rejected Nebbia's contentions, and in so doing effectively retired the distinction between public and private enterprise. "[T]here is no closed class or category of businesses affected with a public interest," wrote Justice Roberts for the majority. "The phrase, 'affected with a public interest' can, in the nature of things, mean no more than that an industry, for adequate reason, is subject to control for the public good."[215]

> So far as the requirement of due process is concerned, and in the absence of other constitutional restriction, a state is free to adopt whatever economic policy may reasonably be deemed to promote public welfare, and to enforce that policy by legislation adapted to its purpose. . . . If the laws passed are seen to have a reasonable relation to a proper legislative purpose, and are neither arbitrary nor discriminatory, the requirements of due process are satisfied. . . . The Constitution does not secure to anyone liberty to conduct his business in such fashion as to inflict injury upon the public at large, or upon any substantial group of the people. Price control, like any other form of regulation, is unconstitutional only if arbitrary, discriminatory, or demonstrably irrelevant to the policy the legislature is free to adopt. . . .[216]

Nebbia's dismantling of the public/private distinction was a milestone in American constitutional development, and its ramifications for national collective bargaining legislation were twofold. First, the category "business affected with a public interest" would no longer operate as an independent constraint on legislative power to regulate the employment relationship. So long as the legislation was not patently arbitrary or capricious, the legislature could regulate the employment relations of any business, irrespective of whether it had in the past been considered a business affected with a public interest.

Second, due to an interdoctrinal relationship formed in the area of commerce clause doctrine, Nebbia augmented the category of enterprises whose employment relations might be deemed to affect interstate commerce directly. From the late nineteenth century through the mid-1930s, the Court had conscientiously maintained a distinction between activities that affected interstate commerce

---

[215] Id at 536.
[216] Id at 537–39.

directly and those that affected such commerce only indirectly.[217] Only activities that affected commerce "directly" were subject to federal regulation.[218] Activities that affected interstate commerce only "indirectly"—such as local sales, mining, agriculture, and manufacturing—were subject only to state regulation. The Tenth Amendment forbade federal regulation of such activities.[219]

However, if an otherwise "local" activity was deemed to be part of a continuous "current" of interstate commerce, that activity might be subjected to federal regulation. On the basis of this "current of commerce" doctrine, the Supreme Court had upheld federal statutes regulating transactions in the nation's major stockyards and grain exchanges.[220] In each instance goods had been shipped from one state to another, where they paused for a local activity, and then moved on to yet another state. The pause for the local activity was not deemed to break the "current" of interstate commerce of which it was a part.

Justices committed to the maintenance of dual federalism[221] recognized that, in an economy becoming increasingly integrated on a national scale, there was virtually no end to the list of business activities that could be conceived as located in a current of interstate commerce. If the traditional regulatory prerogatives of the states were to be preserved, some means would have to be found to restrict the scope of the current of commerce doctrine. The means settled on by the Court was ingenious. Conflating the direct/indirect distinction of commerce clause jurisprudence with the public/private distinction of due process jurisprudence, the Court consistently found that only businesses affected with a public interest could be located in a federally regulable current of interstate commerce. A business affected with a public interest had the power to affect commerce directly; a purely private business did not. The current of commerce was thus conceived as a sequence of interstate

---

[217] See Corwin, *Commerce Power versus States Rights* 189–208 (Princeton Univ, 1936).

[218] See id at 198–208.

[219] See id at 189–93; *Carter v Carter Coal Co.*, 298 US 238 (1936); *United States v Butler*, 297 US 1 (1936).

[220] Compare *Swift & Co. v United States*, 196 US 375 (1905); *Stafford v Wallace*, 258 US 495 (1922); *Chicago Board of Trade v Olsen*, 262 US 1 (1923); *Tagg Bros. & Moorhead v United States*, 280 US 420 (1930) with *Hopkins v United States*, 171 US 578 (1898). See Cushman, note 12.

[221] See Corwin, note 11, at ch 1.

business activities connected by intrastate business activities affected with a public interest. As long as the class of businesses affected with a public interest had remained small and select, the channel cut by the current of commerce had remained narrow.[222]

Nebbia, however, had thrown the class of businesses affected with a public interest wide open. The internal logic of the current of commerce doctrine thus impelled the Court toward recognition of a broader conception of the current of commerce. *Nebbia* made it possible to conceptualize what had previously been considered purely private businesses as businesses affected with a public interest. This in turn made it possible to locate such business activities in a current of interstate commerce. These business activities could now be seen to have the capacity to affect interstate commerce directly. And because these businesses could now be seen as standing astride a current of interstate commerce, the impact that a disruption in their labor relations might exert on the flow of that current could provide the commercial police power rationale for federal regulation of the employer's liberty of contract.[223]

The dissenting Four Horsemen, however, had balked at the Court's abandonment of the formalist public/private distinction in due process jurisprudence. As a corollary, they were not committed to the consequences *Nebbia* implied for current of commerce jurisprudence. The intellectual structure of this Nebbian split would be reflected in the pattern of decision in the Wagner Act cases.

VII. The Wagner Act Cases

Capping off the flurry of labor legislation enacted in the 1930s was the National Labor Relations Act, otherwise known as the Wagner Act.[224] Section 7 of the Act secured to employees "the right to self-organization, to form, join, or assist labor organizations, to bargain collectively through representatives of their own choosing, and to engage in concerted activities, for the purpose of collective bargaining or other mutual aid or protection."[225]

---

[222] Cushman, note 12, at 114–24.

[223] Id at 130–31.

[224] 49 Stat 449 (74-1), ch 372.

[225] 49 Stat 449, 452.

Section 8 described certain "unfair labor practices" in which employers were forbidden to engage. Sections 8(1) and 8(2) sought, as had their statutory predecessors, to preserve workers' freedom of association. Section 8(1) forbade the employer "to interfere with, restrain, or coerce employees in the exercise of the rights guaranteed in section 7."[226] Section 8(2) sought to preserve employer neutrality among unions and to outlaw company unions by forbidding any employer "[t]o dominate or interfere with the formation or administration of any labor organization or contribute financial or other support to it."[227] Section 8(3) constituted a frontal assault on *Adair* and *Coppage*, and a bet that the *Texas & New Orleans* case had overruled them. Resurrecting in substance Section 10 of the Erdman Act, Section 8(3) forbade any employer "[b]y discrimination in regard to hire or tenure of employment or any term or condition of employment to encourage or discourage membership in any labor organization."[228] Section 8 thus clearly proscribed the nemeses of labor associationalism: anti-union discrimination in hiring and firing, company unions, and yellow-dog contracts.[229]

In the hearings and debates on the bill, opponents relied heavily on *Adair* and *Coppage* as precedents standing for the proposition that Section 8 violated the Fourteenth Amendment.[230] Proponents of the bill, however, contended that those precedents were no longer applicable. "The power of Congress to guarantee freedom of organization, to prohibit the company-dominated union, and to prevent employers from requiring membership or nonmembership in any union has been upheld completely" in the *Texas & New Orleans* case, declared Senator Wagner. "[W]e cannot doubt that *Coppage v. Kansas* and *Adair v. U.S.* have been overruled."[231] Time

---

[226] Id.

[227] Id.

[228] Id.

[229] See Thomas R. Fisher, *Industrial Disputes and Federal Legislation* 273 (New York, 1940).

[230] See, e.g., remarks of Sen. Hastings, 2 *Legislative History of the National Labor Relations Act* 2403–11 (Government Printing Office, 1949) [hereinafter cited as *NLRB, Legislative History*]; Statement of James A. Emery, Hearings before the Senate Committee on Education and Labor on S 1958 (74-1) at 854, reprinted in *NLRB, Legislative History* at 2240.

[231] Statement of Senator Wagner, Hearings before the Senate Committee on Education and Labor on S 1958 (74-1) at 52–53, reprinted in *NLRB, Legislative History* at 1428–29. See also S Rep 573 (74-1) at 17, reprinted in *NLRB, Legislative History* at 2317; remarks of Senator Wagner, *NLRB Legislative History* at 2338; Statement of Professor Milton Handler, Hearing of the Senate Committee on Education and Labor on S 1958 (74-1) at 233, reprinted in *NLRB, Legislative History* at 1613.

would show that Wagner's proclamation of *Adair*'s demise was, if not incorrect, at least exaggerated.

The Act's introductory "Findings and Policy" linked its commercial police power rationale to the rhetoric of associational liberty.[232]

> The inequality of bargaining power between employees who do not possess full freedom of association or actual liberty of contract, and employers who are organized in the corporate or other forms of ownership association substantially burdens and affects the flow of commerce. . . . It is hereby declared to be the policy of the United States to eliminate the causes of certain substantial obstructions to the free flow of commerce and to mitigate and eliminate those obstructions when they have occurred by encouraging the practice and procedure of collective bargaining and by protecting the exercise by workers of full freedom of association. . . .

In the floor debates, moreover, proponents defended the Act in associational terms.[233] But despite its evocation of associational rhetoric, the Wagner Act did not embrace the symmetrical protections for workers' associational freedom provided by earlier labor legislation. In the Senate debates on the bill, Senator Millard Tydings of Maryland sought to amend Section 7 to read: "Employees shall have the right to self-organization, to form, join, or assist labor organizations, to bargain collectively through representatives of their own choosing, and to engage in concerted activities, for the purpose of collective bargaining or other mutual aid or protection *free from coercion or intimidation from any source.*"[234] The notion that workers ought to be entirely free from coercion in making associational decisions was a logical outgrowth of the associational paradigm embraced by Congress throughout the preceding decade; and the supporters of the amendment mixed associational rhetoric with citations to the Norris-LaGuardia Act in their remarks on the floor.[235] "Is this not still the kind of country," Senator Tydings asked, "where a man can select, without coercion or intimidation,

---

[232] 49 Stat 449, 450 (74-1), ch 372. See Comment, 30 Ill L Rev 884, 906 (1936) ("the protection of employees in their right of freedom of association is reasonably calculated to promote the amicable settlement of disputes").

[233] See Irving Bernstein, *The Turbulent Years* at 332–33 (cited in note 183).

[234] NLRB, *Legislative History* at 2357 (emphasis in original).

[235] See remarks of Senators Tydings, Couzens, and Hastings, *NLRB, Legislative History* at 2357–96.

the kind of organization to which he shall belong?"[236] "A laborer ought to be entitled without coercion from any side to say whether he wants to join this, that, or the other union, and if it is wrong for the employer, as it is wrong, to coerce labor or intimidate labor, it is equally wrong for somebody else to coerce laborers and intimidate them."[237] Opponents of the amendment were hard put to disagree with the logic of Tydings's arguments; but fearful that judges hostile to labor might interpret "coercion" to include peaceful picketing and persuasion, even Senator Norris spoke against it.[238] The arguments of Wagner and Norris carried the day, and the amendment was defeated by a vote of 50–21.[239]

The rejection of the Tydings amendment was not the only evidence of the Senate's retreat from symmetrical associationalism. Section 9(a) of the Act provided that the representative selected by the majority of the employees in a unit would be the exclusive representative of all unit employees in negotiating the terms of employment: minority workers dissatisfied with the outcome of a certification election could not designate their own representatives to bargain on their behalf.[240] President Roosevelt himself had rejected the principles of majority rule and exclusive representation on the grounds that they interfered with freedom of association when he had mediated the automobile industry settlement in 1934.[241] Moreover, Section 8(3) broke with the policy of the Railway Labor Act by adopting a permissive posture toward the closed shop. The proviso to that section stipulated that "nothing in this Act . . . shall preclude an employer from making an agreement with a labor organization . . . to require as a condition of employment

[236] NLRB, Legislative History at 2359.

[237] Id at 2361.

[238] See remarks of Senator Norris, NLRB, Legislative History at 2380–87; see id at 2357–96 for the remarks of Senators Wagner, Barkley, and Walsh.

[239] NLRB, Legislative History at 2399–2400. Tydings's amendment was rejected in the House without debate, id at 3216, and was later rejected by the conference committee despite the importunings of the Secretary of Commerce. Bernstein, note 182, at 127; Cortner, The Wagner Act Cases 84 (Univ Tennessee, 1964).

[240] 49 Stat 449, 453. For Senator Hastings's unsuccessful associational objections to this provision, see NLRB, Legislative History at 2361, 2389–93. See Blumberg, The National Labor Relations Act: A Presentation of Some Constitutional and Economic Objections, 41 Com L J 136, 138 (1936); Chandler, The National Labor Relations Act, 22 ABA J 245, 250, 281–82 (1936); Comment, 30 Ill L Rev 884, 919 (1936).

[241] Irving Bernstein, The Turbulent Years at 184–85 (cited in note 183).

membership therein. . . ."[242] In the debates over the Tydings amendment, Senator Daniel Hastings of Delaware condemned the asymmetry of the Act's protections for workers' associational liberty. The proviso, he argued, permitted "the reverse, as I understand, of the 'yellow dog' contract which has been so roundly and properly condemned in this body."[243] "Does it not say, in so many words, that if the employer so desires, and the majority of the labor union so desires, they may make an agreement whereby no one may be employed in the establishment unless he belongs to that union, and will not that provision in this bill compel a minority of employees in that particular shop or that particular unit to join that union, whether they wish to or not, and pay all the fees which the union may desire to charge?"[244] But advocates of the proviso would not engage Hastings in associational terms. Associational rhetoric had carried them as far toward their goals as it could. At this juncture, the associational rationale was abandoned; as a result, the asymmetry of the *Coppage* era was revived in inverted form.

The attorneys at the NLRB were aware that these provisions of the Act did not square as neatly as had the Railway Labor Act with the associational ideology expressed in the *Texas & New Orleans* opinion, and they crafted their litigation strategy accordingly.[245] Preparing to defend the constitutionality of the Wagner Act before the Supreme Court, the NLRB lawyers sought out test cases that would not bring before the Court these more problematic provisions of the Act.[246] Each of the test cases selected therefore involved an instance in which an employer had been found guilty of an unfair labor practice under Section 8(3) because it had discharged one or more of its employees for engaging in legitimate

---

[242] 49 Stat 449, 452.

[243] *NLRB, Legislative History* at 2394.

[244] Id at 2395. Several members of the Senate also had misgivings toward the Act's imposition of the duty to bargain. In 1934, the Senate Committee on Education and Labor had shelved Wagner's bill, S 2926, and had instead reported favorably a substitute bill introduced by Senator David I. Walsh, Democrat of Massachusetts. "Walsh believed that the government should only protect the civil right of association in a voluntary organization and that Wagner had gone too far in urging affirmative encouragement of collective bargaining." Bernstein, *The Turbulent Years* at 195 (cited in note 183).

[245] James Gross, *The Making of the National Relation Board* 187 (State Univ of NY, 1974).

[246] Id

union activities.[247] Such cases cleanly presented instances in which a worker's associational liberty had been compromised, and permitted the NLRB attorneys to mobilize associational rhetoric with the greatest effect.

The NLRB lawyers were also careful to select test cases in which an employer's labor relations could be said to have a direct effect on the flow of interstate commerce. Ultimately, they selected and prepared five cases (the so-called "Wagner Act cases") through which to test the constitutionality of the Act. The Washington, Virginia & Maryland Coach Company was a small interstate transit company. The Associated Press was a national wire service utilizing interstate channels of communication. In each of these two cases, the nexus with interstate commerce was fairly clear. In addition to these cases, the NLRB also moved against three manufacturing operations: the Jones & Laughlin Steel Corporation in Aliquippa, Pennsylvania; the Fruehauf Trailer Company in Detroit, Michigan; and the Friedman-Harry Marks Clothing Company in Richmond, Virginia. In each of these manufacturing cases, the plant in question acquired its raw and semifinished materials from points outside its home state. After transforming these materials into a finished product, each plant shipped the bulk of its products to points outside its home state. These three cases had been carefully selected because they could be argued as current of commerce cases; and, indeed, the NLRB lawyers briefed and argued the cases under that theory.[248]

The Wagner Act cases[249] were argued at the same time as the *Virginian Railway* case. The Washington, Virginia & Maryland Coach Company was admittedly a common carrier engaged in interstate commerce. Apparently recognizing that the *Texas & New Orleans* case was controlling, the company offered only a token due process argument.[250] None of the other businesses was so para-

---

[247] Id.

[248] For a detailed discussion of the case selection, briefing, arguing, and resolution of the commerce clause issues in the Wagner Act cases, see Cushman, note 12, at 139–56; Irons, note 4, at ch 11–13.

[249] *NLRB v Jones & Laughlin Steel Corp.*, 301 US 1 (1937); *NLRB v Fruehauf Trailer Co.*, 301 US 49 (1937); *NLRB v Friedman–Harry Marks Clothing Co.*, 301 US 58 (1937); *Associated Press Co. v NLRB*, 301 US 103 (1937); *Washington, Virginia & Maryland Coach Co. v NLRB*, 301 US 142 (1937).

[250] Brief for the Petitioner, at 10, 23–24, 41, *Washington, Virginia & Maryland Coach Co.*, 301 US 142.

digmatically public, however, and each emphasized its essentially private nature in its briefs and arguments. The *Texas & New Orleans* case, argued counsel for Jones & Laughlin, was distinguishable from the instant case because the former involved "an interstate carrier, which is a public utility."[251] Congress possessed broad powers to regulate the employment practices of such enterprises. Jones & Laughlin, however, was not a business affected with a public interest, and Congress was therefore without authority to regulate its common law prerogatives.[252]

The *Texas & New Orleans* case, contended counsel for the Friedman-Harry Marks Clothing Company, could not "be cited in any way as authority for the proposition that the Federal Government may place any limitation upon the right of an employer conducting a *private business*, to hire and fire with impunity. . . ."[253] The Railway Labor Act, the company argued,[254]

> applied only to common carriers engaged in the transportation of commerce between the several states, whose businesses are affected with a great national public interest. . . . (This difference is of the greatest significance and importance in a consideration of the National Labor Relations Act, which is applicable to inherently intrastate enterprises affected with no public interest, the internal regulation and continuance of which is admittedly of only private concern.)

John W. Davis, arguing on behalf of the Associated Press, contended that "regulation of the right to contract in respect of a private business, is arbitrary and therefore void unless confined to the exigencies of a real emergency."[255] The Wagner Act did "not even pretend to establish or follow a distinction between public and private business, [or] between public and private employment. . . ."[256] On the contrary, the Act outlawed "all private and individual bargaining in respect of private enterprise in private industry."[257] The Act as applied to the Associated Press was "an

---

[251] Brief for the Respondent at 33, *Jones & Laughlin Steel Corp.*, 301 US 1.

[252] Id at 33, 112, 116–17.

[253] Brief for Respondent at 68, *Friedman–Harry Marks Clothing Co.*, 301 US 58 (emphasis in original).

[254] Id at 68–69.

[255] Brief for the Petitioner at 68, *Associated Press Co.*, 301 US 103.

[256] Id at 70.

[257] Id.

invasion of freedom of contract between an employer and an employee who are engaged in a wholly private occupation."[258]

The Act's defenders responded, of course, by mobilizing *Nebbia v New York*. The distinction between public and private business was no longer pertinent, and the strand of due process doctrine from which that distinction had emerged no longer constituted a restraint on the exercise of governmental regulatory power. "The Fifth Amendment," argued the attorneys for the NLRB, "serves to invalidate legislation only so far as 'the means selected' are 'unreasonable, arbitrary or capricious', and have no 'real and substantial relation to the object sought to be attained' [citing *Nebbia*]."[259] The AFL cited *Nebbia* to the same effect in its amicus brief in *Washington, Virginia & Maryland Coach Co.*[260] The purpose of the Act, argued Solicitor General Stanley Reed, was to prevent interruptions to the free flow of interstate commerce caused by labor disputes, and the means selected by the Act to achieve this end were "reasonable and proper in their character."[261] The due process issue was accordingly completely controlled by the *Texas & New Orleans* case.[262]

The NLRB attorneys also mobilized associational rhetoric in defense of the Act. The Labor Board's brief in the *Associated Press* case contended that "the protection of employees in their freedom of association has been for a long time a recognized and fundamental part of the policy of the Federal Government in all aspects of labor relations subject to its control or legislative authority, and has been approved as just and reasonable."[263] The amicus brief filed by the American Newspaper Guild in the *Associated Press* case crystallized the defense of the Act in a single statement: "in the public interest, it is essential to enforce freedom of association for the purpose of negotiating the terms upon which labor is willing

---

[258] *Arguments*, note 192, at 67.

[259] Brief for the Respondent at 89, *Associated Press Co.*, 301 US 103.

[260] Brief of the American Federation of Labor, Amicus Curiae, at 15–16, *Washington, Virginia & Maryland Coach Co.*, 301 US 142.

[261] *Arguments*, note 192, at 130–31.

[262] Id at 129.

[263] Brief for Respondent at 96, *Associated Press Co.*, 301 US 103; see also id at 93, 99–100; Arguments, note 192, at 86, 89.

to sell its services to the end that there may be peace instead of war in matters affecting interstate commerce."[264]

The opinion in the *Washington, Virginia & Maryland Coach* case was, predictably, unanimous. The company was a common carrier engaged in interstate transportation, and its common law employment prerogatives were, like those of the Texas & New Orleans Railroad and the Virginian Railway, subject to reasonable regulation in the public interest. In the remaining cases, however, the Justices split 5–4 on the due process issue. The rationales for each position were stated in the *Jones & Laughlin* majority opinion and dissent.[265]

The principal issue before the Court was whether the labor relations of the enterprises in question were sufficiently related to the free flow of interstate commerce to warrant federal regulation under the commerce power. In the course of resolving this issue, the opinion of Chief Justice Hughes outlined the commercial police power rationale justifying the statute's intrusion upon the employer's common law prerogatives. The stoppage of Jones & Laughlin manufacturing operations "by industrial strife," wrote Hughes,[266]

> would have a most serious effect on interstate commerce. In view of respondent's far-flung activities, it is idle to say that the effect would be indirect or remote. It is obvious that it would be immediate and might be catastrophic. . . . When industries organize themselves on a national scale, making their relation to interstate commerce the dominant factor in their activities, how can it be maintained that their industrial labor

---

[264] Brief of the American Newspaper Guild, Amicus Curiae, at 22, *Associated Press Co.*, 301 US 103.

[265] The majority opinions in the *Fruehauf* and *Friedman–Harry Marks* cases simply recited the facts and summarily sustained the application of the Act on the authority of the *Jones & Laughlin* decision. 301 US 49 (1937); 301 U.S. 58 (1937). The Four Horsemen offered a single consolidated dissent from the three manufacturing cases. 301 US at 76. Justice Roberts wrote the majority opinion in the *Associated Press* case, in which he summarily rebuffed due process objections, citing *Jones & Laughlin* and the *Texas & New Orleans* case. 301 US 103, 133 (1937). The Four Horsemen, having offered their liberty of contract objections to the Act in their consolidated dissent from the manufacturing cases, confined themselves to dissenting from Roberts's opinion on the ground that the application of the Act to the Associated Press violated the First Amendment. 301 US at 133.

[266] *Jones & Laughlin*, 301 US at 41. For a detailed discussion of the commerce clause dimensions of Hughes's opinion, see Cushman, note 12, at 146–55.

relations constitute a forbidden field into which Congress may not enter when it is necessary to protect interstate commerce from the paralyzing consequences of industrial war?

Revealing the extent to which the wartime experience had exposed the *Adair* Court's naivete, Hughes concluded:[267]

Experience has abundantly demonstrated that the recognition of the right of employees to self-organization and to have representatives of their own choosing for the purpose of collective bargaining is often an essential condition of industrial peace. Refusal to confer and negotiate has been one of the most prolific causes of strife. This is such an outstanding fact in the history of labor disturbances that it is a proper subject of judicial notice and requires no citation of instances.

Hughes's opinion also drew extensively on the associational rhetoric he had employed seven years earlier. Citing *Texas & New Orleans* and *Virginian Railway*, Hughes held that the Act merely secured[268]

a fundamental right. Employees have as clear a right to organize and select their representatives as the respondent has to organize its business and select its own officers and agents. Discrimination and coercion to prevent the free exercise of [those employee rights] is a proper subject for condemnation by competent legislative authority.

The *Texas & New Orleans* decision had clearly established that an employer's discriminatory discharge of employees constituted a coercive interference with its employees' rights of association. And with the decision in *Nebbia*, it was clear that the Fifth Amendment did not limit governmental power to safeguard those rights from such coercion. Deploying the post-*Nebbia* language of due process, the Court found that restraint of the employer's common law prerogatives "for the purpose of preventing an unjust interference with that right cannot be considered arbitrary or capricious."[269] In the conflict between liberty of contract and freedom of association, the Court had again awarded victory to the latter.

Yet as it had in *Texas & New Orleans* and *Virginian Railway*, the

---

[267] 301 US at 42.

[268] Id at 33.

[269] Id at 44.

Court minimized the Act's imposition on the employer's contractual liberty. The Act, wrote Hughes,[270]

> imposes upon the respondent only the duty of conferring and negotiating with the authorized representatives of its employees for the purpose of settling a labor dispute. . . . The Act does not compel agreements between employers and employees. It does not compel any agreement whatever. It does not prevent the employer 'from refusing to make a collective contract and hiring individuals on whatever terms' the employer 'may by unilateral action determine.' [citing *Virginian Railway*].

Accordingly, *Adair* and *Coppage* were again "inapplicable." The Act did not[271]

> interfere with the normal exercise of the right of the employer to select its employees or to discharge them. The employer may not, under cover of that right, intimidate or coerce its employees with respect to their self-organization and representation, and, on the other hand, the Board is not entitled to make its authority a pretext for interference with the right of discharge when that right is exercised for other reasons than such intimidation and coercion.

It was by now quite clear that "inapplicable" was a highly euphemistic way of describing the status of *Adair*. *Adair* and *Coppage* had embraced a thoroughgoing liberty of contract unchecked by a countervailing right to free association. The voluntary waiver theory of the *Coppage* Court had elided the conflict between these two liberal rights; and this elision was possible only against a backdrop of assumptions about the employment relationship that the Court no longer entertained. Changes in the structure of the labor market undoubtedly informed the Court's concept of coercion. But it is important to recognize that the distance from *Adair* to the Wagner Act cases was traversed within a framework of liberal rights discourse. Liberty of contract had not simply been abandoned as unworthy or anachronistic. It had instead been curtailed in order to safeguard the countervailing liberal right of free association.[272]

---

[270] Id at 44–45.

[271] Id at 45–46.

[272] See Corwin, note 5, at 124–25; Corwin, *Constitutional Revolution, Ltd.* 66–67, 79 (Claremont, 1941); Samuel Hendel, note 165, at 260; Virginia Wood, *Due Process of Law, 1932–1949* 160–61 (Kennikat, 1951).

The Four Horsemen were not prepared to accept this accommodation in the three manufacturing cases, and we cannot understand their reasons for doing so without attention to doctrinal detail. Like the majority, the dissenters continued to work within the analytical model fashioned in *Adair*. Unlike the majority, however, the dissenting Justices did not see that model as having been modified by *Nebbia*. Having dissented in *Nebbia*, the dissenters disagreed with the majority over the types of situations into which the federal government might project its authority in order to adjust the competing claims of contractual and associational freedom. The Four Horsemen thought that Congress might legitimately so project its authority in cases involving both a business affected with a public interest (as that concept had been understood before *Nebbia*) and a commercial police power rationale—this much the cases involving interstate common carriers made clear.[273] But in the absence of these two factors, Congress was in their view powerless to intervene in the competition. Thus, despite their concurrences in the *Texas & New Orleans*, *Virginian Railway*, and *Washington, Virginia & Maryland Coach* cases, the dissenters believed that *Adair* and *Coppage* still retained some vitality.

Justice McReynolds's lengthy discussion of the commerce power issue certainly would have sufficed as a front for a dissent motivated by crude anti-labor sentiment. Yet the dissenters went on in a separate section to condemn the application of the Wagner Act to the three manufacturing establishments as a violation of the Fifth Amendment. The manner in which they did so is eloquent testimony to the continuing vitality the *Adair* model held for them, and to the extent to which they continued to embrace pre-*Nebbian* notions of public and private.

As far as the Four Horsemen were concerned, the *Texas & New Orleans* case was "not controlling."[274] There, Justice McReynolds wrote, the Court had been considering "an act definitely limited to common carriers engaged in interstate transportation over whose affairs Congress admittedly has wide power. . . ."[275] That case had clearly dealt with a pre-*Nebbia* business affected with a public

---

[273] *Washington, Virginia & Maryland Coach Co. v NLRB*, 301 US 142 (1937); *Virginian Railway Co. v System Federation, No. 40*, 300 US 515 (1937); *Texas & New Orleans Railroad Co. v Brotherhood of Railway and Steamship Clerks*, 281 US 548 (1930).

[274] *Friedman–Harry Marks Clothing Co.*, 301 US at 101.

[275] Id.

interest and an obvious commercial police power rationale. In the
instant cases, however, the dissenters were not satisfied that the
activities of the enterprises in question could directly affect interstate commerce. Because they viewed those enterprises as purely
private businesses not affected with a public interest, the Four
Horsemen could not accept the current of commerce theory urged
by the government.[276] Nor could they see any other theory under
which the enterprises in question were anything other than simply
local manufacturing operations immune from federal regulation.[277]
Accordingly, the impact of those employers' labor relations on interstate commerce could not provide the necessary rationale for
federal police power regulation of contractual liberty.

Moreover, the businesses in which the various enterprises were
engaged were not, the dissenters believed, affected with a public interest. Accordingly, the common law prerogatives of those
employers to hire and fire at will were not subject to legislative abridgement. Citing *Adair* and *Coppage*, Justice McReynolds
opined:[278]

> The right to contract is fundamental and includes the privilege
> of selecting those with whom one is willing to assume contrac-
> tual relations. This right is unduly abridged by the Act now
> upheld. A private owner is deprived of power to manage his
> own property by freely selecting those to whom his manufac-
> turing operations are to be entrusted. We think this cannot
> lawfully be done in circumstances like those here disclosed.

The disagreement between the majority and the dissent over
whether the Wagner Act violated the Fifth Amendment thus was
a disagreement over two basic issues. First, whether the labor relations of the employers directly affected interstate commerce (the
commercial police power issue); and, second, whether the businesses in which the enterprises were engaged were affected with a
public interest. The disagreement over this first issue was essentially the disagreement expressed by the two sets of Justices in
Nebbia v New York.[279] The controversy over the second issue was

---

[276] *Friedman–Harry Marks Clothing Co.*, 301 U.S. at 97–99, 103. See Cushman, note 12,
at 154–55.

[277] See Cushman, note 12, at 154–55.

[278] *Friedman–Harry Marks Clothing Co.*, 301 US at 103.

[279] See Cushman, note 12, at 146–56.

likewise comprehended within that same Nebbian fracas. Thus, the fundamental issues that would divide the Justices in the seminal labor cases of modern American constitutional law were decided not in response to the political pressures of 1937,[280] but in a 1934 dispute over the price of milk in upstate New York.

VIII. Conclusion

In preparing to defend the Wagner Act, the NLRB attorneys had been forced to select their test cases and legal arguments with close attention to doctrinal detail. The Court's commerce clause jurisprudence counseled them that only businesses whose labor relations exerted a "direct" effect on interstate commerce would fall under the federal government's commercial police power. As the Four Horsemen were replaced with Roosevelt appointees, however, it appeared that the Court was taking a broader view of the federal power to regulate commerce. The Court's 1941 decision in *United States v Darby*[281] marked a significant step in this progression; with the decision in *Wickard v Filburn*[282] the following year, the federal commerce power became virtually plenary. Taken in conjunction with the Court's decision in *Nebbia*, this expansion of the commercial police power made it clear that *Adair*'s analytical model had dissolved. In 1941, Hughes's final year on the Court, Justice Frankfurter stated what must have been obvious to all. "The course of decisions in this Court since *Adair v. United States* and *Coppage v. Kansas*," he wrote, "have completely sapped those cases of their authority."[283]

As the ultimate expositor of the Wagner Act, the Court would continue to define the extent of the Act's associational and contractual protections. The fundamental right of association was secure, but the legitimate concerted activities of labor associations were not without limits.[284] Similarly, the abandonment of *Adair* and

---

[280] See Cushman, note 6.

[281] 312 US 100 (1941).

[282] 317 US 111 (1942).

[283] *Phelps-Dodge Corp. v NLRB*, 313 US 177, 187 (1941) (citations omitted).

[284] See Karl Klare, *Judicial Deradicalization of the Wagner Act and the Origins of Modern Legal Consciousness, 1937–1941*, 62 Minn L Rev 265, 318–25 (1978); Nowak, Rotunda & Young, note 8, at 967–69.

Coppage did not signal a loss of all solicitude for employers' contractual prerogatives.[285] The Court's constitutional accommodation between associational and contractual rights had taken place within a framework of liberal rights discourse, and the terms of that discourse would continue to inform its construction of the statute. After 1937, however, the extent of the Court's protection of those rights was no longer a matter beyond congressional control. The constitutional revolution in labor law had been consolidated.

It is a commonplace that the Hughes Court era was the period during which the Supreme Court receded from its traditional solicitude for economic liberty and began to turn its attention instead to noneconomic forms of civil liberty. Yet the story is conventionally told as if the two forms of liberty were merely ships passing in the night: one on the ascendant, the other in decline.[286] In the context of the yellow-dog contract, however, the more appropriate image was the face-off. Assimilating unionism to other forms of voluntary association, labor's advocates successfully brought liberty of contract into a face-to-face conflict with freedom of association. Prefiguring and exemplifying the jurisprudential transformations for which it would become known, the Hughes Court from its inception consistently resolved this conflict in favor of associational liberty. The tale of the yellow dog thus was not just a sideshow in the demise of "laissez-faire" constitutionalism. It was emblematic of the Hughes Court's pivotal role in the recasting of American liberalism.

---

[285] Klare, supra at 293–310.

[286] For a discussion of historians' assessment of the Hughes Court, see Parrish, *The Hughes Court, the Great Depression, and the Historians*, 40 The Historian 286 (1978).

PHILIP A. HAMBURGER

EQUALITY AND DIVERSITY: THE EIGHTEENTH-CENTURY DEBATE ABOUT EQUAL PROTECTION AND EQUAL CIVIL RIGHTS

Living, as we do, in a world in which our discussions of equality often lead back to the desegregation decisions, to the Fourteenth Amendment, and to the antislavery debates of the 1830s, we tend to allow those momentous events to dominate our understanding of the ideas of equal protection and equal civil rights. Indeed, historians have frequently asserted that the idea of equal protection first developed in the 1830s in discussions of slavery and that it otherwise had little history prior to its adoption into the U.S. Constitution.[1] Long before the Fourteenth Amendment, however—long before even the 1830s—equal protection of the laws and equal civil rights were hardly notions unknown to Americans, who used these different standards of equality to address problems of religious diversity. In late eighteenth-century America—a na-

Philip A. Hamburger is Professor of Law and Legal History, the National Law Center, George Washington University.

AUTHOR's NOTE: The author gratefully acknowledges the generous financial support of the Lynde and Harry Bradley Foundation and the very helpful suggestions of Robert L. Birmingham, Boris I. Bittker, Barbara Black, Thomas E. Buckley, S.J., Stephen J. Heyman, Peter C. Hoffer, Richard S. Kay, William Letwin, William G. McLoughlin, Bruce H. Mann, and Kent Newmyer.

[1] For example, Howard J. Graham, *The Early Anti-Slavery Background of the Fourteenth Amendment*, in *Everyman's Constitution*, Leonard W. Levy, ed (State Historical Soc of Wisc, 1968) ("*Everyman's Constitution*"); Jacobus Ten Broek, *Equal Under Law* (Collier Bks, 1951, republished 1965) (Ten Broek, "*Equal Under Law*").

scent nation in which territories, peoples, and religions were multiplying—Americans employed ideas of equal protection and equal civil rights to discuss their heterogeneity, and the ways in which they did this cannot help but be of interest. By examining how Americans used different standards of equality to address their diversity, we will be able, among other things, to observe the early development of ideas that have become increasingly central to our perceptions of ourselves and our polity and thereby have affected the development of our nation. Although more spacious than two hundred years ago, America is also more crowded with people and their perceptions of their differences, and, therefore, the history of how we addressed our heterogeneity in the eighteenth century may be of greater interest now than at any time before.

It is unavoidable that this inquiry concentrate on eighteenth-century debates concerning religious liberty. During the nineteenth century, Americans engaged in a variety of controversies—most dramatically that concerning slavery—in which they discussed versions of the ideas of equality examined here: equal protection and equal civil rights. Nonetheless, slavery will not be the focus of this article, for, in the eighteenth century, it was the diversity of Christian sects rather than racial differences that prompted Americans to contend over equal protection and equal civil rights.[2] The familiarity of much of the clergy with the state-of-nature analysis, the alignment of interests among religious sects, and the nature of the controversy about religious freedom permitted eighteenth-century Americans to engage in remarkably sophisticated, albeit polemical debates about equal protection and equal civil rights. Therefore, to study the early history of these notions of equality, we must turn to the eighteenth-century debates about religious freedom.[3]

In recent decades, historians have produced a substantial and important body of literature on equality. Historians of the Fourteenth Amendment, including Howard Jay Graham, Jacobus Ten Broek, and Earl Michael Maltz, have shown that equal protection

---

[2] Of course, religious differences frequently were associated with ethnic and other social differences.

[3] The Massachusetts controversy about equal rights of suffrage is of great interest to historians of equality, but it did not generate debate between advocates of equal protection and advocates of equal civil rights.

was discussed in connection with slavery already in the 1830s.[4] They have not, however, traced the idea back to the eighteenth-century disputes about religious equality. In contrast, historians of religious liberty in the eighteenth century have discussed the general notion of equality, yet they have not focused on the idea of equal protection. For example, Nathan Hatch has traced the "democratization" of religion in America, including the attempts of late eighteenth- and especially early nineteenth-century preachers to encourage religious sentiments among all Americans.[5] In eliciting expressions of religious feeling among a wide variety of Americans, these preachers drew upon desires for political and social equality that, although hardly new, had new potency as a result of America's changing demographics. Of particular importance for this article is the work of William G. McLoughlin and Thomas E. Buckley, who have examined how legal developments came to reflect expectations of equality.[6] Buckley has shown that the notion of equality was of central importance in the Virginia debates about religious freedom, and McLoughlin has traced in rich detail its crucial role in New England. On the whole, however, just as scholars of equality have not sufficiently explored the eighteenth-century debates about religion, so students of religious liberty have not attempted systematically to differentiate the standards of equality for which various religious groups were contending. In particular, they have not examined the idea of equal protection or how it differed from the notion of equal civil rights. Thus, the eighteenth-century history of the idea of equal protection remains unknown to historians of the Fourteenth Amendment and unexplored by historians of religion.[7]

---

[4] Howard J. Graham, *The Early Anti-Slavery Background of the Fourteenth Amendment*, in *Everyman's Constitution*; Ten Broek, *Equal Under Law*; Earl M. Maltz, *Fourteenth Amendment Concepts in the Antebellum Era*, 32 Am J Legal Hist 305 (1985). J. R. Pole writes that "Jackson introduced the phrase 'equal protection.' " J. R. Pole, *The Pursuit of Equality in American History* 146 (U of Calif, 1979). Obviously, Pole could have pursued equal protection farther than he did.

[5] Nathan Hatch, *The Democratization of American Christianity* (1989).

[6] William G. McLoughlin, *New England Dissent, 1630–1833* (Harv U, 1971) (McLoughlin, *"New England Dissent"*); Thomas E. Buckley, S.J., *Church and State in Revolutionary Virginia, 1776–1787* (U of Va, 1977) (Buckley, *"Church and State in Revolutionary Virginia"*). See also Thomas J. Curry, *The First Freedoms* (Oxford U, 1986).

[7] For a brief recognition of the connection, see Michael A. Paulsen, *Religion, Equality, and the Constitution: An Equal Protection Approach to Establishment Clause Adjudication* 61 Notre Dame L Rev 311, 326 (1986). Paulsen notes Madison's use of equal protection in his 1785

A joint examination of these two subjects—religion and equality—provides an opportunity for each to be illuminated by the other. For example, in eighteenth-century debates about religious liberty, Americans employed the ideas of equal protection and equal civil rights and, in so doing, repeated and refined formulations that remain familiar and that have contributed much to our perceptions of equality and our response to the variegated character of our nation. Conversely, eighteenth-century discussions of equality can reveal much about early views of religious liberty. Indeed, an examination of how eighteenth-century Americans understood different standards of equality can shed light on some of their various state and federal guarantees of religious freedom.

It cannot be over-emphasized that modern egalitarian assumptions must be put aside. Americans debated about equal protection and equal civil rights during the ferment of the Great Awakening and then, more prominently, during the revolutionary turmoil of the 1770s, when, having begun to demand equal rights from Britain, Americans increasingly also sought equal rights from their domestic governments. In the context of these stirrings of egalitarian desires and these suggestions that equality could and should be demanded as a right, eighteenth-century Americans who claimed equality with respect to religion can be viewed as having contributed to the much broader social and cultural developments that have made egalitarianism so important for our understanding of American law. Yet eighteenth-century Americans often gave their ideas of equality a relatively narrow focus. Among other things, when they adopted positions on equality, they tended to assume that government had relatively limited purposes and capabilities. Therefore, we should not be surprised if the ideas eighteenth-century Americans called "equal protection" and "equal civil rights" were less egalitarian or were egalitarian in different ways than the ideas we associate with these phrases.[8]

A willingness to put aside modern assumptions is particularly

---

Memorial but appears to equate equal protection with an equality of civil rights. For scholarship on the use of equal protection in the nineteenth century, see note 173 and accompanying text.

[8] This study is in accord with Professor Stanley N. Katz's argument that eighteenth-century Americans typically did not seek to establish social equality by law. Stanley N. Katz, *The Strange Birth and Unlikely History of Constitutional Equality*, 75 J Am Hist 747 (1988). Katz writes that "[t]here was a constant attempt to rein in the notion of social equality." Id at 752.

important if we are to distinguish between "equal protection" and "equal civil rights." Today, these phrases are often considered almost interchangeable labels for an undefined, broad egalitarianism. In the eighteenth century, however, these terms referred to two distinct standards of equality, the one requiring equality with respect to only a portion of the legal rights for which equality was required by the other. Equal civil rights was a standard demanding that civil law treat individuals the same—that it not distinguish among individuals on the basis of their religious differences.[9] By comparison, equal protection of the laws was a lesser degree of equality—an equality only of the protection provided by civil law for natural liberty. As a result of this definition, equal protection allowed preferences or unequal privileges—that is, it permitted inequalities in rights not existing in the state of nature.[10] Thus, equal civil rights was a standard so rigorous it prevented civil laws from allocating either protection or privileges on the basis of religious differences, and equal protection was so lax it generally permitted civil laws to distribute privileges unequally. The struggle between dissenters and establishments over these two standards of equality and over related approaches for harmonizing religious differences is the primary subject of this study.

I. The State-of-Nature Analysis
and the Idea of Protection

When eighteenth-century Americans spoke about equal protection, they drew upon a political theory derived from assumptions about the state of nature. On the assumption that natural

---

[9] Today, the phrase "civil rights" refers to only some of our legal rights; in the eighteenth century, at least in the context of the debates about religious liberty, it often referred to all legal rights—the rights held by individuals under the civil laws of civil government. (This usage was related to English discussion of the need to end the "civil disablities" of dissenters—to give them the same "civil capacities" as Anglicans.) Already in the eighteenth century, however, the phrase "civil rights" could, in many circumstances, be ambiguous. Although it sometimes clearly referred to legal rights in general, it also could refer either to privileges or merely to the natural rights held under civil government. The last of these usages prevailed in the nineteenth century. See text at notes 229–33.

[10] Americans often used the word "privileges" to refer to rights individuals could only acquire by leaving the state of nature—those rights held under the laws of civil government that could not be enjoyed in the state of nature. It is in this sense that the word is used here. In contrast, it should be noted, Americans often used the word to refer to natural rights or rights in general.

liberty was the freedom of individuals in the state of nature, many Americans held that individuals sought protection for their natural liberty by submitting some of it to government to be controlled or "restrained" by the laws. Protection thus was the protection for natural liberty obtained by means of government and its legal restraints on the sacrificed portion of such freedom. More generally, Americans who discussed the protection of natural liberty appear to have assumed that it was a goal of government rather than a legally enforceable right to a particular degree of liberty or of protection.[11] They seem to have taken for granted that the different laws of different societies would protect natural liberty in varying ways and to varying degrees.[12]

Although the word "protection" will be described here as a term of art in the state-of-nature or contract theory of government, it hardly requires to be noted that Americans also often used the word in other ways. For example, any constitution or law could be said to protect various rights. Moreover, all legal rights were protected by courts and judicial process. These ordinary senses of the word "protection" must be distinguished from the specialized sense discussed in the following pages, that is, the protection of government and its laws for natural liberty.[13]

---

[11] Although protection certainly was, in a sense, a "benefit" of government, it was not a legal right or legally enforceable benefit of government. See text at notes 44–46.

[12] The importance of the state-of-nature analysis for the idea of protection has been recognized by Stephen J. Heyman, who points out that protection was considered the initial purpose, duty, or obligation of government and, accordingly, was a right of individuals. Steven J. Heyman, *The First Duty of Government: Protection, Liberty and the Fourteenth Amendment* 41 Duke L J 507 (1991) (Heyman, "*First Duty of Government*"). Although Heyman's discussion of the idea of protection is detailed and interesting, another point of view is possible. For example, Heyman argues that protection was typically understood to be a potentially enforceable legal right of individuals to an ascertainable degree of what might otherwise be considered discretionary police intervention or "protection." Yet the American and English material emphasized by Heyman and the American sources discussed here indicate, on the contrary, that protection, as such, was considered a "moral" rather than a legally enforceable right and that protection was not typically understood to be a particular degree of protection. (See text at notes 25–49 & 184–90.) Second, although Heyman focuses on historical evidence concerning protection rather than equal protection, his argument assumes that *equal* protection was the right of each individual to a particular degree of protection. Yet, as will be seen, Americans who talked about equal protection appear to have assumed that equal protection was merely an equality of such protection as was provided by government and the laws. (See text at notes 185–89.) Third, Heyman assumes that protection, in the sense of police or, more generally, executive branch intervention, was the protection of the laws mentioned in the Fourteenth Amendment. In the nineteenth century, however, Americans, particularly those who campaigned against slavery, often distinguished between the protection of the laws and the protection of government—and only the second of these categories included police or executive protection. (See text at notes 174–84.)

[13] This article focuses on the common notion that government was instituted for the

The eighteenth-century Americans who discussed "protection" each, surely, talked about this subject on the basis of somewhat different assumptions. Nonetheless, large numbers of these Americans appear to have shared at least some assumptions relating to protection, and it is these commonly held views that this article will attempt to elucidate. Of course, religious and political differences divided the Americans who talked in terms of the state-of-nature analysis, but these religious and political distinctions do not appear to have prevented such Americans from sharing many ideas about the state of nature and about the protection of natural liberty. Although some Baptists and some new lights, for example, did not use the relatively secular, state-of-nature analysis as frequently or with as much sophistication as did some other Protestants,[14] and although individuals of different theological persuasions tended to use the analysis for different reasons and in different ways, more or less all who employed the theory appeared to have done so on the basis of some common suppositions, and these are what will be examined here.[15]

---

protection of natural rights. Some writers also argued that, once government was established, it acquired other, additional obligations, which could be discussed in terms of protection. In particular, some writers pointed out that government had to protect itself. See, e.g., quotation from the 1780 Massachusetts Constitution in note 46. So too, government was expected to protect individuals in the rights they had under its laws, including privileges. Nonetheless, as a term of art, "protection" typically referred to the protection of natural rights.

[14] For example, readers may question whether the Baptist leader, Isaac Backus, employed the state-of-nature analysis. Yet he could propose a bill of rights that began: "All men are born equally free and independent, and have certain natural, inherent and unalienable rights, among which are the enjoying and defending life and liberty, acquiring, possessing, and protecting property, and pursuing and obtaining happiness and safety." *Isaac Backus's Draft for a Bill of Rights for the Massachusetts Constitution, 1779* § 1 in William G. McLoughlin, ed, *Isaac Backus on Church, State and Calvinism* 486 (Harvard U, 1968) ("*Backus on Church, State, and Calvinism*"). See also §§ 2, 4, & 7, id at 486–87. Other Baptists, moreover, such as John Leland and Samuel Stillman, employed the state-of-nature analysis with considerable sophistication. John Leland, *The Rights of Conscience Inalienable* (1791), in *The Writings of the Late Elder John Leland* 179–81 (1845) ("*Writings of Leland*"); Samuel Stillman, *A Sermon* 8–10 (Mass election sermon 1779) (Evans 16537).

Although the division between supporters and opponents of establishments will receive much attention in this account, more detailed distinctions relating to religion are approached here with considerable caution, for the theological opinions of late eighteenth-century Americans cannot always be summarized with brief and convenient labels. For example, among Congregationalists, theological divisions were extensive and subtle, and only the broadest differentiations can be captured by distinguishing between new lights and old lights or between "consistent Calvinists" and so-called "Arminians." Theological differences among the persons quoted will be mentioned only occasionally, when the differences seem particularly relevant.

[15] Of course, some Americans expressly rejected the notion of a state of nature, and yet they did not thereby necessarily abandon the analysis traditionally drawn from suppositions

Following European writers, large numbers of Americans assumed that individuals established government to obtain protection for the liberty enjoyed in the state of nature.[16] In the state of nature, said Americans, individuals were equally free.[17] The 1776 Virginia Declaration of Rights, for example, declared that "all Men are by nature equally free and independent."[18] This equal freedom

---

about the state of nature. For example, in 1794, Timothy Ford argued that the state of nature was a "fairy tale." "Americanus" [i.e., Timothy Ford], *The Constitutionalist: Or, An Inquiry How Far It Is Expedient and Proper to Alter the Constitution of South Carolina*, City Gazette and Daily Advertizer (Charleston, 1794), in 2 *American Political Writing of the Founding Era, 1760–1805* 902 (Liberty Press, 1983) (hereafter "*American Political Writing*"). Even while denying the existence of the state of nature, however, he argued on the basis of the assumption that "[t]he natural rights of men undoubtedly form the rational foundation of the social compact." Id at 906. As he explained, he did not consider the state of nature an essential part of the analysis: "It is not requisite to frame the fanciful system of a *state of nature*, in order to learn what these [natural rights] are . . . ." Id. For a brief discussion of how Americans could reject the idea of the state of nature but still retain much of the rest of the state-of-nature analysis, see note 197.

Note that this article draws evidence of the state-of-nature analysis and the idea of protection largely from the states in which Americans debated equal protection. To avoid reproducing familiar sources and to illustrate the extent to which American ministers were acquainted with the state-of-nature analysis, this article frequently quotes sermons. Evidence of the state-of-nature analysis could have been taken, however, from a broader array of states and from a great number of exclusively secular sources.

[16] Incidentally, the word "men" is used here to refer to individuals without regard to their sex. In modern analysis relating to the state of nature, the word "individual" is useful for its greater clarity. In descriptions of eighteenth-century accounts of that analysis, "men" can be useful for its capacity to suggest eighteenth-century conventions and, sometimes, ambiguities.

[17] Note that Locke wrote: "Though I have said . . . *That all Men by Nature are equal*, I cannot be supposed to understand all sorts of *Equality* . . . [T]he *Equality* I there spoke of, as proper to the Business in hand, [was] that *equal Right* that every Man hath, *to his Natural Freedom*, without being subjected to the Will or Authority of any other Man." John Locke, *Two Treatises of Government*, bk II, ch vi, § 54, at 346, Peter Laslett, ed (Mentor, 1963) (Locke, "*Two Treatises of Government*").

[18] Va Decl of Rights of 1776, § 1. It continued: "and have certain inherent rights, of which, when they enter into a state of society, they cannot, by any compact, deprive or divest their posterity . . . ." Id. This language was designed to reflect an assumption that slaves were not parties to the compact and had not become members of society.

So common was the assumption of equal freedom in the state of nature that "[n]o man denies but that *originally* all were equally *free*." Samuel Webster, *A Sermon* 22 (Mass election sermon 1777) (Evans 15703). In the 1787 Constitutional Convention, Luther Martin addressed the issue: "In order to prove that individuals in a State of nature are equally free & independent he read passages from Locke, Vattel, Lord Summers—Priestly." Max Farrand, ed, 1 *Records of the Federal Convention of 1787* 437 (Madison's notes, June 27, 1787) (Yale, 1974) (hereafter "Farrand"). At Princeton, Witherspoon lectured that "men are originally and by nature equal, and consequently free." John Witherspoon, *An Annotated Edition of Lectures on Moral Philosophy*, Lect X, at 124, ed Jack Scott (U of Del, 1982) (Witherspoon, "*Lectures*"). A leading Anti-Federalist, "Brutus," wrote: "If we may collect the sentiments of the people of America, from their own most solemn declarations, they hold this truth as self evident, that all men are by nature free." "Brutus," Herbert J. Storing, ed, 2 *The Complete Anti-Federalist* 372 (Chicago, 1981) ("*Complete Anti-Federalist*"). Quoting Locke, the Rev. Stillman—a Baptist—said that ". . . 'creatures of the same species and rank, promiscuously born to all the same advantages of nature, and the use of the same faculties, should

of individuals in the state of nature from subordination to other humans was the basis of their natural liberty—what frequently was described as their life, liberty, and property, or more simply (in the language of Locke) their property.[19] Unfortunately, if individuals in the state of nature had no common superior, some would use their freedom to injure other individuals. The state of nature was, therefore, if not a "state of war," at least a situation of "inconvenience," in which natural liberty was insecure.[20] On this account,

---

also be equal one amongst another without subordination or subjection . . .' . . . we ought firmly to maintain the *natural equality* of all men." Samuel Stillman, *A Sermon* 8 (Mass election sermon 1779) (Evans 16537). Many examples have survived in the election sermons of establishment New England ministers: Israel Evans, *A Sermon* 9–10 (NH election sermon 1791) (Evans 23358); Asa Burton, *A Sermon* 110 (Vt election sermon 1786) (Evans 19536); Peter Powers, *Jesus Christ the True King and Head of Government* 10 (Vt election sermon 1778) (Evans 16019); Gershom C. Lyman, *A Sermon* 6 (Vt election sermon 1784) (Evans 18566); Jonas Clark, *A Sermon* 9 & 11 (Mass election sermon [1781]) (Evans 17114); Henry Cumings, *A Sermon* 6 (Mass election sermon 1783) (Evans 17899).

[19] Locke, *Two Treatises of Government*, bk II, ch v, § 27, at 328. For American illustrations, see note 22.

[20] In the tradition of Hobbes, some Americans said that the state of nature was a state of war. E.g., "Philodemus" [i.e., Thomas Tudor Tucker], *Conciliatory Hints* (Charleston, 1784), in 1 *American Political Writing* 613. Many examples of this point of view have been preserved among the printed sermons of New England ministers. E.g.: "Government is necessary, . . . is founded in the corruption and vices of human nature; for if mankind were in a state of rectitude there would be no need of the sanctions of human laws . . . . But in the present disordered state of our nature there would be no safety of life or property without the protection of law. A state of nature would be a state of continual war and carnage." Samuel McClintock, *A Sermon* 44 (1784) (Evans 18567). See also: Joseph Lyman, *A Sermon* 9 (Mass election sermon 1787) (Evans 20469); Zabdiel Adams, *A Sermon* 35 (Mass election sermon [1782]) (Evans 17450); William Welsteed, *The Dignity & Duty of the Civil Magistrate* 32 (Mass election sermon 1751) (Evans 6793). For the influence of Hobbes, see Walter Berns, "The New Pursuit of Happiness," Const Comm 65, 67–69 (1987).

Many other Americans, including many New England ministers, described men as social, but these authors also viewed society as safer than the state of nature. E.g., "[T]he social Nature of Man, and his natural Desire of Happiness, strongly urge him to Society as eligible;—to which, if we add, the natural Principle of Self-Preservation, the Dangers Mens Lives and Properties are exposed to, when considered as unconnected with others, Society will appear necessary." Abraham Williams, *A Sermon* 4 (Mass election sermon 1762) (Evans 9310). See also: Noah Hobart, *Civil Government the Foundation of Social Happiness* 1, 15, and 16 (Conn election sermon 1750, printed 1751) (Evans 6692); "The Preceptor" II in Mass Spy (May 21, 1772), in 1 *American Political Writing* 176.

Even with differing views of the state of nature, American commentators often emphasized either the violence or at least the sinfulness of men in the state of nature, as this permitted the commentators to describe the necessity of government in terms of man's fallen character. For example, Thomas Paine wrote that "[s]ociety is produced by our wants, and government by our wickedness; . . . Government, like dress, is the badge of lost innocence; . . ." Thomas Paine, *Common Sense* 65, ed Isaac Kramnick (Penguin, 1986) (Paine, "*Common Sense*"). New England ministers were particularly eloquent on the subject. E.g.: "Were mankind perfect in wisdom and virtue, civil laws and rulers would be needless." Gershom C. Lyman, *A Sermon* 6 (Vt election sermon 1782, printed 1784) (Evans 18566). "[W]hile this womb of hell, the selfish heart, is ever pregnant, and ever bringing forth such trains of destructive evils, there can be no safety in the enjoyment of the blessings of heaven in a *state of nature*. In any state, men, like beasts, would destroy each other, unless the

as Americans noted again and again, individuals sought protection for their natural freedom by sacrificing a portion of it for the creation of government. According to a common maxim, "[w]hen people enter into society, they must, in order to obtain protection, give up some part of their natural liberty, in order to secure the rest."[21] Put another way, individuals created government to protect their "life, liberty, and property,"[22] to secure happiness, or to enable themselves to pursue happiness.[23]

---

corrupt heart is under some powerful restraint. This was the case in fact in the early ages of the world, before government was formed . . . 'the earth was *filled with violence.*' In such a state neither the lives, liberty, rights, or property, or any thing man possesses is secure or safe one moment." Asa Burton, *A Sermon* 9–10 (Vt election sermon 1785, printed 1786) (Evans 19536). "Government then is a necessary evil; a scheme invented to supply the want of *true virtue* . . . ." Id at 11. "[A]ll the social affections concur to urge the importance of civil government. But . . . these arguments . . . would be, at best, but a feeble support to the peace and order of society,—would never have availed to establish government, over the lawless lusts of vicious, aspiring, or blood-thirsty men.—It is *Necessity, Necessity alone,* which combines men in society . . . ." Jonas Clark, *A Sermon* 8–9 (Mass election sermon [1781]) (Evans 17114). See also: Josiah Whitney, *The Essential Requisites* 11 (Conn election sermon 1788) (Evans 21601); Timothy Stone, *A Sermon* 9 (Conn election sermon 1792) (Evans 24820).

[21] "Publicola" [Archibold Maclaine], *An Address to the Freemen of North Carolina* (State Gaz of NC, March 20, 1788), in John P. Kaminski et al, eds, 16 *Documentary History of the Ratification of the Constitution* 437 (State Historical Society of Wisconsin, 1986) ("*Documentary History*").

[22] For some relatively unfamiliar, clerical examples from New England, see the following: "[T]he great and only design of government," said the Rev. Webster, was "*the security* of the *lives, liberty* and *property* of the people." Samuel Webster, *A Sermon* 12 (Mass election sermon 1777). "And the most barbarous heathen nations have found it necessary to have established rules and customary laws strictly observed for the punishment of vice, and for the safety of life, and preservation of property. . . . The people of any nation, country or community, have an undoubted right to set upon such form of government as they judge will most effectually secure their safety, prosperity and happiness . . . ." Peter Powers, *Jesus Christ the True King and Head of Government* 12 (Vt election sermon 1778) (Evans 16019). "Were there no civil government, laws, magistracy, nor *Shields of the earth,* for the preservation of peace, the guard of liberty, the protection of property and the defence of life, it is easy to see . . . that anarchy, confusion, blood and slaughter, waste and destruction, would soon take place in the earth." Jonas Clark, *A Sermon* 8 (Mass election sermon [1781]) (Evans 17114). "The protection of life, liberty and property, is the principal object of law and government." William Morrison, *A Sermon* 13–14 (NH election sermon 1792) (Evans 24563). See also Noah Hobart, *Civil Government the Foundation of Social Happiness* 9 & 16 (Conn election sermon 1750, printed 1751) (Evans 6692).

Some spoke of protection for "property." E.g., "The great Design of mens coming *into Society,* and making up one civil Polity, is the preservation of their Property, which in the *state of Nature,* they could not Singly, and each one by himself Defend." Benjamin Lord, *Religion and Government Subsisting Together in Society, Necessary to their Compleat Happiness and Safety* 26 (Conn election sermon for 1751, printed 1752) (Evans 6868). Thomas Paine wrote of "man" that "he finds it necessary to surrender up a part of his property to furnish means for the protection of the rest; . . ." Paine, *Common Sense* 65. He added that "security" is "the true design and end of government." Id.

[23] According to the Pennsylvania Constitution, "all men . . . have certain natural, inherent and inalienable rights, amongst which are, the enjoying and defending life and liberty,

Of course, the necessity of sacrificing natural liberty in order to secure it was no paradox. Individuals seeking protection for their natural liberty from the depredations of others sacrificed a portion of it in a constitution, which authorized government to impose legal obligations in restraint of the sacrificed portion of their natural liberty. Some of these restraints were, for example, the laws prohibiting violence and the laws requiring military service and payment of taxes.[24] By restraining some natural lib-

---

acquiring, possessing and protecting property, and pursuing and obtaining happiness and safety." Pa Const of 1776, Declaration of Rights, Art 1. In emphasizing the differences among writers, one began by admitting that they agreed about happiness: "Although all writers agree in the object of government, and admit that it was designed to promote and secure the happiness of every member of society, yet their opinions, as to the systems most productive of this general benefit, have been extremely contradictory." "A Native of this Colony" [i.e., Carter Braxton], *An Address to the Convention of the Colony and Ancient dominion of Virginia* . . . (1776), in 1 *American Political Writing* 330. See also Declaration of Independence; "Brutus," in 2 *Complete Anti-Federalist* 373; James Iredell, Charge to the Grand Jury of the Circut Court for the District of Massachusetts (Oct 12, 1792), in Maeva Marcus, ed, 2 *Documentary History of the Supreme Court of the United States* 310 (Columbia U, 1988) ("*Documentary History of the Supreme Court*"); Morton White, *The Philosophy of the American Revolution* 162–64 (Oxford U, 1978).

For the views of New England ministers of varying religious perspectives, see, e.g., the following: "Public Happiness is the original Design and great End of Civil Government." Noah Hobart, *Civil Government the Foundation of Social Happiness* 3 (Conn election sermon 1750, printed 1751) (Evans 6692). "[T]he true original end of civil government was, the safety and happiness of the people; that every man, so far as possible, might enjoy his immunities and privileges in peaceable and quiet possession." Peter Powers, *Jesus Christ the True King and Head of Government* 11 (Vt election sermon 1778) (Evans 16019). "As their leaving a state of nature for a state of civil society, is a matter of their own choice, so they are equally free to adopt that form of government which appears to them the most eligible, or the best calculated to promote the happiness of themselves and of their posterity." Samuel Stillman, *A Sermon* 9 (Mass election sermon 1779) (Evans 16537).

Some writers said that safety was the original reason for establishing government and that happiness became a purpose of government only subsequently. Typically, this distinction is not apparent in American writing. Note, however, this example: "The *immediate end* of government was then at first designed, as it is now, to be a restraint upon the human heart, to keep it from breaking forth into violent outrages . . . . But the *ultimate end* of government is the happiness or well-being of men in this world. In order to this, it is not only necessary that mens lives, property, and natural rights should be safe guarded; but also, that they should discharge the duties, and grant that help and assistance which they in justice owe each other. Government then by restraining the selfish heart, and by obliging men to perform acts of kindness and benevolence, (seemingly so if no more) and to discharge the duties they owe each other, reaches its final term, *the promotion of the happiness and well-being of the world.*" Asa Burton, *A Sermon* 10 (Vt election sermon 1785, printed 1786) (Evans 19536).

[24] Civil "restraints" on natural liberty included not only negative commands but also other laws controlling or restricting an individual's liberty as it existed in the state of nature. Thus, such restraints consisted of all civil obligations, if these are understood as the duties imposed by law on individuals—not including, however, conditions on privileges.

Of course, the obligations included moral duties. In this regard note that ministers of established churches, at least in New England, sometimes suggested that dissenters took a position on religious liberty that was incompatible with moral regulation. In response to dissenters' arguments that civil governments should only regulate civil matters, some mem-

erty, these laws protected or at least facilitated protection of the
remainder.

As has already been suggested, the sacrifice of natural liberty
was assumed to occur by means of a contract, fundamental law, or
constitution, in which the people stipulated what they gave up
and what they retained.[25] In the words of one Anti-Federalist, "[a]

---

bers of establishments justified state support for their establishments by saying, inter alia,
that the regulation of morality was a regulation of religion and that, therefore, civil government had to be able to regulate religion in order to achieve its civil purposes. With this
argument, establishment writers could simultaneously justify an establishment and could
suggest that dissenters were against moral regulation. E.g., "[I]t is the duty of rulers to give
all that countenance and support to religion that is consistent with liberty of conscience.
And it is perfectly consistent with that liberty and equal protection which are secured to
all denominations of christians, by our excellent constitution, for rulers in the exercise of
their authority to punish profane swearing, blasphemy, and open contempt of the institutions of religion, which have a fatal influence on the interests of society, and for which no
man, in the exercise of reason, can plead conscience." Samuel McClintock, *A Sermon* 33
(1784) (Evans 18567). "With respect to articles of faith or modes of worship, civil authority
have no right to establish religion. The people ought to choose their own ministers, and
their own denomination, as our laws now permit them; but as far as religion is connected
with the morals of the people, and their improvement in knowledge, it becomes of great
importance to the state; and legislators may well consider it as part of their concern for
the public welfare, to make provision that all the towns may be furnished with good teachers . . . ." Samuel Langdon, *A Sermon* 47–48 (NH election sermon 1788) (Evans 21192).

Few canards were more annoying for dissenters than to suggest that their opposition to
government tax support for religion would destroy the state's right to regulate morality.
Dissenters, illustrated by the two Baptists quoted below, tended to justify moral regulation
as relating to civil interests. According to Caleb Blood, the government's obligation to
treat people equally notwithstanding religious differences "by no means prohibits the civil
magistrate from enacting those laws that shall enforce the observance of those precepts in
the christian religion, the violation of which is a breach of the civil peace; viz. such as forbid
murder, theft, adultery, false witness, and injuring our neighbor, either in person, name,
or estate. And among others, that of observing the Sabbath, should be enforced by the civil
power. . . . As to the aid of the civil power to force men to support gospel ministers, I
humbly conceive that it can never be necessary." Caleb Blood, *A Sermon* 35 (Vt election
sermon [1792]) (Evans 24126). When Stillman—a leading Baptist—preached an election
sermon, establishment critics allegedly said: " 'That upon the principles contained in the
sermon, the civil magistrate ought not to exercise his authority to suppress actions of immo-
rality.' " Stillman responded that had his words been "properly observed, this objection had
been superseded. Immoral actions properly come under the cognizance of civil rulers, who
are the guardians of the peace of society. For then I beg leave to observe in the words of
Bishop Warburton, 'That the magistrate punishes no bad actions, as sins or offenses *against
God*, but only as crimes injurious to, or having a malignant influence on society.' " Samuel
Stillman, *A Sermon* 20 note (Mass election sermon 1779) (Evans 16537).

[25] A contrary interpretation, according to which Americans desired or assumed an unwritten constitution, has been suggested by Bernard Bailyn, Gordon Wood, Thomas Grey,
and, more recently, Susanna Sherry. Bernard Bailyn, *The Ideological Origins of the American
Revolution* 175–89 (1967); Gordon Wood, *The Creation of the American Republic 1776–1787*
259–305 (1969); Thomas Grey, *Do We Have an Unwritten Constitution*, 27 Stan L Rev 703,
715–16 (1975); Susana Sherry, *The Founders' Unwritten Constitution*, 54 U Chi L Rev 1127
(1987). See, however, Walter Berns, *Judicial Review and the Rights and Laws of Nature*, 3
Supreme Court Review 49 (1982); Isaac Kramnick, *Republican Revisionism Revisited*, 87 Am
Hist Rev 629 (1982); Helen K. Michaels, *The Role of Natural Law in Early American Constitu-*

people, entering into society, surrender such a part of their natural rights, as shall be necessary for the existence of that society. . . . They are conveyed by a written compact, expressing those which are given up, and the mode in which those reserved shall be secured."[26]

Because the people sacrificed their natural liberty by means of constitutions made by themselves, they could exercise their remaining natural liberty—it was protected—only in accord with

---

tionalism: Did the Founders Contemplate Judicial Enforcement of 'Unwritten' Individual Rights? 69 NC L Rev 421 (1991); Ronald M. Peters, Jr., *The Massachusetts Constitution of 1780: A Social Compact* (1978); Rozann Rothman, *The Impact of Covenant and Contract Theories on Conceptions of the U.S. Constitution*, Publius 149 (Fall 1980); see also Gary J. Schmitt and Robert H. Webking, *Revolutionaries, Antifederalists, and Federalists: Comments on Gordon Wood's Understanding of the American Founding*, Political Sci Reviewer 195 (Fall 1979).

A brief sampling of some the evidence can be presented here. In 1771, Josiah Tucker preached that "the fundamental laws, which are the basis of government, and form the political constitution of the state,—which mark out, and fix the chief lines and boundaries between the authority of Rulers, and the liberties and privileges of the people, are, and can be no other, in a free state, than what are mutually agreed upon and consented to." Josiah Tucker, *An Election Sermon* (Boston, 1771), in 1 *American Political Writing* 162. After urging that a "continental conference" should meet, Thomas Paine said that "their business" should "be to frame a CONTINENTAL CHARTER, or Charter of the United Colonies; (answering to what is called the Magna Charta of England) fixing the number and manner of choosing members of Congress, members of Assembly, . . . Securing freedom and property to all men, and above all things the free exercise of religion, according to the dictates of conscience . . . ." Paine, *Common Sense* 97. This charter was a "constitution." Id at 98. See also id at 109. Another author wrote: "The constitution is a social covenant entered into by express consent of the people, upon a footing of the most perfect equality with respect to every civil liberty." "Philodemus" [i.e., Thomas Tudor Tucker], *Conciliatory Hints* (1784), in 1 *American Political Writing* 612. On the commencement of the New Hampshire Constitution, the Rev. McClintock preached: "Were it necessary, I might shew with what precision the rights belonging to men in a state of society are defined in the *Declaration of Rights*, and the life, liberty and property of the subject guarded with a jealous care against oppressive power . . . ." Samuel McClintock, *A Sermon* 23–24 (1784) (Evans 18567). Witherspoon said: "Society I would define to be an association or compact of any number of persons, to deliver up or abridge some part of their natural rights, in order to have the strength of the united body, to protect the remaining, and to bestow others." Witherspoon, *Lectures*, Lect X, at 123. Nathaniel Chipman wrote: "In the exercise of this right of free consent by the people, . . . constitutions of government are formed. The constitution is no other than the fundamental law made and ratified by such compact." Nathaniel Chipman, *Sketches of the Principles of Government* 116 (1793). Thomas Reese—a Presbyterian minister in Salem, South Carolina— noted that "[i]f Mr. Locke, and the American politicians, argue right, all legitimate government is originally founded on compact." Thomas Reese, *An Essay on the Influence of Religion in Civil Society* 20 (1788) (Evans 21418). See also notes 26–29 & 39.

[26] "John De Witt," 4 *Complete Anti-Federalist* 21. He continued: "Language is so easy of explanation, and so difficult is it by words to convey exact ideas, that the party to be governed cannot be too explicit. The line cannot be drawn with too much precision and accuracy." Id. He also wrote that the only difference between a constitution for the United States and an individual state is "in the numbers of the parties concerned; they are both a compact between the Governors and Governed, the letter of which must be adhered to in discussing their powers. That which is not expressly granted, is of course retained." Id

the varying demands of different constitutions. As the Rev. Moses Hemmingway told the Governor and legislature of Massachusetts:

> Though the *natural rights* of men may, in general, seem much alike, they being, in this respect, "all FREE and EQUAL;" yet it is in different degrees that they are permitted to use them. According to the different civil constitutions which men are under, their *civil liberty* is larger, or more restricted.[27]

Anti-Federalists had frequent occasion to use this analysis. For example, a constitution that granted broad powers and failed to mention freedom of the press worried Anti-Federalists because "[t]he people's or the printers claim to a free press, is founded on the fundamental laws, that is, compacts, and state constitutions. . . . The people, who can annihilate or alter those constitutions, can annihilate or limit this right." "Federal Farmer," 2 *Complete Anti-Federalist* 329. The "Federal Farmer" also wrote: "The constitution, or whole social compact, is but one instrument, no more or less, than a certain number of articles, or stipulations agreed to by the people, whether it consists of articles, sections, chapters, bills of rights, or parts of any other denomination, cannot be material." Id at 323; see also id at 325. Another Anti-Federalist wished "that the freedom of the press may be *previously* secured as a *constitutional* and *unalienable right*, and not left to the precarious care of popular privileges [i.e., public opinion about rights] which may or many not influence our new rulers." "Cincinnatus," 6 id at 11. Speaking of natural rights in general, the "Impartial Examiner" wrote: "There can be no other just origin of civil power, but some such mutual contract of all of the people: and although their great object in forming society is an intention to secure their natural rights; yet the relations arising from this *political union* create certain duties and obligations to the state, which require a sacrifice of some portion of those rights and of that exuberance of liberty, which obtains in a state of nature.—This, however, being compensated by certain other adventitious rights and privileges, which are aquired by the social connection; . . . they ought to give up no greater share than what is understood to be absolutely necessary:—and they should endeavor so to organize, arrange and connect it's several branches, that when duly exercised it may tend to promote the *common good* of all, . . . It is evident, therefore that they should attend most diligently to those sacred rights, which they have received with their birth, and which can neither be retained to themselves, nor transmitted to their posterity, unless they are *expressly reserved:* for it is a maxim, I dare say, universally acknowledged, that when men establish a system of government, in granting the powers therein they are always understood to surrender whatever they do not so expressly reserve." "Impartial Examiner," 5 *Complete Anti-Federalist* 176; see also id at 177 & 185. According to "An Old Whig," "To define what portion of his natural liberty, the subject shall at all times be entitled to retain, is one great end of a bill of rights." "An Old Whig," 3 id at 33. "Brutus" wrote that "the portion of their natural liberty, which they give up for the enjoyment of civil government, should be expressly mentioned, in the constitution." "Brutus," in 8 *Documentary History* 212. Federalists did not disagree that natural rights were retained only to the extent they were reserved in the Constitution, but they argued that the unamended federal Constitution adequately reserved natural liberty and that the spirit of the people was a more important means of preserving rights than any paper guarantees.

[27] Moses Hemmingway, *A Sermon* 29–30 (Mass election sermon 1784) (Evans 18526). See also id at 13–14. Josiah Whitney said: "Nations or states are left to chuse and adopt such [forms of government] as are most agreeable to their genius and circumstances. [New ¶] Some natural rights are to be given up into the hands of one, or more, for the preservation of the rest. [New ¶] One form may be best for one people, and a different one for another. In general, that ought to have the preference, which best secures the lives, liberties, and properties of men." Josiah Whitney, *The Essential Requisites to Form the Good Ruler's Character* 12 (Conn election sermon 1788) (Evans 21601).

Similarly, when George Washington transmitted the product of the 1787 Constitutional Convention to the Congress, he mentioned the difficulties the framers had encountered in attempting to delineate the sacrifice of natural rights to the Federal government:

> Individuals entering into society, must give up a share of liberty to preserve the rest. The magnitude of the sacrifice must depend as well on situation and circumstance, as on the object to be obtained. It is at all times difficult to draw with precision the line between those rights which must be surrendered, and those which may be reserved; and on the present occasion this difficulty was encreased by a difference among the several States as to their situation, extent, habits, and particular interests.[28]

More generally, in the words of Jefferson's 1790 official opinion on the right of Congress to adjourn itself: "It is a natural right and, like all other natural rights, may be abridged or regulated in it's exercise by law."[29] The degree of natural liberty protected and enjoyed under government depended upon the varying requirements of the constitutions and other laws adopted in different societies.

According to Americans who employed the state-of-nature analysis, the limited natural liberty permitted and protected by the laws of civil government was much preferable to the insecure liberty enjoyed in the state of nature.[30] Because of civil government and because of the obligations or "restraints" of civil laws, such natural liberty as the civil laws left to individuals was protected. Moreover, because of this security, liberty was more assured when

---

[28] George Washington, letter to the President of Congress, Sept. 17, 1787, in 1 *Documentary History* 305.

[29] Thomas Jefferson, Opinion on the Constitutionality of the Residence Bill, 17 *Papers of Thomas Jefferson* 197, Julian P. Boyd, ed (Princeton U, 1965). He also wrote: "This like all other natural rights, may be abridged or modified in it's exercise, by their own consent, . . . but so far as it is not abridged or modified, they retain it as a natural right . . . ." Id at 195. Jefferson also wrote that "our rulers can have authority over such natural rights, only as we have submitted to them." Thomas Jefferson, *Notes on the State of Virginia*, Paul L. Ford, ed, Question 17, at 197 (1894).

[30] In this sense, Americans were not exclusively "individualistic" or "communitarian," and, for this reason, it can be anachronistic to speak of competing ideologies of liberalism and republicanism. See Thomas L. Pangle, *The Spirit of Modern Republicanism: The Moral Vision of the American Founders and the Philosophy of John Locke* (U of Chi, 1988). The differences among most eighteenth-century Americans on these issues can easily be overdrawn or depicted in modern terms that obscure the extent to which those older Americans held shared assumptions.

subject to government than when it was not; there was a greater enjoyment of liberty under the restraints of law than independent of law.[31] What typically was discussed in terms of liberty could also be addressed in terms of interests: "In vain would it be for individuals to have distinct interests, were they not preserved in the enjoyment of them, by the combined power of the whole."[32]

Of course, not all types of natural liberty could be sacrificed to obtain protection; Americans often denied that there could be any restraints upon the natural right of free exercise of religion. Drawing on Locke, eighteenth-century Americans said that each individual possessed, as part of his equal freedom in the state of nature, an inalienable liberty to worship or to exercise his religion as he pleased. Dissenters and even, increasingly, members of establishments opined that a person's relationship to his Maker was so "personal" and important that it could not be surrendered to the control of society. It was a matter of which an individual had an inalienable right "to judge for himself."[33] This argument that the natural right

---

[31] Zephaniah Swift—later Chief Justice of Connecticut—wrote that "the natural rights which we sacrifice are of but very little value, when compared with the civil rights we acquire in a free and well regulated government." Zephaniah Swift, 1 *A System of the Laws of the State of Connecticut* 16 (1795). According to a Massachusetts minister, "it is indeed much for the People's Good that they are put in Subjection to the Power of the Magistrate; that they are certainly more effectually secured of their Lives, Liberties & Estates, under the Direction & Restraint of Laws and Government, than they possibly could be without. For *if there were not king in Israel, every Man might do what was right in his own Eyes.*" William Welsteed, *The Dignity and Duty of the Civil Magistrate* 22 (Mass election sermon 1751) (Evans 6793). A Connecticut minister preached: *"Men . . . are by no means, to remain in a State of Nature;* each one to possess by himself, and use for himself his natural Rights & Liberties, without any borrowed Strength and Advantage from others by Compact: . . ." Benjamin Lord, *Religion and Government Subsisting Together in Society, Necessary to their Compleat Happiness and Safety* 2 (Conn election sermon for 1751, printed 1752) (Evans 6868). Also: "Every Member may have the Strength of the whole employed for the Security of his own Life and Property. And also rejoyce in his Neighbours having the same Protection and Advantage with himself: So that, the Privileges of Society must be vastly greater than all the Rights of Nature separately Consider'd and Used. . . ." Id at 3. The Rev. Hemmingway said: "It is true, the interests of society require subordination: but this deprives none of liberty, but helps all to enjoy it better." Moses Hemmingway, *A Sermon* 27 (Mass election sermon 1784) (Evans 18526). See also id at 16.

[32] Zabdiel Adams, *A Sermon* 35 (Mass election sermon [1782]) (Evans 17450). On the same page, he added a Hobbesian flourish: "Althou' a state of nature may have some attendant advantages; yet the inconveniences of it are a thousand times greater.—It is a state of war." Id.

[33] For example, in Massachusetts dissenters petitioned that "God hath given to every Man an Unalienable Right in Matters of His Worship to Judge for himself as his Conscience reserves ye Rule from God." 1749 Petition to the Mass Assembly from the Separate congregations in 17 towns in Anson Phelps Stokes, 1 *Church and State in the United States* 422 (Harper, 1950). The Baptist leader Isaac Backus wrote: "In civil states particular men are

of religious judgment and worship was inalienable was reinforced by another argument, based on assumptions about the secular purpose of government. The principle of self-preservation—the assumed goal of humans to preserve themselves—suggested that men formed government to secure their "secular Welfare." Thus, an establishment minister preached: "The Nature of civil Society or Government, is a temporal worldly Constitution, formed upon worldly Motives, to answer valuable worldly Purposes."[34] So common was the assumption that men formed civil government by consent "to promote their *temporal interests*" that a leading Baptist minister could mimic his own use of the state-of-nature analysis by saying of heaven that "[t]hey who enter into this kingdom do it voluntarily, with a design of promoting their spiritual interests."[35] Having been established for secular purposes, civil government

---

invested with authority to judge for the whole; but in Christ's kingdom each one has an equal right to judge for himself." Isaac Backus, *A Fish Caught in His Own Net* (1768), in William G. McLoughlin, ed, *Isaac Backus on Church, State, and Calvinism* 198 (Belknap, 1968) (*"Backus on Church, State, and Calvinism"*). See also id at 332, 335. Another Baptist leader, Samuel Stillman, also asserted that religion was a "right of private judgment." It was a matter "in which every man is *personally* interested; and concerning which every man ought to be fully persuaded in his own mind." Samuel Stillman, *A Sermon* 25 (Mass election sermon 1779) (Evans 16537). In Virginia, Presbyterians petitioned: "The thoughts, the intentions, the faith, and the consciences of men, with their modes of worship, lie beyond their reach, and are ever to be referred to a higher and more penetrating tribunal. These internal and spiritual matters cannot be measured by human rules, nor be amenable to human laws." Memorial of the Presbytery of Hanover to the General Assembly of Virginia (Oct 1784), in William A. Blakely, ed, *American State Papers* 109 (Religious Liberty Assoc, 1911) (*"American State Papers"*). Later, Presbyterians said: "Religion is altogether personal, and the right of exercising it unalienable; and it is not, cannot, and ought not to be, resigned to the will of the society at large; and much less to the legislature, which derives its authority wholly from the consent of the people, and is limited by the original intention of civil associations." Memorial of the Presbyterians of Virginia to the General Assembly (Aug 13, 1785), in *American State Papers* 113–14. See also Witherspoon, *Lectures*, Lect XIV, at 160. Madison wrote that this right "is unalienable, because the opinions of men, depending only on the evidence contemplated in their own minds, cannot follow the dictates of other men." James Madison, Memorial and Remonstrance (1785), *American State Papers* 120–21. An establishment minister in New Hampshire preached: "As the conscience of man is the image and representative of God in the human soul; so to him alone it is responsible." Israel Evans, *A Sermon* 6 (NH election sermon 1791) (Evans 23358). Another preached that, "as piety and our mode of faith are matters only between GOD and our own souls, we ought to be amenable to no human tribunal; but only answerable to GOD and our consciences." Samuel Shuttlesworth, *A Discourse* 14 (Vt election discourse 1791, printed 1792) (Evans 24788). For additional evidence of both dissenting and establishment opinion, see Philip A. Hamburger, *A Constitutional Right of Religious Exemption: An Historical Perspective*, 60 Geo Wash L Rev 933–38 (1992).

[34] Abraham Williams, *A Sermon* 8 (Mass election sermon 1762) (Evans 9310).

[35] Samuel Stillman, *A Sermon* 33 & 26 (Mass election sermon 1779) (Evans 16537). See quotation of the Rev. Booth in note 149.

arguably lacked authority to deny an individual's free exercise of religion. On the basis of these arguments, dissenters and their allies could insist that the natural right of religious freedom was "exactly the same" in civil society as in the state of nature.[36] Although some establishment writers argued that government had a right to deny religious liberty to persons whose religious opinions might pose a threat to civil government, this point of view increasingly was questioned.[37] In the decades following 1776, the natural right of the free exercise of religion was, to large numbers of dissenters and even many members of establishments, a right simply beyond the reach of civil government.

In contrast, Americans did not typically consider most other natural rights—even "inalienable" natural rights—immune from government restraints. Life, liberty, property, and the pursuit of happiness were inalienable natural rights but were to be protected under the regulations of civil government. So too, freedom of speech was governed by the laws concerning, among other things, defamation, blasphemy, and fraud.[38] Taking up the cause of South Carolina's dissenters, the Rev. William Tennent—a Presbyterian—acknowledged that individuals could give government the power to regulate the rights often described as inalienable—the only exception being in matters of religion: "I can communicate to my representative, a power to dispose of part of my property, for the security of the remaining part: I may give him a right to resign a part of my personal liberty to the obligation of good laws, as a means of preserving the rest,—but, cannot,—I say it is out of my power, to communicate to any man on earth, a right to dispose of my conscience, and to lay down for me what I shall believe and

---

[36] Stillman wrote of the "Rights of Conscience" that "in a state of nature, and of civil society [they] are exactly the same. They can neither be parted with nor controled, by any human authority whatever." Samuel Stillman, *A Sermon* 11 (Mass election sermon 1779) (Evans 16537). See also the opinion of the Connecticut Separate, Israel Holly, *A Word in Zion's Behalf* 18 ([1765]) (Evans 10005). Madison wrote "that in matters of religion no man's right is abridged by the institution of civil society, and that religion is wholly exempt from its cognizance." James Madison, Memorial and Remonstrance, *American State Papers* 121. See also quotations in note 39 and accompanying text.

[37] Philip A. Hamburger, *A Constitutional Right of Religious Exemption: An Historical Perspective*, 60 Geo Wash L Rev 915, 918–26 (1992).

[38] The right of contract also was subject to variation by civil laws. Zephaniah Swift, 1 *A System of the Laws of the State of Connecticut* 16 (1795). For a later example, see the dissent of Marshall in *Ogden v Saunders*, 12 Wheat 213, 345 (1827).

practice in religious matters."[39] Whereas the free exercise of religion might be "exactly the same" under government as in nature, other inalienable natural rights were different under government and therefore were inalienable in a rather qualified way. In order to obtain protection for their natural rights, individuals could submit even "inalienable" natural rights to particular legal forms or restraints.[40]

Not surprisingly, Americans frequently associated protection with obedience and allegiance. According to an establishment clergyman in Massachusetts, "[a]s every Subject has a Right or Claim to be protected by the Magistrate, so the Magistrate has an equal

---

[39] William Tennent, *Mr. Tennent's Speech on the Dissenting Petition, Delivered In the House of Assembly, Charles-Town, South-Carolina, Jan. 11, 1777* 6 (1777) (Evans 15612). He also said: "The rights of conscience are unnalienable [sic], and therefore, all laws to bind it, are, *ipso facto,* null and void." Id at 6–7. After defining property to include "everything to which a man . . . may have a right," Madison wrote that "[c]onscience is the most sacred of all property; other property depending, in part, on positive law, the exercise of that [conscience] being a natural and unalienable right." James Madison, "On Property" (1792), in *American State Papers* 159. According to Jefferson, "our rulers can have authority over such natural rights, only as we have submitted to them. The rights of conscience we never submitted, we could not submit. We are answerable for them to our God." Thomas Jefferson, *Notes on the State of Virginia,* P. L. Ford, ed, 197 (1894). In presenting their draft to the public, the 1782 New Hampshire Constitutional Convention explained of the Bill of Rights: "We have endeavor'd therein to ascertain and define the most important and essential natural rights of men. We have distinguished betwixt the alienable and unalienable rights: For the former of which, men may receive an equivalent; for the latter, or the RIGHTS of CONSCIENCE, they can receive none." *An Address of the Convention for Framing a New Constitution or Form of Government for the State of New Hampshire* 15 (1782) (Evans 17616). Nathaniel Chipman quoted Paine: "The natural rights, which he [i.e., an individual] retains, are all those, in which the power to execute is as perfect in the individual as the right itself: Among this class are . . . all intellectual rights, or rights of the mind; consequently Religion is one of those rights. The natural rights, which are not retained, are all those, which, though they are perfect in the individual, the power to execute them is defective." Nathaniel Chipman, *Sketches of the Principles of Government* 107 (1793). Later, Alexander Addison wrote: "The right of conscience is a natural right of a superior order for the exercise of which we are answerable to God. The right of publication is more within the control of civil authority, and was thought a more proper subject of general law." Alexander Addison, *Analysis of the Report of the Committee of the Virginia Assembly* (1800), in *American Political Writing* 1090. See also Zephaniah Swift, 1 *A System of the Laws of the State of Connecticut* 16 (1795); McLoughlin, 1 *New England Dissent* 610.

[40] This summary of how Americans analyzed restraints on inalienable natural rights has, for the sake of simplicity, described only the physical natural freedom or power of individuals in the state of nature to do as they pleased. When discussing the moral liberty of individuals, Americans said that this moral freedom did not include a liberty to infringe the equal rights of others or otherwise to violate natural law. With respect to an individual's moral freedom in the state of nature, Americans could say that no natural rights—alienable or inalienable—were sacrificed to society.

Claim and Right to be obeyed by every Subject."⁴¹ Another preached:

> as by the social compact, the whole is engaged for the protection and defence of the life, liberty and property of each individual; so each individual owes all that he hath, even life itself, to the support, protection and defence of the whole, when the exigencies of state require it. And no man, whether in authority or subordination, can justly excuse himself from any duty, service or exertions, in peace or war, that may be necessary for the publick peace, liberty, safety or defence, when lawfully and constitutionally called thereto.⁴²

Protection required submission to law.⁴³

By the same token, however, a constitution's or government's failure to provide satisfactory protection justified disobedience. "Nothing is more true," wrote Theophilus Parsons, "than that ALLEGIANCE AND PROTECTION ARE RECIPROCAL."⁴⁴ With this double-edged maxim, Americans explained not only obedience to the restraints that provided protection for natural liberty but also the repudiation of constitutions that did not adequately supply protection. For example, the North Carolina Constitution began by declaring that "[w]hereas allegiance and protection are, in their nature, reciprocal, and the one should of right be refused when the other is withdrawn, . . ."⁴⁵ Similarly, the Massachusetts Constitution described the protection or safety of individuals in the enjoyment of their natural rights as at least one of the purposes of government, and said that "whenever these great objects are not obtained, the people have a right to alter the government, and to take measures necessary for their safety, prosperity and happi-

---

⁴¹ William Welsteed, *The Dignity and Duty of the Civil Magistrate* 40 (Mass election sermon 1751) (Evans 6793).

⁴² Jonas Clark, *A Sermon* 29 (Mass election sermon [1781]) (Evans 17114). He also said, "every member is engaged for the peace, safety and defence of the state; and the whole for the peace, safety and protection of every member . . . ." Id at 21.

⁴³ It was a common sentiment. Among others, Swift wrote: "Every citizen owes obedience to the laws of the state, and is entitled to protection and security in his life, liberty, and property. The duties of protection and allegiance, are reciprocal." Zephaniah Swift, 1 *A System of the Laws of the State of Connecticut* 13 (1795). See also Calvin's Case, 7 Coke 1 (1608), cited by Earl M. Maltz, "The Concept of Equal Protection of the Laws—An Historical Inquiry," 22 San Diego L Rev 499, 507 (1985); Thomas Hobbes, *Leviathan*, ch ii, § 21, at 153, and Review & Conclusion, 491, Richard Tuck, ed (Cambridge U, 1991).

⁴⁴ *The Essex Result* (1778), in Theophilus Parsons, *Memoirs of Theophilus Parsons* 367 (1861).

⁴⁵ NC Const of 1776.

ness."[46] The people had subjected some of their natural liberty to civil government through a constitution, and if, by so doing, they did not obtain protection for the rest of their natural liberty, they could alter their mode of government—by constitutional amendment or even revolution. The protection of natural liberty, far from being a legal right with a remedy at law, was a purpose of government the people achieved by establishing and, if necessary, changing the system of law.

The balance between restraint and liberty that constituted the desired protection was not always entirely clear. Protection required a sacrifice of liberty to legal obligations, but an excess of these obligations could endanger the very liberty they were de-

---

[46] Mass Const of 1780, preamble. This quotation was preceded by the following: "The end of the institution, maintenance and administration of government, is to secure the existence of the body-politic; to protect it; and to furnish the individuals who compose it, with the power of enjoying, in safety and tranquility, their natural rights, and the blessings of life:". Id. The New Jersey Constitution declared that "allegiance and protection are, in the nature of things, reciprocal ties, each equally depending upon the other, and liable to be dissolved by the others being refused or withdrawn." NJ Const of 1776, preamble. The Virginia Declaration of Rights proclaimed "[t]hat Government is, or ought to be, instituted for the common benefit, protection, and security of the people, nation, or community; of all the various modes and forms of government, that is best which is capable of producing the greatest degree of happiness and safety, and is most effectually secured against the danger of maladministration; and that, whenever any government shall be found inadequate or contrary to these purposes, a majority of the community hath a indubitable, inalienable, and indefeasible right to reform, alter, or abolish it, in such manner as shall be judged most conducive to the public weal." Va Decl of Rights of 1776, § 3.

The Apostle Paul, according to the Rev. Goodrich, "well knew the rights of human nature," and, after quoting the Apostle on the subject of submission to civil authority, Goodrich said: "When a constitutional government is converted into tyranny, and the laws, rights and properties of a free people are openly invaded, there ought not to be the least doubt but that a remedy consistent with this doctrine of the apostle, is provided . . . for their preservation; nor ought resistance in such case to be called rebellion. . . . Civil society can exist no longer, than while connected by its laws and constitution: These are of no force, otherwise than as they are maintained and defended by the members of the commonwealth. This regular support of authority is the only security, a people can have against violence and injustice, feuds and animosities, in the unmolested enjoyment of their honest acquisitions: Hence the very end of civil society demands, that the orders of government be enforced." Elizur Goodrich, *The Principles of Civil Union* 25 (Conn election sermon 1787) (Evans 20393). In other words, the principle of self-preservation required revolution if government so abandoned its obligations as to invade rather than secure liberty, but, in normal circumstances, security or protection was achieved through enforcement of the laws of civil society. According to Moses Hemmingway, "no man has ever any rightful liberty to consent to any constitution or compact inconsistent with his own safety and welfare, and that of his fellow men: for instance, to authorize any to govern unrighteously and oppressively. . . . and if any people have been so imprudent and blameable as to consent to, and put themselves under a tyrannical government, they are so far from being bound in honor or conscience to support it, that it is their duty to overthrow and abolish it as soon as they can." Moses Hemmingway, *A Sermon* 14–15 (Mass election sermon 1784) (Evans 18526).

signed to protect. On the ground that individuals established government to protect natural liberty, Americans frequently said they did not want more legal restraints on natural liberty than were necessary.[47] Yet even the Americans who said this recognized that substantial legal obligations were necessary to the degree required for self-preservation—for the protection of individual liberty and interests.[48] The challenge was to create constitutions and laws that restrained natural liberty as little as possible but that, nonetheless, imposed restraints adequate for the preservation of such liberty.[49]

Thus, protection—in the sense of protection for natural liberty—was the protection individuals obtained by sacrificing part of their natural liberty for the creation of civil government and its

---

[47] See note 225. James Madison's cousin, the Rev. James Madison, wrote to him that one of the "Principles common to Am[erican]ns" was "ye Desire of enjoying all the Advantages of Gov[ernment] at ye least possible Expense to Natural Liberty." Rev. James Madison, Letter to James Madison (Feb 9, 1788), in 8 *Documentary History* 358. See also "Publicola" [Archibold Maclaine], *An Address to the Freemen of North Carolina* (State Gaz of NC, March 20, 1788), 16 *Documentary History* 437.

[48] E.g., Noah Hobart, *Civil Government the Foundation of Social Happiness* 7–8 (Conn election sermon 1750, printed 1751) (Evans 6692); Israel Evans, *A Sermon* 10 (NH election sermon 1791) (Evans 23358); "Brutus," 2 *Complete Anti-Federalist* 373; "Impartial Examiner," 5 id at 176; Zephaniah Swift, 1 *A System of the Laws of the State of Connecticut* 13 (1795). See also William Blackstone, 1 *Commentaries* 125–26 (1765).

[49] In the words of an Anti-Federalist: "To yield up so much, as is necessary for the purposes of government; and to retain all beyond what is necessary, is the great point, which ought, if possible, to be attained in the formation of a constitution." "An Old Whig," 3 *Complete Anti-Federalist* 33. Similarly, "Brutus" wrote: "[I]t was necessary that a certain portion of natural liberty should be surrendered, in order, that what remained should be preserved: how great a proportion of natural freedom is necessary to be yielded by individuals, when they submit to government, I shall not now enquire. So much, however, must be given up, as will be sufficient to enable those, to which the administration of government is committed, to establish laws for the promoting the happiness of the community, and to carry those laws into effect." "Brutus," 2 *Complete Anti-Federalist* 373. A supporter of a Congressional ticket that included Anti-Federalists wrote that "we ought to preserve our liberties, if possible, so far as they may consist with our essential protection." "A Friend to Liberty and Union," "To the Freemen of Pennsylvania," Federal Gazette (Phila.) (Nov 7, 1788, No. 33). Justice James Iredell told a grand jury: "True liberty certainly consists in such restraints, and no greater, on the actions of each particular individual as the common good of the whole requires. The exact medium it may be difficult to find, . . ." James Iredell, Charge to the Grand Jury of the Circuit Court for the District of Massachusetts (Oct 12, 1792), in 2 *Documentary History of the Supreme Court* 310. In this sense, Paine had written that "'[t]he science of the politician consists in fixing the true point of happiness and freedom.'" Paine, *Common Sense* 97–98. James Witherspoon said that "The end of union should be the protection of liberty, as far as it is a blessing." Witherspoon, *Lectures*, Lect X, at 124. In its instructions to its delegates to the Connecticut ratifying convention, the town of Preston ungrammatically observed that "We are willing to give up such share of our rights as to enable government to support, defend, and preserve the rest. It is difficult to draw the line." Instructions of the Town of Preston, Nov. 26, 1787, in 3 *Documentary History* 439. See also notes 27–28.

laws. In order to protect natural liberty, government and its laws had to restrain a portion of it, and the balance between the liberty protected and the restraints on liberty varied from one society to another, according to their different constitutions and laws. Rather than a legally enforceable right to a particular degree of protection or natural liberty, protection was a purpose of government and, in this sense, was a moral claim on government enforced by the power of the people to alter their constitutions by amendment or even revolution. This specialized idea of protection—protection for natural liberty—was distinct from ordinary notions of protection, and it was this specialized idea of protection that came to be of such importance for American debates about equality. If individuals obtained protection for their natural liberty by submitting to legal restraints on a portion of that freedom, then equal protection may have been an equality of these restraints or civil obligations—and, concomitantly, an equality of the natural liberty protected.

II. EQUAL PROTECTION

The idea of equal protection was the position of establishments, which increasingly conceded an equal protection of the laws for natural rights but did not want to give up the possibility of unequal "privileges." Whereas dissenters typically demanded equal civil rights—not only equal protection but also equal privileges—establishments frequently asserted that the only equality government was obliged to provide was equal protection.

Put more concretely, equal protection appealed to establishment writers who sought to justify a combination of privilege and toleration—who wanted to retain the "privileges" of their religion but were willing to allow dissenters an equality of natural rights and obligations under civil law. Proponents of equal protection typically said that government should provide their established religion with financial support or other privileges not available to dissenters. These advocates of equal protection, however, tended to criticize the intolerant governments that not only distributed privileges unequally among religions but also imposed unequal legal restraints on the natural liberty of dissenters.[50] Such governments, according to increasing numbers of establishment writers, did not equally

---

[50] E.g., if dissenters had to pay penalties or if dissenters could not enforce contracts.

protect the natural rights of individuals with respect to their religious differences. These tolerant establishment writers condemned unequal legal restraints as violations of equal protection and justified their unequal privileges as compatible with that standard.

Although the alternative standard of equality—equal civil rights—will not be discussed until later, it must be mentioned at this point, because equal protection was an idea that was contrasted to equal civil rights. In both England and America, dissenters of varying sects sought equal civil rights—an equality of rights under civil law. They thereby were requesting not only an equality of the natural liberty permitted and protected under civil law but also an equality of legal privileges. It was as an alternative to equal civil rights that establishment authors, in England and then America, proposed equal protection—a standard with which they could advocate toleration without sacrificing their unequal privileges.

American establishment writers who borrowed the idea of equal protection ordinarily did not alter it, but they put that idea to varying uses, according to the circumstances in which they found themselves. In the middle of the eighteenth century, supporters of American establishments advocated equal protection in a context in which it was a relatively tolerant standard: they used equal protection as a basis for condemning unequal legal restraints on dissenters. Later, particularly by the time of the Revolution, when dissenters had obtained equal legal obligations and sought, in addition, equal privileges, supporters of establishments employed the idea of equal protection to defend their unequal privileges against the claims of dissenters. With the idea of equal protection, an establishment could provide dissenters an egalitarian reassurance that no one would be subjected to greater legal obligations or "restraints" than anyone else on account of his or her religion, but an establishment did not thereby promise to share equally or to forgo its privileges, such as state financial support. In short, equal protection required equal obligations and permitted unequal privileges; it was a greater degree of equality than many American dissenters had in the middle of the eighteenth century but less than they increasingly demanded; it was a tolerant establishment position that establishments could employ both against establishment penalties on dissent and against dissenting demands for equal privileges.

The typical eighteenth-century understanding of equal protection appears to have been drawn in most instances from the auda-

cious Anglican apologist, William Warburton.[51] Equal restraints
on natural liberty and even "equal protection" had been discussed
by English political theorists of the previous century, sometimes in
connection with religious liberty and sometimes as a more generally
applicable standard, but it was Warburton's analysis of religious
liberty that eighteenth-century Americans most clearly drew upon
in their debates about equal protection.[52] In the 1730s, Warburton

---

[51] Warburton eventually became Bishop of Gloucester. For the English controversies
concerning Warburton, see Arthur W. Evans, *Warburton and the Warburtonians* (Oxford U,
1932). It is not possible to measure the use of Warburton's ideas in America simply by
counting citations. In addition to the usual difficulties with this approach, it should be noted
that the strongest American establishments were Congregationalist and that the Anglican
establishments were politically weak. For these reasons, Americans often did not cite the
controversial Bishop even when directly borrowing his arguments. Nonetheless, it seems
clear that many American writers drew upon Warburton's ideas.

[52] For an early discussion of equal protection, see *Englands Safety in the Laws Supremacy* 5
(1659). The anonomous pamphleteer urged "such a settlement where every man may be as
to Law and publick Countenance, in a equal capacity (except by past actions for a time
disabled) and alike protected in the enjoynment of propriety and exercise of honest Industry." Id. This sort of language was related to earlier complaints about monopolies and, as
will be seen, was employed in the eighteenth and especially the nineteenth century both to
criticize monopolies and to describe a generally applicable standard of equal protection.
   In connection with religion, Richard Hooker had written: "As for such abatements of
civil state as take away only some privilege, dignity, or other benefit which a man enjoyeth
in the commonwealth, they reach only unto our dealing with public affairs, from which
what should let but that men may be excluded and thereunto restored again, without
diminishing or augmenting the number of persons in whom either church or commonwealth consisteth? He that by way of punishment loseth his voice in a public election of
magistrates, ceaseth not thereby to be a citizen. A man disenfranchised may nothwithstand-
ing enjoy as a subject the common benefit of protection under laws and magistrates." Richard
Hooker, *Hooker's Ecclesiastical Polity Book VIII*, Raymond A. Houk, ed, ch 1, at 164–65
(Columbia Univ, 1931).
   More generally, European theorists—including Hobbes and Pufendorf—argued that an
equality of taxes, of punishments, and, more generally, of civil constraints was an important
means of avoiding dangerous resentments and disturbances. E.g., Pufendorf said that "an
equality is to be observed in punishments, namely, that those who are equally guilty should
suffer equally, and the misdeed which in the case of one is punished, should not in the case
of the other be condoned, without a very weighty cause; since, forsooth, an inequality of
that kind frequently furnishes matter for dangerous disturbances to commonwealths . . . ."
Samuel Pufendorf, 2 *Elementorum Jurispurdentiae Universalis Libri Duo* bk I, ch xxi, § 11, at
205 (Oxford U, 1931). See also: Samuel Pufendorf, *Of the Laws of Nature and Nations* bk
VIII, ch v, §§ 5–6, at 828–29 (1710) (re taxes); Thomas Hobbes, *Philosophical Rudiments
Concerning Government and Society*, in William Molesworth, ed 2 *Works* Of Dominion, ch xiii,
§ 10, at 173 (1841) (re public burdens). Others discussed the necessity of equal restraints
on natural liberty without mentioning the danger of disturbances. In a very late assertion
of leveller ideas, an anonomous pamphleteer wrote that "the Laws ought to be the Protectors
and Preservers, under God, of all our Persons and Estates." *The Leveller* (1659), in 4 *Harleian
Miscellany* 515–16 (1808). He sought "equal justice and safety." Id at 518. Sydney said that
"the equality in which men are born is so perfect, that no man will suffer his natural liberty
to be abridged, except others do the like: I cannot reasonably expect to be defended from
wrong, unless I oblige myself to do none; or to suffer the punishment prescribed by the
law, if I perform not my engagement." Algernon Sidney, *Discourses Concerning Government*

laid the foundation for his controversial reputation by publishing two tracts, *Alliance Between Church and State* (1736) and *The Divine Legation of Moses Demonstrated* (1737), in which he prominently used the idea of equal protection to argue both for a "free toleration" of religious worship and for an established church supported by a test.[53] At the heart of Warburton's arguments was the distinction between "*the sanctions of reward and punishment.*"[54] Reasoning that temporal punishments were in many instances inappropriate and that the civil government could not efficaciously alter the behavior of individuals by distributing temporal rewards, Warburton proved, he thought, the necessity of an alliance between church and state. The church supplied the sanction of future rewards necessary for the success of the state, and the state attended to the interests of the church.

Warburton discussed equal protection when arguing for the proposition that "by the *original constitution* of civil government, the sanction of rewards *was not* enforced."[55] In accord with the state-of-nature analysis, Warburton assumed that individuals formed government to obtain protection and that this protection was "*security to our temporal liberty and property.*"[56] "In entering into society," he wrote, "it was stipulated, between the magistrate and people, that *protection* and *obedience* should be reciprocal conditions."[57] Consequently, punishment could include a denial of protection. Yet a withdrawal of protection was not an appropriate punishment for all types of disobedience: "for though all obedience

---

548, Thomas G. West, ed (Liberty Classics, 1990). It is not altogether clear, however, whether he assumed each individual would have the same protection.

For somewhat ambiguous suggestions of a greater degree of equality—equal legal rights— see John Locke, *A Letter Concerning Toleration* 24 & 55 (Bobs Merrill, 1955); Benjamin Hoadly, *The Original and Institution of Civil Government Discuss'd* 162 (1710) (re an equality with respect to civil government but particularly legal restraints).

[53] William Warburton, 1 *Works*, ed Richard Hurd, 13 (1811) (Warburton, "*Works*"). Note, however, that he qualified his support for toleration. Like Locke, Warburton excepted from complete toleration any "sects" that threatened the state in certain ways; unlike Locke, he had a detailed list of such undesirable groups and varied the restraints upon them: "The ATHEIST, the ENGLISH PAPIST, the GERMAN ANABAPTIST, and the QUAKER, all hold opinions pernicious to civil society. But these having different degrees of malignity, must have different degrees of restraint." 7 id at 255.

[54] *Alliance Between Church and State*, in id at 32.

[55] Id.

[56] Id at 36.

[57] Id at 32–33.

be the same; and so, *uniform protection* a proper return for it; yet disobedience being various both in kind and degree, the withdrawing protection would be too great a punishment for some crimes, and too small for others."[58] Thus, Warburton assumed that individuals deserved "uniform protection" for their obedience. Moreover, he propounded this uniformity as part of an argument for both a toleration and a government alliance with an established church.

Incidentally, in contrast to this uniform protection for individuals of varied religions was the state's rather different protection of the established religion, "which was under the more *immediate* protection of the civil Magistrate, in contradistinction to those which were only TOLERATED."[59] Thus, the uniform protection, which amounted to a toleration, concerned the specialized idea of protection drawn from the state-of-nature analysis, but the magistrate's protection of the establishment was a "more *immediate* protection" of the sort expected from a monarch traditionally known as "the defender of the faith." Of course, this more immediate protection of the establishment consisted not only of "uniform protection" or toleration but also of various unequal "rewards," including a test (to assure that government would be in the hands of the established church) and the provision of "a settled maintenance for its ministers."[60]

In response to dissenters who were clamoring for equal civil rights—for equal rewards as well as uniform protection—Warburton offered only the uniform protection he had derived from the state-of-nature analysis:

> [T]his pretended *right of every qualified subject to a share of the honours and profits in the disposal of the supreme magistrate* is altogether groundless and visionary.
>
> Let it be remembered, that, . . . it hath been proved at large, that REWARD IS NOT ONE OF THE SANCTIONS OF CIVIL SOCIETY: the only claim which subjects have on the magistrate, for *obedience*, being protection.
>
> Now the consequence of this is, that all places of honour and profit, in the magistrate's disposal, are not there in the nature of a TRUST; to be claimed, and equally shared by the subject: but of the nature of a PREROGATIVE; which he may dispose

---

[58] Id at 33.

[59] *The Divine Legation of Moses Demonstrated*, in 2 id at 264.

[60] Id at 278.

of at pleasure, without being further accountable, than for having such places *ably* supplied.[61]

On account of the obedience of its subjects, the state was obliged to provide protection—"uniform protection"—but it was not obliged to distribute rewards equally. Therefore, although it had to offer uniform protection, it could use unequal "rewards" to secure its alliance with the established church.[62]

To Warburton, this combination of equal protection and unequal rewards—of toleration and establishment—held out the promise of religious harmony. Religious disturbances, argued Warburton, had tended to arise when sects were denied toleration or when all were tolerated but they quarrelled to achieve supremacy in a state. Therefore, he reasoned, a state could end such disturbances only by tolerating different religions and establishing one in a way that precluded the political ambitions of the others:

> What persecutions, rebellions, revolutions, loss of civil and religious liberty, these intestine struggles between sects have occasioned, is well known even to such as are least acquainted with the history of mankind.
>
> To prevent these mischiefs was . . . one great motive for the state's seeking *alliance* with the church. For the obvious remedy was to *establish* one church, and give a *free toleration* to the rest.[63]

In the course of advocating a tolerant establishment as a solution to religious discord, Warburton adumbrated the role equal protection would have for decades to come. Yet—notwithstanding the abstract quality of his argument—we may wonder whether he foresaw that his ideas would be adopted by establishments so distant and different from that which he defended.

Relying upon the conventional understanding of protection—that government was established to protect natural liberty—Warburton used the idea of a uniform protection to justify establishments; in contrast, however, a small number of Protestant anti-establishment writers attempted to resist that conventional un-

---

[61] *Alliance Between Church and State*, in 7 id at 252.

[62] For one of the more detailed American arguments based on Warburton's analysis, see Thomas Reese, *An Essay on the Influence of Religion in Civil Society* (1788) (Evans 21418). Among other things, the Rev. Reese speculated that "[i]t may perhaps be said that protection is the reward conferred on every individual for his observance of the laws." Id at 7, note. He then explained that this was a "mistake" or misnomer. Id.

[63] *Alliance Between Church and State*, in Warburton, 7 *Works* 250.

derstanding. Between 1735 and 1738, in England, *The Old Whig*—a series of radically anti-establishment essays—argued that individuals should be equally protected in their rights, whether natural or acquired under civil government. That individuals should have equal civil rights—neither extra restraints nor extra privileges on account of their religion—was a radical but not unusual position. *The Old Whig*, however, associated this with the words "equal protection." According to one of the essays, men entered into society

> with a view to their *better security* in the possession of [their most valuable and sacred rights], whether natural or acquired; and think that the great end of all *just law* and government is the full and *intire protection* of all those who contribute by a peaceable and useful behaviour to the common welfare, and do not by any wilful violation of the public peace forfeit those privileges, which they have otherwise an *equal claim* to with the rest of mankind.[64]

This was an explicit attempt to redefine protection to include privileges. Later, *The Old Whig* urged its readers "to deliver our constitution from every foreign or domestic insult . . . and secure it to our children's children by such laws as may give equal liberty and equal protection to all its friends, however differing from us in trifling opinions, or in useless ceremonies."[65] Apparently, *The Old Whig* came close to associating the phrase "equal protection" with equal civil rights—with an equality both of natural rights and of privileges. As will be seen, this approach was occasionally repeated in subsequent decades but remained a minority view. Far more often, dissenters plainly demanded equal civil rights, and establishments preserved their unequal privileges by offering only equal protection.

The idea of equal protection that Warburton used to defend England's establishment permitted unequal privileges but generally forbade unequal restraints on natural liberty, and therefore it could be used by tolerant supporters of establishments not only to defend

---

[64] 1 *The Old Whig* 15 (1739). The first essay is dated March 13, 1735; the final essay is dated March 13, 1738. 2 id at 440.

[65] 2 *The Old Whig* 431. Incidentally, the periodical appears to have been concerned with "common" rights: "And 'tis equally ridiculous to imagine, that a man can forfeit any of the common rights of the subjects, because he scruples a bit, a gesture, or particular form of words, that others may think fit to make use of . . . ." 1 id at 16. For the significance of this, see note 239.

their unequal privileges but also to condemn the unequal restraints of excessively severe establishments. In his 1758 treatise, Vattel, like Warburton, discussed two types of protection. Vattel argued that a prince should encourage devotion to the established religion[66] and, indeed, that it was a condition of his wearing the crown that he "protect and maintain the religion of the state."[67] This was the protection that could not be equal. Vattel, however, also urged toleration, and, in this regard, he talked about the other sort of protection—the protection that was to be equal.[68] He preceded his discussion of equal protection by noting that the prince should not force compliance with the established religion, for "by constraint" the prince could only "produce uneasiness or hypocrisy."[69] He then explained:

> [I]n general . . . the most safe and equitable means of preventing the disorders that may be occasioned by difference of religion, is an universal toleration of all the religions that have nothing dangerous in them, either with respect to manners, or the state. . . . Holland and the states of the king of Prussia furnish a proof of this: Calvinists, Lutherans, Socinians, Jews, Catholics, Pietists, all live in peace, because they are equally protected by the sovereign; and none are punished, but the disturbers of the tranquility of others.[70]

To prevent religious disputes, individuals of these different religions were to be "equally protected"; they were to be punished for disturbing others but not on account of their religion.

Americans similarly could use the idea of equal protection to argue against unequal restraints on dissenters without questioning establishment privileges. Eighteenth-century Connecticut had one

---

[66] Emmerich de Vattel, *The Law of Nations*, bk I, ch xii, §§ 133–34, at 116–17 (1820).

[67] Id, bk I, ch xii, § 138, at 118.

[68] Of course, the equal protection provided to individuals of varied religions was quite different from the prince's protection of the state religion. Equal protection was an equality of constraint—"protection" being a term of art in the state-of-nature analysis that referred to protection of natural liberty. In contrast, the prince's protection of the "true" religion was protection in an ordinary and broader sense. It concerned the prince's role as defender of the faith and obviously required more of him than that he merely avoid imposing greater legal restraints on that favored religion than on others.

[69] Id, bk I, ch xii, § 134, at 117.

[70] Id, bk I, ch xii, § 135, at 117–18. For a continental discussion of equal protection in connection with taxation, including an attempt to reconcile equal protection with a graduated tax, see Jean Jacques Burlamaqui, 2 *Principles of Natural and Political Law* pt III, ch 5, §§ 14–16, at 148 (1807).

of America's most intransigent establishments.[71] Not only did the government provide financial assistance and other privileges to Congregationalists but also, particularly in reaction to the Great Awakening, it restricted and penalized the increasing numbers who wished to separate from establishment churches. In 1742, the Connecticut legislature prohibited individuals from going into a parish and preaching, unless they had permission from the minister and a majority of the church of the parish.[72] In 1743, the legislature enacted that dissenting congregations had to obtain its permission to hold meetings, and it further indicated, what hardly required saying, that new light and other Congregational requests for such permission would not be considered favorably.[73]

By far the most eloquent attack on this intolerance came in an anonymous 1744 pamphlet, *The Essential Rights and Liberties of Protestants*, possibly by Elisha Williams—a member of the Connecticut General Assembly and eventually a judge of the Colony's Superior Court. Like Warburton and Vattel, Williams had no quarrel with an establishment that consisted of government support for a particular religion. What Williams objected to was the imposition of a religion upon individuals:

> . . . if by the word *establish* be meant only an approbation of certain articles of faith and modes of worship, of government, or recommendation of them to their subjects; I am not arguing against it. But to carry the notion of a religious establishment so far as to make it a rule binding to the subjects, or on any penalties whatsoever, seems to me to be oppressive of Christianity, to break in upon the sacred rights of conscience, and the common rights and priviledges of all good subjects.[74]

---

[71] It provoked Ebenezer Frothingham to inveigh: "The Most High hath condescended to speak heavy things to Connecticut." Ebenezer Frothingham, *A Key to Unlock the Door* 194 (1767) (Evans 10621).

[72] An Act for Regulating Abuses and Correcting Disorders in Ecclesiastical Affairs, §§ 2, 4, & 5 (May 1742), in 8 *Public Records of the Colony of Connecticut* 456 (1874). Violators who were not ordained ministers could (merely upon complaint to a J.P.) be bound over to their peaceable and good behavior in an amount of 100 pounds, and a noninhabitant or person not ordained who violated the law could be "sent (as a vagrant person) . . . out of the bounds of this Colony." Id at §§ 4 & 5.

[73] "An Act Providing Relief Against the Evil and Dangerous Designs of Foreigners and Suspected Persons" (May 1743), in 8 *Public Records of the Colony of Connecticut* 522 (1874), discussed by McLoughlin, *New England Dissent* 362.

[74] [Elisha Williams?], *The Essential Rights and Liberties of Protestants* (Boston, 1744), in Ellis Sandoz, ed, *Political Sermons of the American Founding Era 1730–1805* 73 (Liberty, 1991) ("*Political Sermons*"). Like so many of the American clergy who wrote after the 1730s,

Opposed to penalties on dissenters, Williams, like Vattel, used the idea of equal protection to encourage the establishment to be tolerant:

> That the civil authority ought to *protect all their subjects* in the enjoyment of *this right of private judgement in matters of religion*, and the liberty of worshipping GOD according to their consciences. That being the end of civil government (as we have seen) *viz.* the greater security of enjoyment of what belongs to every one, and *this right of private judgment*, and worshipping GOD according to their consciences, being the *natural and unalienable right of every man*, what men by entering into civil society neither did, nor could give up into the hands of the community; it is but a just consequence, that they are to be protected in the enjoyment of this right as well as any other. A worshipping assembly of Christians have surely as much right to be protected from molestation in their worship, as the inhabitants of a town assembled to consult their civil interests from disturbance *&c.*[75]

Because individuals had not sacrificed to government their natural right of worship and judgment in matters of religion, they were to be equally protected by government in this right as in any other, secular freedom. Of course, the molestation that concerned Williams here was that which occurred under the laws restricting separatist and new light preaching.[76] Drawing on an historical example, Williams added that

> the right of private judgment in matters of religion being unalienable, and what the civil magistrate is rather oblig'd to protect his subjects equally in, both Wickliff, and they who desired to hear him, had a just right to remain where they were, in the enjoyment of that right, free from all molestation from any persons whatsoever . . .[77]

Williams appears to have been familiar with Warburton's arguments in favor of establishment.

[75] Id at 97.

[76] Williams talked about molestation by individuals, but he clearly understood such individuals to be acting through the legal system. He was complaining about the inequality of legal restraints or obligations rather than a failure to enforce those restraints. Incidentally, the description of religious intolerance as "molestation" was quite common. For an example in an equal protection clause, see article 33 of the 1776 Maryland Constitution, reproduced in the text below at note 88.

[77] Id at 115.

Individuals did not submit their natural right of judgment in religious matters to civil government, and individuals were to be equally protected by civil government in that right. Consequently, according to Williams, individuals had a right to enjoy their natural right of judgment, without molestation from anyone. Whereas Warburton had said that individuals should be equally protected in their natural liberty, regardless of their religious differences, Williams talked about equal protection for the natural liberty of worship and judgment, and, in this respect, he slightly recast and narrowed the idea of equal protection to focus it on Connecticut's prohibition of certain religious meetings.[78] In other regards, however, Williams employed an understanding of equal protection consistent with that of Warburton.

As one might expect, many dissenters were not satisfied to claim a mere equal protection of their natural liberty but demanded, in addition, equal privileges, which, together with equal protection, would have given them a full equality of civil rights. In 1750, a prominent Connecticut dissenter, Ebenezer Frothingham, employed the idea of equal protection, not to ask for equal protection only of natural rights, but to insist upon an "equal protection" of the privileges of government and thereby a full equality of civil rights:

> The moral Rule, and civil Power, is to protect every one; that supposing there is in one Society, some of the Church of *England*, and them that profess the *Seabrook* Regulation, and them that are Congregationals, and Baptists, and Quakers: Now all these ought equally to be protected by this moral Rule, or civil Power, in their proper Rights and Privileges, and each one be left to support their own Worship . . . [79]

Like *The Old Whig*, Frothingham argued for equal "protection" of civil rights. Yet the end of government was typically understood to be the protection of natural rights, and therefore Frothingham's

---

[78] Of course, the laws of Connecticut did protect the natural liberty of individuals unequally, but, because they did so by directly prohibiting certain religious meetings, Williams was able to focus his argument on the unequal protection of a particularly valuable portion of natural liberty, the freedom of worship.

[79] Ebenezer Frothingham, *The Articles of Faith and Practice* 296 (1750) (Evans 6504). The "Seabrook regulation" is, of course, the "Saybrook Platform"—representing the position in 1708 of Connecticut's Congregational establishment. He also said he favored "the Protecting and Defending every Man . . . in their moral and civil Rights and Privileges." Id.

argument was vulnerable to being turned against him. Indeed, the response did not take long.

In the 1751 Connecticut election sermon, the Rev. Benjamin Lord used the idea of equal protection to defend the religious role of Connecticut's civil government. Whereas Williams had discussed equal protection in order to urge intolerant establishments to abandon their unequal restraints on dissenters, now, when dissenters prominently demanded equal privileges, Lord could employ the idea of equal protection to defend the establishment against these claims for greater equality. Like Frothingham, Lord defined the purpose of government in terms of protection, but, unlike Frothingham, Lord conformed to the conventional view that government was created to protect the life, liberty, and property of the members of the community—their natural liberty rather than their privileges.[80] Moreover, according to Lord, "[e]very Member may have the Strength of the whole employed for the Security of his own Life and Property. And also rejoyce in his Neighbours having the same Protection and Advantage with himself . . . ."[81] Apparently in reaction to Frothingham's demand that Connecticut provide equal civil rights on grounds of "equal protection," Lord handily pointed out that the Colony already provided equal protection—equal protection of natural liberty—which was a sufficient basis for ending dissentions. As it happens, Lord's position was not as convincing as it might have been, for Connecticut, in fact, still penalized Congregational dissenters, and consequently Lord had to devote much of his sermon to an explanation that separation was a threat to the state—indeed, a danger akin to "anarchy"—and so, perhaps, was to be prohibited rather than protected.[82] Nonetheless,

---

[80] "[A]ll civil Government of the right Stamp, must be agreeable to Scripture and Reason, and so to the Nature and Ends of a civil Community, the Preservation of the Lives, Liberties & Estates of all the Members thereof, against the force of Rapine, Injustice & all manner of destructive Violence." Benjamin Lord, *Religion and Government Subsisting Together in Society, Necessary to their Compleat Happiness and Safety* 28 (Conn election sermon for 1751, printed 1752) (Evans 6868).

[81] Id at 3. The word "advantage" does not necessarily relate to anything other than natural rights. The immediate context, a discussion of rights in the state of nature and their preservation under government, suggests this limited meaning. At the very least, Lord did not want equal privileges for dissenters.

[82] Lord passionately asserted that the separations of dissenters were an anarchical threat to civil government, see note 150, and he seems to have understood this threat to be grounds for denying toleration, though he said so only indirectly. Id at 23, 34–35, 40–41. Lord's ambiguity or, perhaps, ambivalence may have been connected to his difficult position in his

Lord clearly had an advantage over Frothingham, for Lord argued
on the basis of the widely-held assumptions that government was
formed to protect natural rights and that natural rights were distinct from privileges. Thus, just as tolerant supporters of establishments used the idea of equal protection against penalties on dissenters, so too establishment writers could use the idea to defend a
supposedly tolerant establishment against dissenters' demands for
equal privileges and equal civil rights.

Even so, it was only after mid-century that American establishments used the idea of equal protection as an important part of
their position in a broad political debate rather than merely as
an occasional argument. Whereas, in England, already in the late
seventeenth century, a substantial number of Anglicans urged tolerance for dissenters, in America, before the 1760s and '70s, relatively few establishment writers were inclined to advocate toleration. It was one thing to be willing to concede an equality of
restraints, but it was another actively to seek such an equality.
Consequently, although the argument that government had to treat
individuals equally only with respect to protection was a useful
establishment response to demands for equal privileges, it was not
likely to be an identifying position of America's mid-century establishments.

In the 1770s, however, many dissenters intensified their claims
for equal civil rights. The Great Awakening and the migrations of
people to and through America had left many colonies with large
numbers of dissenters of various denominations, some of whom
formed majorities in their localities. In the turbulence of the 1770s,
emboldened by the freedom and equality claimed for America as
a whole, some dissenting sects began to feel their strength and
importuned colonial and then state legislatures for equal rights.[83]
Throughout America, the justice of their claims, their strength,
and the sympathy they elicited from members of establishment

---

parch. In 1748, Separates in Lord's parish "obtained a majority and were able to block a
vote to levy the annual taxes for Lord's salary and for the . . . new meeting house."
McLoughlin, 1 *New England Dissent* 373. It is difficult to resist speculating that Lord's
unusual difficulties in his parish may have affected the peculiar tone of his sermon and even
other aspects of his life. For Lord's years of controversy and his eventual poverty, insanity
and death, see id at 373–76.

[83] H. J. Eckenrode, *Separation of Church and State in Virginia* 41–73 (Da Capo, 1971 reprint
of 1910 edition) (Eckenrode, "*Separation of Church and State in Virginia*"); Buckley, *Church and
State in Revolutionary Virginia* 177 & passim.

religions created a climate of opinion in which establishment ministers often sought, rather defensively, to show that they too were against "persecution." A constitutional guarantee of the natural right of free exercise was rapidly becoming the minimal degree of religious liberty one could respectably acknowledge.

In these new circumstances, in which restraints on natural liberty on account of religious differences were no longer possible and establishment privileges were at risk, some establishments defended their privileges by asserting their support for religious freedom and equality—but only the free exercise of religion and equal protection. What, for Lord, had been a useful argument against equal civil rights now became a central principle for several American establishments. By acknowledging the natural right of free exercise and offering an equal protection, establishments could take an attractively egalitarian position and thereby could resist demands for equal civil rights; establishments could be for equality and yet could retain their unequal privileges. Thus, in several states, the Revolution was accompanied by a struggle in which anti-establishment forces demanded equal civil rights, and establishments offered, instead, equal protection.

The importance of equal protection to the position of establishments is apparent from three state constitutions. In 1776, the Maryland Constitution guaranteed that "all persons, professing the Christian religion, are equally entitled to protection in their religious liberty."[84] In 1780, the Massachusetts Constitution promised equal protection to Christian sects, and New Hampshire in 1784 copied this provision and others from its neighbor's constitution.[85]

The Anglican church in Maryland was the first establishment to use an equal protection clause to help fend off claims for equal rights. Having long received government support, Maryland's Anglicans in 1776 attracted considerable resentment. Indeed, with George III as head of their church, Anglicans had particular difficulty resisting egalitarian and anti-establishment demands.[86] At the November 1776 convention, however, Anglicans constituted a ma-

---

[84] Md Const of 1776, Art 33.

[85] See note 92 and accompanying text.

[86] Arthur Pierce Middleton, *From Daughter Church to Sister Church: The Disestablishment of the Church of England and the Organization of the Diocese of Maryland*, in 79 Md Hist Mag 189, 191 (1984).

jority, and, of the committee responsible for drafting the Declaration of Rights, all members but one were Anglican.[87] Therefore, although Anglicans apparently felt obliged to sacrifice their old tax privileges, they at least had an opportunity, in drafting the Maryland Declaration of Rights, to preserve some opportunities for a future establishment. Article 33 said:

> . . . all persons, professing the Christian religion, are equally entitled to protection in their religious liberty; wherefore no person ought by law to be molested in his person or estate on account of his religious persuasion or profession, or for his religious practice; . . . nor ought any person to be compelled to frequent or maintain, or contribute, unless on contract, to maintain any particular place of worship, or any particular ministry; yet the Legislature may, in their discretion, lay a general and equal tax, for the support of the Christian religion; leaving to each individual the power of appointing the payment over of the money, collected from him.[88]

In other words, Anglicans abandoned exclusive claims on tax support. The best they could retain for themselves with respect to financial assistance was to leave open the prospect of a tax to support all Christian denominations. As for other privileges, however, the possibility of an inequality even among Christians was left intact. Indeed, in the first half of the 1780s, Anglicans sought tax support for Christians and incorporation for themselves. Yet these attempts encountered substantial and ultimately successful opposition. That the Anglicans of Maryland failed after 1776 to obtain much from government was a consequence of political resistance rather than the provisions of their state's Constitution.[89]

Of the two northern constitutions that contained equal protection clauses, that of Massachusetts may be taken as an example, for extensive information about that constitution is available.[90] After guaranteeing the right of individuals to worship according to conscience, the Massachusetts Bill of Rights, in article three, required

---

[87] Id at 190.

[88] Md Const of 1776, Art 33.

[89] 79 Md Hist Mag 193–94; Norman K. Risjord, *Chesapeake Politics 1781–1800* 211–13 (Columbia U, 1978). For the documents produced by the Anglicans in 1783 and 1784, see William Smith, 2 *The Works of William Smith* 509–23 (1803).

[90] Unfortunately, there is little evidence concerning contemporary interpretation of New Hampshire's religion clauses. See McLoughlin, 2 *New England Dissent* 846. See, however, quotation of McClintock in note 24.

legislation ensuring that towns would tax individuals for the support of Protestantism—an arrangement that was advantageous for the most numerous sect in each town, typically the Congregationalists.[91] According to article three and the scheme created under it, individuals who did not wish to support the dominant sect in their locality could direct their tax payments to their own religious society, but, in order to do this, they had to take the initiative to have themselves recognized as members of dissenting denominations. Consequently, the taxes paid by dissenters unwilling or unable to get such official recognition ended up in the pockets of Congregationalists, who thereby received what was considered an unequal government privilege. A subsequent clause of article three of the Massachusetts Bill of Rights—the Christian-denominations clause—provided that "every denomination of christians, demeaning themselves peaceably, and as good subjects of the Commonwealth, shall be equally under the protection of the law." A second half of this clause added: "And no subordination of any one sect or denomination to another shall ever be established by law."[92]

The authors of the Massachusetts Constitution apparently understood the first, equal-protection half of the Christian-denominations clause to require equal protection for rights existing in the state of nature. The natural rights context of equal protection is apparent in article ten of the Massachusetts Bill of Rights, which explained that "[e]ach individual of the society has a right to be protected by it [i.e., the society] in the enjoyment of his life, liberty and property, according to standing laws."[93] Individuals sacrificed some of the liberty they enjoyed in the state of nature—some of their "life, liberty and property"—and, by means of this sacrifice,

---

[91] The legislation was to apply "in all cases where such provision shall not be made voluntarily." Mass Const of 1780, Bill of Rights, Art 3. In practical terms, this meant that Boston was exempted.

[92] Mass Const of 1780, Bill of Rights, Art 3. When addressing the establishment of religion, the New Hampshire Constitution approximately followed the Massachusetts provisions, including the Christian-denomination passage already quoted: "And every denomination of christians, demeaning themselves quietly, and as good subjects of the state, shall be equally under the protection of the law: and no subordination of any one sect or denomination to another, shall ever be established by law." NH Const of 1784, Bill of Rights, Art 6.

Whereas the religion provisions in Maryland used the idea of equal protection in connection with individuals, the provisions in Massachusetts and New Hampshire used the notion of equal protection in connection with denominations.

[93] Mass Const of 1780, Bill of Rights, Art 10.

they obtained the protection of society or government "according to standing laws." As the similar New Hampshire Constitution said, "[w]hen men enter into a state of society, they surrender up some of their natural rights to that society, in order to insure the protection of others."[94] An equality of natural freedom in society and a concomitant equality of legal obligations or "restraints" is also suggested by the communication of the largely Congregationalist town of Gorham to the Massachusetts drafting convention: "That no Restriction be laide on any Profession of Christianity or denomination of Christians, but all Equally intiteled to protection of the Laws."[95]

The second half of the Massachusetts Christian-denominations clause (which said that "no subordination of one sect or denomination to another shall ever be established by law") looked, at first glance, as if it provided an equality of at least privileges or benefits,

---

[94] NH Const of 1784, Bill of Rights, Art 3.

[95] Oscar & Mary Handlin, eds, *Popular Sources of Political Authority—Documents on the Massachusetts Constitution of 1780*, at 430 (Belknap, 1966) ("*Popular Sources of Political Authority*"). Since 1820, Gorham has been part of the state of Maine. For the power of Congregationalists in Gorham, see Hugh D. McLellan, *History of Gorham, Me.* ch 9–10, at 169–221 (1903). In addition to the general information found in this volume, note the following. In 1781, at least 66 men sought certification as Baptists so as to be free of paying taxes in support of the Congregational ministry. Id at 206–7. To these Baptists must be added an indeterminate number of new lights. Id at 204. However, Gorham's tax records for 1780 indicate an adult (over 16) male population of approximately 380. Id at 336.

The constitutional guarantee of equal protection for all Christian denominations posed some difficulties with regard to Catholicism. In a meeting to consider ratification of the Massachusetts Constitution, the town of Dunstable recognized that the guarantee extended to Catholicism and was uncomfortable with this: "[T]hese Sentences are so general as to Engage full Protection to the Idalatrous worshippers of the Church of Rome [and] therefore they wore not Clear in their judgment to give so much Incoragement to Idol worship as to Engage any full protection in their Idolatry[,] for if the government should not Disturbe such in their pretended worship it would be as much as they might Expect without our being under special obligation to protect them there in by the laws of the land." *Popular Sources of Political Authority* 641. In contrast, George Washington was not reluctant to grant Catholics equal protection. He wrote to American Catholics that "[a]s mankind becomes more liberal they will be more apt to allow that all those who conduct themselves as worthy members of the community are equally entitled to the protection of civil government." George Washington, letter to the Roman Catholics in the U.S., March 15, 1790, in William B. Allen, ed, *George Washington: A Collection* 546 (Liberty Classics, 1988). Like so many other late eighteenth-century supporters of establishments, Washington approved of government financial benefits for Protestantism and gladly conceded equal protection. (For Washington's position on establishments, note his letter to Mason, in which he refused to sign Madison's 1785 *Remonstrance*: "Although no man's sentiments are more opposed to any kind of restraint upon religious principles than mine are, yet I must confess, that I am not amongst . . . those, who are so much alarmed at the thoughts of making people pay towards the support of that which they profess." Quoted by Eckenrode, *Separation of Church and State in Virginia* 105.)

and thus, if taken together with the first half of the clause—which concerned equal protection—it seemed to concede equal civil rights. Yet the no-subordination language only proscribed the subordination of one sect to another; it did not forbid a scheme that established in each town whichever sect formed a majority there. Indeed, as has been seen, earlier paragraphs of article three of the Bill of Rights authorized tax support for Protestantism through a system that gave privileges to persons whose religion constituted a majority in a locality. Of course, it was no coincidence that such persons tended to be Congregationalists. Thus, an establishment minister could quote the equal-protection and no-subordination language of the Constitution and claim with satisfaction that it prohibited the establishment of any one church over others: "Any denomination of Christians, who would endeavor to bring the Civil Authority of the State to grant any peculiar privileges to their church, and to give it a pre-eminence over others, ought to be watched over and guarded against. . . . While this frame of Government continues, no one church or denomination of Christians can oppress another with constitutional law on their side."[96] Although he was correct that no church had been given peculiar privileges—that no particular sect had been established—he omitted to mention that privileges had been granted to local majority churches. In other words, the no-subordination requirement had been carefully drafted to permit the establishment of majority sects. As the town of Middleborough observed, "in saying that no Subordination etc. Shall ever be Established by Law: and in another part of the same article: in Saying, that all monies paid by the Subject etc; where it must be understood: if any thing can be Learnt by it: that individuals may at some Times and under Some Circumstances be obliged to pay money as aforesaid, Contrary to the Dictates of their Consciences for the Support of Teachers as aforesaid."[97] To meet egalitarian pressures while retaining some unequal privileges, Maryland

---

[96] Joseph Willard, *Persecution Opposite to the Genius of the Gospel*, sermon preached at Harvard on Sept. 7, 1785, Widener Library Archives, Harvard Univ, as quoted by James H. Smylie, *Protestant Clergy, the First Amendment and Beginnings of a Constitutional Debate, 1781–91*, in Elwyn A. Smith, ed, *The Religion of the Republic* 116, 130 (Fortress, 1971).

[97] *Popular Sources of Political Authority* 693. Isaac Backus had a parish that included part of Middleborough or Middleboro, and eventually the town had additional Baptist churches. Although Congregationalists remained dominant, the complaint quoted above appears to reflect some deference to the views of the Baptists. The rest of the town's return, however, was less accommodating. McLoughlin, 1 *New England Dissent* 629.

had used the idea of equal protection, and now, for similar purposes, Massachusetts used both equal protection and a very narrow guarrantee against the subordination of "any one sect . . . to another."

Thus, the men who drafted the constitutions of Massachusetts, New Hampshire and Maryland used the idea of equal protection to preserve establishments. Whereas a constitutional right to the free exercise of religion was a right to a particular degree of freedom, a constitutional right of equal protection was, apparently, not a legal right to enjoy natural liberty or any portion of it to any particular degree, but simply the right to enjoy the same natural liberty in civil society and to be subjected to the same legal obligations as other persons. Therefore, to a constitution that already guaranteed the natural right of free exercise of religion, an equal protection clause added a clarification or reassurance that the document prohibited discriminatory restraints on natural liberty; an equal protection clause made clear that the document not only forbade direct denials of free exercise but also forbade unequal restraints, on account of religion, of other natural liberty. An equal protection provision did this, moreover, with a phrase that gave the constitution an egalitarian luster—that secured the political advantages of discussing religious liberty in terms of equality. But equal protection did not give the equality of benefits or privileges so many dissenters desired. The constitutions of Maryland, Massachusetts, and New Hampshire employed egalitarian language but did not preclude unequal privileges.[98]

Dissenters and other opponents of establishment understood that they had not achieved full equal civil rights with respect to religion. They knew they had obtained guarantees of their natural right of free exercise and clarifying prohibitions against unequal protection of natural liberty but not a provision for equal privileges. Recollecting his work in drafting most of the Massachusetts Constitution, John Adams observed that "[t]he Article respecting Religion . . .

---

[98] In Massachusetts and New Hampshire, tax support could vary according to religious differences among Christian sects. In Maryland, only benefits other than tax support could vary among such denominations. The idea of equal protection was also used to describe Connecticut's religious liberty. Zephaniah Swift, 1 *A System of the Laws of the State of Connecticut* 144 (1795). For the limited character of such equality, see id at 146 & 144 n. As observed above, relatively little information survives concerning the contemporary interpretation of New Hampshire's religion clauses.

was the only Article which I omitted to draw."[99] Later he explained
that he "could not sketch [it], consistent with my own sentiments
of perfect religious freedom, with any hope of its being adopted
by the Convention, so I left it to be battled out in the whole
body."[100] Although in a minority, John Adams was not alone.
During ratification of the Massachusetts Constitution, the mostly
Baptist town of Swansea complained that "[t]he Legislature cannot
act agreeable to such a Power as is Vested in them by the third
article [which included the equal protection clause] without Rendering individuals unhappy who have an Equal Right to the Blessings of government."[101] The town of Bellingham—which also had a
Baptist majority—suggested replacing the third article with several
brief statements, including: "Nor can any man who acknowledges
the being of a God Be justly abridged or Deprived of any Civil
Right as a citizen on account of his Religious Sentiment or Peculiar
mode of Religious Worship."[102] Dissenters sought equal civil rights
and were fobbed off with equal protection.

III. Equal Civil Rights

In the 1770s, when many Americans claimed equal rights
from Britain, increasing numbers of dissenters demanded equal
rights with respect to religion from their American governments.[103]
As already observed, the requests of these dissenters for equal civil
rights prompted some establishments to obtain equal protection
clauses in state constitutions. Rather than accept mere equal protection, however, dissenters continued to press for equal civil rights.

---

[99] John Adams, letter to William D. Williamson, Feb 28, 1812, quoted in Gregg L. Lint
et al, eds, 8 *Papers of John Adams* 262, n 12 (Harvard U, 1989) ("*Papers of John Adams*"). He
continued: "I could not satisfy my own Judgment with any Article that I thought would be
accepted: and farther that Some of the Clergy, or older and graver Persons than myself
would be more likely to hit the Taste of the Public." Id. Later, there were unconfirmed
suggestions that Parsons had drafted Article 3. E.g., Independent Chronicle (Boston), June
13, 1811 (XLIII, No 3147). These may have been based merely on Parson's committee
assignment in the drafting convention.

[100] Josiah Quincy's diary (entry for May 31, 1820), as quoted by Edmund Quincy, *Life of
Josiah Quincy* 379 (1867), in 8 *Papers of John Adams* 262, n 12.

[101] *Popular Sources of Political Authority* 530. For the Baptist majority, see McLoughlin, 1
New England Dissent 675; see also id at 628.

[102] *Popular Sources of Political Authority* 740. For the Baptist majority, see McLoughlin, 1
New England Dissent 675; see also id at 628.

[103] A useful collection of Massachusetts discussions of equality and suffrage may be found
in *Popular Sources of Political Authority*.

Dissenters did not repudiate the idea of equal protection, because an equal protection for natural liberty was something they wanted and, indeed, had already largely achieved in practice, if not in name; yet they also, in addition to equal protection, desired an equality of privileges. Among other things, dissenters tended to resent state systems of tax support that in one way or another favored other denominations over their own. Even plans that allowed dissenters to direct their payments to their own sects were often understood to establish unequal benefits.[104] By requiring dissenters to inform the civil government that they were not of the majority sect, such plans signified government approbation of the established religion and, moreover, transferred the tax payments of noncomplying dissenters to the establishment. In opposition to these unequal privileges, many dissenters demanded equal privileges, which, together with the equal protection they already had, would have given them equal civil rights. They insisted that all civil laws rather than merely those protecting natural freedom avoid inequalities on account of religion.

Demands for what amounted to equal civil rights with respect to religion took several forms, each of which used different language to refer to the desired type of equality. Often, dissenters treated these different forms or modes of analysis as equivalents and employed them interchangeably. A brief survey of the most common of these approaches for discussing equal civil rights can, perhaps, illustrate the extent of anti-establishment demands.

Some analysis was explicitly in terms of an equality of civil rights. For example, the Pennsylvania Constitution of 1776 declared: "Nor can any man, who acknowledges the being of a God, be justly deprived or abridged of any civil right as a citizen, on account of his religious sentiments or peculiar mode of religious worship."[105] Similarly, at least with respect to a narrower class of individuals, the New Jersey Constitution said "[t]hat there shall be no establishment of any one religious sect in this Province, in preference to another; and that no Protestant inhabitant of this

---

[104] Incidentally, Americans may have distinguished between general taxes and taxes raised to support specific government benefits. An unequal distribution of the benefits supported by general revenues was an inequality of privileges and was not considered contrary to notions to equal protection. In contrast, a tax system for support of religion may have been considered a form of special assessment. If so, then a mechanism permitting an individual at least to direct his payment to his own religious society may have been necessary to avoid a constraint of natural liberty that discriminated among religions.

[105] Pa Const of 1776, Art 2.

Colony shall be denied the enjoyment of any civil right, merely on account of his religious principles; but that all persons, professing a belief in the faith of any Protestant sect . . . shall fully and freely enjoy every privilege and immunity, enjoyed by others their fellow subjects."[106]

Another, far more common approach was to distinguish natural rights from the privileges, advantages, benefits, or emoluments of civil government—that is, from rights not existing in the state of nature. There were numerous variations in the language with which this approach was described. For example, although many Americans used the words "right" and "privilege" interchangeably to denote either a natural right or a right existing only under civil government, they often employed these words to distinguish between the two types of rights and demanded not only the right to the free exercise of religion but also equal privileges. For purposes of this bifurcated analysis, they also used the words "discrimination" and "preference." Thus, in New York, where anti-establishment sentiment found strength in the state's religious diversity, the 1777 Constitution prohibited an establishment by requiring that "the free exercise and enjoyment of religious profession and worship, without discrimination or preference, shall forever hereafter be allowed . . . ."[107] Not only would the natural right of free exercise be shielded from discriminatory restraints—in the document's words, "without discrimination"—but also preferences on account of religious differences would be prohibited. Anti-establishment Americans frequently attempted to use versions of this bifurcated analysis of equal civil rights in order to guarantee the free exercise of religion and then prohibit an establishment.[108]

---

[106] NJ Const of 1776, Art 19. For other examples, note the following. The 1778 South Carolina Constitution provided that Protestants "shall enjoy equal religious and civil privileges." SC Const of 1778, Art 38. In this context, the word "privileges" appears to have been interchangeable with "rights." Among other things, the presbytery of Hanover, Virginia, wanted government "to restrain the vicious and to encourage the virtuous, by wholesome laws equally extending to every individual." Memorial of the Presbytery of Hanover to the General Assembly of Virginia (Oct 24, 1776), in *American State Papers* 94; see also the same language in the Memorial of April 25, 1777 in id at 97.

[107] NY Const of 1777, Art 38.

[108] E.g., in 1790, South Carolina employed the same language as New York to prohibit an establishment. SC Const of 1790, Art 8, § 1. As suggested in the text, the bifurcated analysis had many variants. In 1788, New York's ratification convention proposed as an amendment to the U.S. Constitution: "That the people have an equal, natural, and unalien-

A third analysis was that civil government had no authority to legislate with respect to religion—a claim commonly assumed to preclude unequal civil rights on account of religion. It will be recalled that large numbers of Americans, following Locke, said that individuals could not relinquish their natural right of free exercise and that civil government was erected for exclusively secular purposes.[109] On the basis of such arguments, some Americans, in addition, insisted that all religious matters were beyond the jurisdiction of civil government.[110] According to these Americans, civil government had no authority to legislate with respect to religion— whether to restrain free exercise and other natural rights or even to give privileges to one or more religions. For example, Madison

---

able right freely and peaceably to exercise their religion, according to the dictates of conscience; and that no religious sect or society ought to be favored or established by law in preference to others." Elliot, 1 *Debates* 328. Virginia's proposal concluded with a similar guarantee: "[A]ll men have an equal, natural, and unalienable right to the free exercise of religion, according to the dictates of conscience, and that no particular religious sect or society ought to be favored or established, by law, in preference to others." 3 id at 659. In Delaware, section 2 of the Declaration of Rights said that Christians "ought . . . to enjoy equal Rights and Privileges in this State, unless, under Colour of Religion, any man disturb the Peace, Happiness or Safety of Society." Del Const of 1776, Bill of Rights, § 3. See also: NJ Const of 1776, Art 19, quoted in text at note 106; proposal of 1788 NC ratification convention, Elliot, 4 *Debates* 244. Israel Holly wanted "civil rulers to tolerate and protect all conscientious professors of religion, and establish none." Israel Holly, *An Appeal to the Impartial* (1778), as quoted in Ezra H. Gillett, *Historical Sketch of the Cause of Civil Liberty in Connecticut 1639–1818*, 4 Historical Magazine 20 (2nd Ser) (July 1868). Some of Virginia's dissenters petitioned that "That your memorialists have never been on an equal Footing with the other good People of this Colony in respect of religious Priviledges, having been obliged by Law, to contribute to the Support of the Established Church." Memorial and Petition of the Dissenters from the Church of England and others in the Counties of Albermarle, Amherst, and Buckingham (Oct 22, 1776), Va State Library, Mfm of Misc Ms 425. Other dissenters in Virginia petitioned that, being "[f]ully Persuaded . . . That the Religion of JESUS CHRIST may and ought to be Committed to the Protection Guidance and Blessing of its Divine Author, & needs not the Interposition of any Human Power for its Establishment & Support[,] We most earnestly desire and Pray that not only an Universal Toleration may take Place, but that all the Subjects of this Free State may be put upon the same footing and enjoy equal Liberties and Privileges." Petition of Divers of the Freeholders and other Free Inhabitants of Amherst County (Nov 1, 1779), Va State Library, Mfm of Misc Ms 425.

[109] See text accompanying notes 33–35.

[110] These Americans were expanding upon the ideas of earlier, European writers. Pufendorf had argued that civil law has no need to inquire as to things merely of the mind or as to things that do not disturb the peace. Samuel Pufendorf, *Elementorum Jurisprudentiae Universalis Libri Duo*, ed W. A. Oldfather, bk I, ch xiii, § 19, at 162 (Oxford U, 1931). Locke wrote: "The commonwealth seems to me to be a society of men constituted only for the procuring, preserving, and advancing their own civil interests. [New ¶] Civil interests I call life, liberty, health, and indolency of body; and the possession of outward things, such as money, lands, houses, furniture, and the like." Locke, *Letter Concerning Toleration* 17. Locke argued, however, that government could prohibit some religions, and he did not explicitly preclude the possibility of some government recognition of an established church.

wrote "that in matters of religion no man's right is abridged by the institution of civil society, and that religion is wholly exempt from its cognizance."[111] This position, that religion was free from civil control and even civil recognition, was a powerful argument against unequal privileges on the basis of religious differences. Indeed, a prohibition of any legislation with respect to religion could have a still broader effect: It could bar even equal privileges.

Any of these three approaches could be generically described by eighteenth-century Americans as freedom of conscience or religious liberty. For a long time, Englishmen and Americans had sometimes called the free exercise of religion "freedom of conscience" or "religious liberty." They also, however, could use these phrases to refer to a right against establishments.[112] For example, some assumed

---

[111] James Madison, Memorial and Remonstrance (1785), in *American State Papers* 121. The Presbytery of Hanover petitioned: "In the fixed belief of this principle, that the kingdom of Christ, and the concerns of religion, are beyond the limits of civil control, we should act a dishonest, inconsistent part, were we to receive any emoluments from any human establishments for the support of the gospel." Memorial of the Presbytery of Hanover to the General Assembly of Virginia (April 25, 1777), in *American State Papers* 98; see also Memorial of Presbytery of Hanover (Oct 24, 1776) in id at 94. Some attributed this position to Locke: ". . . any Majestrait or Legislative Body that takes upon themselves the power of Governing Religion by human Laws Assumes a power that never was commited to them by God nor can be by Man for the Confirmation of which Opinion we shall Cite no less Authority than the Great Mr: Lock who says 'that the whole Jurisdiction of the Majestrait reaches only to civel Concernments and that all civel power Right and Dominion is bounded and confined to the only care of promoting these things' which is so Pertinent that we need not Expatiate on it Onely say that if you can do any thing in Religion by human laws you can do every thing if you can this Year take five Dollars from me and give it to A Minister of any Denomitation you may next year by the same Rule take Fifty or what not and give it to one of another or to them of all other Denominations." Petition of Sundry of the Inhabitants of Rockingham County (Nov 18, 1784), Va State Library, Mfm of Misc Ms 425. (Note, however, that the petitioners admired South Carolina's equal establishment of Protestant sects. In other words, the no-legislation-repsecting language may sometimes have been interpreted simply to require equality among Protestants.) A petition from Rockbridge, Virginia, said: "Let the Ministers of the Gospel of all denominations enjoy the Privileges common to every good Citizen protect them in their religious exercises in the Person and Property and Contracts and that we humbly conceive is all they are entitled to and all a Legislature has power to grant." Petition from Rockbridge County, Virginia in Eckenrode, *Separation of Church and State in Virginia* 97. The Baptist leader John Leland wrote that "[t]o indulge [ministers] with an exemption from taxes and bearing arms is a tempting emolument. The law should be silent about them; protect them as citizens, not as sacred officers, for the civil law knows no sacred religious officers." John Leland, *The Rights of Conscience Inalienable, and, Therefore, Religious Opinions Not Cognizable By Law* (1791), in *Writings of Leland* 188. See also notes 119–22 and accompanying text.

[112] Americans frequently spoke of "free exercise" or "free exercise, according to conscience." "Free exercise," however, tended to be understood to suggest the natural right. Therefore, the broader degree of liberty—not only the natural right but also equal civil rights or freedom from government legislation with respect to religion—often was said to be freedom of conscience or freedom of religion.

that these phrases referred to equal civil rights among Christians or, at least, among Protestants. On this basis, in the South Carolina Assembly, the Rev. William Tennent said: "My first, and most capital reason, against all religious establishments is, that *they are an infringement of Religious Liberty.*"[113] For yet other Americans, "freedom of consicence" and "freedom of religion" could refer to an absence of laws respecting religion or to an unspecific absence of establishments. These phrases could be used as convenient catch-alls.[114]

With a somewhat more descriptive label, dissenters, particularly Baptists, generically claimed equal liberty or equality of religious liberty. For example, Samuel Stillman—a prominent Baptist—preached in a Massachusetts election sermon that the governor should secure to all peaceable Christians "the uninterrupted enjoyment of equal religious liberty." Such language (like the phrase "freedom of conscience" or "religious liberty") could be ambiguous,

---

[113] William Tennent, *Mr. Tennent's Speech on the Dissenting Petition, Delivered in the House of Assembly, Charles-Town, South-Carolina, Jan. 11, 1777* 5 (1777) (Evans 15612). Tennent made it clear that he understood religious liberty in terms of equality. See John Wesley Brinsfield, *Religion and Politics in Colonial South Carolina* 107–8, 116, 120–22 (Southern Historical Press, 1983). Recalling how he had collected signatures for the petition supported by Tennent, Colonel William Hill later wrote of himself that, "in order to get as many names as possible—(and not believing in the doctrine of the turks that women have no souls) he got the women to sign their names with the men." Id at 111.

[114] For some uses of these phrases against establishments, see the following. According to a minority of the Pennsylvania ratification convention, "[t]he right of conscience shall be held inviolable." "The Address and Reasons of Dissent of the Minority," 2 *Documentary History* 623. In 1779, Isaac Backus prepared a draft Bill of Rights for the Massachusetts Constitution. Among other things, it said that "every person has an unalienable right to act in all religious affairs according to the full persuasion of his own mind, where others are not injured thereby." *Backus on Church, State, and Calvinism* 487. In 1780, Backus wrote: "Our Convention at Cambridge passed an act last Wednesday to establish an article in our bill of rights which evidently infringes upon the rights of conscience." McLoughlin, 1 *New England Dissent* 604. Also in Massachusetts, Joseph Hawley wrote: "Pray give over the impossible (task) of endeavoring to make a religious establishment, (consistent with the unalienable Rights of Conscience." Joseph Hawley, *Protest to the Constitutional Convention of 1780*, in Mary C. Clune, ed, *Joseph Hawley's Criticism of the Constitution of Massachusetts*, in 3 Smith College Studies in Hist 50 (1917). According to Leland, "[t]he question is, 'Are the rights of conscience alienable, or inalienable?'" John Leland, *The Rights of Conscience Inalienable* (1791), in *Writings of Leland* 180. Although he discussed this as an inalienable natural right, he had a broad view of it, apparently considering it a freedom from all legislation concerning religion, including taxes in support of religion. See also J. Leland, *The Yankee Spy* (1794), in id at 239; *Popular Sources of Political Authority* 693. For a much narrower understanding of "religious rights," see Noah Hobart, *Civil Government the Foundation of Social Happiness* 30 (Conn election sermon 1750, published 1751) (Evans 6692). In many of these writings, the precise definiton of the "right of conscience" or the "right of religion" was not altogether clear.

for it could refer either to the equal natural right of free exercise or to a religious liberty involving equal civil rights. Stillman, however, clarified that, for him, "equal religious liberty" was an equality of civil rights with respect to religion:

> The authority by which he [i.e., the "magistrate"] acts he derives alike from *all the people*, [and] consequently he should exercise that authority *equally* for the benefit of *all*, without any respect to their different religious principles. . . .

Stillman wanted *"equal treatment of all the citizens."*[115]

Of course, these various modes of analysis were often used together, as may be illustrated by the First Amendment to the Constitution of the United States. Like some earlier constitutional provisions concerning religion, the First Amendment drew upon the bifurcated approach that distinguished between natural rights and government privileges. As indicated above, the bifurcated analysis took various forms. Some state constitutions, for example, protected the natural right of free exercise in one clause and proscribed unequal privileges in a second. Other constitutional provisions— including New Hampshire's 1787 proposal to amend the United

---

[115] Samuel Stillman, *A Sermon* 29 (Mass election sermon 1779) (Evans 16537). Stillman also said that "as all men are equal by nature, so when they enter into a state of civil government, they are entitled *precisely* to the same rights and privileges; or to an *equal degree* of political happiness." Id at 11. For other uses of the phrase "equal liberty" or "equal religious liberty" to refer to an equality of civil rights, see the following. In Virginia, Baptists petitioned that "the full equal and impartial Liberty of all Denominations, may be indubitably secured." Petition of the Ministers and Messengers of the Baptist Denomination assembed at Noel's Meeting House in Essex County on May 3, 1783 (May 30, 1783), Va State Library, Mfm of Misc Ms 425. Baptists also told the legislature: "Your Memorialists have hoped for a removal of their Complaints, and the enjoyment of equal Liberty; . . . And that in every Act, the bright beams of equal Liberty, and Impartial Justice may shine, . . ." Memorial of the Committee of Several Baptist Associations, Assembled at Dover Meeting House, Oct 9, 1784 (Nov 11, 1784), Va State Library, Mfm of Misc Ms 425. The Presbyterians of Hanover, Virginia, tendentiously interpreted the 1776 Declaration of Rights as "declaring that equal liberty, as well religious as civil, shall be universally extended to the good people of this country." Memorial of the Presbytery of Hanover to the General Assembly of Virginia (April 25, 1777), in *American State Papers* 96. An anti-establishment Virginian said: "When every society of Christians is allowed full, equal, and impartial liberty, what can they desire more?" *The Freeman's Remonstrance Against an Ecclesiastical Establishment . . . By a Freeman of Virginia* 5 (1777) (Evans 43750).

In contrast, the July 1789 House Committee Report on the Bill of Rights may have equated equal rights of conscience merely with the natural right of free exercise: "No religion shall be established by law, nor shall the equal rights of conscience be infringed." House Committee Rep of July 28, 1789, in *Creating the Bill of Rights* 30. The phrase concerning establishment may have made unnecessary any further anti-establishment clause, and therefore, perhaps, the "equal rights of conscience" here may have referred only to equal rights of free exercise.

States Constitution, and, later, the First Amendment—took a similar bifurcated approach, yet, in place of the clause prohibiting unequal privileges, these provisions more broadly forbade legislation with respect to religion.[116]

Incidentally, a prohibition of all legislation with respect to religion may have been considered too broad. In particular, it might have precluded legislation protecting the free exercise of religion. Americans of many persuasions, both dissenters and members of establishments, had argued that government should protect their right freely to exercise their religion,[117] and, in effect, they thereby added a caveat to their claim that government was created only to protect civil or temporal interests. In the words of some of Virginia's more prominent Presbyterians, "The end of civil government is security to the temporal liberty and property of mankind,

---

[116] The New Hampshire ratification convention proposed that "Congress shall make no Laws touching Religion, or to infringe the rights of Conscience." *Creating the Bill of Rights* 17. Typically, as has been seen, it was dissenters who sought a prohibition of legislation with respect to religion, but, for purposes of the federal government, this position of dissenters may have also appealed to state establishments. See note 122.

[117] For example, Witherspoon, who thought that "[t]he magistrates . . . have a right to instruct, but not to constrain," argued that "[t]he magistrate ought to defend the rights of conscience, and tolerate all in their religious sentiments that are not injurious to their neighbors." Witherspoon, *Lectures*, Lect XIV, at 160–61. He added that, "At present, as things are situated, one of the most important duties of the magistracy is to protect the rights of conscience." Id. The Presbyterian Synod of New York and Philadelphia declared that, "It having been represented to Synod, that the Presbyterian Church suffers greatly in the opinion of other denominations from an apprehension that they hold intolerant principles, the Synod do . . . declare, that they ever have, and still do renounce and abhor the principles of intolerance; and we do believe that every member of society ought to be protected in the full and free exercise of their religion." *Records of the Presbyterian Church in the United States of America* 499 (1904), as quoted in James H. Smylie, *Protestant Clegy, the First Amendment and Beginnings of a Constitutional Debate, 1781–91* in Elwyn A. Smith, ed, *The Religion of the Republic* 116, 141–42 (Fortress, 1971). See also David Parsons, *A Sermon* 13 (Mass election sermon 1788) (Evans 21360).

In related language, Americans could request that government equally protect individuals in their religious liberty. For example, an Anti-Federalist minority in the Maryland ratification convention proposed as an amendment to the Constitution: "That there be no national religion established by law; but that all persons be equally entitled to protection in their religious liberty" (April 21, 1788), Elliot, 2 *Debates* 553. Of course, Federalists argued that, even without a bill of rights, the Constitution provided equal protection: "Partiality to any sect, or ill treatment of any, is neither in the least warranted by the constitution, nor compatible with the general spirit of toleration; an equal security of civil and religious rights, is therefore given to all denominations, without any formal stipulations; which, indeed, might suggest an idea, that such an equality was doubtful. If the constitution must at all have any amendment on this subject, it should be to guarantee to every state in the union perfect liberty of conscience; because it is much more probable that superstition, mingled with political faction, might corrupt a single state, than that bigotry should infect a majority of the states in Congress." [Nicholas Collin], *Remarks on the Amendments to the Federal Constitution* (No 9), in Federal Gazette (Phila) (Nov 18, 1788, No 42).

and to protect them in the free exercise of religion."[118] Therefore, when dissenters came to argue against establishments that government should not legislate concerning religion, some of these dissenters—at least, many Presbyterians in Virginia—hastened to add as a caveat that government should, of course, be able to provide protection for the inalienable natural right of free exercise.[119] For example, in 1777, a petition from the Presbytery of Hanover asked that "the civil magistrates no otherwise interfere [in religion], than to protect them all [i.e., "every individual"] in the full and free exercise of their several modes of worship."[120] Similarly, in 1785, the Presbyterians of Virginia petitioned that "it would be an unwarrantable stretch of prerogative in the legislature to make laws concerning it [i.e., religion], except for protection."[121] Perhaps, to permit legislation protecting the free exercise of religion, the First Amendment merely forbade legislation "respecting an establishment of religion."[122]

---

[118] Memorial of the Presbyterians of Virginia (Aug 13, 1785), in *American State Papers* 113.

[119] This was not exclusively a Presbyterian position. Thomas Paine wrote that "[a]s to religion, I hold it to be the indispensible duty of all government, to protect all conscientious professors thereof, and I know of no other business which government hath to do therewith." Paine, *Common Sense* 108–9.

In contrast, however, many dissenters wanted government to promote and, in this sense, protect religion rather than just the free exercise of religion, provided the goverment did not discriminate among Christian or, at least, Protestant sects. Buckley, *Church and State in Revolutionary Virginia* 177 (re Presbyterians); McLoughlin, 1 *New England Dissent* 610. For example, the New York and Philadelphia Synod of the Presbyterian Church said, in 1792, that "Civil Magistrates may not assume to themselves the administration of the word and sacraments . . . or, in the least, interfere in matters of faith. Yet, as nursing fathers, it is the duty of civil magistrates to protect the church of our common Lord, without giving the preference to any denomination of christians above the rest." *The Constitution of the Presbyterian Church in the United States of America* 35 (1792) (Evans 24711). Incidentally, in their introduction to their 1787 draft, the Synod had revealed some sympathy for the more liberal position: "They do not even wish to see any religious constitution aided by the civil power, further than may be necessary for protection and security, and, at the same time, may be equal and common to all others." *A Draught of the Form of the Government and Discipline of the Presbyterian Church in the United State of America* iii (1787) (Evans 20658).

[120] Memorial of the Presbyterians of Hanover to the the General Assembly of Virginia (April 25, 1777), in *American State Papers* 97.

[121] Memorial of the Presbyterians of Virginia to the General Assembly (Aug 13, 1785), in *American State Papers* 114. Immediately preceding the passage quoted in the text was the following: "We never resigned to the control of government our right of determining for ourselves in this important article [i.e., religion], and acting agreeably to the convictions of reason and conscience in discharging our duty to our Creator. And therefore . . . ." According to Eckenrode, this Memorial was drafted by William Graham. Eckenrode, *Separation of Church and State in Virginia* 107.

[122] Indeed, already in 1784 Madison had attributed to anti-establishment forces in Virginia the position that there should be no legislation concerning an establishment of religion. In

With numerous minor variations, the types of analysis reviewed above were used to claim at least equal civil rights. Of course, some dissenters demanded, not merely equal civil rights, but, more generally, an absence of legislation respecting religion. Many other dissenters ungenerously insisted upon equal civil rights only for Christians—or, alternatively, only for Protestants—rather than for all persons.[123] Large numbers of dissenters even were willing to be content with a lesser right than that which they might request in general terms. Subject to these caveats, however, dissenters employed some common modes of analysis and described their hopes for at least an equality of civil rights—an equality both of restraints on natural liberty and of privileges.

---

a letter to Richard Henry Lee, Madison summarized the opposition to an assessment bill as being based, among other grounds, "on the general principle that no Religious Estabts. was within the purview of Civil authority." J. Madison, letter to Robert Henry Lee (Nov 14, 1784), in Robert S. Alley, ed, *James Madison on Religious Liberty* 53 (Prometheus, 1985). He continued by pointing out that the Presbyterians "do not deny but rather betray a desire that an Assessment may be estabt. but protest agst. any which does not embrace all Religions . . . ." Id at 54. When attributing to opponents of assessment the principle that "religious establishments" were not within the "purview" of civil authority, Madison may have been summarizing the views of Baptists and western and other Presbyterians who were reluctant to compromise on the question of establishment. Certainly, some such Presbyterians in the 1780s held that government should not interfere with religion, except to protect the free exercise of it. For such a position, taken about nine months after Madison wrote his letter, see text at note 121.

Madison's subsequent writings seem to confirm that he considered his own position to be different from the principle that "religious establishments" were not within the "purview of civil authority." Madison's notes for the debates on the 1784 assessment bill state: "*Rel:* not within purview of Civil Authority." R. A. Rutland et al, eds, 8 *Papers of James Madison* 198 (U of Chi, 1973). Similarly, a year later, an ameliorated assessment bill provoked Madison in his famous Memorial and Remonstrance to say that "religion is wholly exempt from [government's] cognizance." Memorial and Remonstrance, in *American State Papers* 121. Madison may have been emphasizing the unqualified character of his claim.

Of course, the radical anti-establishment position adopted by Madison coincided with the Federalist view that the federal government, being a government of delegated powers, had no power with respect to religion. In the Virginia ratification convention, Madison said: "There is not a shadow of right in the general government to intermeddle with religion. Its least interference with it would be a most flagrant usurpation." J. Madison in Va Rat Convention (June 12, 1788), in Elliot, 3 *Debates* 330. Some historians have claimed that the "no law respecting" language merely reflected the federal character of the government of the United States. E.g., Joseph M. Snee, *Religious Disestablishment and the Fourteenth Amendment*, Wash U L Q 371 (1954). This is belied by the extensive evidence that such language had been used for some time at the state level to describe one of the most radical of the anti-establishment positions. See text at notes 109–11 & 117–22.

[123] Thus, they could consistently assume that civil government should inculcate the principles of Christianity. Even those who sought equal rights for persons of all religions could explain that government was able to promote the principles of Christianity to the extent such principles were in accord with natural religion. On this basis, many claimed that government could enforce observance of the Sabbath.

Among the most intriguing discussions about equal civil rights
were the arguments of dissenters and their supporters in states in
which establishments and establishment constitutions had conceded only the right of free exercise or free exercise and equal
protection. Disappointed with these guarantees, dissenters and
their confederates attempted to couch their demands for equal civil
rights in terms of the meager language available to them. In Virginia, where the 1776 Declaration of Rights merely guaranteed free
exercise and did not prohibit an establishment, it is possible to
trace in considerable detail how dissenters and their supporters
adapted their arguments to make the best of what little had been
yielded to them.

For example, many dissenters in Virginia claimed equality by
denouncing "separate privileges." During the Revolution, various
state bills of rights, including Virginia's, prohibited separate privileges, emoluments, or honors, unless in exchange for services—
these prohibitions being addressed to the fear that aristocratic or
economic interests separate from the common interest of society
would seek to enrich themselves through legislation.[124] Not having
a better constitutional foundation for their claims to equal privileges, many Virginia dissenters rested their case on the separate
privileges clause of the Declaration of Rights.[125] For various rea-

----

[124] According to the Virginia clause, "no man, or set of men, are entitled to exclusive or
separate emoluments or privileges from the community, but in consideration of publick
services; which, not being descendible, neither ought the offices of magistrate, legislator, or
judge to be hereditary." Va Decl of Rights of 1776, § 4. See text at notes 216–17.

[125] For example, Presbyterians petitioned: "[W]e ask no ecclesiastical establishment for
ourselves, neither can we approve of them and grant it to others: this, indeed, would be
giving exclusive or separate emoluments or privileges to one set (or sect) of men, without
any special public services, to the common reproach or injury of every other denomination."
Memorial of the Presbytery of Hanover to the General Assembly of Virginia (Oct 24, 1776),
in *American State Papers* 94; see also id at 100 & 118. With an unusual touch of dry humor,
Baptists petitioned "That your Memorialists firmly believe as they are taught in the Declaration of Rights 'that no Man or set of Men are entituled to exclusive or seperate Emoluments
or Privileges from the Community, but in Consideration of publick Services' [and] That
they cannot see that for a Person to call himself a Church-Man and to conform to the Rites
and Ceremonies of the Church of England, is doing the State any publick Service." Memorial of the Baptist Association (June 3, 1782), Va State Library, Mfm of Misc Ms 425. See
also the following petitions from Va State Library, Mfm of Ms 425: Memorial of the
Committee of Several Baptist Associations, Assembled at Dover Meeting-House, Oct 9,
1784 (Nov 11, 1784); Petition of the Inhabitants of Cumberland County (Oct 26, 1785);
Petition of the Inhabitants of the County of Buckingham (Oct 27, 1785); Petition of the
Inhabitants of the County of Henry (Oct 27, 1785); Petition of the Inhabitants of the County
of Surry (Oct 26, 1785); Memorial & Remonstrance of the Inhabitants of the County of
Charlotte (Oct 27, 1785); Petition of the Inhabitants of the County of Isle of Wight (Oct
28, 1785). Note that the petitions of October 26 and 27 listed here employed versions of a

sons, however, such arguments were of limited appeal or usefulness. Among other things, although "separate interests" and "unequal laws" were ideas applicable to religious interests, they were traditionally associated with social and economic interests. Even with respect to economic interests, moreover, at least some Americans were becoming cautious about prohibiting unequal laws or special privileges for separate interests; many Americans accepted the inevitability of separate interests and sought political as much as merely legal obstacles to unequal laws.[126] Last but not least, dissenters wanted a greater equality than mere "equal laws." To provide equal civil rights, laws had to avoid making any distinction among different religions; the laws had to treat individuals the same, regardless of religion. In contrast, equal laws were laws that did not unjustly benefit or penalize any separate interest, and this was not the strict equality needed by dissenters.[127]

Even more interesting than the anti-establishment use of the separate-interests language was the anti-establishment attempt to claim equal civil rights in terms of the free exercise of religion. George Mason's draft religion clause for the 1776 Virginia Declaration of Rights adverted to toleration rather than a right of free exercise and did not preclude an establishment. In response, Madison drafted an alternative clause, similar to that which would appear in most state constitutions, asserting the free exercise of religion as a right rather than something merely to be tolerated. He also, however, sought to make an equality of privileges seem a necessary consequence of the far more acceptable right of free exercise. Madison wrote that:

> all men are equally entitled to the full and free exercise of it [i.e., religion], accord[ing] to the dictates of Conscience: and therefore that no man or class of men ought on account of religion to be invested with peculiar emoluments or privileges: nor subjected to any penalties or disabilities . . . .[128]

---

single text. For evidence that Jefferson may have had a hand in some of these petitions, see Declaration of the Va Association Baptists (Dec 25, 1776), in Thomas Jefferson, 1 *Papers*, 660, Julian P. Boyd, ed (Princeton U, 1950).

[126] See, of course, *Federalist* No 10.

[127] Thus, much later, Emerson wrote about "the Spartan principle 'of calling that which is just, equal; not that which is equal, just.'" Ralph W. Emerson, *Politics*, in his *Essays: Second Series* 193, 197 (1854).

[128] He indicated that it should continue: "unless, under colour of religion, any man disturb the peace, the happiness, or safety of society." Robert Scribner & Brent Tarter, eds, 7

Madison described equal emoluments and an absence of penalties as a necessary result of the equal right to the free exercise of religion.

Madison's proposal failed. Supporters of Virginia's Anglican establishment recognized the implications of the phrase concerning "peculiar emoluments or privileges"—that it was "a prelude to an attack on the Established Church."[129] They therefore insisted on dropping the second half of Madison's language. As a result, the Declaration protected only the natural right: "all men are equally entitled to the free exercise of religion, according to the dictates of conscience . . . ."[130]

In the next session of the Virginia legislature, dissenters petitioned for equal civil rights. For example, on October 16, 1776, a petition was presented in which some dissenters described their desire for "every religious denomination being on a level" and their hope that the legislature would interfere "only to support them in their just rights and equal privileges."[131] On October 22, two petitions were presented—from Albermarle, Amherst, and Buckingham counties—praying that "every religious denomination may be put upon an equal footing."[132] Another, on November 9, from the Committee of Augusta County, complained of "unequal treatment."[133]

Some of the 1776 Virginia petitions acknowledged that the Declaration of Rights, in speaking of "free exercise . . . according to . . . conscience," had not abolished the establishment, and these petitions asked the legislature to finish the task. In what may have been the first petition of the session on behalf of dissenters, the legislature was requested "to complete what is so nobly begun."[134]

Revolutionary Virginia: Independence & the Fifth Convention, 1776, A Documentary History 457 (U Press of Va, 1983) ("*Revolutionary Virginia*").

[129] 7 *Revolutionary Virginia* 457.

[130] Va Const of 1776, Decl of Rights, § 16.

[131] Charles F. James, *Documentary History of the Struggle for Religious Liberty in Virginia* 69 (Da Capo, 1971 reprint of 1900 edition) (James, "*Struggle for Religious Liberty in Virginia*").

[132] Id at 70.

[133] Id at 74.

[134] Id at 68–69. Such acknowledgements continued long after 1776. In 1780, Baptists seeking legislative reforms said that "the Completion of Religious Liberty is what as a Religious Community your Memorialists are particularly interested in." Memorial of the Baptist Association Met at Sandy Creek in Charlotte, Oct 16, 1780 (Nov 8, 1780), Va State Library, Mfm of Misc Ms 425. In 1784, the Presbytery of Hanover petitioned: "The security

Before the end of the month, however, some petitions exhibited a
rather lawyerly tendency to demand in terms of what was granted
that which had been denied. Some, as noted above, argued that
the "separate privileges" clause had prohibited an establishment of
religion. Others, however, made arguments more similar to Madison's that the free exercise of religion required equal privileges.[135]
As the historian H. J. Eckenrode noted, these petitions "advanced
the theory that the Bill of Rights had put an end to the establishment."[136]

---

of our religious rights upon equal and impartial ground, *instead of being made a fundamental
part of our constitution as it ought to have been*, is left to the precarious fate of common law. A
matter of general and essential concern to the people is committed to the hazard of the
prevailing opinion of a majority of the assembly at its different sessions." Memorial of the
Presbytery of Hanover to the General Assembly of Virginia (May 1784), in *American State
Papers* 101. In 1785, the Presbyterians of Virginia petitioned: "We regret that full equality
in all things, and ample protection and security to religious liberty were not incontestably
fixed in the Constitution of the government." Memorial of the Presbyterians of Virginia to
the General Assembly (Aug 13, 1785), in id at 118.

[135] Some dissenters argued against an establishment that their hopes had "been raised &
confirmed by the Declaration of your Hon[ora]ble House in the last Article of rights which
we beg leave to recite, viz. 'That Religion or the Duty we Owe to our Creator . . . .' It will
hence unavoidably follow that No Laws which are indefensible & incompatible with the
Rights of Conscience should be suffered to remain unrepealed." They believed that "religious liberty in its fullest extent" was one of the "rights of human Nature." Petition of the
Dissenters from the Ecclesiastical Establishment, Berkeley County (Oct 25, 1776), Va State
Library, Mfm of Misc Ms 425. Others petitioned that "it would be a violation of the rights
of the Good People of this state[.] our Bill or Rights Particularly Points out that religion is
the duty we owe to our Creator and the manner of dischargeing it can only be directed by
reason and Conviction not by Force or violence, therefore as all men are Equally Intitled
to the free Exercise of Religion according to the dictates of Conscience &c &c We your
Petitioners beg leave to represent . . . that we think . . . that even to force a man to support
this or that teacher of his own religious Persuation, [sic] is a depriving him of that liberty
of giving his Contributions to the Particular Pastor whose Morals he would make his Patron
[sic?], whose Powers he feels most Persuasive to Rightousness would be wrong, Cruel, and
Oppressive." Petition of Sundry Freeholders and other Inhabitants of the County of Bedford
(Oct 27, 1785), Va State Library, Mfm of Misc Ms 425.

[136] Eckenrode, *Separation of Church and State in Virginia* 47; Buckley, *Church and State in
Revolutionary Virginia* 24. Already on October 11, 1776, "a letter from Augusta County
quoted the free exercise clause . . . and asked that it be carried into effect immediately by
placing all religious groups on the same basis 'without prefcrence or preeminence' given to
any one church." Va Gaz (Purdie, Oct 11, 1776), as quoted in id at 24. Presbyterians of
Hanover, Virginia, based their complaints against the establishment on the Declaration of
Rights and, in the following paragraph, noted that they "annually pay large taxes to support
an establishment from which their consciences and their principles oblige them to
dissent,—all which are confessedly violations of their natural rights, and in their consequences a restraint upon freedom of enquiry and private judgment." Memorial of the Presbytery of Hanover to the General Assembly of Virginia (Oct 24, 1776), in *American State Papers*
92. In 1785, Presbyterians claimed of a proposed statute: "The bill is also a direct violation
of the Declaration of Rights, which ought to be the standard of all laws. The sixteenth
article is clearly infringed . . . ." Memorial of the Presbyterians of Virginia to the General
Assembly (Aug 13, 1785), in id at 116.

What was tendentious in ordinary petitions was an opportunity for ingenuity in the writing of Madison and Jefferson.[137] Already in 1776, as has been seen, Madison proposed unsuccessfully that the free exercise of religion required that there be no "peculiar emoluments or privileges." In 1779, in his Virginia Act for Establishing Religious Freedom, Jefferson took a similar approach, and, because Jefferson provided a lengthier explanation than had Madison, his proposal can be examined in greater detail. Eventually enacted in 1785, Jefferson's statute declared, among other things, that the profession of religious opinions by men "shall in no wise diminish, enlarge, or affect their civil capacities."[138] The prefatory clauses explained

> that our civil rights have no dependence on our religious opinions, more than our opinions in physics or geometry; that, therefore, the proscribing any citizen as unworthy the public confidence by laying upon him an incapacity of being called to the offices of trust and emolument, unless he profess or renounce this or that religious opinion is depriving him injuriously of *those privileges and advantages to which in common with his fellow-citizens he has a natural right*; . . .[139] [italics added].

If civil government had been established for exclusively secular ends, and if religion was, moreover, not susceptible to civil control, then, indeed, it could be argued that civil government had no power to deny a man office because he would not swear, for example, to the 39 Articles. Yet it was a paradox—a clever and arresting solecism—to assert that the refusal of office was a denial of "privileges and advantages" to which a man had a natural right. According to the state-of-nature theory discussed in part I and that was so popular in America, a denial of a right that did not exist in the state of nature would not normally be a denial of a natural right. Nonetheless, the prefatory clauses of Jefferson's statute suggested that a denial of such a right on grounds of religion could be viewed as an infringement of natural right, because the exercise of religion was a natural right. This suggestion of the preface was

---

[137] Many petitions may have drawn upon the ingenuity of these two Virginians but without their sophistication.

[138] Jefferson's language about civil capacities probably reflected his familiarity with English debates about religious liberty.

[139] 12 William Waller Hening, ed, *Collection of the Laws of Virginia* 85 (U Press of Va, 1969 reprint of 1823 edition).

repeated in the body of the Act, and, indeed, this second pro-
nouncement reveals why, even when successfully achieving equal
civil rights, Jefferson went out of his way to stretch traditional
notions of natural right:

> And though we well know that this Assembly, elected by the
> people for the ordinary purposes of legislation only, have no
> power to restrain the acts of succeeding Assemblies, constituted
> with the powers equal to our own, and that therefore to declare
> this act irrevocable would be of no effect in law, yet we are
> free to declare, and do declare, that the rights hereby asserted
> are of the natural rights of mankind, and that if any act shall
> be hereafter passed to repeal the present or to narrow its opera-
> tion, such act will be an infringement of natural right.[140]

To restrain future Assemblies, Jefferson declared that a denial of
civil rights on grounds of religion—including a denial of some
rights existing only under civil government—would be a violation
of natural right. Jefferson was appropriating for equal civil rights
the inviolability associated with an aspect of natural liberty, particularly the inalienable natural right of free exercise of religion.

In 1785, Madison came close to repeating the sophisticated solecism that he and Jefferson each had made in, respectively, 1776
and 1779, but Madison appears to have been quite careful in 1785
to avoid saying that a denial of equal civil rights was a violation of
natural right. In his *Memorial* of 1785, Madison argued against
legislation that he described as contrary to, among other things, the
natural right of free exercise of religion guaranteed by the Virginia
Declaration of Rights. Conceivably, therefore, Madison's *Memorial*
may be understood to suggest that he thought the bill's unequal
privileges violated the natural right of free exercise. Yet, in the
Memorial, Madison did not directly say this, and, indeed, at one
point he seems to have gone out of his way to avoid such a statement. Immediately after denouncing the bill's violations of the
equal natural right of free exercise, he warned against the special
exemptions and other privileges the bill created:

> As the Bill violates equality by subjecting some to peculiar
> burdens, so it violates the same principle, by granting to others,
> peculiar exemptions. Are the Quakers and Menonists the only
> sects who think a compulsive support of their Religions unnec-

---

[140] Id at 86.

essary and unwarrantable? . . . Ought their Religions to be
endowed above all others with extraordinary privileges by
which proselytes may be enticed from all others?[141]

Note that Madison did not say that peculiar exemptions or privileges would violate the natural right of free exercise; rather, they
would violate the "principle" of "equality." By cleverly shifting the
foundation of his argument from the equality of the natural right
of free exercise of religion to the principle of equality, he avoided
the somewhat strained position he and Jefferson had earlier espoused.[142]

It has been seen that opponents of establishments frequently
stretched the conventional understanding of separate privileges or
of free exercise in order to justify their claims for equal civil rights.
Strikingly, however, they attempted to use the idea of equal protection for this purpose much less frequently. Only very occasionally
did they claim equal civil rights in terms of equal protection. It
will be recalled that Ebenezer Frothingham wrote about equal protection in order to justify equal civil rights. According to Frothingham, persons of different sects "ought equally to be protected
by . . . civil Power, in their proper Rights and Privileges, and each
one be left to support their own Worship . . . ." Civil power, he
added, "knows nothing about the different Professions there is [sic]
among Mankind."[143] Later, other opponents of establishments
sometimes demanded equal civil rights on grounds of equal protection. For example, during ratification of the Massachusetts Constitution, the town of Leicester described that Constitution's compulsory support for religion as a violation of conscience and a
"Persecuting or Compeling" of individuals. This, they said, "is
inconsistent with the Last Paragraph [according to which] Every
Denomination of religious Societys Demeaning themselves Peace-

---

[141] James Madison, Memorial and Remonstrance, in 8 *Papers* 300, Robert A. Rutland, ed
(U of Chi, 1977). On the political maneuvers of Madison in 1784 and 1785, see Norman K.
Risjord, *Chesapeake Politics 1781–1800* 205–10 (1978).

[142] Later, however, when not writing to garner political support for legislation, Madison
continued to assert that an establishment was a violation of natural right. For example, in
1792, Madison used a very broadly defined notion of property to argue that a tax in support
of religion was a taking of property. James Madison, "Of Property," *American State Papers*
158. His argument was as follows: property embraces everything to which a man may attach
a value and have a right; a person has a property of particular value in his religious opinions;
government is instituted to protect property, including the rights of individuals; if government imposes a test or taxes individuals to support religion, it violates the property rights
individuals have in their opinions.

[143] Ebenezer Frothingham, *The Articles of Faith and Practice* 296 (1750) (Evans 6504).

ably and as Good Subjects Should be Equally under the Protection of Law."[144] Relatively few Americans, however, demanded equal civil rights in terms of equal protection with as much clarity as did the men of Leicester.[145]

In sum, the exigencies faced by dissenters sometimes prompted them and their supporters to base their claims for equal civil rights on unconventional and, in this sense, strained interpretations of less generous but more widely accepted standards. They sometimes argued that establishment privileges were separate privileges or a denial of a natural right. They also occasionally said that equal protection included equal privileges; yet they made this assertion relatively infrequently and rarely in an unambiguous fashion.

Dissenters understood that they needed guarantees of equal civil rights rather than only equal protection. In Massachusetts, in the decades following the adoption of the 1780 Constitution, dissenters repeatedly went to court to challenge the constitutionality of religious assessments, but they did so on the basis of language other than that relating to equal protection—and even so they ultimately failed.[146] Where they had the power—in Delaware, Pennsylvania,

---

[144] *Popular Sources of Political Authority* 836. McLoughlin describes Leicester as one of the Massachusetts towns in which Baptists, although a minority, were on relatively "good terms" with their neighbors. McLoughlin, 1 *New England Dissent* 516 & 628.

[145] For what may be another Massachusetts example, see *Popular Sources of Political Authority* 694. In Virginia, dissenters and their supporters appear occasionally to have used this argument but not clearly or systematically. E.g., the Presbytery of Hanover said: the legislature should be "the common guardian and equal protector of every class of citizens in their religious as well as civil rights." Memorial of the Presbytery of Hanover to the General Assembly (May 1784), in *American State Papers* 103. Yet, in the same Memorial, the Presbytery also said that "an equal share of the protection and favour of government to all denominations of Christians, were particular objects of our expectations and irrefragable claim." Id at 100. This bifurcated analysis was in accord with the conventional understanding of equal protection. In his Memorial, Madison may have treated equal protection as an equality of civil rights: "Such a government will be best supported by protecting every citizen in the enjoyment of his religion with the same equal hand which protects his person and property; by neither invading the equal rights of any sect, nor suffering any sect to invade those of another." J. Madison, Memorial and Remonstrance, in id at 126. Whether this passage employs the conventional understanding of equal protection is not altogether clear.

The argument that equal protection was an equality of legal rights—of both natural rights and privileges enjoyed under government—was revived, as one might expect, shortly after the adoption of the Fourteenth Amendment to the U.S. Constitution. E.g., in 1872, Senator Oliver Morton of Indiana argued that "the word 'protection,' as there used, . . . is substantially in the sense of the equal benefit of the law . . . ." See Earl A. Maltz, *The Concept of Equal Protection of the Laws—A Historical Inquiry*, 22 San Diego L Rev 499, 528 (1985).

[146] McLoughlin, 1 *New England Dissent* 636–59, especially 637, 639; Isaac Backus, *A Door Opened for Equal Christian Liberty* 4–5 [1783]; *Kendall v Kingston*, 5 Mass 524, 529 (1809); *Barnes v Inhabitants of 1st Parish of Falmouth*, 6 Mass 401, 416–17 (1810) (the whole of the Christian denominations clause quoted but the equal protection language apparently not relied upon). Many of the challenges in Massachusetts are described in Nathan Dane, 2 *A General Abridgment of American Law* 329–48 (ch 48) (1823).

North Carolina, South Carolina, New Jersey, and New York—opponents of establishments sought and obtained constitutional guarantees of equal privileges or equal civil rights. In contrast to establishments, which used equal protection clauses to preserve unequal privileges, opponents of establishments insisted that privileges also should be equal—that there should be an equality of civil rights.

Dissenters and other opponents of establishments tended to proclaim their egalitarian aspirations in relatively perspicuous language, and this account of how they sought equal civil rights rather than merely free exercise and equal protection can best be concluded in their own words. For example, in 1790, in New Hampshire, where the Constitution of 1784 promised equal protection rather than equal civil rights with respect to religion, a dissenting Anglican minister, John Cosens Ogden, was asked to preach the election sermon. He praised the tolerance of American governments and noted that "all religions are most justly tolerated, and ought and are promised to be protected." But he gently suggested that there should be a still greater equality:

> [A]ll are to enjoy every advantage, which law can afford to preserve, and whose professors are each determined to defend and maintain their own privileges. Upon this head, the conduct of our civil rulers in every part of this continent, for many years, has been founded upon the purest justice, and most perfect policy, in not only protecting and guarding all from spoil and incursions, but striving to remove all cause of heartburnings, and jealousies, by preferring one before another, either by an open or implied partiality . . . .[147]

After declaring his hope for "a more equal practice in Newengland," he went on to complain of unequal state support for ministers: "If God . . . extends his care to all, let us not be inattentive to his will, nor appear to limit his mercies or our favours by any unnecessary partialities; or debar them an equal opportunity to inculcate the great duties we owe each other."[148] In a 1791 Fourth

---

[147] John C. Ogden, *A Sermon* 17–18 (NH election sermon 1790) (Evans 22747). He then praised the legislature for encouraging the principle of "protecting all denominations of professors" and attributed "the honour done me in calling me to lead the devotions of this day" to the "beginning [of] a more equal practice in Newengland, according to the opinion and wish of so large a part of our country, . . ." Id at 19.

[148] Id at 20.

of July sermon, the sometime congressional chaplain, William Linn of New York City, voiced a similar appreciation of equality when discussing the United States Constitution. He praised the new Constitution and then proceeded to exclaim about the extent of religious liberty: "Here no particular modes of faith, or worship are established. . . . Every one stands upon equal footing, and can prove successful, only by the piety, virtue, learning, and liberality of its professors."[149]

IV. EQUALITY AND DIVERSITY

The eighteenth-century Americans who struggled over standards of religious equality understood that their debate concerned not only their legal rights but also the character of their society, and, in defense of their different positions, each side argued that its own standard of equality would allow Americans to overcome the discord so often associated with religious diversity. Americans were attempting to delineate the civil consequences of

---

[149] William Linn, *The Blessings of America* 18–19 (Fourth of July sermon given at request of Tammany Society 1791) (Evans 23504). In the ellipses, he said: "No undue preference is given to one denomination of religion above another." In fact, it may be doubted whether Linn expected any religious preferences under the U.S. Constitution. Incidentally, note that, in a July 4 sermon in 1794, David Ramsay—President of the South Carolina Senate—preached: "While the government, without partiality to any denomination, leaves all to stand on equal footing, none can prove successful, but by the learning, virtue, and piety of its professors." David Ramsay, *An Oration Delivered on the Anniversary of American Independence . . . in St. Michael's Church in Charleston, South Carolina* 9 (London, Daniel Isaac ["swinish multitude"] Eaton 1795). Earlier, a petition to the Virginia General Assembly, presented on October 11, 1776, asked that "all church establishments be pulled down . . . and each individual [be] left to rise or sink by his own merit and the general laws of the land." James, *Struggle for Religious Liberty in Virginia* 69. The Dutch Reformed Church concluded the preface to the publication of its Constitution by observing that "Whether the Church of Christ will not be more effecutally patronized in a civil government where full freedom of consience and worship is equally protected and insured to all men, and where truth is left to vindicate her own sovereign authority and influence, than where men in power promote their favorite denominations by temporal amendments and partial discriminations, will now, in America, have a fair trial." *The Constitution of the Reformed Dutch Church, in the United States* vii–viii (1793) (Evans 26065). Even before ratification of the Bill of Rights, the Rev. Shuttleworth—an establishment minister—preached to the Vermont legislature: "[T]hat which most of all distinguishes this excellent constitution, and adds a glory to the whole, is that religious liberty, candour, and catholicism therein exhibited. . . . The legislature of our nation, . . . are setting us the example; [they] have put all denominations of christians on a level." Samuel Shuttlesworth, *A Discourse* 14 (Vt election discourse 1791, printed 1792) (Evans 24788). The Rev. Abraham Booth mimicked this sort of analysis in his description of the "privileges and honors enjoyed by the subjects of th[e heavenly] kingdom," which, he said, would not be unequal: "Nor are they confined to a few distinguished favorites of our celestial Sovereign; for they are common to all his real subjects." Abraham Booth, *An Essay on the Kingdom of Christ* 99 (1791) (Evans 23213).

religious disagreement, including the relationship of contentious religious groups to the larger polity, and therefore, not surprisingly, their views on diversity and equality were connected to their perceptions of social unity. Having been challenged to explain how a harmonious, unified political society was to be achieved if it were to contain diverse and discordant religious sects, dissenters insisted that an equality of civil rights would remove the sources of controversy. In contrast, some establishment ministers, once they had accepted as inevitable and even attractive a degree of legal equality, suggested that legal equality—even an equality of all civil rights— could not, by itself, produce unity. On this ground, they urged Americans to recognize the Christian sentiments and morals they had in common and, at least by implication, justified government support for religion as a means of encouraging shared opinions. Thus, dissenters who claimed equal civil rights and establishments that defended a lesser equality understood and sometimes justified their positions in terms of their somewhat different conceptions of unity in a diverse society.

Establishment writers had long argued that separation from the established church undermined the unity and harmoniousness of society. Particularly during the Great Awakening, they pointed to the dangers of separation. In Connecticut, for example, Benjamin Lord went to the extreme of associating the colony's religious divisions with a selfish, anarchical individualism: "In the Exercise of *Anarchy*, Men seem to be dissolving Community it self, and going back to the state of Nature: to do every one what is Right in his own Eyes; which a greatly privileg'd People are often, but too prone unto. As if a Government form'd for *Liberty*, to the Subjects, gave them a *License*, to act for themselves abstracted from Relation to Society and without concern for the common Good."[150]

---

[150] Benjamin Lord, *Religion and Government Subsisting Together in Society, Necessary to their Compleat Happiness and Safety* 27 (Conn election sermon for 1751, printed 1752) (Evans 6868). He continued: "Verily, 'tis a Principle near akin to Anarchy, that prompts men in a Community, to act, as Individuals with levelling Designs; forgetting how sacred are the bonds of civil Society, which the have taken upon them, and objecting against any settled form of Government at all." Id at 27–28. According to Lord, separation was an assertion of private interest against the interest of society: "If Persons are Ignorant of the Distinction there is between the State of Men; as *Individuals*, and as *Members* of Community: If they are Insensible of the Bonds of Society, and the sacred Obligations arising thence, to act with unselfish, steddy Views of the common Good: But are ready to separate their own private Interest from that, and so practically Renounce their Relation to the Body Politic; this hurts it greatly. If they Imagine, they may seek their own private Good, abstracted from any Regard

Religious divisions were, for Lord, a threat to social and political unity.

In contrast, dissenters frequently defended their ambitions for equal civil rights on the ground that legal equality would produce social harmony. Establishment writers occasionally employed this argument to justify equal protection or, sometimes, an equal establishment of Christianity,[151] but, on behalf of their greater degree of equality, dissenters could take the approach more frequently and more effectively. Frothingham wrote:

> I think it will not weaken the hands of civil rulers, that rule for God, to have different professions [of religious belief] in a town

to the whole Community; or, as if their own particular Interest must be the Standard by which, to measure the public Good; and hence, frame their Schemes of Conduct to suit them, only, this is Mischievous to Society. For now, when they come to act as Members of Society, the *great Question* with them is, What is good for *me?* and what will suit *my Interest?* Not what is good for the *Community*, or proper for *them?* And this governs their Vote and Conduct; which is a Violation of the duty of Members, a betraying their Trust, and breaking their solemn bonds. . . . And this, I suppose upon a just Examination, will be found one great spring of the hurtful Divisions in Church and State." Id at 48–49. Although Lord's language was extreme, even for Connecticut, it sounded a widely known theme. In Connecticut, the Rev. Bartlett preached that "there is nothing, tends more directly and effectually, to cast a Blemish upon Christianity, than the following seducing Teachers, and receiving such Errors from them, as tend to break the Bands of christian Charity, and to crumble christian Societies and Communities into Sects and Parties; and to lay a Foundation for unchristian Strifes, Divisions, Separations, and Schisms . . . ." Moses Barlett, *False and Seducing Teachers* 46 (1757) (Evans 7842).

[151] E.g., in Massachusetts, Zabdiel Adams defended the supposedly equal support for Protestant denominations as a means of ending dissension: "Nothing gives life and spirit to any corporate body; nothing induces them ["constituents"] to submit to burdens with greater alacrity than to find they are necessary and levied in equal proportions." Zabdiel Adams, *A Sermon* 29 (Mass election sermon [1782]) (Evans 17450). In Virginia, petitioners for an equal establishment of Christians argued "That a System of Worship Simple Pure & Tolerant Formed On the Broad Basis of Gospel Liberty & Christian Charity—Divested of past Prejudices & Bigotry—And Dictated by a true Catholick Spirit would meet with a General Acceptance and Approbation. . . . No Proud or lordly Prelate, No bigoted Presbytery can Awe your Deliberations: . . . That you may Form such a System as may Reconcile all those Petty Jars & truifling Differences which . . . have hitherto so unhappily Divided the Protestants Amonst us. . . . promote an Happy Union by Comprehending All the Sincere & pious Christians of every Denomination at present Among us . . . lay a Foundation for the Exercise of Christian Love . . . and exhibit such a Spectacle to the Wondering World as hath not appear[e]d since the first Ages of Christianity." Petition of Sundry Inhabitants of the County of Amherst (Nov 27, 1783), Va State Library, Mfm of Misc Ms 425. In Connecticut, Benjamin Lord used such arguments on behalf of equal protection. See text at note 81. More generally, Governor Wolcott of Connecticut wrote that "the late Bishop of London was of Opinion, that the Religious State of this Country is founded upon an equal Liberty of all Protestants; none can claim a national Establishment, nor any Superiority over the rest. . . . as far as I can know anything about it, this Government is of the Same opinion & that this is the best Foundation of Love & Peace. [Y]et it is certain the Charter grants us a Power to govern the People religiously," which he thought meant "a Power to Set up the Gospel & Support it & to oblige the people to attend the Publick ordinance of it . . . ." Roger Wolcott to E. Punderson (Jan 30, 1752), *The Wolcott Papers* 145 (1916).

> or colony. For consider persons in different professions, finding
> themselves favoured with an equal share of liberty, with the
> rest of their neighbors, and fellow subjects, it will in my opin-
> ion have a natural tendency to knit their affections, and dutiful
> regard to their rulers, stronger, if it can be, than if they was
> all of one opinion in religion. . . . [152]

Indeed,

> instead of the colony's being ruined by enacting full and free
> liberty of conscience, it is the most likely, if not the only rem-
> edy to save it from confusion, and final ruin: for such a liberty
> has a natural tendency to unite all parties in good neighbor-
> hood, to strive together in all civil things for the good of the
> whole civil body, and the contrary for its ruin.[153]

According to Frothingham and many other dissenters, only "an
equal share of liberty" could unify a diverse society.[154]

---

[152] Ebenezer Frothingham, *A Key to Unlock the Door* 155–56 (1767) (Evans 10621)."[N]ow
for civil rulers to set up and establish the sect that pleases them, and deprive all the rest of
their equal share of liberty, and force their neighbours to go against the light of their
consciences, . . . Sure I am, that nothing is more likely to alienate good subjects from due
affection, and dutiful regard to their civil rulers, than such a practice; . . ." Id at 156.

[153] Id at 159.

[154] E.g.: "Upon Trial it hath been found that where Ministers have been settled by the
Power of the established Constitution, in many Instances it hath occasioned warm Debates,
Divisions, and Separations unavoidably. . . ." Strict Congregational Churches in Connecticut, *An Historical Narrative* 15 (1781) (Evans 17115). "It is inequality that excites jealousy
and dissatisfaction." William Tennent, *Mr. William Tennent's Speech on the Dissenting Petition*
19 (1777) (Evans 15612). In Virginia, some Presbyterians petitioned that by removing unequal civil rights with respect to religion, the legislature "will remove every real ground of
contention, and allay every jealous commotion on the score of religion." Memorial of the
Presbytery of Hanover to the General Assembly (May 1784), in *American State Papers* 105.
Baptists urged "the Expediency of removing the Ground of Animosity, which will remain
while Preference is given, or particular Favours are granted in our Laws to any particular
Religious Demoninations." Memorial of the Baptist Association (June 3, 1782), Va State
Library, Mfm of Misc Ms 425. Baptists expressed their "hope . . . that no Species of religious
Oppression may remain to . . . alienate the Affections of the different Denominations
from each other." Address of the Ministers and Messengers of the Churches of the Baptist
Denomination Associated in Amelia County, May 12, 1783 (May 31, 1783), Va State Library, Mfm of Misc Ms 425. Dissenters argued that if "every Religious Denomination"
were "on a Level," then "animosities may cease." Petition of Dissenters (Oct 16, 1776) (the
so-called "Ten-Thousand Name" Petition"), Va State Library, Mfm of Misc Ms 425.
Charles Carroll—a Catholic—wrote that "were an unlimited toleration allowed and men of
all sects were to converse freely with each other, their aversion from difference of religious
principles would soon wear away." Charles Carroll, letter to Edmund Jennings, Aug 13,
1767, in *Unpublished Letters of Charles Carroll of Carrollton* 143, Thomas M. Field, ed (U.S.
Catholic Historical Soc, 1902). A sympathetic establishment minister preached: "With respect to articles of faith or modes of worship, civil authority have no right to establish
religion. The people ought to choose their own ministers, and their own denomination, as

Λ prominent Baptist minister, Samuel Stillman, not only argued that legal equality was the means to achieve unity amid diversity but also that unequal law was the cause of a diversity of interests. Like other dissenters who attacked establishments by demanding greater equality, Samuel Stillman accepted the common eighteenth-century assumption that "[u]nion in the state is of absolute necessity to its happiness" and that this unity was something "the magistrate will study to promote." Like other dissenters, he argued that unity would exist only under a plan of "a *just and equal treatment of all of the citizens*":

> For though christians may contend amongst themselves about their religious differences, they will all unite to promote the good of the community, because it is their interest, so long as

---

our laws now permit them; but as far as religion is connected with the morals of the people, and their improvement in knowledge, it becomes of great importance to the state; and legislators may well consider it as part of their concern for the public welfare, to make provision that all the towns may be furnished with good teachers . . . . Perhaps a little addition to the law already in force in this state might sufficiently secure the continuance of religious instruction, enlarge rather than diminish liberty of conscience, and prevent envyings, contentions, and crumbling into parties." Samuel Langdon, *A Sermon* 47–48 (NH election sermon 1788) (Evans 21192). See also Nathaniel Ward, *The Simple Cobler of Aggawam in America*, in Clarence L. Ver Steeg & Richard Hofstadter, eds, *Great Issues in American History* 207 (1969).

Sometimes such views about equality were associated with arguments that diversity would create a competition for virtue among sects. Concerned that other sects feared Presbyterians, the Synod of New York and Philadelphia declared in a Pastoral Letter: "No denomination of Christians among us have any reason to fear oppression or restraint, or any power to oppress others. We therefore recommend charity, forbearance, and mutual service. Let the great and only strife be who shall love the Redeemer most, and who shall serve him with greatest zeal." *A Pastoral Letter from the Synod of New York and Philadelphia . . . May 24, 1783* ([1783]) (Evans 44445). Jefferson wrote: "Difference of opinion is advantageous in religion. The several sects perform the office of a Censor morum over each other." Thomas Jefferson, *Notes on the State of Virginia* Query XVII, at 198–99, Paul L. Ford, ed (1894). According to a New Hampshire Anglican, ". . . let us beware of infidelity and Laodicean indifference; and show our gratitude to God and our country, and prove our love to religion and its professors, by each living up to the rules and professions of his own order; and the emulation be, who shall best know, defend, and practice the truth." John C. Ogden, *A Sermon* 18 (NH election sermon 1790) (Evans 22747). See also note 158.

In response to dissenters' demand for an equality of privileges, Warburton had argued that a complete equality was a danger to the state, because sects would struggle for supremacy. William Warburton, *Alliance Between Church and State*, in Warburton, 7 *Works* 99–100. Similarly, after arguing that the established church "has shewn no Disposition to restrain [dissenters] in the Exercise of their Religion," some of the established clergy in Virginia argued that "[t]hey cannot suppose, should all Denominations of Christians be placed upon a Level, that this Equality will continue, or that no Attempt will be made by any Sect for the Superiority; & they foresee that much Confusion, probably civil Commotions, will attend the Contest." Memorial of a Considerable Number of the Clergy of the Established Church in Virginia (Nov 8, 1776), Va State Library, Mfm of Misc Ms 425.

they all enjoy the blessings of a free, and equal administration of government.[155]

Extending this analysis, that equal treatment could produce a unity of interests, Stillman drew the even more dramatic conclusion that unequal rights were what created a division of interests:

> [I]f the magistrate destroys the equality of the subjects of the state on account of religion, he violates a fundamental principle of a free government, establishes separate interests in it, and lays a foundation for disaffection to rulers, and endless quarrels among the people.[156]

According to Stillman, legal inequalities created "separate interests."[157]

---

[155] Samuel Stillman, *A Sermon* 30 (Mass election sermon 1779) (Evans 16537). In the election sermon of the previous year, Phillips Payson had argued that "[t]he variety and freedom of opinion is apt to check the union of a free state." Phillips Payson, *A Sermon* 22 (Mass election sermon 1778) (Evans 15956).

[156] Id. He continued: "Happy are the inhabitants of that commonwealth, in which every man sits under his vine and fig-tree, having none to make him afraid.—In which all are *protected*, but none *established*." Id at 30.

[157] Stillman made explicit what was at least suggested by the writings of many others. E.g., in Virginia, Baptists said that, by neglecting to remove injustices, the legislature "does but increase suspicion and disaffection." Memorial of the Baptist Association met at Noels Meeting House, May 8, 1784 (May 26, 1784), Va State Library, Mfm of Misc Ms 425. It also was argued that "when one is by law exalted to dominion above the rest, this lays the foundation of envy, and debate, and emulation, and wrath, and discord, and confusion; if not of war, bloodshed, and slaughter, in the end:—Being all indulged alike, as children of the same family (though differing in size, feature, complexion, &c.) what cause can they have to quarrel with one another?" *The Freeman's Remonstrance Against an Ecclesiastical Establishment . . . By a Freeman of Virginia* 5 (1777) (Evans 43750).

Incidentally, the "Freeman" was not the only dissenter to make the argument about differences of size or complexion. See, e.g., William Tennent, *Mr. Tennent's Speech, on the Dissenting Petition* 7–8 (1777) (Evans 15612). In New England it was written that: "'It is great pity, . . . as charity is our distinguishing mark as christians, that we exercise it much less in religion, than in the common affairs of life. Agreeable to which, says an author, I do not believe that there are two men upon earth who think exactly alike upon every subject; and yet our different tastes in meat, drink, building and dress make not the least difference in humans society; nor is it likely that they ever will, unless we establish by law, and tack preferments to one particular mode of eating, drinking, building and dressing . . . .'" *Some Remarks upon Mr. President Clap's History* 56–57 (1757) (Evans 7881), as quoted by Isaac Foster, *A Defence of Religious Liberty* 184 (1780) (Evans 16775). See also Isaac Watts, *A New Essay on Civil Power in Things Sacred*, in 6 *Works of . . . Isaac Watts* 42 (1811); Jefferson as quoted in note 158.

Nor was the warning about potential bloodshed unique. E.g., in 1794, in response to a statute that used the proceeds from the sale of western lands to support Christian sects, Connecticut's Baptists met in Hartford during the meeting of the next General Assembly and declared that they were prepared "to shed their blood" on behalf of their liberty. Ezra H. Gillett, *Historical Sketch of the Cause of Civil Liberty in Connecticut, 1639–1818*, 4 Historical Magazine 28 (2nd Ser, July 1868) (citing interview with participant in 1794 meeting).

Just as dissenters viewed diversity and equal civil rights as compatible with the unity of society, so establishment clergymen perceived the unity of society in a way that reflected their distress about religious differences and their conviction that establishment was a means of producing rather than destroying harmony. Establishment clergymen emphasized, among other things, the need for Christian charity. In conjunction with their arguments for equal civil rights, various dissenters had urged a tolerance of religious differences,[158] but members of establishments turned this theme against them. Particularly after conceding what they thought a generous degree of equality,[159] many establishment clergymen felt that the strident self-righteousness and contentiousness of dissenters was unseemly at best. They exhorted dissenters to be more humble, charitable, tolerant, and, in these senses, more Christian.[160]

---

[158] Stillman urged establishments to accept the inevitability of diversity: "In fine. Seeing the body of christians, however divided into sects and parties, 'are entitled precisely to the same rights,' it becomes them to rest contented with that equal condition, nor to wish for pre-eminence. Rather they should rejoice to see all men as free, and as happy as themselves. [new ¶] They should study to imbibe more of the spirit of their divine Master, to love as brethren, and to preserve the unity of the spirit in the bonds of peace. In the present state of ignorance and prejudice, they cannot expect to see eye to eye. There will be a variety of opinions and modes of worship among the disciples of the same Lord; men equally honest, pious, and sensible, while they remain in this world of imperfection. Let them therefore be faithful to their respective principles, and kind, and forbearing towards one another." Samuel Stillman, *A Sermon* 37–38 (Mass election sermon 1779) (Evans 16537). From a rather different perspective, Thomas Paine described the diversity of sects as a test of Christian kindness: "it is the will of the Almighty, that there should be diversity of religious opinions among us: It affords a larger field for our christian kindness. Were we all of one way of thinking, our religious dispositions would want matter for probation; and on this liberal principle, I look on the various denominations among us, to be like children of the same family, differing only, in what is called their Christian names." Paine, *Common Sense* 109. Jefferson asked: "But is uniformity of opinion desireable? Nor more than of face and stature." T. Jefferson, *Notes on the State of Virginia* 198, ed Paul L. Ford (1894).

Incidentally, note that, at Harvard, in 1784, Isaias-Lewis Green argued affirmatively on the question: "An diversitas opinionum, inter homines, ad felicitatem corum [copy defective]." Harvard University, *Quaestiones Sub Reverendo Josepho Willard* (1784). Nathan Read argued affirmatively on the question: "An tolerantia cujusque religionis ad veram religionem promovendam tendat." Id.

[159] Although an attempt to preserve unequal privileges, the establishment of Christianity or, at least, Protestantism in various states was also a tangible manifestation of establishment latitudinarianism.

[160] E.g.: "It is however greatly to be lamented that there is not a more catholick and comprehensive spirit among different denominations of christians. Bigotry and censoriousness sour the temper and interrupt the happiness of society. . . . among people of knowledge, though of different communions, a harmonious intercourse commonly takes place. With madmen and enthusiasts there can be no agreement, except among people as distracted as themselves." Zabdiel Adams, *A Sermon* 42 (Mass election sermon [1782]) (Evans 17450).

Some of the establishment clergy who pleaded for charity and moderation in disputes among Christians suggested that legal equality—whether equal protection or equal civil rights—could not, by itself, harmonize the conflicting interests and passions of diverse sects. Whereas Stillman and other dissenters tended to emphasize that individuals "cannot expect to see eye to eye" and that they therefore should "be faithful to their respective principles, and kind, and forbearing toward one another,"[161] some establishment clergy declared their hopes for an amelioration of differences among Christians.[162] They urged their fellow Christians to accept

---

According to Ezra Stiles, religious denominations, having "no superiority as to secular powers and civil immunities, they will cohabit together in harmony, and I hope, with a most generous catholicism and benevolence. The example of a friendly cohabitation of all sects in america, proving that men may be good members of civil society, and yet differ in religion." Ezra Stiles, *The United States Elevated to Glory and Honor* 55 (Conn election sermon 1783) (Evans 18198). Speaking of religious disputes among "people who before lived in harmony," Jonathan Boucher—a loyalist and a relatively tolerant Anglican—preached that, "though religious disputes ought, of all others, to be carried on with good temper and mildness, they seem, as conducted by these persons, apt to excite bitterness and rancour." Jonathan Boucher, "On Schisms and Sects" (1769), in *A View of the Causes and Consequences of the American Revolution* 81 (1797). He also noted that, "[a]gainst the ministers of the established Church their censures are particularly sharp and severe." Id at 82. (This was preached in various places, including "once (not in any church, but *sub dio*) in the Back Woods, near the Blue Ridge." Id at 46, n.)

[161] See note 158.

[162] Of course, they assumed that sects other than their own required moderation. Zabdiel Adams hoped the diversity of sects would ameliorate fanaticism: "If coercion would bring mankind to a uniformity of sentiment, no advantage would result therefrom. It is on the contrary best to have different sects and denominations live in the same societies. They are a mutual *check* and *spy* upon each other, and become more attentive to their principles and practice. Hence it has been observed that where *Papists* and *Protestants* live intermingled together, it serves to meliorate them both. The same may be observed of any other sects." Zabdiel Adams, *A Sermon* 41–42 (Mass election sermon [1782]) (Evans 17450). Nathan Strong preached: "If we look thro the christian sectaries, who differ in ceremonies and words, candor will perceive that the greatest number of them unite, in the weighty matters of faith, piety, religion and justice, towards GOD and towards men. A diffusion of knowledge is now advancing a liberal spirit. May the Great Head of the Church hasten the period, when those who think alike, concerning a divine love, justice, faith and truth, may join their hands and hail a future meeting in Heaven, where ceremonies and modes of expression will not separate brethren. Experience hath taught, that tolerancy in these things is the most powerful means of union . . . ." Nathan Strong, *A Sermon* 21 (Conn election sermon 1790) (Evans 22913). For earlier discussions in Massachusetts about Christian unity, see, inter alia, McLoughlin, 1 *New England Dissent* 278–300.

Of course, such sentiments were not confined to establishment writers or New England. Nonetheless, these opinions appear to have had particular appeal to writers who—whether because of their religious traditions or their political circumstances—either did not fear an acknowledgment of unity or, at least, felt the resentment of dissenters. For a Catholic example from Maryland, see John Carroll, Letter to Joseph Berington (July 10, 1784), 1 *John Carroll Papers* 148 (Notre Dame, 1976). For an Anglican example from Virginia, see Petition from Amherst County quoted in note 151.

the unity of their faith—an old theme with which increasing numbers of dissenters did not disagree.

Even without a reconcilation of sectarian differences, some of the establishment clergy urged at least a recognition of America's common Christianity or, even less ambitiously, its common religiosity and morals. They emphasized shared religious values not merely as a means of overcoming sectarian differences but also as a solution to the broader problem of separate or private interests in American society. In Connecticut, for example, the Rev. Nathan Strong eloquently described the varieties of private interests and then preached:

> It is the business of government to hold the balance between them, to check the overbearing and point them to a common good, and for this it needs the assistance of some pervading social bond, and this bond can be no other than religion. . .
>
> In all rational society there needs some cementing principle of the heart, by which the minds who compose it may be united, have one interest, one common good, and one happiness. . . .
>
> Christian love in its comprehension of virtues, is the supreme tie of social connexion.[163]

Strong was not alone. After noting that "a community like ours" was "spread out over such an immense continent, divided by so many local governments, prejudices and interests," the Rev. David Tappan of Massachusetts observed: "A people so circumstanced, can never be firmly and durably united, under one free and popular government, without the strong bands of religious and moral principle, of intelligent and enlarged patriotism."[164] By acknowledging

---

[163] Nathan Strong, *A Sermon* 11–12 (Conn election sermon 1790) (Evans 22913). The preceding passage was as follows: "The great end of political associations is best answered where there is the most perfect union, and those principles are most essential to government, which have the greatest tendency to produce union. The interests of individuals, are by the emergencies of time thrown into many situations. We live with many others whose passions are complicated, various and pointed to their own personal ends. Every lesser district, every family, and individual in the family, hath interests of its own. If these private interests have a supreme influence the utmost evils will ensue." Id at 11.

[164] David Tappan, *A Sermon* 37 (Mass election sermon 1792) (Evans 24481). He disclaimed a desire for establishment. He quoted: "Take away the law-establishment, and religion re-assumes its original benignity. In America a Catholic Priest is a good citizen, a good character, and a good neighbor; an Episcopalian Minister is of the same description; and this proceeds from there being no law-establishment in America." Id at 20. Nonetheless, he thought there was "in many respects, a natural alliance between intelligent, virtuous Magistrates and Ministers, in a free and christian State." Id. For sentiments concerning

the Christianity, religiosity and morals they had in common, these Americans attempted to bind together a vast and variegated nation, and they thereby contributed to the establishment—the voluntary or moral establishment—of a virtuous, religious, and Christian nation.[165] Although developed in New England, "[t]he enormous practical success of the voluntary social establishment reached the farthest corners of the expanding nation; it dominates the Protestant mind in large sections of the nation to this day."[166]

Yet what may have been platitudinous in discussions of the diversity of interests in general was still somewhat controversial with respect to religious divisions. Establishment writers often emphasized the importance of shared values, and they thereby disparaged the necessity of shared rights. By implication, unequal rights were the necessary means of establishing shared values and unity. In

---

republican unity and the role of the people in the Christian polity, see Alan Heimert, *Religion and the American Mind* 540–49 (1966).

[165] Elwyn A. Smith, *The Voluntary Establishment of Religion*, in Elwyn A. Smith, ed, *The Religion of the Republic* 154, 155 (1971); Sydney E. Ahlstrom, 1 *A Religious History of the American People* 463–65 (1975); see also Carol Weisbrod, *Charles Guiteau and the Christian Nation*, 7 J L & Relig 187 (1989). It may be suspected that the idea of a Christian nation was merely a nationalist and Protestant rejection of Catholocism. It appears, however, to have developed, at least in part, as a response to sectarian diversity chiefly among Protestants. Even when discussing a somewhat later period than that considered here, Perry Miller wrote of the attempt by some Americans to make "the voluntary principle . . . a mechanism not of fragmentation but of national cohesion." Perry Miller, *The Life of the Mind in America* 44 (Harcourt Brace 1965). See also id at 70–72.

The clergy who addressed the problems of diverse interests and sects occasionally spoke in terms of common religiosity and morals rather than in terms of a common Christianity. An emphasis on virtue rather than Christianity was more typical of the very frequent assertions in election sermons that nations, Christian or infidel, would be blessed or punished in this world according to their virtue or, in some accounts, according to their conformity to natural religion. This idea could be expressed in terms of a national religion: "Let no man take an alarm as if by a national religion, I would recommend the establishment of any modes or forms in preference to others. . . . By a national religion I would be understood to mean, an acknowledgement of the being, perfections and providence of one supreme GOD; a sense of his moral government both in this and a future State; and a careful observance of the eternal laws of justice, truth and mercy in all our public conduct." Jeremy Belknap, *An Election Sermon* 34 (NH election sermon 1785) (Evans 18927). Of course, nonestablishment clergy could still be worried about the possibility of a national establishment. For example, Abraham Booth of New York said: "If all the subjects of Christ be real saints, it may justly be queried whether any *National religious establishment* can be a part of his kingdom. . . . is it not plain, that a National church is inimical to the spirit of our Lord's declaration. *My kingdom is not of this world?* Does not that . . . saying compel us to view the church and the world in a *contrasted* point of light." Abraham Booth, *An Essay on the Kingdom of Christ* 38–39 (1791).

[166] Elwyn A. Smith, *The Voluntary Establishment of Religion*, in Elwyn A. Smith, ed, *The Religion of the Republic* 154, 156 (1971).

contrast, dissenters frequently argued that equal civil rights would produce harmony among individuals of different religions. Although hardly adverse to a recognition of America's common Christianity, dissenters wanted to preserve their distinctiveness— they wanted to be "faithful to their respective principles"—and therefore they stressed common rights rather than a common Christianity as the means of achieving unity.

Thus, Americans pursued their dispute about religious diversity and different standards of equality within the context of a wider disagreement about harmoniousness and unity in American society. Dissenters and establishments not only formulated standards of equality that preserved their interests and reflected their perspectives on religious diversity but they also sometimes justified their positions concerning equality in terms of the social unity that they said would result from their distinct approaches to diversity. Whereas those who lacked legal equality said unequal civil rights were a source of discord, those who benefited from unequal privileges saw these as the means of establishing the shared religious values that would produce harmony in American society. By making such arguments, which contrasted shared rights to shared values, these Americans seem to have developed—at least for purposes of this dispute—rather different assumptions about what constituted unity and harmony among persons of varied denominations.

In Congregationalist New Hampshire, an Anglican, John Cosens Ogden, optimistically combined the positions of dissenting and establishment writers.[167] He had an interest in equality typical of dissenters, and yet he adhered to the establishment position that an equality of rights alone could not produce harmony. After noting that "[w]e have one common country and kindred to provide for," and, after explaining the political usefulness of piety and moral behavior, he spoke about the significance of a common religion:

---

[167] Similarly, when arguing in the *Federalist* that the states "should never be split into a number of unsocial, jealous, and alien sovereignties," John Jay had found evidence of American unity in sentiments and in rights: "Similar sentiments have hitherto prevailed among all orders and denominations of men among us. To all general purposes, we have uniformly been one people. Each individual citizen everywhere enjoying the same national rights, privileges, and protection." John Jay, *The Federalist* 9 (No 2) (Everyman, 1937). For Jay, the unity of Americans was manifest in their similar sentiments and similar rights.

> A similarity of religion, language, and laws, have ever availed much to spread peace and prosperity: and unless the first binds our hearts in love, and restrains our unruly passions, we shall ever be exposed to confusion and tumult.[168]

What all Christians had in common—Christian sentiment and virtue—were particularly important in a nation in which diverse sects were to be treated equally:

> The preservation of a religious, pure heart, is not less important; but becomes much more so in a country where all religions are most justly tolerated, and ought and are promised to be protected . . . .[169]

He then demanded, as seen in part III, a greater equality of rights for dissenters and reminded his audience that dissenters were "determined to defend and maintain their own privileges."[170] Nonetheless, Ogden also emphasized the importance of a "similarity of religion." He appears to have thought a harmonizing similarity—in particular, "a religious and pure heart"—was possible and even necessary amid the sectarian diversity he defended.

As dissenters sensed their victories, they came to acknowledge the possibility that the nation could be unified by its religious sentiments. Until the New England establishments abandoned their special privileges, their claims that they sought a moral rather than a legal establishment remained suspect, at least within their own states. In the 1790s, however, and especially in the early nineteenth century, as Americans abolished their remaining establishments, they recognized with gratification their voluntary or moral establishment of a Christian nation.[171] They considered themselves blessed by a unity of Protestant sentiment and by an equality of rights—a unity that, although now based on mere sentiment rather than doctrine, was enough to bind Americans together,

---

[168] John C. Ogden, A Sermon 17 (NH election sermon 1790) (Evans 22747).

[169] Id. Of course, it is no coincidence that Ogden was an Anglican.

[170] Id at 18. See text at note 147.

[171] Until the influx of large numbers of Catholics in the nineteenth century, many Americans felt little need to emphasize the Protestant character of their Christian nation. Of course, the growing religious diversity of nineteenth-century America prompted numerous challenges to the establishment of Protestant Christianity—not least to its remaining legal privileges—but this article focuses on the earlier debate that occurred largely among Protestant sects.

and an equality of rights that, by removing the grounds for dissention, allowed Americans to acknowledge their religious unity.

V. AN EPILOGUE CONCERNING EQUAL PROTECTION

Thus far, I have examined the ideas of equal protection and equal civil rights as standards developed by eighteenth-century Americans to address their religious diversity. In the nineteenth century, however, Americans employed the idea of equal protection in connection with racial differences and eventually even adopted that standard in the United States Constitution. They thereby gave that idea a prominence and legal significance that remains with us and that makes any information about equal protection in the nineteenth century seem unusally interesting.

An epilogue to this history of equal protection in the eighteenth century is especially warranted because other histories of equal protection commence their accounts in the 1830s. Equal protection has its origins, we are sometimes told, in Andrew Jackson's 1832 Bank veto.[172] Howard Jay Graham, Jacobus Ten Broek, and others have added that the ideas of protection and equal protection were developed in the antislavery debates of the mid-1830s.[173] In light of the mid-nineteenth-century focus of this older scholarship, two basic questions need to be examined: First, how did nineteenth-century Americans define equal protection? In particular, did they employ an idea of equal protection similar to that used by their predecessors? Second, if nineteenth-century Americans did draw upon the earlier notion of equal protection, how did they come to do so? How did an idea used in eighteenth-century discussions of religious diversity come to play a role in nineteenth-century debates about slavery and eventually in the U.S. Constitution?

---

[172] E.g., J. R. Pole, *The Pursuit of Equality in American History* 146 (U of Calif, 1979).

[173] Howard J. Graham, *The Early Anti-Slavery Background of the Fourteenth Amendment*, in *Everyman's Constitution*; Ten Broek, *Equal Under Law*; William M. Wiecek, *The Sources of Antislavery Constitutionalism in America, 1760–1848* 155 (1977). Professors Earl A. Maltz and Steven J. Heyman have pointed out that the notion of protection was discussed in prior centuries, but they seem to be unaware of the eighteenth-century debates concerning equal protection. Earl A. Maltz, *The Concept of Equal Protection of the Laws—A Historical Inquiry*, 22 San Diego L Rev 501 (1985); Steven J. Heyman, *The First Duty of Government* 41 Duke L J 507 (1991). Raoul Berger was aware of the the equal protection clause in the 1780 Massachusetts Constitution but did not pursue it. Raoul Berger, *Government by Judiciary* 168 (Harvard, 1977) (Berger, "*Government by Judiciary*").

What, then, was the nineteenth-century definition of equal protection? Although the evidence bearing on this question is extensive and requires further study, the materials I have examined suggest the possibility that Americans in the nineteenth century typically defined the idea of equal protection very much as they had in the eighteenth. Of course, historians unaware of the eighteenth-century history of equal protection have not even purported to discuss the relationship between the eighteenth- and the nineteenth-century understandings of that idea, but they have taken positions on various aspects of the meaning of equal protection in the nineteenth century and their views must now be considered.

Howard J. Graham, Jacobus Ten Broek and Steven J. Heyman have argued that the protection involved in the idea of equal protection was a right of individuals to have government protect rights not only by passing laws but also by taking otherwise discretionary actions.[174] In support of their position, these historians point to instances in which Americans argued that they needed police or other executive intervention to "protect" their rights.[175] For example, when abolitionists were beset by mobs, they complained about the failure of the states to apply the laws against murder, arson, and other injurious behavior; they pointed out that, when the victims of popular violence were abolitionists, the law was not enforced, and, therefore, they asked that government provide equal protection of, for example, their right of free speech and press.[176] Some of these instances involved a failure of judicial process—an issue that, as will be discussed below, came to be addressed in terms of equal protection.[177] In other instances, however, abolitionists complained, not about unequal legal restraints, not about a failure of judicial process, but about unequal government intervention to prevent violence or otherwise to enforce legal restraints.[178] So too,

---

[174] Howard J. Graham, *The Early Anti-Slavery Background of the Fourteenth Amendment*, in *Everyman's Constitution* 153; Ten Broek, *Equal Under Law* 21, 51–52; Steven J. Heyman, *The First Duty of Government*, 41 Duke L J 507, 545 (1991).

[175] See, e.g., notes 178 & 180.

[176] E.g., Ten Broek, *Equal Under Law* 37–38. See note 181 & accompanying text.

[177] See text at notes 207–10.

[178] Ten Broek, for example, quotes James G. Birney, who complained of mob violence against abolitionists: "Law has lost its honor; it is in the dust; none do it reverence; its authority to restrain, to punish, to protect, is mocked at." James G. Birney, Letter to Joshua Leavitt and Others (Jan 10, 1842), in Dwight L. Dummond, ed, 2 *Letters of James Gillespie Birney 1831–1857* 653 (Peter Smith, 1966 reprint of 1938 edition), quoted in Ten Broek, *Equal Under Law* 37.

Chancellor Kent identified the "preventive" arm of the government as a "further" form of protection: "While the personal security of every citizen is protected from lawless violence by the arm of government and the terrors of the penal code, and while it is equally guarded from unjust and tyrannical proceedings on the part of the government itself, by the provisions [of constitutions], every person is also entitled to the preventive arm of the magistrate, as a further protection from threatening or impending danger."[179] Tracing a similar usage, Heyman has drawn attention to the 1858 Congressional debates about police forces in the District of Columbia, during which some Congressmen discussed the necessity of police "protection" for life, liberty, and property.[180] Clearly, nineteenth-century Americans sometimes used the term "protection" to refer to their need for executive-branch intervention.

Nonetheless, it should be noted that the abolitionists and others who complained about unequal executive enforcement of the law tended to talk about the necessity of protection or equal protection from government but did not typically demand for themselves equal protection *of the laws* or equal *legal* protection. As noted in Part I, eighteenth-century Americans frequently said that individuals obtained protection for their natural liberty from government. Although they typically focused on protection of the laws for natural rights, their language was not entirely free from ambiguity. On the one hand, many of their discussions indicate that they understood protection for natural liberty to be provided by laws that restrained a portion of it; on the other hand, they often spoke in generalities that permitted protection to be understood more broadly to include government enforcement of such laws. This broader usage of the word "protection" as a term of art in the state-of-nature theory certainly was in accord with the unspecialized or ordinary usage of the word "protection," and, consequently, nineteenth-century writers could easily talk about unequal government enforcement of laws in terms of the obligation of government to provide protection or equal protection. They tended,

---

[179] James Kent, 2 *Commentaries* Pt IV, Lect xxiv, at *15.

[180] Steven J. Heyman, *The First Duty of Government*, 41 Duke L J 507, 544–45 (1991). For example, Heyman quotes Senator Crittenden, who said that Congress had an obligation "to provide for an adequate and efficient police in this city, so as to preserve the peace and secure the lives and property of individuals." Id, quoting *Congressional Globe*, 35th Cong. 1st Sess. 1465 (1858).

however, not to address this problem in terms of equal protection of the laws.[181]

Moreover, Americans who talked about ending slavery by securing "equal protection"—particularly, Americans who sought to end slavery by securing "equal protection of the laws"—were not typically speaking about executive action to enforce laws protecting natural liberty. Although the unequal policing of the laws was the problem of protection that most seriously affected abolitionists in their efforts against slavery, it was hardly the problem of protection that most seriously affected slaves or ex-slaves. Prior to 1868 and (for some purposes) even later, the law itself, not merely the executive enforcement of the law, was what was unequal. As Henry B. Stanton said in 1837, when speaking of domestic relations among slaves, "[t]here is not the shadow of legal protection for the family state among the slaves of the District."[182] In other words, the unequal protection *of the laws* was the more obvious inequality with respect to slavery. Indeed, the equal protection of the laws was one of the things that distinguished free persons from slaves. Northern abolitionists remained free men and women even when deprived of government protection, in the sense of government enforcement of the laws. In contrast, slaves remained slaves even when provided with such protection, for they did not have a more basic type of protection, the equal protection of the laws. It is no coincidence

---

[181] For example, William Goodell sarcastically wrote that "we are generously offered protection on condition that we shall renounce our principles and cease to disseminate them . . . . We are to be protected, not in the enjoyment of our civil and religious liberties as free citizens; but if we will relinquish those rights, then we are to be unmolested in our persons and our property . . . . [New ¶] The protection we ask is a protection different from all this; and it is a protection we supposed we had a right to claim, as free American citizens . . . . the protection most highly appreciated by us, is that which protects the freedom of speech and of the press . . . ." Ten Broek, *Equal Under Law* 38, n 6, quoting *The Emancipator* (July 22, 1834). Lovejoy pleaded to a committee of the people of Alton: "I, Mr. Chairman, have not desired, or asked any compromise. I have asked for nothing but to be protected in my rights as a citizen—rights which God has given men, and which are guaranteed to me by the constitution of my country. . . . the question to be decided is, whether I shall be protected in the exercise and enjoyment of those rights—*that is the question, sir;*—whether my property shall be protected, whether I shall be suffered to go home to my family at night without being assailed, and threatened with tar and feathers, and assassination . . . . " Id, quoting Joseph C. and Owen Lovejoy, *Memoir of the Rev. Elijah Lovejoy; Who Was Murdered in Defence of the Liberty of the Press, at Alton, Illinois* 279–80 (1838). In addition to the abolitionists, note Kent's *Commentaries* and the 1858 police debate quoted in text at notes 179–80. For other illustrations see Ten Broek, *Equal Under Law* 38–39 & notes, and Heyman, *The First Duty of Government*, 41 Duke L J 507, 537–45. Of course, Ten Broek and Heyman take a rather different view of the evidence than is presented here.

[182] Quoted in Ten Broek, *Equal Under Law* 46.

that Stanton recommended that slaves be given equal *legal* protection:

> [T]he slave should be legally protected in life and limb, in his earnings, his family and social relations, and his conscience. To give impartial legal protection in that District, to all its inhabitants would annihilate slavery. Give the slave then, equal legal protection with his master, and at its first approach slavery and the slavery trade flee in panic, as does darkness before the full-orbed moon.[183]

Although abolitionists were often denied equal protection, in the sense of equal government enforcement of the laws protecting their natural rights, slaves were denied the equal protection of the laws, and this was essential to their status as slaves.[184]

Graham, Ten Broek and Heyman also suggest that protection was a particular degree of protection.[185] Yet it was the failure of the idea of protection to indicate any particular degree of protection that made the idea of equal protection so much more precise and so much more useful as a legal standard. In political declarations, some Americans demanded, for example, "complete and ample protection."[186] They had to specify that their protection was to be complete and ample because the word "protection" did not, by itself, necessarily refer to an extensive protection.[187] On the basis of a similar understanding of the word, Southerners sometimes justified their peculiar institution by explaining that their laws afforded protection for each individual—not the same protection for

---

[183] Quoted in Ten Broek, *Equal Under Law* 46–47.

[184] Thus, Birney asked: "What is our object? Liberty . . . . We contend for liberty as she presents herself in the Declaration of American Independence . . . . We struggle for her reception, her installation. We long to see the first work of her reign—the abolition of slavery, and the protection of every human being in the land by just and impartial laws." James G. Birney, letter to Joshua Leavitt and Others (Jan 10, 1842), in Dwight L. Dumond, ed, 2 *Letters of James Gillespie Birney 1831–1857* 645 (Peter Smith, 1966 reprint of 1938 edition). Incidentally, note that abolition and protection by impartial laws was hardly the sum of Birney's goals, but it would be, he thought, the "first" manifestation of liberty.

[185] Howard J. Graham, *The Early Anti-Slavery Background of the Fourteenth Amendment*, in *Everyman's Constitution* 152; Ten Broek, *Equal Under Law* 21, 51–52; Heyman, *The First Duty of Government*, 41 Duke L J 545.

[186] E.g., Democratic Platform, § 4 (1840), in Thomas H. McKee, ed, *The National Conventions and Platforms of All Political Parties 1789–1905* 41 (Friedenwald Co, 1906). This was "complete and ample protection from domestic violence, or foreign aggression." Id.

[187] Even "complete and ample protection" was so imprecise that it was more often employed as a political slogan rather than as a legal standard.

blacks as for whites, but, nonetheless, protection, varying from one class of persons to another according to what was appropriate.[188] Hence, the significance of "equal" protection.[189]

Nineteenth-century Americans tended not even to consider protection, as such, a legally-enforceable right. Many nineteenth-century writers assumed, as was conventional already in the eighteenth century, that civil government and its legal restraints on natural liberty were the means by which individuals obtained protection for their remaining natural liberty and that if government and its laws failed to provide adequate protection, they could be altered by the people. Therefore, when exposed to murder, theft, and other assaults on those portions of their natural liberty that typically were protected by legal restraints, nineteenth-century Americans argued that government should protect them. But this is not to say that nineteenth-century courts enforced this right of protection or that many Americans expected the courts to do so.[190] Graham, Ten Broek, and Heyman have not provided any evidence that Americans typically understood protection to be more than the idea of protection drawn from the state-of-nature analysis—the protection individuals obtained for their natural liberty by sacrificing some of that liberty to government and its laws.

The nineteenth-century idea of equal protection was also similar to that of the eighteenth century in that it concerned an equality of natural liberty protected by civil laws rather than an equality of all legal rights, including privileges. Just as eighteenth-century Americans differentiated between equal protection and equal civil rights, so too, as Professor Maltz has pointed out, nineteenth-century Americans distinguished equal protection from an equality of all legal rights.[191] For example, whereas some opponents of slav-

---

[188] William Sumner Jones, *Pro-Slavery Thought in the Old South* 113–15 (U of NC, 1935); see also Earl M. Maltz, *Fourteenth Amendment Concepts in the Antebellum Era*, 32 Am J Legal Hist 305, 329–31 (1988). Another approach was to say that slaves were not members of civil society. For an early example, see 7 *Revolutionary Virginia* 454, n 16.

[189] Incidentally, both eighteenth- and nineteenth-century sources not infrequently use the phrase "the same protection" as a synonym for "equal protection." This may illuminate the significance of the word "equal" in the latter phrase.

[190] Heyman suggests that protection was a potentially enforceable right but cites no case in which such a claim succeeded. Heyman, *First Duty of Government*, 41 Duke L J 538–41. Instead, he argues, among other things, that statutes, such as the American versions of the English Riot Act of 1714, were what "reaffirmed the community's duty of protection and made it the basis of a legal action." Heyman, 41 Duke L J at 542.

[191] Earl M. Maltz, *Fourteenth Amendment Concepts in the Antebellum Era*, 32 Am J Legal Hist 305, 324; Earl M. Maltz, *The Concept of Equal Protection of the Laws—An Historical*

ery were content to argue for equal protection, others also advocated equal privileges.[192] Of course, free blacks tended to demand equal rights or equal privileges rather than mere equal protection.[193]

Consistent with the claims for equal protection were arguments similarly based on assumptions about the equal freedom of humans in the state of nature. Typical of these related arguments was William Thomas's observation that "[w]e declare that 'all men are born free and equal.' . . . . [W]e can find no difference between black and white, as respects their natural rights."[194] In language as varied as that of William Channing and Abraham Lincoln, Americans frequently spoke of their common humanity and natural freedom.[195] Although not stated in terms of "equal protection," this

---

Inquiry, 22 San Diego L Rev 499, 506–7 (1985). In contrast, most historians of the Fourteenth Amendment largely ignore this distinction. E.g., William E. Nelson, *The Fourteenth Amendment from Political Principle to Judicial Doctrine* (Harvard U, 1988) (Nelson, "*Fourteenth Amendment*").

According to both Graham and Ten Broek, nineteenth-century Americans typically defined equal protection in terms of protection for natural rights, yet both historians apparently attribute to abolitionists a very broad understanding of what constituted natural rights. These historians apparently consider natural rights to have included important privileges in addition to the liberty existing in the state of nature.

Of course, some nineteenth-century Americans adopted definitions of natural liberty that deviated from the conventional version described in the text here. For example, some Americans argued that agency and therefore representation was a natural right, and, subsequently, some opponents of slavery made use of this argument.

[192] See Earl M. Maltz, 22 San Diego L Rev 499, 506 (1985). Of course, defenders of slavery could also use the idea of equal protection. See Ten Broek, *Equal Under Law* 42; Earl M. Maltz, 32 Am J Legal Hist 305, 329–34 (1988). Incidentally, Ten Broek says "slavery and the concomitant discriminations against free Negroes and abolitionists were to be described by abolitionists, as early as 1835, as denials of rights to the equal protection of the laws . . . ." Ten Broek, *Equal Under Law* 34. In fact, the analysis of equal protection was not first applied to the question of slavery in the 1830s, let alone by the abolitionists. For example, see a Fourth of July oration published at Gettysburg, David M'Conaughy, *The Nature and Origin of Civil Liberty* 5–6 (1823).

The 1833 *Declaration of Sentiments of the American Anti-Slavery Society* did not clearly require equality, although it may have been so understood: "Every man has a right to his own body—to the products of his own labor—to the protection of law—and to the common advantages of society." Declaration of Sentiments of the American Anti-Slavery Convention (1833), in William L. Garrison, *Selections from the Writings and Speeches of* . . . 68 (Negro Universities, 1968 reprint of 1852 edition). Note the ambiguity of "common advantages," which left room for some unequal rights. Note also that Garrison was familiar with the use of the idea of equal protection in the context of religious freedom. William L. Garrison, *Penal Observance of the Sabbath*, in id at 101.

[193] See, e.g.: Philip S. Foner & George E. Walker, eds, 1 & 2 *Proceedings of the Black State Conventions, 1840–1865* (Temple U, 1979–80); C. Peter Ripley, ed, 3–5 *The Black Abolitionist Papers* (U of NC, 1991).

[194] Defensor [i.e., William Thomas], *The Enemies of the Constitution Discovered, or An Inquiry into the Origin and Tendency of Popular Violence* 109 (1835).

[195] Charles Edward Merriam observed the contrasting ways in which these and other

type of argument attacked slavery by assuming that all individuals had equal natural rights not only in the state of nature but also under civil government—the same assumption upon which the idea of equal protection was founded. Consequently, the argument about the equal humanity of each individual could easily merge into discussion of equal protection.[196] Thus, William Channing, who gently criticized the extreme measures of abolitionists, wrote of human rights: "The great end of civil society is to secure rights . . . . The community is bound to take the rights of each and all under its guardianship. It must substantiate its claim to universal obedience by redeeming its pledge of universal protection."[197] If all men are equally human, he argued, then the liberty they have as humans—that is, the liberty they have as individuals, independent of government—should be protected by government, regardless of race. Although not an equality of all rights held under civil laws, an equality of natural rights—or, more important for our puposes, an equality of protection for natural rights—would bring slavery to an end.

This very traditional understanding of equal protection as a minimal degree of equality—the equality all persons should have as individuals—is apparent in the debates about the Fourteenth Amendment. In Congress and elsewhere, Americans repeatedly associated equal protection with "life, liberty and property"—these

---

Americans espoused this position, quoting Lincoln as saying that "[t]he Fathers 'did not mean to say all were equal in color, size, intelligence, moral development or social capacity.' What they did mean was that 'all men are equal in the possession of certain inalieable rights among which are life, liberty, and the pursuit of happiness.' " Charles E. Merriam, *A History of American Political Theories* 222 (Kelly, 1969 reprint of 1903 edition), quoting Abraham Lincoln, 1 *Works* 232 (1894). For Channing, see text at note 197.

[196] This is not to say, however, that these arguments were the same or were considered to be equally efficacious. See John Jay's views in note 215.

[197] William E. Channing, *Slavery* 48 (1835). See also id at 17–19, 37, & 39. For his views on abolitionists, see id, ch 7. Note that he thought obedience and protection were reciprocal obligations.

Note also that, by Channing's time, some Americans had altered their vocabulary and spoke of human or personal rights rather than of natural rights. Although not exclusively or even chiefly a historical theory, the state-of-nature analysis was, in the eighteenth century, increasingly questioned for its historical inaccuracy. Some Americans responded to this difficulty by talking about human, individual or personal rights—meaning the rights an individual had as a human or person, independent of civil society and government. Incidentally, they thereby adopted at least one phrase—"personal rights"—already used for other purposes and so managed to avoid an irrelevant historical inaccuracy by employing langugage likely to cause significant analytic confusion.

being well understood as the components of natural liberty.[198] Although, as one might expect, Congressmen and Senators sometimes spoke about equal protection without defining it and sometimes loosely said, without elaboration, that an equal protection clause would provide for equality,[199] their particular examples tended to be consistent with the standard definition of equal protection—with the idea of equal protection of the laws for natural rights.[200] That equal protection concerned natural rights—life, liberty, and property[201] —was the assumption upon which Senator Howard could say: "Is it not time, Mr. President, that we extend to the black man, I had almost called it the poor privilege of the equal protection of the law?"[202] Today, we may, perhaps, regret that our predecessors established in our Constitution only a mininal degree of equality. Yet this should no more surprise us than that, to do so, they first had to fight a civil war.

Alexander Bickel, Alfred H. Kelly, William E. Nelson, Louis H. Pollock and William W. Van Alstyne have emphasized that equal protection of the laws was a vague, amorphous and therefore potentially expansive idea.[203] In taking this position, these scholars have suggested that the indeterminacy of the 1866 understanding of equal protection of the laws permitted judicial development of equal protection doctrine—that the text of the Fourteenth Amendment in effect authorized judicial formation of the requirements of the Equal Protection Clause.[204] Yet, to support their conclusion,

---

[198] Berger, *Government by Judiciary* 169–92; Earl M. Maltz, *Civil Rights, the Constitution and Congress, 1863–1869* 93–120 (U of Kansas, 1990).

[199] For another possible explanation, see note 235.

[200] See, e.g., speech of Senator Howard at *Congressional Globe* 2766 (1866), discussed by Berger, *Government by Judiciary* 174.

[201] Berger, *Government by Judiciary* 166–92; Earl M. Maltz, *Civil Rights, the Constitution and Congress, 1863–1869* 93–120. See also the quotations in Herman Belz, *A New Birth of Freedom* 140–41 (Greenwood, 1976). Belz, however, appears to assume that equal protection was an equality of all non-political rights held against government. Id at 142–43.

[202] *Congressional Globe* 2766 (1866).

[203] Alexander M. Bickel, *The Original Understanding and the Segregation Decision*, 69 Harv L Rev 1, 60–61 (1955); Alfred H. Kelly, *The Fourteenth Amendment Reconsidered: The Segregation Question*, 54 Mich L Rev 1049, 1084–86 (1954); Nelson, *The Fourteenth Amendment* 8, 9, 21 (1988); Louis H. Pollock, *Racial Discrimination and Judicial Integrity: A Reply to Professor Wechsler*, 108 U Pa L Rev 1 (1959); William W. Van Alstyne, *The Fourteenth Amendment, The 'Right' to Vote, and the Understanding of the Thirty-Ninth Congress*, Supreme Court Review 33, 72 (1965).

[204] See note 203. For example, Nelson writes that his history "directs judges to cease

these scholars hardly look beyond the post-Civil War Congressional debates. Kelly, for example, writes that "equal protection had virtually no antecedent legal history."[205] As has been seen, however, the earlier evidence about equal protection is extensive, and it does not suggest the sort of vagueness Bickel, Pollock, Kelly, and others, following them, have claimed. Although Nelson cites various mid-nineteenth-century discussions of equality, he does not even attempt to distinguish among the various different standards of equality Americans may have been discussing. By now it should be clear that Americans claimed more than one type of equality, and that equal protection of the laws cannot simply be lumped together with other standards of equality. Far from being a vague and therefore flexible commitment to equality in general, equal protection of the laws was a specific type of equality, and it was defined with relative precision.[206]

In only one respect did the nineteenth-century definition of equal protection differ from the eighteenth-century definition: In the nineteenth century, the words "equal protection" often referred to the idea of equal *judicial* protection of legal rights. Yet even this usage did not greatly alter the idea of equal protection, which remained a contrast to equal civil rights. Englishmen and Americans had often said that courts should treat individuals equally—that is, with the same process. More generally, they assumed that, although established to protect natural rights, government, including its courts, should protect all rights held under law. In the late eighteenth century, being increasingly familiar with the phrase "equal protection," some Americans began to speak of equal protection by the courts for legal rights—that is, all such rights as a person had under law. This notion of equal protection—equal judi-

---

searching in the amendment's legislative history for specific binding resolutions of the particular issues they face." Nelson, *Fourteenth Amendment* 11. See also text at 242.

[205] Alfred H. Kelly, *The Fourteenth Amendment Reconsidered: The Segregation Question*, 54 Mich L Rev 1049, 1052 (1954). Incidentally, Kelly, who contributed to the NAACP brief in *Brown v Bd. of Ed.*, has subsequently written that it "manipulated history in the best tradition of American advocacy, carefully marshalling every possible scrap of evidence in favor of the desired interpretation and just as carefully doctoring all the evidence to the contrary, either by suppressing it when that seemed plausible, or by distorting it when suppression was not possible." Alfred H. Kelly, *Clio and the Court: An Illicit Love Affair*, Supreme Court Review 119, 144 (1965).

[206] Of course, there is an extensive literature on the ways in which the idea of equality and other, similar ideas can be vague. Particularly elegant is Nelson Goodman, *Seven Strictures on Similarity*, in *Experience and Theory* 19 (U of Mass, 1970).

cial protection for such legal rights as one had—amounted to an equality of process or an equality before the courts. As Maltz has shown, this definition of equal protection was not unusual in mid-nineteenth-century America.[207]

Increasingly, Americans appear to have combined this notion of equal protection by the courts—an equality of process—with the idea of equal protection for natural rights. American advocates of equal protection for natural rights often appear to have assumed an equal protection by the courts. In nineteenth-century America, however, the idea of equal protection by the courts typically concerned an equal protection of all civil rights, whether originally natural or acquired only under government, and Americans sometimes explicitly combined this broad idea of equal judicial protection with the older idea of equal protection for natural rights. Thus, nineteenth-century Americans continued to use the phrase "equal protection" to refer to an equal protection of natural rights,[208] but they also, instead, sometimes used those words to refer to an equality of judicial process[209] or a combination of these two ideas. Incidentally, the phrase "equal protection" was also occasionally used in its ordinary sense rather than as a label for a specific idea about natural rights or about judicial protection.[210] In general, there is

---

[207] Earl M. Maltz, *Fourteenth Amendment Concepts in the Antebellum Era*, 32 Am J Legal Hist 305, 324–25.

[208] The Federal Circuit Court for the District of New Jersey said of a property owner that "he may devote [his property] to whatever purposes he pleases, in which the law protects him equally with any other proprietor." *Bonaparte v Camden & A.R. Co.*, 3 F Cas 821 (Cir Ct NJ 1830) (Fed Case 1,617). When a "negro John Brooks" was charged with disturbing and hindering "the congregation of the African meeting-house in Washington county . . . by cursing and swearing, and loud and profane talking and noise," the Circuit Court for the District of Columbia overruled a motion in arrest of judgment. Among other things, it observed that although it might be said that the Christian religion was not a part of the commmon law, "[e]very religious sect is equally protected by our laws." *US v Brooks*, 24 F Cas 1244 (Cir Ct DC 1834) (Fed Case 14,655).

[209] For an early example, note that, in *Chisholm v Georgia*, Chief Justice Jay said that "by securing individual citizens as well as States, in their respective rights," the extension of the judiciary power of the United States in that case "performs the promise which every free Government makes to every free citizen, of equal justice and protection." *Chisholm v Georgia*, 2 US 419, 479 (1793). This was the equal protection by the courts for such rights as a person had under civil laws. For a much earlier, English example, see John Rogers, *A Vindication of the Civil Establishment of Religion* 83 (1728).

[210] E.g., in Wisconsin, the Democratic members of the 1846 Constitutional Convention resolved in favor of, inter alia, "[e]qual, just, and humane protection to the social rights alike to debtors and creditors." Resolutions (Dec 30, 1846), in Milo M. Quaife, ed, *The Struggle Over Ratification 1846–1847*, 206 (1920).

little difficulty distinguishing the different uses of "equal protection."

Equal protection was not, evidently, a very different idea in the
nineteenth century than it had been in the eighteenth. It required
a type of equality rather than a particular degree of substantive
rights, and the equality it required was an equal protection for
natural rights, plus, occasionally, an equality of judicial process.
Because equal protection did not require an equality of privileges,
it often was contrasted to an equality of all rights. One kind of
equal protection was the equal protection of the laws, and this type
of equal protection did not include a right to executive-branch
intervention. Moreover, in the absence of some constitutional or
other positive law providing a legal right to equal protection,
Americans did not consider the "right" of equal protection legally
enforceable. Although there were other, nonspecialized definitions
of the phrase "equal protection," and although this term was sometimes used imprecisely, the evidence suggests that, in mid-
nineteenth-century America, the phrase "equal protection" could
and, typically, was understood as a term of art in the state-of-
nature analysis with the standard definition described here. It was
this standard definition that Americans appear to have taken for
granted in the 1860s.

If nineteenth-century opponents of slavery employed a notion of
equal protection similar to that used by eighteenth-century Americans in debates about religious liberty, it may be asked how the
idea of equal protection was transmitted to the campaigners against
slavery or, for that matter, to other Americans, such as the champions of the South who claimed equal protection for their natural
right of property. All of these Americans could use the same idea
of equal protection, because they were drawing upon a notion that
had long been part of theoretical discussions about politics and
law. Having employed the idea of equal protection to address their
religious differences, Americans, particularly Federalists, used that
idea beginning c. 1790 to justify differences in acquisitions and
wealth. In so doing, these Americans adopted the idea of equal
protection as part of their general political theory, and they thereby
came to use equal protection as a broadly applicable standard of
equality not tied to any particular characteristic or type of diversity. Consequently, in the 1820s and '30s, when ever-larger numbers of Americans wrestled with the issue of slavery, they could

apply, among other notions of equality, the idea of equal protection.

Like the establishment clergy in the previous decades, Federalists in the 1790s sought to stave off demands for equal rights, and one of the ways they could do so was by promoting the alternative type of equality, equal protection, which they, among others, had discussed in connection with religious liberty.[211] Unlike the establishment clergy, however, these Federalist advocates of equal protection were less concerned about the preservation of unequal privileges than about the possibility that, under the guise of "equal rights," government would, in fact, provide inadequate or unequal protection. Federalists particularly feared the notion of equal rights when it was associated with demands for equal political rights or was asserted as the basis for an equalization of property. To be precise, they suspected that "French"-style equal rights would lead to severe and even, perhaps, unequal restraints on property or other natural rights,[212] and they tended to employ the idea of equal protection as a defense against this leveling egalitarianism. They emphasized that government was designed to protect natural liberty equally and extensively—leaving individuals to pursue their natural liberty according to their various unequal talents and circumstances.[213] For example, after descanting on the different re-

---

[211] In some states, Federalists were closely associated with the religious establishments. Of course, although Federalists in the 1790s found the idea of equal protection particularly useful for some of their arguments, it is not suggested that they were the only persons who found the idea attractive. The idea reflected commonly held assumptions. Incidentally, note that one Anti-Federalist said he favored "the peaceable and equal participation in the rights of nature." "A Columbian Patriot," Observations on the New Constitution and on the Federal and State Conventions (1788), 4 *Complete Anti-Federalist* 274.

[212] The alternative possibility, that government would attempt to equalize the condition of individuals by providing either massive or unequal benefits, was not frequently even considered. Warburton wrote that "*society could not* reward, *though it should* discover *the objects of its favour;* the reason is, because no society can ever find a fund sufficient for that purpose, without raising it on the people as a tax, to pay it back to them as a reward." William Warburton, *Alliance Between Church and State*, in Warburton, 7 *Works* 35. In a similar vein, James Witherspoon told his classes at Princeton: "It has been often said, that government is carried on by rewards and punishments; but it ought to be observed, that the only reward that a state can be supposed to bestow upon good subjects in general is protection and defence. Some few, who have distinguished themselves in the public service, may be distinguished by particular rewards; but to reward the whole is impossible, because the reward must be levied from those very persons to whom it is to be given." Witherspoon, *Lectures*, Lect XII, at 141.

[213] This aspect of Federalist thought was not always discussed in terms of "equal protection." For example, in *Federalist* No 10, Madison discussed protection, but his approach to the factionalism caused by inequality did not rely upon a simple legal requirement, such as

wards men would reap on account of their unequal talents,[214] Zephaniah Swift—the future Chief Justice of Connecticut—insisted
that "[w]hether men possess the greatest, or the smallest talents,
they have equal claims to protection, and security in their exertions, and acquisitions."[215]

By applying the notion of equal protection to differences other
than those of religion, Federalists popularized an understanding
that the idea of equal protection concerned differences in general.
Already in the seventeenth century, it had been argued that "every
man" should be "alike protected in the enjoyment of propriety and
exercise of honest Industry."[216] At least some Federalists appear to
have been aware of such generalized discussions of equal protection

---

equal protection. When speaking of "men in society, previous to civil government," Wilson
discussed "the laws of God and nature" and said that, "[b]y these laws, rights, natural
or acquired [i.e., acquired before establishment of government—more commonly called
'adventitious rights'], are confirmed, in the same manner, to all; to the weak and artless,
their small acquisitions, as well as to the strong and artful, their large ones. If much labor
employed entitles the active to great possessions, the indolent have a right, equally sacred,
to the little possessions, which they occupy and improve." James Wilson, *The Works of James
Wilson*, 241, Robert G. McCloskey, ed (Belknap, 1967). (Incidentally, in examining this
passage, Professor Jenifer Nedelsky appears to be of the opinion that it concerned the laws
of civil government. Jenifer Nedelsky, *Private Property and the Limits of American Constitutionalism* 105.) Although the approach described here was typically employed by Federalists, it
was also used by others. See, e.g., "Federal Farmer," 2 *Complete Anti-Federalist* 261. For an
early antecedent, see Thomas Hobbes, *Philosophical Rudiments Concerning Government and
Society*, Of Dominion, ch xiii, § 11 in 2 *Works* 174, ed William Molesworth (1841).

[214] "Men at their birth are all vested with equal rights, but are endowed with unequal
powers. There is a great difference between their intellectual, as well as corporeal faculties,
which is the origin of the inequality of mankind. . . . The man who possesses uncommon
talents for accumulating property, will grow rich, while the opposite character, with equal
advantages will remain poor. Those who are blest with the powers of eloquence . . . . will
acquire a fame that cannot be reached by men of moderate capacity. . . ." Zephaniah Swift,
1 *A System of the Laws of the State of Connecticut* 17 (1795).

[215] Id. For his discussion of religious liberty, see id at 144. Chief Justice John Jay distinguished equal protection from the protection and equal rights declared in bills of rights. It
will be recalled that many state constitutions contained, typically in their bills of rights,
statements that all men had equal liberty or rights in the state of nature and that governemnt
was established to protect such liberty. In a charge to a grand jury, Jay argued that such
declarations were not, by themselves, adequate: "It is not sufficient to tell men by a Bill of
Rights, that they are free, that they have equal Rights, and that they are entitled to be
protected in them—men will not believe they are really free, while they experience oppression—they will not think their title to equal Rights, realized, until, they enjoy them; nor
will they esteem that a good Government, whatever may be its Name, which does not
uniformly, impartially and effectually protect them." John Jay, Charge to the Grand Jury
of the Circuit Court for the District of Virginia, May 22, 1793, 2 *Documentary History of the
Supreme Court* 390.

[216] *Englands Safety in the Laws Supremacy* 5 (1659).

and of related early debates about monopolies, and Federalists now used the concept of equal protection in a similarly generalized way.

A particularly lengthy and elegant example of the Federalist approach to equal protection may be taken from an anonymous essay on equality published in 1804 in the *Connecticut Courant*. It is somewhat atypical (though hardly unusual) for its association of equal protection with the idea of equal or equitable laws—that is, laws that were not partial to separate or private interests. Whereas the idea of equal protection (or, for that matter, equal civil rights) was familiar from a controversy in which equality was demanded with respect to a particular characteristic—religion—the notion of equal laws had long been discussed with regard to the full variety of interests in society. In other words, for a long time, Americans had associated equal protection with religious differences and had associated equal laws with the problem of differing interests in general. Thus, the *Courant*'s essayist may have been inclined to draw upon the idea of equal or equitable laws precisely because he was elucidating equal protection as an idea concerning differences in general. Otherwise, however, he was orthodox in his argument that inequality was inevitable and that equal protection left individuals with an equal and very extensive degree of natural freedom.

The essayist began his analysis by noting that republican laws should recognize the rights of human nature without partiality. All men, according to the Courant,

> have equally a right to the gifts of nature and to all their honest acquirements, whether of learning or property, and to enjoy, or in any wise appropriate the fruits of their industry as they themselves may deem proper. . . . These rights of human nature, which, under arbitrary governments, are either withheld or granted with a partial hand, are recognized expressly or virtually by those republics which acknowledge the people to be the source of power. While such free republics continue pure, they are constantly making a *practical* acknowledgement of the equal rights of human nature by the equity of their laws and the impartiality of their courts of justice; meting the same measure to the rich and poor, protecting good citizens and punishing evil doers, without any respect of persons.[217]

---

[217] *Dissertations on the Deceptive Arts of Demagogues* No 7 (concerning equality), in 40 Conn Courant, No 20, p 1 (Sept 19, 1804).

This "equity" or nonpartiality of law with respect to the rights of human nature was compatible with the natural inequality or differences of humans:

> In various other respects, men are created *unequal*, and by the improvement, the neglect, and the misimprovement of their talents, as well as by innumerable providential occurrences, the native inequalities between them are further diversified and considerably increased. . . . This order of nature tends to effect a necessary degree of subordination and at the same time, so to diversify the occupations and pursuits of men as to promote the general interests of society. . . . Yet, [even] if all men were equal in the gifts of nature, in their educations, and in their industry and prudence, there still would be great inequalities in their circumstances, effected by causes hidden from their sight and beyond their controul.[218]

Thus, individuals were unavoidably unequal both in their abilities and in their circumstances. By protecting individuals equally or nonpartially in their natural freedom, republican laws left individuals free to pursue their own interests and to make the best of their varied abilities and circumstances:

> Now amidst all the diversity of human talents, amid the constantly shifting circumstances of men living under a free government when every one has the power of self-direction as to the improvement of his talents and the pursuits of life, *the true republican equality* consists in the whole body politic guarding with the same care all its members, by enacting equitable [i.e., nonpartial] laws and executing those laws with strict impartiality. This kind of equality is practicable and salutary; . . . it is the great spur to general industry, and is a spring of life to a free commonwealth. In such a state of things, the rich and the poor are equally protected in their persons and reputations, in their honest acquisitions and in all their rights; and they are at liberty to employ for their own benefit the faculties which have been given them by the God of nature.[219]

According to the *Courant*'s essayist, equal protection permitted and was the means of attaining a high degree of individual liberty in civil society. With equal protection, Federalists thought they could reconcile equality and individual freedom, and therefore they made

---

[218] Id.

[219] Id.

that idea their egalitarian response to the demands for equality that appeared to portend an equalization of condition.[220]

---

[220] A few other illustrations may be useful. Supreme Court Justice William Cushing charged a grand jury: "The great end of government, you know, is peace and protection; peace with nations, protection against foreign force:—peace and order within; protection of individuals, of all classes of men, whether poor or rich, in the undisturbed enjoyment of their just rights, which are comprehended under a few, but important words—*security of person and property*, or, if you please, *rights of man*." William Cushing, Charge to the Grand Jury of the Circuit Court for the District of Rhode Island (Nov 7, 1794), in 2 *Documentary History of the Supreme Court* 491. He also said that: "Where people are not permitted to enjoy these blessings, *security of person and property*, unmolested, there is tyranny, whether it arises from monarchy, aristocracy, or a mob. Where all men are equally and promptly protected in the free exercise of these rights, there is liberty and equality;—liberty, to do whatever just laws made by a free respresentative allow; equality, that is, as to right of protection respecting the great objects of life, liberty and property, when not forfeited to the state by criminal conduct; respecting property, which a man has fairly and honestly obtained—not that which is unrighteously taken or forced from another;—not equality in regard to quantity; for that seldom, if ever, can happen, owing, under providence, to the infinitely various faculties and diligence of different individuals;—not a right for the indolent to rob the laborious—to share equally the fruits of the virtuous industry of others; such ideas being founded in extravagance of enthusiasm and delusion, or in downright dishonesty and depravity of mind—subversive of the first principles of justice, and the great ends of society." Id at 492. In response to the idea of "equality," Jonathan Maxcy wrote: "When the road to acquisition is equally open to all—when the laws equally protect every man's person and property—all men will not make exertions equally great—all will not possess the same spirit of enterprize—all will not obtain accession of wealth, of learning, virtue and honour, equally extensive and important. . . . That men in the social state are equal as to certain rights—that they ought to be protected in their persons and property, while they conduct [themselves] as good citizens, will undoubtedly be admitted. This, however, is a very different kind of equality from that which the promulgers of this pernicious doctrine [of equality] intended to introduce." Jonathan Maxcy, *An Oration* (1799), in 2 *American Political Writing* 1048. According to Noah Webster, "That one man in a state, has as good a right as another to his life, limbs, reputation and property, is a proposition that no man will dispute. Nor will it be denied that each member of society, who has not forfeited his claims by misconduct, has an equal right to protection. But if by *equality*, writers understand an equal right to distinction, and influence; or if they understand an equal share of talents and bodily powers; in these senses all men are *not* equal." Noah Webster, *An Oration on the Anniversary of the Declaration of Independence* (1802), in 2 *American Political Writing* 1229. According to Timothy Ford, "To what then does this term equality relate? I will answer in the words of the French constitution; 'men are born and always continue free, and equal in respect of *their rights*.' Thus, my personal liberty is equal to that of any other man; my life is *equally* sacred and inviolable, my bodily powers are *equally* my own; my power over my own actions is *equally* great and *equally* secured from external restraint; my will is *equally* free; what I acquire, be it greater or less, I have an *equal* right to possess, to use and to enjoy. I have an equal claim upon the protection of the laws; an *equal* right to serve my country, and an *equal* claim to be exempted from service. . . ." "Americanus" [i.e., Timothy Ford], *The Constitutionalist* (1794), in 2 *American Political Writing* 930. For the significance of Ford's use of the phrase "personal liberty," see note 197. Responding to claims for equalization of property and of political rights, Fisher Ames wrote: "The philosophers among the democrats will no doubt insist that they do not mean to equalize property, they contend only for an equality of rights. If they restrict the word equality as carefully as they ought, it will not import that all men have an equal right to all things, but, that to whatever they have a right, it is as much to be protected and provided for as the right of any persons in society. In this sense nobody will contest their claim. . . . [new ¶] As the common law secures equally all the rights of the citizens, and as the jacobin leaders loudly decry this system, it is obvious that

In connection with their argument that equal protection was the sort of equality desireable under a free government, Federalists sometimes modified the standard description of the purpose of government so that it incorporated the notion of equal protection. For example, in a charge to a grand jury, John Jay said that "impartially to give Security & Protection to all" was "among the most important Objects of a *free* Government."[221] The end of government, once described simply as the protection of life, liberty, and property for every individual, increasingly could be described as "the equal protection of life, liberty, and property, to every individual."[222] By the middle of the nineteenth century, some state constitutions had declared of the "people" that "Government is instituted for their equal protection and benefit."[223]

Eventually, Americans used the notion of equal protection not only to define the purpose of republican government but also to define "civil liberty." Increasingly, during the eighteenth century, Americans described liberty or civil liberty as the natural liberty enjoyed under civil laws. Americans were educated in the assumption that civil government was instituted to protect natural liberty,

---

they extend their views still farther. . . . Am I then to have, in the new order of things, an equal right with you? Certainly not, every democrat of any understanding will reply. What then do you propose by your equality? You have earned an estate; I have not; yet I have a right, and as good a right as another man, to earn it. I may save my earnings and deny myself the pleasures and comforts of life till I have laid up a competent sum to provide for my infirmity and old age. All cannot be rich, but all have a right to make the attempt; and when some have fully succeeded, and others partially, and others not at all, the several states in which they then find themselves become their condition in life; and whatever the rights of that condition may be, they are to be faithfully secured by the laws and government. This, however, is not the idea of the men of the new order of things, . . ." Fisher Ames, *Equality* II, in The Palladium (Nov 20, 1801), in 1 *Works of Fisher Ames* 240–42, William B. Allen, ed (Liberty Classics, 1983). See also Nathaniel Chipman, *Sketches of the Principles of Government* 177–82 (1793). Of course, some of the individuals who used this analysis were not strictly Federalists.

[221] John Jay, Charge to the Grand Jury of the Circuit Court for the District of Virginia, May 22, 1793, 2 *Documentary History of the Supreme Court* 381.

[222] *Constitutional History*, 29 North Am Rev. 265, 280 (1829). A Connecticut minister argued: "The end of government is the general happiness. It is not that a few may riot in affluence at the expense of the rest; but that all may enjoy equal security and liberty." Joseph Lathrop, *The Happiness of a Free Government and the Means of Preserving It* 10 (July 4th sermon 1794) (Evans 27200). In 1828, South Carolina protested against the tariff that its unequal and oppressive operation was "incompatible with the principles of a free government and the great ends of civil society, justice, and equality of rights and protection." SC Protest Against the Tariff, Dec. 19, 1828, in Richard Hofstadter, ed, *Great Issues in American History* 277 (1958).

[223] Ohio Const of 1851, Art 1, § 2; Kan Const of 1855, Art 1, § 2. The latter was the anti-slavery constitution produced in Topeka.

and therefore they could easily conclude that civil liberty was the natural liberty held under the laws of civil government.[224] Indeed, some of them may have found this narrow definition of civil liberty a convenient response to the growing demands for equal civil rights. In a variant of this definition of civil liberty, Americans described civil liberty as the largest possible degree of natural freedom held under civil laws—not a particular set of civil rights, but rather, more generally, the character of the liberty desirable under civil government and its laws. In the terse phrase of an anonymous pamphleteer, "Civil liberty is the exemption from useless restraint."[225] Of course, such a notion of civil liberty could be defined in terms of protection. For example, a Federalist wrote that "[w]hen people enter into society, they must, in order to obtain protection, give up some part of their natural liberty, in order to secure the rest—the more we retain in our hands, consistent with that protection, which is necessary for society, will be so much the better, and this is called civil liberty."[226] Similarly, if the purpose of government was equal protection, civil liberty could be defined in terms of *equal* protection for the greatest possible natural freedom. In 1822, for example, Daniel Chipman wrote:

> To establish civil liberty, and render the enjoyment of it certain and uniform with all classes of people, is, or ought to be the

---

[224] For example, James Iredell told a grand jury: "Let it be remembered that civil Liberty consists not in a Right to every Man to do just what he pleases—but it consists in an equal Right to all the Citizens to have, enjoy, and to do, in peace Security and without Molestation, whatever the equal and constitutional Laws of the Country admit to be consistent with the public Good." John Jay, Charge to the Grand Jury of the Circuit Court for the District of New York (April 12, 1790), in 2 *Documentary History of the Supreme Court* 30. See also Thomas Rutherforth, *Institutes of Natural Law*, bk II, ch vii, at 444 (1832) (first published 1756).

[225] [Zephaniah Swift?], *The Security of the Rights of Citizens of Connecticut* 9 (1792) (Evans 24776) (citing Paley on *Moral and Political Philosophy*). For the tentative attribution to Swift, see Pierce W. Gaines, ed, *Political Works of Concealed Authorship 1789–1810* 32 (Shoe String 1965). Of course, this approach was drawn from the other side of the Atlantic. Blackstone had written that "Political, therefore, or civil liberty, which is that of a member of society, is no other than natural liberty so far restrained by human laws (and no further) as is necessary and expedient for the general advantage of the public." W. Blackstone, 1 *Commentaries* 125 (1765). See also Thomas Rutherforth, *Institutes of Natural Law*, bk II, ch vii, at 444–45 (1832) (explaining the necessity of this modified definition). Francis Lieber observed that "when the term Civil Liberty is used, there is now always meant a high degree of mutually guaranteed protection . . . ." Francis Lieber, *Civil Liberty and Self-Government* 24 (1859), cited by Heyman, *The First Duty of Government* 41 Duke L J 507, 530.

[226] "Publicola" [Archibold Maclaine], "An Address to the Freemen of North Carolina" (Mar 20, 1788), 16 *Documentary History* 437. For a nineteenth-century example, see quotation of Lieber in note 225. See also James Kent, 2 *Commentaries* pt IV, lect xxiv, at *1.

great end of all governments; that is, to secure all classes of
society alike in the enjoyment of their rights, without any other
restraint upon natural liberty, than that which is imposed upon
all by equal and expedient laws for the general safety and welfare of the whole community.[227]

Later, Francis Lieber was more succinct: "Liberty of social man
consists in the protection of unrestrained action in as high a degree as the same claim of protection of each individual admits
of . . . ."[228]

Incidentally, the definition of civil liberty in terms of protection
for a large degree of natural liberty was not without its costs.
Among other things, it contributed to a redefinition of the phrase
"civil rights." In the eighteenth century, the phrase "civil rights"
had often been used to refer variously to all rights held under the
laws of civil government, to the portion of such rights acquired
under the laws of civil government, or to the natural rights held
under the laws of civil government. As noted in Part III, the first
and broadest definition had been reflected in dissenters' claims of
equal civil rights.[229] Already in the eighteenth century, however,
and expecially in the nineteenth, the phrase "civil rights" increasingly came to be understood to refer only to the natural rights
protected by civil laws and, sometimes, certain rights of process.[230]
Of course, Americans still occasionally used the phrase "civil
rights" to refer to all rights under civil laws or to privileges, but,

---

[227] Daniel Chipman, *An Essay on the Law of Contracts for the Payment of Specific Articles* iii
(1822). In 1791, the Rev. Israel Evans said that "where the rights of man are equally
secured in the greatest degree, there is the greatest happiness—AND THAT IS OUR
COUNTRY." Israel Evans, *A Sermon* 18 (NH election sermon 1791) (Evans 23358).

[228] Francis Lieber, *Civil Liberty and Self-Government*, as quoted by Thomas M. Cooley, *A
Treatise on the Constitutional Limitations Which Rest Upon the Legislative Power of the States of the
American Union* 485 n 2 (1890). Lieber continued: "or in the most efficient protection of his
rights, claims, interests, as a man or citizen, or of his humanity manifested as a social being."
Id.

[229] See text at notes 105–6. See also Samuel Pufendorf, *Of the Relation Between Church and
State* § 13, at 27 (1719).

[230] The increasingly dominant natural-rights definition and some of the ambiguities are
revealed in this definition by Zephaniah Swift: "Civil rights may therefore be defined to be
the exercise and enjoyment of natural rights, in that limited qualified manner which is
prescribed by law and is necessary to their security, and the peace and good order of society,
and by reason of which he acquires certain other civil rights, resulting from the social state."
Zephaniah Swift, 1 *A System of the Laws of the State of Connecticut* 176–77 (1795).

by the nineteenth century, they typically no longer did so.[231] As a result, by the 1860s, "equal civil rights" normally denoted only an equality of natural rights and judicial process. On this basis, when, in 1866, Congress enacted guarantees of various natural rights and judicial process, it could say that the bill assured Americans of their "civil rights,"[232] and, shortly afterward, Senators and Representatives could say that the Equal Protection Clause of the Fourteenth Amendment required an equality of civil rights.[233] Thus, in the middle of the nineteenth century, the phrases "equal civil rights" and "equal protection" both referred to an equality of judicial process and of the natural rights protected under civil government. Unlike for the phrase "equal protection," for the phrase "equal civil rights," this was a truncated definition. Of course, even this diminished meaning has since been lost, and the phrase "civil rights" now refers, not to legal rights, nor even to protected natural rights, but more vaguely to important or fundamental rights.

Just as Federalists and others used the idea of equal protection to define, in powerfully egalitarian terms, republican equality, the

---

[231] This may be why dissenters increasingly did not talk about their demands in terms of "equal civil rights." Apparently to avoid ambiguity, they often asked for "equal rights" or for a combination of free exercise and "equal privileges."

[232] An Act to Protect All Persons in the United States in their Civil Rights, and Furnish Means of Their Vindication (1866), 14 *Statutes at Large* 27 (1866). In explaining the Civil Rights Bill, Representative Wilson asked, "What are civil rights? I understand civil rights to be simply the absolute rights of individuals, such as [in the language of James Kent] 'the right of personal security, the right of personal liberty, and the right to acquire and enjoy property.'" *Congressional Globe* 1117 (1866). As has been shown by Berger and Maltz, this was the standard interpretation of the Civil Rights Bill. Berger, *Government by Judiciary* 27–28, 169–71; Earl M. Maltz, *Civil Rights, the Constitution, and Congress, 1863–69* 67–68.

[233] Berger, *Government by Judiciary* 172. As Berger points out, Americans also said that the Civil Rights Bill would require equal protection. Id at 169–70.

In connection with suffrage for former slaves, Republican Representative James W. Patterson of New Hampshire spoke of the military heroism of "these despised chattels" and asked: "Have not such deeds redeemed the race from dishonor and distrust, and entitled them, not only to a protection of their civil rights, but to an impartial enjoyment of the privileges of citizenship?" Id at 2695 (1866). Democratic Representative Lewis W. Ross of Illinois said of the Freedmens' Bureau that he was "unwilling to vote a tax on my constituents to support in idleness any class of people, white or black." He was "opposed to any law discriminating against ['the unfortunate colored people'] in the security and protection of life, liberty, person, property and the proceeds of their labor. These civil rights all should enjoy. Beyond this I am not prepared to go." Id at 2699 (1866).

Incidentally, Raoul Berger has concluded that the Fourteenth Amendment's equal protection "was limited to the rights enumerated in the Civil Rights Act of 1866." Berger, *Government by Judiciary* 169. This seems to suggest that a constitutional right was defined in terms of a statutory enumeration of rights. For another interpretation, see my text.

purpose of government, and the extent of civil liberty, so too, some Americans used the idea to describe the limited economic role of government. For example, at South Carolina College, the President and Professor of Political Economy, Thomas Cooper, used the idea against monopolies. Although a privilege for the monopolist, a monopoly was also an unequal restraint on the talents, industry, and, more generally, the natural liberty of other individuals. According to Cooper (who appears to have been familiar with some of the pre-eighteenth-century discussions of equal protection) individuals forming government would "endeavour to provide" for "the equality of protection in the earning and enjoyment of the fruits of their honest industry."[234] In rather stronger language, an anonymous essay of 1841 emphatically disclaimed any role for government, except equal protection. It asserted that "human legislation . . . has conferred neither rights, nor privileges, nor powers—but protected all, and all alike."[235] According to the essay, "The boast of the laws should be . . . that they have neither advanced nor retarded any man; but that they let him alone to work out his happiness in the exercise of his own true nature. . . .

[234] Thomas Cooper, *Lectures on the Elements of Political Economy* 249 (1830). When explaining the benefits of abolishing monopolies, the eighteenth-century English controversialist, Josiah Tucker, noted that "[t]he Government and Administration, which . . . considers itself as the *equal* Protector *of*, and *equally* related *to* all its Subjects, would soon find the Effects of its Paternal Care in the growing Industry of the People." Josiah Tucker, *The Elements of Commerce and Theory of Taxes*, in Josiah Tucker, *A Selection from His Economic and Political Writings*, ed, Robert Livingston Schuyler, 180 (Columbia U, 1931).

[235] "A Phrenologist," *On Rights and Government*, 9 Democratic Rev 568, 575 (Dec 1841). The author was, apparently, a New Yorker, who combined in his writing the state-of-nature analysis, a severe version of laissez-faire theory, and considerable religious enthusiasm. Most remarkable was a passage in which he said that man "comes into society with the capital which God has given him, and he demands 'free trade.' " Id at 576. He also said: "The most perfect human laws claim no higher merit, than that they have followed nature; not having conferred the rights of humanity, but guarantied and defended them; not having bestowed any powers upon any man, but having kept him free from obstruction in the exercise of his natural faculties." Id at 575.
  Incidentally, by assuming that government should protect individuals in their natural rights and should not confer privileges, this author could quite consistently say that his scheme treated all persons equally. For example, he wrote that "*the laws shall be general in their scope and application, equal and impartial to all*." Id at 575. Also: "if the laws . . . apply to all men alike, or are general, affecting all men alike, then all men are equally regarded, protected, and punished by those laws, and legal equality is established." Id at 575. In other words, if a government confined itself to equal protection and thus did not give any privileges, such a government could be said to have laws that were "equal and impartial to all." This understanding of the limited role of government may, perhaps, explain some of the occasional statements, during the Congressional debates about the Fourteenth Amendment, to the effect that the Equal Protection Clause would require states to treat individuals alike, regardless of racial differences.

Government has nothing to bestow upon any man; it can only serve to protect him in all he hath."[236] The essay not only argued that government should provide equal protection but also explicitly stated that equal protection was the sole purpose of government.

It was in the context of the Federalist-derived analysis of equal protection that Andrew Jackson demanded equal privileges in his 1832 Bank veto.[237] Using language that could have been borrowed from a Federalist, Jackson acknowledged equal protection:

> Distinctions in society will always exist under every just government. Equality of talents, of education, or of wealth, cannot be produced by human institutions. In the full enjoyment of the gifts of heaven, and the fruits of superior industry, economy, and virtue, every man is equally entitled to protection by law.

Only after he had accepted the inequality of individuals and the equality of protection, did Jackson insist on equal privileges:

> But when the laws undertake to add to these natural and just advantages, artificial distinctions, to grant titles, gratuities, and exclusive privileges . . . , the humble members of society, . . . who have neither the time nor the means of securing like favors to themselves, have a right to complain of the injustice of their government. . . . If [government] would confine itself to equal protection, and as Heaven does its rains, shower its favors alike on the high and the low, the rich and the poor, it would be an unqualified blessing. . . .
>
> . . . Many of our rich men have not been content with equal protection and equal benefits.[238]

The equality demanded by Jackson consisted of both equal protection and equal "favors," "benefits," or "privileges." Jackson did not argue against equal protection any more than did religious dissenters of the previous century or abolitionists of the coming decade.

---

[236] Id at 575–76.

[237] Amos Kendall and others drafted it.

[238] Andrew Jackson, Bank Veto (1832), in *The Addresses and Messages of the Presidents of the United States* 409–10 (1839). A locution similar to Jackson's had been employed by Virginia's Presbyterians in 1785 when complaining about a proposed assessment in support of Christianity. The assessment, they wrote, "exalts to a superior pitch of grandeur, as the church of the State, a society which ought to be contented with receiving the same protection from government which the other societies enjoy, without aspiring to superior notice or regard." Memorial of the Presbyterians of Virginia to the General Assembly (Aug 13, 1785), in *American State Papers* 117.

Like many of them, he simply asked for an additional degree of equality.[239]

By insisting upon both equal protection and equal "favors," Jackson drew upon and encouraged popular suspicions about the distribution of economic benefits from an increasingly wealthy and powerful federal government.[240] While government was understood to have been created to provide protection, and while government distributed relatively few economic privileges, Americans could still aspire, with respect to economic matters, simply to have equal protection. Indeed, by urging that government should confine itself to equal protection, some Americans signaled the limited role they desired for government.[241] Nonetheless, Americans perceived that government was increasingly a source of substantial economic favors, and therefore many Americans now demanded that these privileges, like protection, be equal.

Opponents of slavery also frequently discussed equal protection and equal privileges, and, as had Jackson, they thereby employed ideas familiar from earlier debates. After using the notion of equal

---

[239] For another illustration of the dependence of Jacksonian analysis upon Federalist discussions of equal protection, see William Leggett (Evening Post, Nov 21 & Dec 13, 1834), in *Democratick Editorials*, Lawrence H. White, ed, 3, 7–9 (1984).

Jackson assumed that unequal benefits would involve "artificial distinctions." In the debates about religious liberty, dissenters sought equality with respect to a single characteristic, religion, and therefore they could be relatively clear about the equality they sought. In contrast, Jackson was discussing equality generally rather than with respect to a single characteristic, and therefore he had to speak of an end to "artificial distinctions."

Abolitionists, unlike Jackson, were concerned about inequalities with respect to a single characteristic, yet they often conformed to the Jacksonian approach. That is, they opposed "artificial distinctions" and sought a right to "common advantages." For example, in 1833, the Declaration of Sentiments of the American Anti-Slavery Society proclaimed: "Every man has a right to his own body—to the products of his own labor—to the protection of law—and to the common advantages of society." Declaration of Sentiments of the American Anti-Slavery Convention (1833), in William L. Garrison, *Selections from the Writings and Speeches of . . .* 68 (Negro Universities, 1968 reprint of 1852 edition). These abolitionists said that each individual had a right to common advantages rather than all advantages because they were not seeking to have race treated differently than any other characteristic. Indeed, only because the equal rights standard was considered generally applicable could abolitionists convincingly argue that individuals should have equal rights regardless of race.

[240] Of course, the Jacksonian requests for equal government benefits were different from many of the earlier demands for equal rights so abhorred by Federalists. By adopting Federalist language about equal protection, the Jacksonians made clear that they were not attempting to reduce all individuals to an equality of condition.

[241] Drawing upon Jackson's language, a leading Jacksonian editor, William Leggett, wrote of government that he desired that "its duties shall be strictly confined to its only legitimate ends, the equal protection of the whole community in life, person, and property." William Leggett (Evening Post, April 22, 1834), in *Democratick Editorials* 24.

protection in their disputes about religious differences, Americans had applied the idea to other differences, such as those of skill, character, and wealth, and they thereby had emphasized that it was generally applicable to the varied distinctions among individuals. For this reason, opponents of slavery could convincingly argue that individuals deserved equal protection without regard to race. Thus, by the time Congress proposed the Fourteenth Amendment to the U.S. Constitution, the idea of equal protection had long been part of American legal and political theory and clearly was applicable to the difficulties facing the nation.

In closing, we should remind ourselves that older ideas of equality may have been rather different from those to which we are accustomed. Too often, historians have examined the development of the notion of equality without attempting to distinguish among the different types of equality that earlier Americans discussed. Conflating ideas eighteenth- and nineteenth-century Americans distinguished, some historians have talked about a single notion of equality. For these historians, the different formulations about equality employed by early Americans and the different implications of those formulations are simply evidence that the idea was ill-defined and amorphous. In the words of one commentator, "[e]quality was thus a vague . . . idea in mid-nineteenth-century America. . . . Equality could mean almost anything."[242]

Another approach, however, is possible, and it sheds light not only on the Fourteenth Amendment but also on eighteenth-century ideas of equality and religious liberty. By tracing how late eighteenth-century Americans responded to their problems of religious diversity, this account has differentiated at least two constrasting standards of equality. Far from being the same, equal protection and equal civil rights were, in the eighteenth century, the carefully defined standards of competing religious interests.

Just as debate about religious freedom provoked Americans to pursue contrasting ideas of equality, so these notions of equality contributed much to American understandings of religious freedom. In their struggles over the legal implications of their religious differences, eighteenth-century Americans often discussed their religious freedom and their religious discord in terms of equality,

---

[242] Nelson, *Fourteenth Amendment* 21.

some seeking equal civil rights and others, equal protection. Although Americans who participated in these debates frequently disagreed as to which standard of equality could secure their freedom and harmonize their differences, they apparently concurred that the standard of equality they adopted would affect the capacity of their society to overcome and survive its divisions.